TERRA

NEW FRANCE

45°N — Sagadahoc River

Sabino Point / Popham Colony

PLYMOUTH COMPANY

Monhegan Island

Cape Cod

Plymouth

Dee River

41°N —

Martha's Vineyard

HEAST PASSAGE?

VIRGINIA

OVERLAPPING
TERRITORY

ANIAN

38°N —

Henrico

Bermuda Hundred

Point Comfort

Chesapeake

Smith's Hundred
Jamestown

Cape Henry

LONDON COMPANY

Roanoke Island

Croatoan Island

angelsk

lmogro

w

Cambalech

CIPANGO

CATHAY

INDIA

Calicut

East Indies

Equinoctial

Mare de
India

Moluccas

Mare Pacifico

London

Blackwall

River Thames

Rotherhithe

Deptford

Woolwich

Greenwich

Dartford

Gravesend

0 Miles   5   10

0 Kilometers   10

ENGLAND

Norwich

Cambridge

Oxford

Harwich

London

Bristol

Windsor   Mortlake

Richmond   Dover

Southampton

Calais

Plymouth

Channel

FRANCE

STRALIS

NEW

WORLD,

INC.

NEW WORLD, INC.

HOW ENGLAND'S MERCHANTS FOUNDED AMERICA AND LAUNCHED THE BRITISH EMPIRE

JOHN BUTMAN & SIMON TARGETT

Atlantic Books
London

To my parents, Olive and Robert — *John*
To my parents, Val and Pete — *Simon*

Contents

Contents

Cast of Characters

Clement Adams (**c. 1519–1587**) was a writer, engraver and tutor. One of William Cecil's Cambridge-educated acolytes, Adams was hired to help Sebastian Cabot engrave an updated version of his 1544 map, featuring new details of the Northwest Passage. This map was reproduced widely and later hung on the wall of Whitehall Palace, and Adams was rewarded with the post of schoolmaster to the king's henchmen — Edward VI's young friends. He subsequently wrote the account of the first Mysterie voyage, after interviewing Richard Chancellor.

Matthew Baker (**c. 1530–1613**) was a royal shipwright who designed and built the *Gabriel*, Frobisher's first vessel. He also designed Edward Fenton's flagship for the aborted voyage to the Spice Islands in 1582. He compiled the first English treatise on ship design — *Fragments of Ancient English Shipwrightry* — which was later collected by Samuel Pepys, the naval administrator and diarist.

George Barne (**c. 1500–1558**) was one of the two "principal doers" — the real architects of the Mysterie. A member of the Haberdashers, he was Lord Mayor of London in 1552–1553. His son, also **George Barne** (**d. 1593**), became governor of the Muscovy Company, a leading investor in overseas ventures (although he withheld his support for Frobisher), and later followed in his father's footsteps as Lord Mayor of London.

George Best (c. 1555–1584) was a writer and sea captain. The son of **Robert Best**, a translator for the Muscovy Company, Best was educated at Eton. He served as a captain in Frobisher's second expedition. His chronicles of Frobisher's three voyages provided the classic account of England's first detailed exploration of the New World. He died in a duel with a peer of the realm.

William Bonde (d. 1576) was a merchant and civic administrator. A member of the Worshipful Company of Haberdashers, he became Sheriff of London in 1567, and was wealthy enough to buy Crosby Hall, one of the city's most prestigious mansions. There, the leading merchants behind the first Frobisher voyage to Cathay met to plan the expedition.

Stephen Borough (1525–1584) was a sea captain and naval administrator. He served as master on Richard Chancellor's ship in the first Mysterie voyage to Cathay. In 1555, he became one of the youngest charter members of what later became known as the Muscovy Company. He made a pioneering voyage to the White Sea along the Northeast Passage to Cathay, but he was among those skeptical of Frobisher's plans to search for the Northwest Passage. By contrast, his brother, **William Borough (1536–1598)**, was actively involved in the organization of Frobisher's voyages.

William Bradford (1590–1657) was one of the Pilgrim Fathers and a founder of the Plymouth Colony. His account of the separatists' story, *Of Plymouth Plantation,* was lost after his death, and only came to light in the mid-nineteenth century, when its publication by Little, Brown rekindled interest in the founding myth of America.

John Brereton (c. 1571–1619) was a clergyman and writer. He accompanied Bartholomew Gosnold on his voyage to the New World. His account, *A Brief and True Relation of the Discovery of the North Part of Virginia,* was the first published account of a voyage to New England (other than Giovanni da Verrazzano's account of his 1524 voyage, published in Italian in 1556).

Sebastian Cabot (c. 1482–1557) was an explorer, navigator, and naval administrator. He accompanied his father, **John Cabot (c. 1451–1498)**, on the successful voyage to the New World in 1497. He later claimed to have discovered the entrance to the Northwest Passage during a voyage in 1508–1509. He served the Spanish as pilot major and later transferred allegiance to England, where he was made governor of the Mysterie (later the Muscovy Company) and oversaw the first voyages in search of a passage to Cathay.

William Cecil (1520–1598) was initially John Dudley's right-hand man before becoming Elizabeth I's long-serving adviser. He became Lord Burghley, and he was connected with many major overseas ventures, first as a leading investor in the Mysterie and later as a prominent courtier behind the Frobisher voyages. His son **Robert Cecil (1563–1612)** became the Earl of Salisbury, served as adviser to James I, and continued his father's support of overseas ventures.

Richard Chancellor (d. 1556) was the pilot major on the first Mysterie voyage to Cathay in 1553. On this visit, he secured trading rights after reaching Moscow and meeting Ivan IV, the tsar later known as "The Terrible." On a second visit, he strengthened commercial ties between England and Russia. But he drowned at sea on the homeward journey, when escorting the first Russian ambassador to England. One of his sons, **Nicholas Chancellor**, was purser on several voyages, including the Frobisher voyages.

Humfrey Cole (d. 1591) was a maker of navigational instruments. He designed the instruments used in the Frobisher voyages.

Thomas Dale (d. 1619) was a soldier and colonial leader. He arrived in Jamestown in 1611 and enforced strict military law, which was codified in the *Lawes Divine, Morall and Martiall*. He oversaw an expansion of the colony beyond Jamestown, founding the city of Henrico, named after James I's son Prince Henry. He also introduced measures that paved the way for the creation of private plantations in Virginia. In 1616, he returned to England, bringing Pocahontas to London. He later served the East India Company and died in India.

John Dee (1527–1609) was a mathematician, cosmographer, and astrologer. A Fellow of Trinity College Cambridge while still a teenager, he was hired to help Richard Chancellor and Martin Frobisher prepare for their voyages across uncharted waters to Cathay. As Elizabeth I's favorite astrologer, he approved the date for her coronation. Also, he made the case for her title to lands in the New World, coining the phrase "British Empire." Humphrey Gilbert gave him the right to all the land north of today's US-Canada border. He never sought to claim these lands, however.

Francis Drake (1540–1596) was an explorer. The first English captain to complete a circumnavigation, he struck a trade deal with the king of Ternate in the Spice Islands; laid claim to the northwest coast of America, which he named Nova Albion; and captured a hoard of Spanish treasure that transformed him into one of the richest men in England. His remarkable success earned him the Spanish nickname "El Draque" and served as a catalyst for a new surge of interest in colonial activity.

Lionel Duckett (1511–1587) was a merchant. A member of the Worshipful Company of Mercers, he was governor of the Muscovy Company and the Company of Mines Royal, and he became Lord Mayor of London in 1572. The business partner of Thomas Gresham, he was an early supporter of the Frobisher voyages to Cathay, going against the consensus held by other leaders of the Muscovy Company.

John Dudley (1504–1553) was a soldier and courtier. He became the Earl of Warwick (1547) and Duke of Northumberland (1551). As Lord President, he was de facto king from 1549 and gave London's merchants the support they needed to embark on the search for new markets. Two of this sons, **Ambrose Dudley (c. 1530–1590)**, who became Earl of Warwick, and **Robert Dudley (c. 1533–1588)**, who became Earl of Leicester and Elizabeth I's favorite, were prominent investors in overseas ventures. Ambrose's wife, **Anne, Countess of Warwick (c. 1548–1604)**, was a supporter of the Frobisher voyages and had an island and a sound named after her.

Richard Eden (c. 1520–1576) was a translator. Educated at Cambridge, where he studied under Thomas Smith, he became secretary to William Cecil, compiling the travel dossier for the first Mysterie voyage to Cathay in 1553. He followed this with an expanded dossier for the second voyage in 1555. In doing so, he introduced several new words into the English language, including "China" and "colony."

Elizabeth I (1533–1603) was the longest-reigning queen until Victoria in the nineteenth century. She presided over a series of overseas ventures that led to the creation of the first British empire, and her nickname—the Virgin Queen—is remembered in the name of America's oldest state: Virginia. Although reluctant to invest money in foreign enterprises, she encouraged colonial development, diverting state monopolies to leading adventurers such as Walter Ralegh.

Martin Frobisher (c. 1535–1594) was a pirate and privateer who became a pioneering navigator and led three epic voyages in search of the Northwest Passage in the 1570s. He left his mark on the landscape—Frobisher Bay is named after him. He later earned a knighthood after distinguishing himself in the defense of England during the battle against the Spanish Armada.

William Garrard (c. 1510–1571) was one of the two "principal doers" of the Mysterie (along with George Barne). A Haberdasher, he became Lord Mayor of London in 1555–56 and governor of the Muscovy Company. His daughter married George Barne's son, George.

Thomas Gates (d. 1622) was a soldier and colonial leader. One of the eight people named in the Virginia Charter, he was among the settlers shipwrecked off the coast of Bermuda. Later, he arrived in Jamestown, which had endured a miserable winter, and took the decision to abandon the colony — only to turn back after meeting a relief supply with new colonists coming the other way. He served as effective governor until 1614.

Humphrey Gilbert (1537–1583) was a courtier, colonist, and adventurer. He studied at Eton and Oxford, and served Elizabeth when she was still a princess before becoming a soldier in the army. He fought in the abortive campaign to win back Calais and tried to establish colonies in Ireland, where he won notoriety (and a knighthood) for the brutal way he put down a rebellion. He is best remembered as the author of the *Discourse of a Discoverie for a New Passage to Cataia* and the leader who claimed Newfoundland for Elizabeth I. His son, **Raleigh Gilbert**, was one of the leaders of the short-lived Popham Colony.

Ferdinando Gorges (1568–1647) was a soldier and colonial investor. Captain of the Plymouth Fort, succeeding Francis Drake in that post, Gorges became fascinated by the New World when he hosted some Indians captured by George Waymouth in 1605. He was one of the prime movers behind the Popham Colony and later led the Council for New England that gave the Pilgrims their letters patent. He was granted the province of Maine but never fulfilled his dream to visit the New World.

Bartholomew Gosnold (d. 1607) was a lawyer and colonial leader. A kinsman of Thomas Smythe, he led an expedition to Virginia in 1602, and gave Cape Cod and Martha's Vineyard their names. He returned with an exotic tree — sassafras — which was believed to have magical medicinal properties. In 1606, he was one of the leaders of the first voyage of the London Company, which led to the founding of Jamestown. He died within a few months of his arrival in the New World.

Richard Grenville (1542–1591) was a naval commander and colonial investor. A kinsman of Humphrey Gilbert and Walter Ralegh, he worked with the first on colonial enterprises in Ireland and South America. When these came to nothing, he worked with Ralegh on the Roanoke Colony, commanding the fleet that escorted the settlers in 1585.

Thomas Gresham (1518–1579) was a leading cloth merchant and financial adviser to three monarchs. A founding member of the Muscovy Company, he was a prominent supporter of the Frobisher voyages. He built the Royal Exchange, England's first bourse, which marked the beginning of London's rise as a global financial center.

Richard Hakluyt (c. 1552–1616) was a clergyman and colonial publicist. As a schoolboy, he was introduced to the glories of cosmography by his cousin, also **Richard Hakluyt (d. 1591)**. After Oxford, he wrote a series of works championing colonization in the New World—above all *Principal Navigations and Voyages,* which first appeared in 1589, and later reappeared in an expanded version in 1598–1600. He was one of eight people listed on the first Virginia charter that led to the founding of Jamestown.

Thomas Harriot (c. 1560–1621) was a mathematician, scientist, and colonist. Hired by Walter Ralegh, he learned the rudiments of Algonquian and traveled on the first English colonial voyage to Roanoke in 1585. There, he prepared notes on the food, commodities, and people, which he later published as *Brief and True Report of the Newfound Land of Virginia.* After returning to England in 1586, he settled on Ralegh's Irish estates and subsequently won acclaim as a mathematician and stargazer, pioneering the use of telescopes.

Christopher Hatton (c. 1540–1591) was a courtier and one of Elizabeth I's favorites. From the 1570s, when he was captain of the queen's bodyguard and an industrious member of the privy council, he wielded great influence in overseas ventures. He supported George Best, Frobisher's chronicler, John Dee, who dedicated his work on the British empire to Hatton, and Francis Drake, who changed the name of his flagship from the *Pelican* to the *Golden Hind*—the defining feature of Hatton's coat-of-arms.

James I (1566–1625) was the son of Elizabeth I's hated cousin, Mary Queen of Scots. He succeeded Elizabeth in 1603 and, guided by Robert Cecil, supported colonial efforts, with the first enduring English colony, and the river on which it was situated, named after him: Jamestown and the James River. His eldest son, **Prince Henry** (1594–1612), was an enthusiastic supporter of colonial activities in Virginia before his untimely death at the age of eighteen.

Robert Johnson (fl. 1586–1626) was a merchant, colonial investor and promoter. A member of the Worshipful Company of Grocers, he was a loyal supporter of Thomas Smythe as deputy treasurer of the Virginia Company. He wrote some renowned pamphlets exhorting people to invest in the Jamestown Colony—notably *Nova Britannia,* published in 1609. He became an alderman of London in 1617 but lost out to Edwin Sandys in the race to succeed Smythe as treasurer of the Virginia Company.

Andrew Judde (c. 1492–1558) was Lord Mayor of London in 1551 when the cloth crisis hit England's capital. Later, he was Mayor of the Staple in Calais, serving in the year that the port was recaptured by the French after more than two centuries in England's possession. He was one of the senior merchants responsible for founding the Mysterie.

Michael Lok (1532–1620) was the son of Sir William Lok, the "king's merchant" in Henry VIII's day. He was the agent of the Muscovy

Company and the leading merchant behind Frobisher's voyages in the 1570s. He lost his family fortune, ending up in a debtor's prison on several occasions. But he remained influential, producing a map of the world that was reprinted by Hakluyt in 1582. He later served as the Levant Company's resident merchant in Aleppo.

Christopher Newport (1561–1617) was a sea captain and privateer. He came to prominence in the sea war with Spain in the 1590s, captaining the ship that seized the rich cargo of the *Madre de Dios* in 1592. He led the first voyage of the London Company to Virginia in 1606, and subsequently made several resupply voyages. Later, he served the East India Company, and he died on the Indonesian island of Java.

Philip II (1527–1598) was a Spanish king and, when he also held the title of king of Portugal, the most powerful man in the world, commanding two global empires. When he was a prince, the Philippines were named after him, and when he succeeded his father in 1556, he was already king of England, having married **Mary I (1516–1558)**. When she died in 1558, he tried to remain king of England, offering to marry Elizabeth. But this never happened, and the two monarchs became enemies, with Elizabeth supporting efforts to establish bases in the New World from which raids could be launched on Spain's prized treasure fleet. Philip launched his Armada in an effort to overthrow her. His death in 1598 signaled the end of a long sea war between England and Spain.

John Popham (c. 1531–1607) was a senior judge and colonial investor. As Lord Chief Justice, Popham presided over some of the most famous court cases—including the trials of Walter Ralegh and the men behind the Gunpowder Plot. He became interested in the New World after he hosted two Indians captured by George Waymouth. With Ferdinand Gorges, he led the Plymouth Company, sponsoring the voyage that led to the establishment of the Popham, or Sagadahoc, Colony in Maine by his nephew **George Popham (1550–1608)**.

Walter Ralegh (1554–1618) was a courtier, colonial investor, and writer. He gave Virginia its name, and organized the first English colony in the New World: Roanoke. He later went in search of El Dorado and sent out several voyages in search of the so-called "Lost Colonists" of Roanoke. A great favorite of Elizabeth I, he was despised by James I, who had him incarcerated in the Tower of London, where he wrote his famous *History of the World*. He was executed in 1618.

John Rolfe (1585–1622) was a colonist and tobacco entrepreneur. He was among the colonists shipwrecked off the coast of Bermuda. There, his wife and newborn child died, and he settled in Jamestown, marrying **Pocahontas (c. 1596–1618)**, who was born Matoaka and took the name Rebecca Rolfe. The match marked the end of the first Anglo-Powhatan War. He successfully pioneered the growing of tobacco in Jamestown—an achievement that put the vulnerable colony on a secure economic footing.

Edwin Sandys (1561–1629) was a parliamentarian and colonial leader. Early on, he was close to Thomas Smythe, and was tasked with drafting the second Virginia charter in 1609. With Smythe, he was involved in the setting up of a legislative body in Jamestown, the House of Burgesses. But these firm friends became entrenched enemies, and in 1619 Sandys staged a corporate coup, seizing control of the Virginia Company and replacing Smythe as treasurer, its effective leader.

Jonas Schütz (1521–1592) was a metallurgist. Also known as Christopher, he was living in England in the 1560s, on temporary leave from his master, the Duke of Saxony. He became one of the two patentees of the newly formed Company of Mineral and Battery Works. In 1577, he was approached to conduct assays on the black stone brought back by Frobisher. In the second voyage, he was sent out to oversee the extraction of hundreds of tons of black ore—which proved worthless.

Henry Sidney (1529–1586) was a courtier and administrator. A close boyhood friend of Edward VI and son-in-law of John Dudley, having married **Mary Dudley (c. 1530–1586)**, who shared her father's and her husband's interest in overseas ventures, Sidney was a founding investor in the Mysterie and became Elizabeth's Deputy Lieutenant, or viceroy, in Ireland. Mary supported the Frobisher voyages, and her son **Philip Sidney (1554–1586)** was a leading supporter of Humphrey Gilbert's colonial venture in 1583.

John Smith (1580–1631) was a soldier, colonist, and chronicler. After fighting in eastern Europe, he helped found Jamestown in 1607. He led exploratory trips into the hinterland and, after being captured by some Powhatans, was—he claimed—saved from a brutal death by a young Indian princess: Pocahontas. He rose to become president of Jamestown and later wrote several accounts of his time in Virginia. A brilliant publicist, he gave New England its name.

Thomas Smith (1513–1577) was a Cambridge University professor turned courtier. He became Secretary of State under Edward VI and Elizabeth I, as well as ambassador in Paris. With his son, he tried—but failed—to establish an English colony in Ireland's Ards Peninsula. But he won lasting fame as the author of the greatest social and economic tract of the sixteenth century: *Discourse of the Common Weal of This Realm of England.*

Thomas Smythe (1558–1625) was a merchant, civic administrator, and ambassador. He served as the governor of several trading companies, including the Virginia Company, the Muscovy Company, and the East India Company. Also, he became Sheriff of London and, after being elevated to a knighthood by James I, ambassador to Russia. His father, also **Thomas Smythe (1522–1591),** was a leading investor in the Mysterie and commonly known as "Customer" Smythe because he was the top customs tax collector for the Port of London. Smythe's grandfather was Sir Andrew Judde.

George Somers (1554–1610) was a privateer and colonial leader. Admiral of the expedition that was struck by a hurricane off the coast of Bermuda, he spotted land and guided the passengers of his stranded ship, the *Sea Venture,* to safety. After nine months, the settlers left for Jamestown, but Somers returned to Bermuda and died there. For many years, the Bermuda Islands were known as the Somers Islands, in his honor.

William Strachey (1572–1621) was a colonial administrator and writer. He traveled on the ill-fated voyage to Jamestown in 1609 when his ship, the *Sea Venture,* was wrecked off the coast of the Bermuda Islands. After reaching Jamestown in a makeshift vessel, he served as secretary of the colony and, drawing on his education at Cambridge and Gray's Inn, helped Thomas Dale codify the colony's rules. He also wrote an account of the Atlantic storm that is widely thought to have provided Shakespeare with the inspiration for his final play, *The Tempest.*

Francis Walsingham (c. 1532–1590) was an administrator and ambassador. Fervently Protestant, he left England during Mary I's reign, only returning after Elizabeth I's accession and later becoming ambassador in Paris and Secretary of State. An enthusiastic investor in the Muscovy Company, Frobisher's voyages, and Drake's circumnavigation of the world, he was among the most important patrons of New World ventures.

George Waymouth (fl. 1587–1611) was a sea captain. In 1602, he led a failed expedition in search of the Northwest Passage before setting out three years later on a voyage to explore Virginia. In advance, he presented James I with *Jewell of Artes,* a practical guide to setting up a settlement in the New World. He returned with five Indians, who were sent to live with Gorges and Popham. **James Rosier** (1573–1609), a young Cambridge graduate and one of the crew, wrote the account of the expedition.

Thomas West (1577–1618) was an aristocrat and colonial governor. The third baron De La Warr, he became Lord Governor and Captain General of Jamestown in 1610, after investing five hundred pounds in the venture. He arrived with a great fanfare, the first nobleman to lead an American colony. But he stayed barely ten months, most of which was spent on board his ship. In 1618, he set off for Jamestown once more but he died en route.

Thomas Weston (died c. 1647) was a merchant. A member of the Worshipful Company of Ironmongers, he was a struggling cloth merchant when he approached a group of Separatists who wanted to leave Holland and establish their own settlement in the New World. He found and supplied two ships, including the *Mayflower,* but he was a ruthless negotiator, forcing the worshippers who would later be known as the Pilgrims to make a punitive agreement. He backed out of the deal after one year. By 1628 he had moved to Virginia, where he acquired a plantation and became a member of the House of Burgesses. In the 1540s he returned to England, where he died.

John White (fl. 1577–1593) was a painter and colonist. He first came to prominence in 1577, when he painted Inuits brought back by Martin Frobisher. Then, in 1585, he was hired by Ralegh to paint pictures of Roanoke and its people, producing more than two hundred watercolors. In 1587, he was made governor of the second Roanoke Colony, where his daughter gave birth to Virginia, the first English baby born on American soil. But after he left Roanoke to get supplies, he never saw his granddaughter again, and she entered American legend as one of the "lost colonists." White returned once more in 1590 but failed to make contact with them.

Hugh Willoughby (d. 1554) was a soldier. He led the first expedition in search of Cathay in 1553, even though he did not have any relevant sailing experience. He and his crew froze to death in the icy wastes of the Arctic, after getting lost in the North Sea and taking the risk of overwintering in a river inlet to the Barents Sea on Russia's north coast.

Edward Maria Wingfield (1550–c. 1619) was a soldier and colonist. One of the eight people named on the original Virginia charter, he was the first leader of Jamestown, having been selected as president of the Council of Virginia.

William Winter (c. 1525–1589) was a naval administrator and colonial investor. A charter member of the Muscovy Company, he was involved in Gilbert's colonial plans in Ireland and was a prominent member of the commission set up to provide oversight of the Frobisher voyages.

John Yorke (d. 1569) was a merchant whose family had a long connection with Calais. He became prominent at the Tower of London mint and later rose to become Sheriff of London and a close friend of John Dudley. He raised his wayward nephew, Martin Frobisher, and set him on his course for a life at sea.

The Prequel to the Pilgrims

On May 6, 1621, the *Mayflower* returned to England from the fledgling American colony of New Plymouth. In the eight months since the little ship left the English coast behind, the seventy investors that had bankrolled the voyage — mostly London merchants — had not received a scrap of news about the fate of their venture. Now, as the ship's master, Christopher Jones, eased the *Mayflower* into its dockage at Rotherhithe, an ancient landing place two miles down the Thames from London that had become a huddle of boatyards, sailors' cottages, and merchants' warehouses,* the financial backers eagerly awaited news about the one thing they cared about most: what saleable cargo the ship had brought back from the New World. Perhaps it carried oak timbers for shipbuilding and barrel-making. Perhaps it contained cedar, which was much prized for the construction of exquisite dining-room furniture. Perhaps there might be great bundles of sassafras, the wildly popular plant that could be decocted into remedies for syphilis, malaria, incontinence, and the common cold. Best of all, and certainly the most lucrative, there might be beaver

---

* Rotherhithe has Saxon origins, its name deriving from Rothra ("a mariner"), and hythe ("a landing place").

pelts for fashioning the hats that had become all the rage with aristocrats and rich merchants. Such commodities could quickly find a
ready market, not only in England but in mainland Europe, and perhaps even in Asia, where they could be traded for the fabulous goods
that the English craved: Chinese silks and velvet and linen, precious
stones and metals, spices, medicines, fine wines and exotic foodstuffs,
and Turkish carpets.

But no. The *Mayflower* carried no goods or commodities, nothing
saleable, nothing of value at all. Instead, the hold groaned with rocks,
loaded as ballast to replace the weight of the 102 settlers left behind
on the far-distant shoreline.

Disappointed and unwilling to throw good money after bad, most
of the investors eventually sold out of the *Mayflower* venture and
washed their hands of the New Plymouth settlers, the people who
later referred to themselves as "pilgrims." Four centuries later, however, the tables have turned. The commercial organizers of the *Mayflower* voyage have long since been forgotten, while the Plymouth
settlers have been enshrined as the true originators, the makers of
America. Indeed, the *Oxford English Dictionary,* that great storehouse
of the English language, defines the Pilgrim Fathers as "the founders
of the United States."[1]

But the story of the making of America actually begins in England
in the mid-1500s—seventy years before the *Mayflower* set out to
brave the westerly gales and cross the Atlantic. At that time, England
was a small kingdom at the margin of Europe, a relatively insignificant participant in world affairs. The island realm faced a daunting
array of social, commercial, and political problems: rising unemployment, failing harvests, a widening gulf between rich and poor, and a
crisis of leadership. A prepubescent boy, Edward VI, nominally led
the country following the death of his father, the tyrant-king Henry
VIII. But a cabal of ambitious noblemen held the real power. A whiff
of rebellion, perhaps even revolution, hung in the air. And to provide
a physical manifestation of the country's precarious health, a virulent

disease known as the sweating sickness returned for the first time in a quarter of a century, destroying lives and devastating communities. You could be dancing in the morning, the saying went, and be dead by noon. In just a few days, nearly a thousand people perished in London.[2]

Throughout the land, conditions had grown so dire that a terrifying question loomed over the kingdom's cosmopolitan capital city as well as its countless rural villages: Can England survive?

As if in answer to that existential question, a constellation of remarkable people, often linked by family ties, emerged over the course of three generations to seek solutions to England's ills. There were courtiers, intellectuals, scientists, writers, artists, and buccaneers. Above all, there were some of England's most prosperous merchants. Although these entrepreneurs rarely ventured overseas themselves, they masterminded a relentless stream of commercial enterprises dedicated to discovery, exploration, development, and settlement. Variously bold, obsessed, hungry for gold and glory, and driven by compelling ideas about social improvement and commercial advantage, they organized, promoted, and supported hundreds of ventures, one after another, until multiple threads of failure began to stitch into a fabric of success.

In the process, they developed many of the elements that shaped America as it grew into the country we know today. They originated new corporate and political institutions workable in the New World, embraced new approaches to leadership and social organization, and applied the latest technologies and the latest thinking. They learned how to raise funding, share risk, and allocate capital in ventures with unpredictable outcomes. And most strikingly, they learned how to overcome seemingly insuperable challenges, accept and learn from failure, and cherish the quality that Americans have come to regard as quintessentially their own: perseverance. In *New World, Inc.*, we tell their story—the prequel to the Pilgrims. And, insofar as their actions helped to usher in the modern world, it is our story, too.

PART I

BEFORE AMERICA

1551–1574

1

———⋙•(◉)•⋘———

WAXING COLD AND IN DECAY

THE STORY BEGINS with sheep.

By the middle of the sixteenth century, there were 11 million sheep throughout England, outnumbering human beings by around four to one.[1] They grazed everywhere—on the tiny tracts of land rented by peasant farmers as well as on the great estates of noblemen, bishops, and abbots. Their ubiquity was attributable to one factor: the age-old importance of wool to the English economy.

The hardy English sheep had long flourished in the cold northerly climate, grazing on land that was, as one contemporary put it, "so fruitful that if overnight a wand or rod be laid upon it, by the morning it shall be covered with grass of that night's growth."[2] In these conditions, they grew a golden fleece of fine, dense fibers that could—once sheared, carded, fulled, tucked, and dried—be spun into a wonderfully warm and weatherproof cloth.[3]

As early as the twelfth century, raw English wool was exported to the Low Countries, then the epicenter of Europe's clothmaking industry, and textile makers there considered it to be the finest in

Europe.* In 1343, King Edward III granted a group of merchants a monopoly on the trade of raw wool with the textile merchants of the Low Countries that transformed the way the business was done.[4] In return for the royal monopoly, the king exacted an export duty that covered a significant portion of the royal budget. Also, soon after, he fixed the official market for the wool trade, known as the "staple," in the port town of Calais, on France's northern coast, which he had recently captured as a trophy of war. There, the merchants, who were incorporated as the Company of the Staple and known simply as the Staplers, conducted their trading activities with foreign merchants. For some time, the Staplers' monopoly ensured that they prospered most from England's greatest natural resource.[†]

But in commerce, nothing stands still: over the next fifty years, the trade in raw wool steadily declined as woven cloth grew in popularity — significantly because the export duty on woven cloth was lower than on raw wool.[5] The cloth dealers now followed the precedent set by the Staplers. In 1407, they founded the Company of Merchant Adventurers and received a royal monopoly for the export of woven cloth to Europe.

The Merchant Adventurers purchased their cloth from regional suppliers who transported it to London's Blackwell Hall, a converted medieval mansion that stood adjacent to the Guildhall at the heart of London's commercial district. Most of the cloth was unfinished—the dyeing and other refining activities were undertaken by textile workers in foreign markets. The classic English product was the broadcloth—a sheet thirty yards long and made from as many as sixty fleeces. Typically woven in East Anglia as well as the West Country counties of Gloucestershire, Wiltshire, and Somerset, it was popular in the cool-climate countries of northern Europe. Another cloth, the kersey—a smaller, cheaper cloth, woven from short-stapled wool,

---

* The Low Countries broadly encompass modern-day Belgium, Luxemburg, and the Netherlands.

† The Staplers were first incorporated in the 1260s.

fulled less extensively and woven to be lighter, and produced in narrower measures—was favored in warmer climates to the south.

English cloth was popular beyond the Low Countries. Venice, Florence, Lucca, and the other city republics of the Italian peninsula were eager purchasers of English cloth. So, too, were Spanish traders, who bought it and then shipped it across the Atlantic to their colonies in the West Indies and other parts of the New World. Meanwhile, merchants from Ragusa (now Dubrovnik) on the Adriatic coast distributed English cloth across the Ottoman empire, which stretched from the Mediterranean to the Caspian Sea, including swaths of what we know today as Turkey, Syria, Iran, Iraq, and the Arabian Peninsula.

By the mid-1500s, almost everyone in England was involved with, benefited from, or was affected by England's dominant industry. In a speech before Parliament, Sir Edward Coke, one of England's most prominent judges, later remarked that if one were to "divide our native commodities into ten parts...nine arise from the sheep's back."[6]

Many of England's leading families built their livelihoods, fortunes, estates, and, in the long run, their legacies, on the cloth trade. One prosperous merchant etched an encomium in a window of his home:

> *I praise God and ever shall...*
> *It is the sheep hath paid for all!*[7]

AMONG THE MOST successful of these families were the Greshams, who originally hailed from Norfolk on England's blustery North Sea coast and who initially prospered as purveyors of hats made from worsted, the cloth named after the local village of Worstead. Then, in the first half of the 1500s, three Gresham brothers—William, Richard, and John—rose to become prominent members of the Worshipful Company of Mercers, the most powerful guild of merchants. They specialized in the import of textiles: linen, fustian, and, above all, silk.[8]

Over time, the Gresham brothers gained renown across Europe—trading with the Low Countries, Spain, and the Levant—and they came to exert an extraordinary influence over the commercial fortunes of London and, indeed, of England.* At various times, they served as masters or wardens of the Mercers. Also, William became governor—chief executive—of the Merchant Adventurers, while Richard and John each served as Lord Mayor of London. The mayoralty was the pinnacle of achievement for any London merchant. As one contemporary noted, there is "no public officer of any city in Europe that may compare in port and countenance" with the Lord Mayor of London.[9] Both brothers were knighted for their service as mayor.

The Greshams' success, built on their unquestioned business acumen, was greatly aided by the growing dominance of London as England's commercial capital. In the early years of the sixteenth century, London had been rivaled in commercial importance by several "outports," commercial and trading centers on England's south, southwest, and northeast coasts, including Bristol, Hull, Newcastle, Plymouth, and Southampton. But as the export of unfinished cloth grew, London's relative proximity and easy access to Antwerp, the staple, or primary trading center, for England's unfinished cloth, gave the city and its merchants, including the Greshams, an advantage over the outports.

Antwerp was northern Europe's greatest entrepôt—a hub for the trading of goods from around the world. Situated near the mouth of the Scheldt river, which rises in France and flows through what is now Belgium and into the North Sea, Antwerp was ideally located to serve as a commercial thoroughfare for the transport and trade of goods throughout Europe. As a nineteenth-century historian wrote, "It was no uncommon sight to see two or three thousand vessels at one time in the Scheldt, laden with merchandise from every quarter of the globe."[10] Here, German merchants traded silver and copper

---

* "The Levant" consists roughly of the lands bordering the eastern Mediterranean Sea. The word derives from the French for "rise" and pertains to the point where the sun rises in the east. See the *Oxford English Dictionary* for "Levant."

from the mines of central Europe, Venetian merchants displayed silks from the Levant and beyond, and Portuguese merchants, fast displacing Venetians as carriers of luxury goods from the East, arrayed their spices. The Greshams and other ambitious English merchants brought their unfinished cloth to market in Antwerp, exchanging it for the luxury products prized by England's wealthiest citizens.

A cosmopolitan metropolis of some 100,000 inhabitants — including William Gresham, who resided in the English community there — the city was a melting pot of cultures and a gabble of languages. While out and about in Antwerp, noted one observer, it was not unusual to meet "a lady who could converse in five, six, or even seven different languages."[11] With so many merchants conducting business and with so much money flowing in and out of the city, Antwerp soon became the financial capital of Europe — and its richest city. Emperors and kings came from across the continent to raise their loans and discharge their debts. Merchants, flush with cash, became bankers. Germans, such as the Fuggers, were preeminent among these, tapping into their networks of merchant-factors with capital to invest and offering a variety of financial mechanisms such as bills of exchange to manage and maintain their accounts. Some English merchants — the Greshams, in particular — became bankers, too.

In the 1540s, when London's trade with Antwerp was booming, Thomas Gresham, Richard's son, emerged as the leader of the next generation. In a portrait dated 1544, when he was twenty-six years old, newly married, and recently admitted to the Worshipful Company of Mercers, Thomas poses in an unadorned black coat with white collar and sleeves, his face characterized by a regal nose, eyes of great clarity, and a modest ginger-colored beard. The impression is of a person both equable and resolute, poised to spend his life — as Greshams before him had — in service to his crown and country.

But even as the Greshams prospered, it was becoming clear that not everyone was benefiting from England's trade boom. A few who had the foresight to look deeply into the matter could see that, on the contrary, England was on the cusp of a great crisis: the cloth trade was faltering, the English presence in Antwerp was threatened, the crown was mired in debt, people were homeless and unemployed, towns were ravaged, and disease raged.

One of the most perceptive analysts of the English situation was a very different sort of character than any of the Greshams—a courtier, a former Cambridge professor, a man with no commercial interests: the brilliant intellectual Sir Thomas Smith.

IN THE SUMMER of 1549, Smith, one of England's two secretaries of state and a member of King Edward's Privy Council—essentially his cabinet of chief ministers and closest advisers—escaped London and the burdens of court. He repaired to Eton College, where he served as provost, a position that brought him an additional salary and the advantage of a fine country retreat. Eton was, and still is, one of England's grandest secondary schools. It is situated some twenty miles west of London, on the banks of the Thames and within sight of Windsor Castle, the mightiest of the royal residences.

Smith was deeply concerned about what he called "the miserable estate, our commonwealth." He had tried assiduously to explain his reasoning and make the case for reforms to Edward Seymour, who was the uncle of the boy-king Edward VI and wielded great state power as effectively regent with the grand title of Lord Protector.[12] But Smith had been ignored by Seymour and, feeling aggrieved, retired from court to spend some time at Eton. Over the course of the long summer months, Smith tried to get the frustration out of his system by putting his ideas down in writing. The resulting work, *A Discourse of the Commonweal of This Realm of England,* is now considered one of the most powerful social and economic tracts of the sixteenth century.

Like the Gresham family, the Smith family was rooted in the cloth industry. They were not cloth merchants, however, but sheep farmers, based in Walden in Essex, fifty miles northeast of London. But Thomas was not destined to follow in his father's footsteps. Showing early prowess as a scholar, he won a place at Queens' College in Cambridge at the age of thirteen. At first, he struggled financially, and came near to abandoning his studies. In the end, however, he persisted, achieved distinction, and, by the age of thirty, he had become not only the first Regius Professor of Civil Law but also the vice-chancellor of the university. But this, it seems, was not enough for him. In February 1547, at the age of thirty-three, Smith relinquished a university career and accepted an invitation to enter Seymour's service. A little over a year later, he was named Secretary of State.[13] It was a meteoric rise.

Smith's *Discourse* manifested his deep understanding of England's travails and expressed his urgent desire to overcome them. The book is written as a dialogue, a popular literary device of the day, in which a husbandman (farmer), a knight, a merchant, a capper (artisan), and, most prominently, a doctor — who clearly speaks for Smith — engage in an extended debate on what ails England. Smith begins by enumerating England's many ills, the most alarming of which, according to the doctor, is the matter of wealth disparity. Although rich landowners, with their large flocks of sheep, and successful cloth merchants such as the Gresham family were making large profits, not everyone in England was prospering in the boom times.

"Poverty reigns everywhere," Smith declared.

One of the root causes of the problem, he wrote, was inflation. Indeed, prices had risen by 50 percent in the first four decades of the sixteenth century, and they continued to rise, especially on goods that were scarce in the realm and were often imported — notably silk, wine, spices, paper, and glass of all kinds. "Every man finds himself grieved" by the rising prices, he wrote.[14]

Smith blamed the inflationary spiral on Henry VIII, who spent recklessly on foreign wars and an extravagant lifestyle and plunged the crown into debt. When Henry could no longer raise sufficient money from taxes, loans, and the sale of monastic land, he turned to financial chicanery: currency manipulation. This involved debasing the coinage by reducing the amount of silver in every coin. Although the crown could spend less on silver, the value of the coins plunged and prices were driven even higher. This was a disaster for everyone. In his *Discourse,* Smith called for an end to this abuse.

Also, Smith identified another factor that he saw as deleterious to the realm: the practice of "land enclosure." England's open lands—the island was a rural patchwork of vast fields and manorial estates—had long done double duty. Generally, arable land was tilled by one owner or tenant, but after the harvest or during an off-season, it was available to everyone and was typically employed for the grazing of sheep.[15]

For landowners who sought relief from the damaging effects of inflation, the temptation was to convert some or all of their arable land into pasture for their own animals to graze exclusively. This involved enclosing their fields with wooden fences, rows of stones and mounds of earth, or hedges—and thereby removing them from common use. Such enclosure made good economic sense for the landowners. Wool for cloth was in high demand, and the cost of grazing sheep was considerably less than the cost of growing grain or corn. Thomas Tusser, an old Etonian Norfolk farmer, reckoned that enclosure made land three times more profitable than when it was made available to everyone.[16] But the effects on local communities could be disastrous. Smith noted that a plot of land that once employed one or two hundred people would, after enclosure, serve only the owner and a few shepherds.[17] Without employment—or even land to grow food or graze small flocks—entire villages were abandoned.

The practice of enclosure was not new. In the fourteenth century, England, like much of Europe, was devastated by the Black Death—an epidemic of bubonic plague that obliterated nearly half the population.[18] With so few laborers available to farm the land, landowners were forced to enclose their property and turn it into pasture for sheep and other animals.

Of course, some unscrupulous landowners took advantage—even as the population started to rise again—and over the years, the crown had sought to curb the most flagrant abuses: two acts of Parliament, in 1489 and 1515, were introduced to limit or regulate the practice of land enclosure, but they had little effect. By the 1540s, when the practice spiked, the Privy Council, led by Edward Seymour, made another attempt to tackle the problem, issuing a royal proclamation that condemned the "unlawful converting of arable land to pastures." A commission for the "redress of enclosures" was established and charged with conducting an inquiry into those who had been transgressors or violators of the anti-enclosure statutes already on the books.

But government intervention had failed before, and as Smith wrote in his *Discourse,* there was little reason to think that it would work now, particularly as it was the avarice of landowners that underlay the recent practice and this seemed unlikely to change. And so, unless they could find a way to solve the problem, the king and his court could expect to face mounting social unrest. It was no surprise, Smith wrote, that given "hunger is a bitter thing to bear," the impoverished majority "murmur against them that have plenty."[19]

His observation was prescient. As he penned these words, the country was on the brink of rebellion. About 150 miles away, in the Gresham family's home county of Norfolk, and just north of Smith's own home county of Essex, the people were preparing to do a great deal more than just murmur about their discontent.

IN THE FIRST week of July 1549, a crowd of villagers gathered at the local chapel of the village of Wymondham to attend a pageant, an all-day festival of "processions and interludes."[20] Emotions ran high because the beloved building was scheduled for demolition as part of Edward's dissolution of church properties—a euphemism for smashing and looting—begun by his father, Henry VIII. In 1534, the king had proclaimed himself supreme leader of the church of England, broken from the Pope and the Catholic Church in Rome, and soon set about stripping ancient monasteries of their treasure, lands, and influence. Between 1538 and 1540, more than two hundred monastic buildings—housing more than 8,000 monks, nuns, and canons (a clergyman or clerk)—were suppressed, their riches seized by the crown and their property sold to raise cash.[21]

Wymondham's churchgoers dearly wished to save the chapel, but their ability to do so against the decree of the king seemed doubtful, if not impossible. As the festival played on, a group of townspeople banded together and marched to nearby Morley, where they began "throwing down" fences erected by landowners there. The fences— and the sheep they enclosed—were, if nothing else, a symbol of the favor shown to the wealthy men who grazed the sheep and whose interests were placed above those of the majority of the local and larger population.

Throwing down the enclosures at Morley did not fully quell the anger of the Wymondham people, and it discontented others. One of these, a significant landowner called Sir John Flowerdew—a lawyer, whose son was a close friend of Thomas Gresham and who lived in the nearby village of Hethersett—was angry that some of his fences had been removed. Seeking a twisted kind of revenge, he offered money to anyone who would be willing to have a go at the enclosures of another local landowner, a man named Robert Kett.[22]

A band of about six men took Flowerdew up on his offer. It is unlikely, however, that they saw Kett as the enemy: he was a local citizen, an ardent supporter of the church, and a tanner by trade. Although a man of rising prosperity, holding property worth about £670, he was no grand figure.[23] So, before dismantling his enclosures, the men entreated Kett to return the land to public use. They spoke, they assured him, not just on their own account, or for Flowerdew, but for the "weal of the Commonalty."

Kett made no attempt to turn them away or defend his enclosures. He did not even defend his right to have them. Instead, he declared his sympathy with the protestors, revealing that "he felt deeply their own misery." The "nobility and gentry," he said, possessed a "power so excessive, avarice so great, and cruelty of every kind so unheard of" that it had to be restrained.

As if to convince the protestors, Kett marched with them into his field, helped remove his enclosures, and then participated in throwing down those in the fields of other landowners in the county. In doing so, he quickly emerged as the rebels' leader. As word of the action spread, the handful of Wymondham men grew into a watershed of protestors, at first trickling and then cascading across the fields and pastures and woodlands of Norfolk, destroying hedges and ransacking villages as they went, until they pooled into a great, raging body—estimated to have reached 20,000 at its peak—on Mousehold Heath, an open area on the outskirts of Norwich, the capital of Norfolk.

From there, where they made camp and established a kind of headquarters, Kett's rebels expanded their activities across large parts of Norfolk. Within days, the small Wymondham protest turned into a prolonged combination of revolt, crusade, campout, and riot. The rebels seized control of Norwich and scoured the countryside for food, slaughtering and devouring 20,000 sheep in the process. They captured members of the local gentry—the few who had not fled their estates—and held them hostage in the woods.

While enclosures were a tangible symbol of the rebels' plight and an easy target for their anger and aggression, Kett and his men knew their removal alone would not restore the England they had once known. So, in their wooded haven at Mousehold Heath, they drew up a petition of twenty-two grievances to be presented to King Edward. It was a laundry list of complaints. One grievance directly addressed the issue of land enclosure, others railed against high and rising prices as well as exorbitant and unregulated rents, and yet others called for revisions to fishing rights, greater standardization of weights and measures used in trade, and questioned the duties of priests.

The rebels made it clear that, despite their grievances, they were loyal supporters of the king, and their only goal was to achieve justice and, again, to "deliver the common-wealth."[24] But Edward Seymour, as regent to the boy-king, saw Kett's action as a serious threat to the sovereignty of the king and the peace of the nation. He ordered William Parr, the Marquis of Northampton, to lead a royal force against the rebels. Extraordinarily, Kett's men rebuffed the attack.[25]

A second royal force was mounted. This time, Seymour, taking no chances, gave command to his long-standing friend and ally on the Privy Council, the dashing forty-five-year-old John Dudley, Earl of Warwick. Dudley was typical of yet another class caught up in England's crisis. Neither a merchant like Gresham nor an intellectual like Smith, Dudley was an aristocrat and a man of action who had won a fine reputation as, among other things, a tournament jouster. John's father, Edmund, had been a close adviser of Henry VII but was executed on trumped-up charges of treason when Henry VIII acceded to the throne. Without a father, John was sent to be raised in the household of one of the king's favorite soldier-courtiers, and he was quickly marked out for great things, receiving a knighthood at the age of nineteen after distinguishing himself on the battlefield against France. Seymour was knighted at about the same time, and the two became companions at arms. Over the next twenty years, Dudley emerged as one of Henry's stalwart supporters, and benefited from gifts of land and offices. In 1543, he joined the Privy Council as Lord Admiral, responsible for England's naval activities. After Henry's death, he was granted the earldom of Warwick by Edward, and over the course of his reign, the boy-king came to think of the earl as a mentor — even a father figure.[26]

Called into action after Kett's unlikely victory, Dudley assembled a much larger force than William Parr had put together. With six thousand foot soldiers and fifteen hundred cavalry — including fourteen hundred mercenary soldiers from Germany and Italy — he rode towards Norwich. As he approached Kett's encampment, he stopped for the night at the home of Thomas Gresham, whose family estate, Intwood Hall, lay just three miles south of Norwich.[27]

The next morning, Dudley set out to engage the Mousehold rebels. But before he unleashed his forces, he sent two emissaries into the rebel camp in an attempt to persuade Kett to surrender and offer them leniency if they did so.[28] It was a notable display of compassion that seems out of character for a commander sent out to quash an act he saw as rebellion. His efforts failed, however. Kett distrusted Dudley and his promises and refused to back down.

Given Kett's unbending response, Dudley had little choice but to order an attack by his royal force. The result was mass slaughter. Kett's ragtag army was no match for Dudley's mercenary soldiers. In a single August day, some three thousand five hundred rebels were killed at a place called Dussin's Dale.[29] Kett, seeing that the cause was lost, fled. When his followers saw him abandoning the battlefield, they too lost heart, and at last surrendered.

The next morning, most of the leaders were rounded up and hanged. In the following weeks, Dudley presided over court proceedings, after which many more of the Mousehold rebels were executed, some in gruesome fashion: "first their privy parts are cut off, then their bowels pulled out alive, and cast into the fire, then their head is cut off, and their body quartered: the head set upon a pole, and fixed on the tops of the Towers of the City, the rest of the body bestowed upon several places, and set up to the terror of others."[30] Eventually, Kett himself was captured, tried, found guilty, and hanged in chains from the top of Norwich Castle.[31]

The punishment meted out to the rebels did not satisfy some of the local gentry, who demanded even greater action. Dudley retorted, "There must be measure kept," even in punishment. Was there, he pleaded, no place for "humble petition" or even "pardon and mercie?"[32] His apparent sympathy may be telling, but he would have known the potential danger that Kett's rebellion posed to the kingdom.

Uprisings were taking place across the country—in neighboring Suffolk, as well as in Cornwall and Devon. The motives varied and overlapped—sheep and enclosures, taxes and subsidies, new religious strictures, laws concerning vagrancy and treason. But at their heart there was a continuing and growing disgust with the avarice of the nobility and gentry, the 2 percent who governed the 98 percent of yeomen and husbandmen, artisans and apprentices.[33]

KETT'S REBELLION SHOOK England to its foundations. Some feared that the country might even descend into civil war. In the febrile atmosphere at court, Seymour started to lose the confidence of the Privy Council, and Dudley, the hero of the hour, emerged as the most powerful royal adviser. It helped that he had not fully disbanded his fighting force and, within a couple of months of suppressing Kett's rebellion, he staged a coup d'état, arresting Seymour, becoming the effective regent, and assuming the title of Lord President.

In his new role, Dudley's tasks were nothing less than to restore confidence in Edward's reign, rescue England from economic calamity, and resolve the damaging social divisions that were being exposed by land enclosure. His job was made immeasurably harder with an abrupt and seemingly catastrophic collapse in demand for cloth from mainland Europe. In 1550, as he took over from Seymour, the cloth trade was buoyant, and total exports numbered 132,767 cloths, as lengths of fabric were called. But in 1551 this slumped to 112,710 cloths, falling to 84,968 the following year.[34] At a time when the monarchy was already heavily in debt, the decline in demand seemed to rule out any hope that royal loans could be paid back with customs revenue from the cloth trade. As one merchant reflected, some years later, England's economy was "waxing cold and in decay."[35]

The situation was made worse by another development. In 1549, as Smith wrote his *Discourse*, Antwerp collapsed as a center for Europe's spice trade. For fifty years, Portuguese merchants had used the Flemish port as its staple, trading spices there for German silver. But now the king of Portugal, João III, had decided that, with sufficient silver pouring into Lisbon from Spanish silver mines in America, he did not need to trade in Antwerp.[36] This disruption left English merchants facing a double hit: the decline of their export business in cloth and the loss of their import business in spices and associated luxuries from Asia.

To help sort out this complex crisis, Dudley called on a number of friends and associates to advise him. These included the merchant Thomas Gresham as well as several scholars, many associated with Cambridge University, including Thomas Smith, Richard Eden, Clement Adams, John Dee, and Ralph Robinson, most of whom were in their late twenties and early thirties. But even with this talented group of advisers, it is doubtful that Dudley would have made much progress without the active involvement and influence of a government administrator of genius, William Cecil, Dudley's right-hand man and, officially, Secretary of State.

Like Gresham and Smith, Cecil also grew up with the sights and sounds of the sheep, wool, and cloth business. Born in 1520, the son of a minor royal servant and local landowner, he was raised in Stamford, a market town in Lincolnshire, one of the centers of the cloth industry: as early as the thirteenth century, merchants from Venice and Lucca were travelling to Stamford to buy scarlet and *halberget,* a richly textured cloth.[37] After attending local schools, Cecil went to St. John's College in Cambridge, founded by Edward VI's great-grandmother. There, from the age of fourteen, he was taught by Thomas Smith and John Cheke, a renowned Greek scholar. Young Cecil was among the first generation to follow the "new learning" introduced to Cambridge by the Renaissance scholar Desiderus Erasmus. This promoted Greek as a way of accessing the rediscovered writings of philosophers such as Pythagoras, Plato, Ptolemy, and Euclid—and, as a result, new subjects such as astronomy, arithmetic, and cosmology.[38]

At the age of nineteen, Cecil advanced to Gray's Inn, the grandest of the four Inns of Court, situated beyond London's old Roman wall. Today, Gray's Inn is one of the professional associations where barristers have their chambers and practice as advocates in the nearby law courts. But in Cecil's day, it was seen as a kind of finishing school for young aristocrats who needed to understand enough about legal documents to manage their estates or for future royal administrators who would be involved in keeping the statute books. There, in an atmosphere very different from the cloistered world of Cambridge, Cecil was able to connect with leading figures at court and in commerce.

He soon followed Smith into royal service, almost certainly through the good offices of John Cheke, whose sister he had married and who had left Cambridge to tutor Edward VI. Initially, he served Edward Seymour, and he was briefly imprisoned when Dudley made his move for power. Unlike Smith, however, who lost his place at court, Cecil, displaying the remarkable political dexterity that would become his trademark, managed to extricate himself from the Tower of London and quickly secured Smith's old job as Secretary of State.

Now, as Cecil pondered how best to advise Dudley and address England's crisis, he may well have considered the ideas of his former tutor. Although Thomas Smith did not publish his *Discourse* in the summer of 1549, he did share it with Cecil. Knowing how potentially explosive his views were, he had urged Cecil not to distribute the treatise. Keep it "between us two," he pleaded.[39]

Nevertheless, Cecil may well have promoted some of Smith's recommendations. And, as it turned out, there were others in this constellation of merchants, intellectuals, courtiers, and government officials who shared Smith's perspective — notably the thirty-three-year-old businessman Thomas Gresham. He was invited to appear before the king and Privy Council to offer his opinion about the most effective way — with the "least charge" — that his majesty might "grow out of debt."[40] As he later recalled, he argued persuasively that a program of reforms was needed.[41]

This program, which included a revaluation of the coinage that Dudley soon put into effect, featured an initiative to give English merchants greater control over English exports by reducing the influence of the powerful German merchants then resident in London. Ever since the 1470s, merchants from Lubeck, Danzig, and other market towns on the Baltic — which formed a commercial confederation known as the Hanseatic League — had enjoyed significant trading privileges in England, thanks to their usefulness in supplying the royal navy with timber, hemp, and other essentials. By the late 1540s, they were handling around 35 percent of England's cloth exports.[42] This, according to Gresham, was a key cause of the cloth crisis, "the chiefest point of the undoing" of the realm. Gresham urged Dudley "to overthrow the Steelyard," the enclave on the banks of the Thames where the Hanse merchants were headquartered — and Dudley did precisely that. In February 1552, the foreign merchants' privileges were withdrawn, and as a result England's merchants managed to capture a greater share of the country's cloth trade.[43]

With these measures, Dudley was able to address some of the causes of England's economic crisis. Yet many of England's political, intellectual, and business leaders felt strongly that something more — and something different — needed to be done to prevent England from falling into decay once again. As Clement Adams, one of Cecil's coterie of Cambridge-educated protégés, put it, many people "perceived" there was not sufficient demand for "the commodities and wares of England" from people in the countries nearest to them.[44]

The situation had to be remedied. But how?

2

———◦◎◦———

THE LURE OF CATHAY

IN THE DARK months towards the end of 1551, as England's economic malaise worsened, a number of London's "grave" citizens—the word signifying their gravitas, although it might have signified their mood, too—came together to discuss ways to remedy what they called the "mischief" of England's decay.[1]

The "great furtherer" of the endeavor—its mastermind, principal architect, and the convener of the group—was the aristocrat and vanquisher at Dussin's Dale, John Dudley, who now bore the title Duke of Northumberland.[2] Two prominent merchants worked with Dudley as leaders, or "principal doers," as John Stow, the contemporary chronicler, described them: George Barne and William Garrard. Both were members of the Worshipful Company of Haberdashers. Barne, in his early fifties, was being talked about as a candidate for Lord Mayor, a position he soon achieved. William Garrard, ten years younger, was described by Stow as "a grave, sober, wise and discreet citizen, equal with the best, and inferior to none of our time."[3] Another key participant in the discussions was Sir Andrew Judde, a member of the Worshipful Company of Skinners.[4] About to turn sixty, he had just stepped down from an exhausting year as Lord Mayor, during which he had dealt with some big issues, including the slump in cloth exports, rising prices, and the sweating sickness.

William Cecil may or may not have attended the discussions among the members of the group, which were referred to as "sit-togethers," but he was almost certainly responsible for bringing forward a timely piece of intellectual analysis for the group to con sider: the first English translation of the book *Utopia,* by Sir Thomas More. A work of brilliant literary invention, the little volume, first published thirty-five years earlier, had originally been written in Latin. The new English version was translated by Ralph Robinson, who dedicated it to Cecil, one of his old school friends. By allowing his name to be associated with this literary endeavor, Cecil seems to have been endorsing the case that fresh thinking and radically new approaches were needed to rescue England.

Utopia tells the story of a fictional traveler, Raphael Hythlodaeus, who lived for five years on an imaginary island called Utopia— More's neologism combining the Greek words for "no" and "place." Although Hythlodaeus is a made-up character, More provides him with a plausible, real-life backstory: he claimed to have voyaged with Amerigo Vespucci, the Florentine explorer, who sailed along the coast of Brazil and South America at the turn of the sixteenth century.

Raphael has much to say about the sorry state of affairs in England. He portrays it as a dystopian place: dominated by a parasitic noble class who "live idle" lives, and who rely on that which "others have labored for," it is a country troubled by rising prices, overrun with sheep, and blighted by the practice of land enclosure. "Your sheep that were wont to be so weak and tame…" says Raphael, "now, as I hear say, become so great devourers and so wild that they eat up and swallow down the very men themselves." He continues: "They con-sume, destroy, and devour whole fields, houses, and cities."[5]

More then goes on to describe, through Raphael's narrative, a land where these social and political problems have been solved: an ideal place called Utopia. It is, in effect, a new England. More was the first Englishman to envision—in print, at least—the enormous potential that the New World held for remaking society.

More's vision, when first published in 1516, may even have been compelling enough to have inspired England's earliest attempt at overseas colonization. The initiative was organized and led by his brother-in-law, John Rastell, a lawyer, author, and printer. In 1517, Rastell embarked with forty soldiers on a voyage to establish a trading post and military camp somewhere in the "New Found Lands," as the New World was typically called in England.[6] Rastell got no farther than Ireland before his crew mutinied, but he did write a play about the expedition, called *A New Interlude,* and lamented a missed opportunity. "O what a thing" it would have been, he wrote, if "they that be Englishmen" had been the first to "take possession" and make "the first building and habitation" in the New World.[7]

The publication of the English translation of *Utopia* in 1551 seems to have been intended to exert a similar catalyzing influence on the grave citizens as they pondered solutions to England's crisis. To ensure the long-term future of the cloth industry, perhaps they would have to go looking for new markets with new customers beyond the familiar European centers. If so, the next question was where? Where would they find the new markets and new customers they desired?

The ideal place, they determined, would be Cathay.

TO LONDON'S MERCHANTS, "Cathay"—which comes from "Khitai," for the land of the Khitans, who held sway in northern China in the tenth century—was shorthand for all that was wondrous: a commercial utopia. Other parts of Asia had their allure: pepper came from India's southwestern coast, cloves and nutmeg from a handful of Indonesian "spice islands." But it was Cathay, dreamy and far-off, that inspired the greatest awe.

Nearly three hundred years earlier, Marco Polo, the Venetian merchant, had traveled to Cathay. He spent more than twenty years in the court of its ruler, Kublai Khan, and then brought back his stories of the kingdom's magnificence. In his *Travels,* Polo reported that the Great Khan's territories overflowed with spices, silver, and silk. One vast city, known as Quinsay, or "the City of Heaven," stretched out over a hundred miles, contained 12,000 bridges, and included a lake thirty miles wide, in the middle of which stood two royal palaces.[8] To many Venetians, Polo's stories were scarcely credible. Indeed, the sheer number of people and places he described defied belief—to the extent that he was mocked as Marco "The Millions" Polo.

Yet much of what he had to say about China was accurate, and by the 1500s the information Polo had gathered was accepted far and wide, as if nothing had changed and as if "the Great Khan" still ruled the country. But Kublai Khan was long dead. A new dynasty, the Ming, was in power. For a while, under their leadership, Chinese culture had blossomed. In a series of remarkable voyages of discovery in the early fifteenth century, a eunuch admiral, Zheng He, took his fleet of giant ocean-going treasure ships—four hundred feet long, with nine masts, nearly one hundred support vessels, and a crew of 28,000 sailors—to the Persian Gulf and the east coast of Africa.[9] But these expeditions were abruptly halted in the 1430s when China turned inward, shunning the outside world. It remained the richest country on earth, however, with an extraordinary gravitational pull on the global economy. By 1500, China accounted for 25 percent of the world's output of goods and services. England, by contrast, accounted for just 1.1 percent.[10]

Through the fifteenth century, a tangled web of trade routes connected Cathay to Europe, stretching five thousand miles across oceans, mountains, steppes, and deserts. Along these routes—which the German explorer Baron von Richtofen labeled the "Silk Road" in the 1870s—all manner of luxury goods were carried by ship, camel, and horse.[11] By the time they reached Europe, their price could have risen by as much as 1000 percent, having been handled by many middlemen—factors, traders, government officials—who charged fees, exacted their portion, skimmed a percentage, imposed taxes and duties, and demanded bribes.[12]

For centuries, it was the Venetians who were the primary importers of Chinese, Indian, and other Asian goods into Europe, collecting them from Arab merchants who had overseen their transportation to the key markets of the eastern Mediterranean—Alexandria in Egypt and Aleppo in what is now Syria. It was a highly profitable business, not least because the Venetians held an effective monopoly. And it was partly to break this Venetian stranglehold on the spice trade that the Portuguese launched a succession of voyages in search of a faster, cheaper trade route to the East. In 1498, after nearly a century of exploration, the Portuguese navigator Vasco da Gama rounded the southern tip of Africa—the Cape of Good Hope—sailed into the Indian Ocean, and reached Calicut, on India's Malabar coast. This port was the great trading center of the East, a fabulous emporium, every bit the equal of Venice and Antwerp, where Indian, Arab, and Chinese merchants came to trade.

The English ruling elite had long been enthusiastic consumers of exotic commodities from the East, and their appetite started to expand in the twelfth century, when crusader-soldiers returned home from the Holy Land with all kinds of luxury goods.[13] Most of the exotic goods native to tropical lands were rarities. Spices, in particular, were special—the words have a common etymology—because so few of them, with the exception of saffron, could be grown at home.* These otherworldly condiments were used not only to preserve and enhance food but also to ward off disease, arouse sexual desire, and summon the gods. Their scarcity value conferred sta-

---

* Useful as both a cooking spice and as a cloth dye, saffron was so successfully cultivated in Walden, where Thomas Smith was born, that the market town came to be known as Saffron Walden.

tus on those who purchased and used them, and for several centuries only monarchs, noblemen, and bishops could afford them.

Yet English merchants made no effort to match the Portuguese and Spanish by trading directly with countries in the East. Indeed, it was not until the crisis of the early 1550s that the English realized they must begin the search for new markets beyond Europe. The trouble was, England did not have the oceangoing expertise of its commercial rivals. Fortunately, John Dudley, who had served as Henry VIII's last Lord Admiral, knew someone who could help, if only he could be persuaded to come back to England.

That someone was Sebastian Cabot, the greatest seafaring expert in all of Europe.

THE NAME CABOT was hardly unknown to the English. It harked back to a time when England had made its first steps towards the New World. In 1497, Sebastian's father, a Venetian called Giovanni or Zuan Cabota—later Anglicized as John Cabot—had initiated a voyage to the New World for the English. King Henry VII had granted him letters patent—the royal document specifying rights and permissions of discovery—"to find, discover, and investigate whatsoever islands, countries, regions or provinces...which before this time were unknown to all Christians."[14]

Henry's sponsorship of Cabot's voyage represented more than a bold initiative—it was a remarkable act of defiance against the dominant powers of the day: not only the kings of Spain and Portugal, but also Pope Alexander VI, the leader of the Catholic Church. After Christopher Columbus first claimed lands in the West Indies for Spain in 1492, the Portuguese had protested. In a negotiation supervised by the Pope, a Spaniard, they struck a deal that was ratified by the Treaty of Tordesillas, named after the village in northern Spain where the deliberations took place. They drew an imaginary line through a meridian near the middle of the Atlantic, dividing the world roughly in half. Spain was granted the rights to any non-Christian territories they had discovered or might discover to the west of the line, Portugal got everything to the east of it. In effect, Spain and Portugal divided up the unexplored world among themselves—with the approval of the Pope, whom Christians believed was God's representative on earth.

Henry's support for John Cabot's voyage was risky not only because of the potential reaction of the Pope, Spain, and Portugal, but also because Cabot was untested. Although he had extensive experience as a mariner in the Mediterranean—as his name, which means "the coaster," suggests—he had no oceangoing experience.[15] But the Venetian was driven and persuasive and obviously willing to take the risk, and Bristol, where he was living, had a growing reputation as a seafaring capital. It was a thriving port, made wealthy through fishing as well as direct trade with Bordeaux, Lisbon, Seville, and the Atlantic islands: Azores, Madeira, and the Canaries. But legend also held that Bristol's sailors had a taste for Atlantic exploration. One Bristolian had supposedly sailed in search of an illusive place known as the Isle of Brasil or High Brasil (not to be confused with Brazil in South America), and two merchants were said to have been "discoverers of the New found lands"—myth, perhaps, but part of the local lore.[16]

It was from this dynamic English port that, in May 1497, John Cabot departed in the *Matthew*, a three-masted caravel, flying the flag of Henry VII.[17] Sebastian Cabot claimed that he, then in his teens, was on board the ship as one of his father's crew of eighteen men.[18] In June, they made landfall, went ashore, and came upon a fire site, a stick "carved and painted with brazil," and a trail into the woods—which suggested the place was or had been inhabited.[19] Cabot and his men set up a cross, raised the banner of Henry VII and the standard of St. Mark of Venice, and took possession of the place on behalf of the English king. Cabot called it *Prima Tierra Vista,* or First Discovered Land. Exactly where this land was, no one knows for sure. Some say Newfoundland, others Nova Scotia.[20]

When Cabot returned to Bristol, he was received with wild acclaim and became something of a celebrity. "He goes dressed in silk," wrote Lorenzo Pasqualigo, a Venetian merchant residing in London, "and these English run after him like mad." Cabot may well have made the claim that he had reached the fabled Cathay. Pasqualigo reported that the "Venetian . . . who went with a small ship from Bristol to find new islands" claimed to have "discovered mainland 700 leagues away, which is the country of the Grand Khan."[21] Henry VII was so delighted that he rewarded Cabot with a royal pension and an impressive title. Great Admiral.

The celebrity did not last, however. The following year, Cabot set out on another voyage, leading a fleet of five ships, again with Henry's support and also the backing of some Bristol merchants. There were great hopes for this enterprise. According to the Duke of Milan's ambassador, the plan was to "form a colony" and, as he explained, "by means of this, they hope to make London a more important mart for spices than Alexandria."[22] But John Cabot and his ship never returned.[23]

IT HAS BEEN speculated that Sebastian sailed on this second voyage, returning to England on one of the ships that did make it home.[24] At any rate, after his father's death, the young Venetian inherited the letters patent granted by Henry VII, and a few years later, when he was in his twenties, he embarked on a voyage across the northern Atlantic. Setting off in 1508, Cabot glimpsed what he considered was a channel of water around the northern coast of America. This, he believed, was the route to Cathay — what became known as the Northwest Passage. He had probably reached what is now called Hudson Strait, more than one hundred years before its eponymous discoverer, Henry Hudson. Cabot later revealed that he would have continued through the passage — to Cathay, as he presumed — if his crew had not threatened mutiny and persuaded him to return to England.[25] When Cabot arrived home, he found that Henry VII had died, and, as the Venetians reported, the new king, Henry VIII, "cared little for such an enterprise" to the New World.[26]

For the next three years following his voyage, Cabot worked in England as a mapmaker. Then, in 1512, he was given royal permission to go to Spain and work for King Ferdinand, Henry VIII's father-in-law. It seems he was lured there by the prospect of "the navigation to the Indies and the Island of the Bacallaos,"* meaning Newfoundland.[27] This hoped-for voyage never happened, but Cabot evidently impressed the Spanish court. In 1518, he landed a plum job as Pilot Major at La Casa de la Contratación—the House of Trade—the official body responsible for managing the practical, political, and economic matters associated with Spain's burgeoning empire in the New World.[28] The Pilot Major was essentially the country's senior navigator, a position created in 1508 and first held by Amerigo Vespucci. Among Cabot's responsibilities was the continual updating of the *Padrón Real,* the Casa's master chart of the world's seas.[29]

Even as he carried out his official duties, Cabot retained his interest in finding a northern passage to the East. In 1519, Cabot—although he was now a Spanish official—was approached by England's Cardinal Thomas Wolsey, Henry VIII's powerful adviser, to lead a "voyage of discovery" to the "newfound island" for Henry's "honour" and "for the general wealth of his realm." It is not clear what kindled Henry's sudden interest in the New World, but he pledged to provide ships for the venture if merchants paid for supplies and sailors' wages. In return for their support, Henry promised to grant a monopoly of trade for ten years and a fifteen-month exemption on paying customs duties.[30]

The merchants considered the proposal. The three Gresham brothers—William, Richard, and John—agreed to invest, as did other members of the Mercers and some Bristol merchants.[31] The majority of London merchants, however, were not convinced. The members of the Worshipful Company of Drapers, a powerful guild

---

* The Spanish word *bacalaos* means "codfish," and the Spanish named this region after the abundant cod found on the Newfoundland banks.

of cloth merchants, were especially dubious, arguing that it made no sense to risk the lives of men and goods on "the singular trust of one man," namely Sebastian Cabot. They questioned his experience and doubted his claims, suggesting that he was just repeating things he had "heard his Father and other men speak in times past."[32] Although Henry tried to keep the mission alive, it eventually fell apart in 1521.

With his hopes dashed, Cabot, now approaching forty, continued his work in Spain as Pilot Major for La Casa. Then, in 1524, another opportunity arose, this time courtesy of Charles V, ruler of the Spanish empire. A consortium of merchants, including Robert Thorne, an English merchant based in Seville whose father had sponsored John Cabot, agreed to fund a voyage to the East with Sebastian as leader. Charles charged Cabot with filling his ships "with all the gold, silver, pearls, precious stones, drugs and spices" that could be found in "eastern China, Tarshish, Ophir, Japan, the islands of the Molluccas, and other lands and islands."[33]

In April 1526, Cabot's fleet set off across the Atlantic. He had been instructed to pass through the Magellan Strait, named for the Portuguese nobleman, Ferdinand Magellan, who had discovered the passage round the southern tip of South America when leading the first circumnavigation of the world five years earlier. But Cabot failed to reach the strait, and when he returned to Spain he was arrested, tried, convicted, and sentenced to exile in Oran, a Spanish-controlled trading city on the north coast of Africa, now Algeria.

In the end, however, he was reprieved and restored to his post as Pilot Major.

HOW MUCH JOHN DUDLEY knew about the details of this turbulent episode in Sebastian Cabot's past in Spain is not clear—but he believed that, whatever his faults, the Venetian was a man of exceptional experience, expertise, and tenacity.

There was no guarantee that Cabot would consider a return to England. He had built a life in Spain, and despite the lingering stain on his reputation Charles V still held him in high regard. But all was not rosy at work. At La Casa, Cabot got caught up in a game of power politics, as an intense debate raged between the advocates of the practical and theoretical aspects of navigation. Cabot was a practical man, suspicious of academic theorists, but he was losing the debate and, with it, his stature as a leader of La Casa.[34]

By now in his late sixties, he might have soldiered on, settling for a distinguished retirement. But in 1547 his beloved Spanish wife died, and suddenly he had no filial ties to keep him in Spain.[35] He soon requested a six-month leave of absence from his duties at La Casa, saying that he intended to visit Brussels, where he needed to attend to some business affairs. It was then that Dudley, knowing that Cabot faced an uncertain future and was leaving Spain, took his opportunity. He and his fellow privy councillors earmarked one hundred pounds "for transporting of one Cabot, a pilot, to come out of Hispania to serve and inhabit in England." By the following year, Cabot was in England, and his reward was an annuity of £166.[36]

Charles was livid at Cabot's departure. In April 1549, he instructed his ambassador to demand Cabot's return, later explaining that the Venetian "must clearly understand that we require his services, and claim a right to them."[37] But Cabot successfully evaded these demands, soon proving that Charles was right to be angry. After his arrival in England, Cabot got involved in the planning of more than one daring overseas project, probably at Dudley's behest. One was an attack on Peru, the source of much of Spain's silver wealth, but this did not materialize. The second was the voyage to Cathay that the English merchants had been considering. As Spain's ambassador noted, "The people of London set a great value on the captain's services, and believe him to be possessed of secrets concerning English navigation."[38]

Cabot may indeed have carried a secret to England, embedded in a map of the world that he brought with him from Spain. He had first created a world map in 1544 as a way of demonstrating his extensive knowledge of the earth's lands and oceans. Like many maps of the day, it combined cartography based on detailed information collected from mariners and merchants along with fanciful illustrations and marginal legends containing large segments of text. There were drawings of ships, strange and wonderful people, animals, buildings, and legends describing monsters with massive ears, birds that could lift an ox, and the funeral practices of the inhabitants of Bengal.[39]

Also, the map presented some information that Cabot did not actually believe. Emblazoned across the entire northern region of the earth are the Latin words *Mare congelatum per totum*—meaning "the entire sea is frozen" and, therefore, presumably impassable. Cabot believed, however, that the sea was perfectly navigable and that there was some kind of northern passage along the northern coast of America. He was not alone in thinking this. In 1507, Martin Waldseemüller, a German cartographer, had published an atlas with a wholly new depiction of the world, called the *Universalis cosmographia secundum Ptholomaei traditionem et Americi Vespucii alioru[m]que lustrationes,* and simply known as the *Cosmographia*. Drawing on the writings of Amerigo Vespucci, who coined the phrase "New World," Waldseemüller rejected the hallowed view of ancient cosmographers who believed the world comprised three continents: Europe, Africa, and Asia. He added a fourth continent: a narrow, scraggly island surrounded by water at the western margin of the world. He gave the continent a name, arguing that since a "fourth part"—adding to Europe, Asia and Africa—had been "discovered by Amerigo Vespucci," there was "no reason why anyone should justly object to calling this part… America, after Amerigo, its discoverer, a man of great ability."[40]

But Waldseemüller's map of North America was largely inspired guesswork, while Cabot's belief in the northern passage was rooted in the voyage he began in 1508, when he claimed to have found the entrance to the sea route. In his early days in Spain, he tried to generate sufficient interest to mount another expedition. But he failed, and despite his best efforts to keep his discovery secret, others picked up on his claim. In 1537, Gemma Frisius, a renowned Dutch cosmographer serving as royal cartographer at the Spanish court, produced a globe that showed an open northern channel trending west and then southwest towards the Pacific Ocean. He labeled it the Strait of the Three Brothers—which may have referred to Cabot and his two brothers, who were all listed on the original royal patent granted to their father. Also, as if to underscore the point, he labeled the southern shore "the land found by the Britons."[41]

Significantly, Cabot had not drawn this northern passage on his map of 1544. But when he came to London in 1547, he set about updating and revising the map, working with Clement Adams, who was an engraver as well as a writer. The revised version (now lost) depicted the northern passageway and quickly became one of the key documents for John Dudley and the London merchant's bold new endeavor to reach Cathay.

3

<hr>

THE MYSTERIE

SOMETIME IN LATE 1552, a group of merchants, courtiers, and intellectuals, in consultation with Sebastian Cabot, drew up plans for a new commercial venture and gave it a rather glorious name: "The Mysterie, Company, and Fellowship of Merchant Adventurers for the Discovery of Regions, Dominions, Islands, and Places Unknown." Its purpose was to enable them to "lay their heads together" to "give their judgments" and to "provide things requisite and profitable" for the venture.[1]

The Mysterie was hardly the first English company. Many of London's medieval guilds—which were associations of merchants who came together to protect and promote their particular trade—had gradually evolved into livery companies. These enjoyed significant privileges granted by the crown and, as their name suggests, they were distinguished by, among other things, their ceremonial dress. The twelve richest of these companies—known as the "Great Twelve" and led by the Worshipful Company of Mercers—were among the most powerful institutions in the country. Through their apprenticeship systems, they determined who could enter their trade. They set standards for quality: the goldsmiths, for example, operated from a hall where they stamped gold they deemed to be of good quality, hence the term "hallmark." Above all, the livery companies conferred upon their members the "freedom" of the city—in other words, citizenship. And without this designation, no person was permitted to trade in London. Anyone who dared to defy the system—by trading without a company's approval—faced being ostracized as an "interloper."[2]

The Mysterie had some characteristics of these traditional livery companies. The word "mysterie"—from the Latin *ministerium* and the Anglo-Norman *mestier,* meaning "art" or "calling"—signified an occupational group, an organization of professionals in a certain discipline or trade.[3] But the term was becoming an anachronism even at this time and obscures the truly transformational character of the new company. Unlike the Great Twelve, the Mysterie was not so focused on a single, homogeneous group. In fact, it brought together in a new way two pillars of England's ruling elite: merchants and courtiers.

To understand the two groups in the commerce-court dynamic, take a look at the geography of London. A map published in 1572 but representing London of the 1550s shows a vibrant place, the Thames busy with high-masted ships and rowing boats.[4] To the east is the City of London, which lay in the shadow of the Tower of London. It is still surrounded by the wall that the Romans built when they first chose Londinium as the site for crossing the river. This was the commercial center, and here the merchants held sway. To the west is Westminster, which was gathered around the precincts of the medieval abbey, where the king resided and the courtiers were dominant. The two conurbations were linked by a long thoroughfare, the Strand, which was fronted by the riverside mansions of the great nobles.

The City and Westminster, the merchants and the courtiers, had long enjoyed a close, symbiotic relationship—the business people filled the royal coffers in return for commercial privileges. But this was transformed in the wake of the dissolution of the monasteries, when, as favored beneficiaries of the crown, they gained substantial wealth and property. Dudley, for example, claimed Durham House, the mansion on the Strand formerly owned by the bishops of Durham. The merchants, too, took advantage of the dissolution. The Mercers, for example, laid claim to the magnificent church, mansion, and associated lands that belonged to the order of Thomas Becket, a former archbishop of Canterbury, right in the heart of the City.[5]

As the merchants from the City and the courtiers from Westminster increased in wealth and enjoyed royal favors, they began to share power, and the Mysterie was one of the first ventures in which they worked together with a new unity of purpose. But what also distinguished the Mysterie was its corporate structure. It was established with what has been called "a revolutionary new form of business organization"—arguably the world's first joint-stock company and certainly the first in England.[6] Until then, English trading voyages—to Antwerp, Bordeaux, Lisbon, Seville, even the eastern Mediterranean—had been funded by individual merchants or small syndicates. Typically, the business was conducted on credit and exchange, requiring relatively little up-front capital. But the Mysterie's proposed voyage to Cathay promised to be altogether more capital-intensive and risky. No one merchant or courtier had the liquid assets to finance it alone, and given the parlous state of Edward VI's finances, none could count on funding from the crown.

It was to solve this problem that the Mysterie leaders chose the joint-stock form, which overcame these difficulties. This may have been at Sebastian Cabot's suggestion, since the joint-stock approach, like so much about business organization, had been pioneered by Italian merchants, and he was deeply familiar with their business practices.[7] Italian merchants devised the fundamental idea of a company, a *compagnia*—which comes from the conjunction of the Latin words *cum* and *panis* and means "breaking bread together." It enabled individuals, usually relatives, to come together for their mutual benefit, devoting their time and money to a single, simple partnership or family firm.[8] The joint-stock form took the company idea a step further. It provided a governance structure and had perpetual corporate status, so that a large number of individual investors—not just family members and not all of them directly involved in company operations—could pool their assets and share the risk over extended periods of time. This made investment highly attractive to courtiers because they could invest and potentially reap profits without having to get involved in the tedious business of management themselves. It also enabled investors to bequeath or sell their shares to other people, ideally at a higher price than they had originally paid.

The Mysterie offered membership in the company to anyone prepared to invest twenty-five pounds, which, in effect, bought them a single share of stock. Although this sum may sound small today, it was far beyond the reach of most people, amounting to between two and three times the average annual salary of a journeyman.* For the richest citizens, however, who might spend twenty-five pounds on a suit of fine armor, the share price was reasonable and even attractive.[9] Where else could you transmute such an amount into such a grand undertaking? As a result, the Mysterie was able to raise a total of six thousand pounds. By way of comparison, when Henry VII invested in John Cabot's second voyage to the newfound land, albeit six decades earlier, he spent just fifty pounds. The names of the investors in the Mysterie have been lost to history, but if every subscriber purchased just one share, it means that 240 people were sufficiently

---

* The average daily nominal wage in the period 1490–1609 was five pence for a semi-skilled worker or journeyman. In 1553, this rose by 60 percent in nominal terms (although the purchasing power actually fell, because of the rising costs of day-to-day commodities). So, assuming a six-day week, the annual salary was around ten pounds. See Steve Rappaport, *Worlds Within Worlds*, 401–7.

excited or convinced to invest a sizeable amount — in a venture that might easily result in a complete loss.

WITH THE ORGANIZATION established and funding secured, the Mysterie members — particularly George Barne, William Garrard, and Andrew Judde — set about organizing the voyage. These three constituted a formidable team. Supremely wealthy, they also possessed substantial administrative experience. Barne and Garrard ruled London, as mayor and sheriff respectively, while Judde, as Mayor of the Staple, oversaw the economy of Calais. Thomas Gresham probably also remained influential, although by this time he had been appointed the king's factor, or merchant, responsible for handling the crown's business affairs in Antwerp.

The first task for the Mysterie organizers was to commission the construction of a fleet of three ships, purpose-built for a long voyage into potentially hostile waters. In doing so, they sought out the latest thinking on maritime design and building. No doubt, they were aided by John Dudley, who had gained a great deal of relevant knowledge during his years as Lord Admiral. The ships were designed to accommodate a large company of merchants and crew, with sufficient storage space for an eighteen-month supply of victuals and equipment, and ample cargo space to hold cloth and other export merchandise as well as the commodities they hoped to bring home.

The merchants took great care in their preparations, making sure to purchase the best materials available, including "very strong and well-seasoned planks." The diligent shipwrights worked "with daily travail, and their greatest skill" to build ships "staunch and firm" that could endure the hardships that certainly awaited them. Together, they tried to prepare for all eventualities. For example, the merchants had learned that the ships might encounter a type of worm known as the *teredo navalis* that could bore through even the staunchest oak planking. To prevent this, the shipbuilders sheathed the keels with thin sheets of lead.[10]

With the ships under construction, the Mysterie began the critical task of recruiting men to lead the expedition, command the ships, and serve as crew and specialists. Unlike their Spanish rivals, the merchants of the Mysterie had no plans to build forts or conquer territories in distant lands. Their goal was to establish friendly relations with the leaders in foreign markets or, in Edward's words, "an indissoluble and perpetual league of friendship."[11] They wanted to establish mercantile headquarters abroad and promote profitable trading relations. To this end, the captain would play a critical role. He might need to deal with hostile people and foreign armies along the way, and he might eventually be required to consort with the fabled king of Cathay, the Great Khan himself. So the captain would ideally be a diplomat, soldier, navigator, and merchant.

There was no obvious English candidate available with such a range of skills. So, the Mysterie decided that the wisest choice for supreme commander and admiral of the fleet would be a gentleman-soldier—a person with a sound family lineage, unimpeachable personal character, and exceptional vitality. Accordingly, they appointed Sir Hugh Willoughby, who was "of goodly personage"—from the right kind of family—and suitably young, probably in his thirties.[12] He had military experience, having been knighted on the battlefield after distinguishing himself in battle against the Scottish. What's more, he keenly wanted the job. As Clement Adams noted, the young knight "earnestly requested" to be given command of the voyage.[13]

Willoughby ticked many of the boxes, but he lacked one important qualification: maritime experience. So the Mysterie agreed to appoint a pilot major, or chief navigator, for the entire fleet. They chose a young man whom Cabot probably endorsed: Richard Chancellor. In 1550, Chancellor had taken part in a training voyage organized by Cabot. The ship *Aucher,* financed by Sir William Aucher, a courtier close to Dudley's family, sailed to the Levant, manned by a cohort of talented young sailors that included Chancellor, the Borough brothers— Stephen and William—as well as Matthew Baker, an aspiring ship-wright.[14] The captain, Roger Bodenham, later reported that all the mariners on his ship had distinguished themselves and were ready to take charge of their own vessels and expeditions.[15]

Chancellor had the eloquent support of the aristocrat Henry Sidney, Dudley's son-in-law and longtime friend of the king, Edward VI. Still in his early twenties, and distinguished by hooded eyes and a delicate mouth, Sidney was a fine orator, and he made a compelling case for Chancellor, who had been raised in his household. "You know the man by report," Sidney told his fellow Mysterie investors, "I by experience; you by words, I by deeds; you by speech and company, but I, by the daily trial of his life, have a full and perfect knowledge of him."

But it was Chancellor's formidable knowledge of the seas, rather than Sidney's rhetorical flourishes, that ultimately persuaded the unsentimental merchants to put their faith in him. They even came to the conclusion that the "great hope for the performance of the business" rested almost entirely on the shoulders of the young navigator.[16]

AS MUCH AS they trusted Chancellor, the Mysterie members wanted to prepare him as thoroughly as possible for his responsibility. To that end, they sent him to work with the foremost cosmographer of the age, Dr. John Dee. Just twenty-five, and well-known to John Dudley as tutor to his children, Dee was charged with helping Chancellor to develop the charts he would need to sail through unfamiliar waters and plot a route to Cathay.

If anyone could help Chancellor in this regard, it was Dee. Praised as a brilliant polymath, Dee was another one of the generation of Cambridge scholars that had come to prominence under the patronage of William Cecil.[17] A merchant's son—his Welsh father was a Mercer—Dee was reportedly "a very handsome man," who was "tall and slender" and had a "very fair, clear complexion." He thrived at Cambridge, where he studied at St. John's, Cecil's beloved college. There, no doubt wearing what would become his trademark attire—a flowing garment "like an Artist's gown, with hanging sleeves"—he developed the intense study habits that he continued throughout his life.[18] He typically worked eighteen hours a day, breaking only "to allow [for] meat and drink (and some refreshing after) two hours every day" and "to sleep four hours every night."[19]

In 1546, when still a teenager, Dee was appointed to a founding fellowship at Trinity College, which was newly established by Henry VIII. Officially, he held his post in the study of Greek, although mathematics was his true calling and greatest strength. The college that would later boast Sir Isaac Newton among its professors did not yet have a lecturer in mathematics. As John Aubrey, the contemporary biographer, put it, "Astrologer, Mathematician and Conjurer were accounted the same things."[20]

In 1547, Dee crossed the English Channel to study civil law at the University of Louvain, in modern-day Belgium, after Cambridge had lost its star law professor with Sir Thomas Smith's move to court. While there, however, he developed a fascination with cosmography. The cosmographers' goal was to describe the overarching principles governing the formation of the universe—not the precise geographic features of the earth or the other planets. Dee took up his study at a time of enormous change in the understanding of the universe. In 1543, a few years before Dee arrived on the European mainland, a book called *De Revolutionibus* had been published. Written by Mikolaj Kopernik, an obscure Polish priest better known as Copernicus, its then heretical theory—that the sun, not the earth, occupied the center of the universe—was starting to be hotly debated in learned circles.

At Louvain, Dee encountered some of the leading lights in the field of cosmography. He befriended Gemma Frisius—the scholar who had incorporated the information about Sebastian Cabot's voyage to the Northwest Passage in one of his globes—as well as Frisius's pupil, Gerard Mercator. During his time with them, Dee copied their maps and came into possession of a pair of Mercator's globes.[21] Returning to England in 1551, as the cloth industry spiraled downward and the country plunged into economic crisis, Dee was soon tutoring not only Dudley's children but also young Edward, a job he landed by proposing a novel way to teach mathematics that required "measuring the size of the universe" — a cosmographical pursuit if ever there was one.

With Richard Chancellor, Dee was not so much teaching as collaborating, although he called the young navigator an "incomparable" student. Together, they tackled the particularly tricky problems of sailing in the far northerly latitudes. The magnetic pull of the North Pole affects the compass, making it difficult to hold a true course. Moreover, the meridians of longitude become compressed the closer ships get to the Pole, so that when following a fixed-compass bearing the sailor may spiral off course. To aid their studies, Dee and Chancellor referred to the Mercator globes Dee had brought from Louvain. Also, they used Dee's own invention, which he called a "paradoxical compass," designed to help mariners correct for longitudinal compression.[22]

During their consultations, Dee and Chancellor must have focused their attention on the various possible routes to Cathay. They were probably able to consult Cabot's revised map of the world, completed in 1549, which showed the Northwest Passage. Given Cabot's lifelong interest in that route, the likelihood is that Dee and Chancellor plotted a course along the margin of North America. Yet, by the time the two men had completed their work, it seems that the Mysterie had agreed that its fleet would take a very different route: the North*east* Passage. Investors were informed that Willoughby and Chancellor would attempt "to sail into the East parts, by the coasts of Norway, Lappia, and Finmarchia, and so by the narrow tract of the sea by the coasts of Groueland, into the frozen sea, called Mare Congelatum, and so forth to Cathay."[23]

FOR ALL THEIR fascination with Cathay, the Mysterie merchants had very little practical information about the people, lands, and seas to the northeast of the British Isles. This was largely because the merchants of the Hanseatic League, from Germany's Baltic coast, held a firm grip on the trade to those markets—not for nothing was the North Sea then known as the *Mare Germanicus*, or German Sea. It was only after Thomas Gresham's assault on the Hanse merchants' privileges in 1552—an action that paved the way for an opening of the sea lanes to English commercial traffic—that the Mysterie merchants could contemplate voyages to the northeast and beyond.

Nevertheless, plenty of information about Cathay and sea routes to the East did exist. In the first fifty years of the sixteenth century, the Portuguese amassed some six thousand documents relating to trade in the East. Most of this material, however, was unpublished, undistributed, or held in secret.[24] A good deal of the published work, if it was not held close by governments or trade organizations, was either too general to be of much use, out of date, or unavailable in English or Latin. The *Decades of the New World,* by Peter Martyr d'Anghiera, an Italian scholar in the Spanish court, chronicled the history of Spain and Portugal's discoveries—but it had first been published in 1516. Another Italian, Giovanni Batista Ramusio, who was based in Venice, published the first volume of his *Navigations & Voyages*, a collection of travelers' tales, in 1550—but it was not readily available to English readers.

Filling the knowledge gap was a library of popular travel narratives, chief among them Marco Polo's *Travels*. Another popular title was *The Eastern Parts of the World Described,* by Odoric of Pordenone, a Franciscan monk who journeyed from Italy into Iran, India, China, and Russia in the 1300s. Friar Odoric marveled at the abundance of pepper available on India's southwestern Malabar coast and wrote that the spice "groweth on plants which have leaves like ivy."[25] He described several Chinese cities, including Censcalan, now the massive industrial city of Guangzhou, which, even in his day, was a sprawling metropolis "as big as three Venices." Here he found a shipping industry "so great and vast in amount that to some it would seem well nigh incredible." Odoric spent three years in the "noble city Cambalech"—present-day Beijing—where the Great Khan, the Chinese ruler, kept a splendid palace. He reported on how the ruler's court worked, provided information for travelers, and explained how news was disseminated—by a form of pony express, but employing camels when the news was particularly urgent.[26]

Even more popular was the *Travels of Sir John Mandeville,* purportedly written by an English knight, describing his experiences in India and China starting in 1322 and continuing for some thirty years. Almost certainly, Mandeville was the nom de plume of a French armchair traveler who derived most of his tales from Odoric's work.[27] Nevertheless, his *Travels* served to engender interest in the Great Khan. Apparently, the emperor and his barons valued woolen cloths more than their "cloth of gold and silken camlet"—which must have perked up the ears of a purveyor of English broadcloth.[28]

To improve their knowledge, the Mysterie organizers started "to inquire, search and seek" for information "concerning the Easterly part or tract of the world."[29] Their inquiry included, quite bizarrely, an interview with two men who worked in King Edward's stable. Adams called them "Tartarians," meaning they came from the land of Tartary, or central Asia, and a term used by Mandeville.[30] The stable hands proved to be useless interviewees. They ultimately admitted they knew little about their homeland, preferring to "toss pots"—that is, drink—than "learn the states and dispositions of people"[31]

To bring them more reliable information, the merchants commissioned Richard Eden, another of Cecil's acolytes and his secretary at the time, to prepare a dossier on "new found lands." The result was *A Treatyse of the Newe India,* which was largely a translation of parts of the *Universal Cosmographie,* a book by Sebastian Munster, a German professor at Basel University in Switzerland. Originally published in 1544, the *Cosmographie* offered information on a variety of foreign lands. But, in a sign that the Mysterie was focused on reaching Cathay, Eden picked out stories about the countries of the East: Calicut, a city on the Malabar Coast and "the most famous market town of India," the "great empire of Cathay," and the "marvelous cities" of Mangi, or southern China. He painted them in a glorious light, contrasting them with the lands conquered by the Spanish in America, which he described in derogatory terms as places with "anthropophagi" (cannibals) and limited commercial opportunities.[32]

Eden's work, dedicated to John Dudley, was more than a collection of translated tales, however. It was in effect a prospectus and brochure for investors in the Mysterie venture. Eden, who has been described as "England's first literary imperialist," urged his readers to see the "reward of noble and honest enterprises"—namely "worldly riches," the glorification of God, and the enlargement of the Christian faith.[33] He further reassured those who may have noticed that a northern passage to Cathay did not appear on most maps. Its absence, Eden explained, was because the cartographers had relied on the outdated calculations of Claudius Ptolemy, the Greek-Egyptian mathematician who produced a "world gazetteer" in AD 150. And, although Ptolemy was "an excellent man," many things were "hid from his knowledge" at that distant time.[34]

Even aided by the information collected in Eden's *Treatyse,* and armed with the knowledge imparted by Cabot and Dee, the Mysterie was still taking a grand and audacious shot in the dark. For all the Mysterie's preparations and investigations, Willoughby and Chancellor barely knew where they were headed, what they might discover, or how they would conduct business with whosoever they might encounter there. As Clement Adams acknowledged, "it was doubtful whether there was any passage or no."[35]

That is why Sebastian Cabot prepared some very precise instructions, which he called ordinances. These constituted a kind of mission statement and employee manual for Willoughby and his crew.

BASED ON HIS tenure as Pilot Major at La Casa as well as on his own extensive seagoing experience, Cabot knew that an expedition could go disastrously wrong without a clear statement of purpose and written rules and regulations. His thirty-three ordinances provided instructions for managing the fleet while at sea, guidelines for behavior when encountering new people in strange places, and advice on methods that would work best when trading in unfamiliar markets.

The first ordinance was general in nature, almost motivational in tone. Cabot entreated the ship's company to be "knit and accorded in unity, love, conformity, and obedience." Only if they avoided the kind of mutinous dissent that "hath overthrown many notable intended and likely enterprises and exploits" would they stand any chance of success.[36] These words had their origins in Cabot's own bitter experience. In 1508, he had faced a mutinous crew when he reached what he believed was the entrance to the Northwest Passage. Then, in 1526, he once again clashed with his crew as he navigated along the coast of South America.

Several of Cabot's ordinances are concerned with seafaring, navigation, and fleet management. In one of them, he specified that the captain, pilot major, and masters must all agree on matters of navigation. He inserted this in order to prevent the ships' becoming separated from one another and to avoid unilateral action on any master's part. In another ordinance, he reinforced this point, making it clear that the "fleet shall keep together and not separate themselves asunder."

Cabot also stressed the importance of chronicling the voyage. He recommended that the merchants "shall daily write, describe, and put in memory the Navigation of every day and night." All the vital information was to be recorded in "a common ledger" so that the Mysterie's leaders could learn from the experience and better prepare the next voyage. The importance of knowledge gathering was further underlined in an ordinance that directed the "steward and cook of every ship" to make weekly — or even more frequent — accounts of "the victuals, as well flesh, fish, biscuit, meat, or bread" and all else, so that "no waste or unprofitable excess be made." The fleet was provisioned with food for eighteen months, though no one knew for sure how long they might actually be away from England.[37] A detailed and accurate record-keeping of the food supplies could mean the difference between life and death.

Given that Willoughby and his crew were sure to meet new peoples, Cabot warned them not to use "violence or force" — the English, it was clear, wanted to be different from the Spanish. In particular, no woman should "be tempted," implying there should be no dalliances, romantic liaisons, or forced sexual encounters between the English and native people. Also, the mariners were to take pains "not to provoke" any foreigners by "disdain, laughing, contempt, or such like," regardless of how strange or unusual their manners and appearance.

If the subject of religion came up, the crew were advised to "pass it over in silence." Even though investors had been assured that the venture would promote the enlargement of the Christian faith, the English wanted to avoid any subjects that might interrupt the peaceful, commercial aims of the voyage. To this point, Cabot added a stern reminder that the company was operating according to new rules: those of a joint-stock company. This meant, he said, that no individual was to conduct business privately, on his own behalf, for his own benefit. Each was only to do business for "the common stock of the company."

Above all, Willoughby and his crew were instructed to remember that they were on a mission for king and country. They were "not to give up," Cabot wrote, "until it shall be accomplished, so far forth as possibility and life of man may serve or extend."

4

———•«◉»•———

A NEWE AND STRANGE
NAVIGATION

ON THE AFTERNOON of Thursday, May 20, 1553, the Mysterie's flotilla of newly constructed ships prepared to set off from Ratcliffe, a village on the north bank of the Thames and about two miles downstream from the heart of London. The flagship, *Bona Esperanza,* was commanded by Hugh Willoughby, the soldier with little maritime experience. Richard Chancellor, the pilot major, commanded the largest of the vessels, the *Edward Bonaventure.* The ships' names—a third vessel was called *Bona Confidentia*—expressed the optimism of the enterprise: Good Hope, Good Fortune, Good Confidence.[1]

The ships sailed with the blessing and good wishes of King Edward, along with a letter of royal introduction. The document, translated into Greek and "diverse other languages," was signed with a flourish and grandly addressed to "all Kings, Princes, Rulers, Judges, and Governours of the earth."[2] In it, Edward announced that he, the king of England, had "licensed the right valiant and worthy Sir Hugh Willoughby" to venture to lands beyond his dominions, to conduct trade and to establish "an indissoluble and perpetuall league of friendship" with trading partners abroad.[3] He promised the foreign kings that, if they allowed his merchants to conduct business in their domains, their subjects would receive reciprocity in England "if at any time they shall come to our kingdoms."[4]

According to the sailing orders, the ships were to progress to the Thames estuary, a journey of some thirty-five miles. Once there, they were to turn north into the North Sea, the *Mare Germanicus,* and then head towards the *Oceanus Deucale*—now known as the Norwegian Sea—that lay beyond Scotland.

After clearing the Norwegian coast, they were to turn east again and continue sailing as far as the wind would take them and the seas would let them. If all went well, they would scud through the northeast seaway, skirt the territory marked on Cabot's map as *Terra Incognita*—unknown land—and reach the hoped-for outlet into the China Sea. From there they would navigate, somehow, to Cathay and the markets of the East, where they would trade English cloth for spices and silks or whatever could be had—and then do it all in reverse.

This was a bold "blue ocean" strategy of the most literal kind.[5] To execute on the plan, Willoughby and Chancellor had assembled a crew of 116 men—sailors, of course, as well as cooks, carpenters, coopers, gunners, surgeons, and a minister. Also aboard was a large contingent of merchants—eighteen of them—who were to be the first English commercial travelers to crack the new overseas markets.[6]

At Ratcliffe, to see them off, was Sebastian Cabot. Now about seventy, his luxuriant hair had gone completely white, and his beard, bifurcated into bushy tufts, extended down to his chest. He was too old to make the voyage himself, but it remained, nevertheless, the realization of his lifetime dream: to prove the existence of a northern passage to Cathay.

AS THE TIDE turned on that May day, the mariners, resplendent in their azure-blue outfits, cut from a cloth produced in the tiny fishing village of Watchet on England's southwest coast, bade farewell to their wives and children, kinfolk, and friends who had gathered to see them off.[7] Then the ships progressed downstream to Deptford, where they anchored for the night. On the second day, the fleet approached Greenwich, and the sumptuous riverside palace where Edward and his court were then in residence. At the sight of the approaching vessels, courtiers ran out of the palace to watch them sail by. Townsfolk swarmed to the river's edge to wave. Members of the Privy Council peered out from the windows of their chamber. Others scurried to the tops of towers to take in the scene. The sailors shouted, scrambled up the rigging, climbed onto the poop, teetered on the spars, and fired the ships' guns so that the "tops of the hills sounded therewith."[8] The procession, according to an eyewitness account, was a "very triumph."[9] Except in one respect. The young king was seriously ill and unable to come to the window. Those attending him feared for his life.

The Willoughby fleet navigated the traffic and currents of the Thames for six days, bumping along from Blackwall to Woolwich to Gravesend, until they reached the outlet to the North Sea. They then sailed up the east coast of England, putting in at the port of Harwich, about fifty miles north of the Thames estuary, where they waited for a favorable wind. At last, in late June, the wind blew up fair from the southwest, and the *Bona Esperanza, Bona Confidentia,* and *Edward Bonaventure* "committed themselves to the sea, giving their last adieu to their native Country, which they knew not whether they should ever return to see again." Uncertain of "what hazards they were to fall" or "what uncertainties of the sea they were to make trial of," the mariners were reported to have "looked oftentimes back, and could not refrain from tears." Even Richard Chancellor, courageous as he was, appeared "somewhat troubled" because "he left behind him his two little sons" who would be "orphans if he speed not well."[10]

THE WILLOUGHBY FLEET followed Cabot's instructions as faithfully as they could and managed to sail "in company" — together, as he had specified. In late July, after more than a month at sea, a massive storm blew up off the coast of Norway. "By violence of wind, and thickness of mists," Willoughby noted in his logbook, "we were not able to keep together within sight."[11] Chancellor feared his comrades were not only lost to him, but to the world: "If the rage and fury of the sea have devoured those good men, or if as yet they live, and wander up and down in strange countries, I must needs say they were men worthy of better fortune."[12]

The next day the crew of Willoughby's *Bona Esperanza* spotted the *Bona Confidentia* on the horizon. Chancellor's *Edward Bonaventure*, however, was nowhere to be seen. Separated from his pilot major, Willoughby decided to proceed to one of the known places on the charts prepared with the help of John Dee—the Wardhouse, the present-day area of Vardø, off the north coast of Norway.[13] It was there that they had agreed to meet should the ships become separated.

But no sooner had Willoughby settled on this plan than he ran into trouble. He was no seafarer, and he lacked the mariner's instincts about weather and the experience of keeping his two ships aright and on course through violent storms. The Wardhouse, as described by a visitor a few years later, was a "castle standing in an island" two miles from the mainland and subject to the king of Denmark. Its isolated inhabitants "live[d] only by fishing."[14] But it was in vain that Willoughby scanned the horizon, and his ships, tacking and wallowing through the sea, sailed far to the northeast until mid-August, then headed southeast before eventually turning back at the end of the month and proceeding west until the middle of September. The path they took, as recorded in Willoughby's logbook, was a desperate zig-zagging course.[15] Without Chancellor, Willoughby was unable to make effective use of his flagship's nautical instruments. "The land," he observed ominously, "lay not as the Globe made mention."[16]

Eventually, in mid-September, four months after leaving London, the *Bona Esperanza* and *Bona Confidentia* put in at a harbor. It was not the Wardhouse, but the sea ran deep into the mainland and provided a safe haven, shelter from the winds, and a secure anchorage. The water teemed with seals and fish, while the land seemed "strange and wonderful." The crew caught sight of bears, deer, foxes, and some "strange beasts." After a week, they "thought best to winter there." The "year [was] far spent" and they feared the onset of "evil weather."[17]

While Willoughby hunkered down for the winter, Chancellor, having survived the storm, sailed the *Edward Bonaventure* on a smooth course to the Wardhouse. He waited there for seven days, keeping watch for any sign of Willoughby's two ships. When none came, he had to make a decision. This time, he could not turn to Cabot's instructions. As Cabot had rightly noted in one of his ordinances, "Of things uncertain, no certain rules may or can be given."[18]

Chancellor decided to follow Cabot's more general exhortation — to "not give up" and "to bring that to pass which was intended." As his sponsor, Sir Henry Sidney, had noted, Chancellor was a supremely brave sailor. Unlike the merchant-investors who stayed at "home quietly with our friends," he had chosen to "hazard his life amongst the monstrous and terrible beasts of the sea," declaring that if he did not succeed, he would "die the death." Sailing on, he "held on his course towards that unknown part of the world, and sailed so far that he came at last to the place where he found no night at all, but a continual light and brightness of the Sun shining clearly upon the huge and mighty Sea."[19]

The constant daylight of the Arctic proved a navigational boon. Even with precise charts and reasonable knowledge of the waters, neither of which Chancellor had, sailing at night is a precarious undertaking. There were no buoys or channel markers, no lights ashore to indicate where a landmass might be. But at last, while Willoughby was still languishing in the North Sea, Chancellor was able to bring his ship into a great bay, perhaps a hundred miles across, with the help of the midnight sun.[20]

Chancellor did not know where he was, but he anchored the *Edward Bonaventure* and soon saw a fishing boat in the distance. With a few of his men, he approached the fishermen, but they hastened away, "amazed with the strange greatness" of the English ship. Sometime later, and mindful of Cabot's instructions to deal courteously with local people, he managed to tempt them back, inviting them on board his ship. He learned that the "country was called Russia, or Moscovie, and that Ivan Vasilivich of Russia (which was at that time their King's name) ruled and governed far and wide in those places."

The "Russes," in return, asked Chancellor and his men "whence they were, and what they came for." They replied that they were Englishmen "sent into those coasts, from the most excellent King Edward the sixth." They assured the fishermen that they sought nothing from Ivan but "traffic," meaning trade, with his people. If such trade could begin, they said, then "they doubted not but that great commodity and profit would grow to the subjects of both kingdoms."[21]

Chancellor—having demonstrated his worth as a pilot—now displayed his skills as a diplomat and negotiator. The Russians told him they could not trade without permission from the tsar, Ivan Vasilyevich. To get instructions from him, they sent a letter by a "sledman" messenger to Moscow and, while waiting for a reply, hemmed and hawed about what they could or could not supply to Chancellor's party. At last, Chancellor, growing impatient, threatened to depart and ditch plans to travel to Moscow. This alarmed the Russians, who had seen some of Chancellor's "wares and commodities as they greatly desired." So, without waiting for word from the tsar, they decided to organize a team of sledmen to transport the Englishmen to Moscow—a journey of some fifteen hundred miles across icy, snow-bound land. En route, they met the sledman messenger coming towards them with a letter of welcome from Ivan written in the "most loving manner." When Chancellor finally arrived in Moscow, he was impressed by what he found: a city "that in bignesse" was "as great as the City of London" with many large buildings, although none as beautiful as those in London.

The emperor, Tsar Ivan IV (who would only later earn the sobriquet "The Terrible"), kept the English party waiting for twelve days before granting them an audience. At last, they were escorted to his residence and through the gates of the court, where they found a hundred courtiers "all appareled in cloth of gold." Then they went into the "chamber of presence" where the tsar sat "aloft, in a very royal throne," wearing a golden crown and robe and holding a "scepter garnished and beset with precious stones." Ivan was attended by his chief secretary and 150 counselors. This display so amazed the English travelers that they might have been thrown "out of countenance," but Chancellor remained calm, presented the letter from Edward VI, and engaged in conversation with the tsar, answering his many questions with few words. Apparently satisfied with their comments, the tsar invited the Englishmen to dinner with him that evening. It proved to be another stunning scene, with gold service and gold tablecloths, and 140 servants, also dressed in gold, seeing to the needs of a hundred guests. After dinner, the tsar impressed the Englishmen by greeting each of his guests by name and conversing with them.[22]

The reception of the English by the tsar was truly a momentous event. Not since the days of King Harold II—who was vanquished by William, Duke of Normandy, at the Battle of Hastings in 1066—had there been official contact between England and Russia. Back then, Harold's daughter had been married off to the Grand Prince of Kiev.[23] But Chancellor had arrived in Muscovy at an opportune moment of change. The Russians were expanding their empire by opening the trade route along the Volga River—which flowed from Moscow to the Caspian Sea—and tapping into the riches of Persia and the Silk Road to China. It had been thirty years since an ambassador from western Europe, representing the Habsburgs, had been seen at the Russian court. Now Ivan was looking for new trading partners. Chancellor's unexpected arrival provided him with an opportunity to reestablish relations with the governments and traders of western Europe — and he seized it.[24]

After several weeks in Moscow, Chancellor was granted what he had come for: a trade agreement from the tsar for King Edward. A letter granted permission to the English merchants to "have their free mart with all free liberties through my whole dominions with all kinds of wares to come and go at their pleasure, without any let, damage or impediment." The tsar, in presenting Chancellor with these commercial rights, had opened the door to what the English hoped could be a significant new market for cloth and other products.[25]

Satisfied with this success, Chancellor decided to return to England, even though he had not achieved the overarching goal of the expedition — to find the passage to Cathay. But perhaps Willoughby had somehow navigated his way through the ice floes and was even now trading with the Great Khan.

BY THE TIME Chancellor guided the *Edward Bonaventure* back along the Thames — about a year after setting off from Ratcliffe — the situation in England had changed. The letter that Chancellor carried from the tsar was addressed to Edward VI, but the young king had been dead for nearly a year, having taken his last breath in the arms of Henry Sidney, not long after the Mysterie ships departed Greenwich.

Also dead was John Dudley, the man who had brought Sebastian Cabot to England. He had been executed for his role in a succession plot to put Lady Jane Grey, his teenaged daughter-in-law, on the throne after Edward's death. For nine days, Lady Jane had reigned as queen, and Dudley hoped she would buttress the cause of Protestantism and bolster his own power. But Mary Tudor, the thirty-seven-year-old Catholic daughter of Henry VIII, seized the throne with an armed force, compelled Dudley to surrender, and condemned him to death.

Many of the merchants who had founded the Mysterie had sided with Dudley, signing the so-called "device" that transferred the throne to Lady Jane Grey. They included Sir George Barne, who was mayor at the time, William Garrard, Sir Andrew Judde, Sir John Gresham, and twelve other Staplers and Merchant Adventurers.[26] But their support for Dudley melted away as Mary exerted her royal authority and they became her willing supporters. Yet these were perilous times, and the merchants had to tread carefully. In January 1554, Mary faced a Protestant rebellion, when a Kentish landowner, Sir Thomas Wyatt, led a force of three thousand to London in a bid to secure the throne for Elizabeth, Mary's younger half-sister. This was effectively quashed. Then, six months later, Mary married Philip, ten years her junior and, as Charles V's son, heir to the Spanish throne. This horrified English Protestants who feared persecution by the Catholic monarch and alarmed English merchants who worried that their trade monopolies might be overturned by the Spanish at court.

These complications thrust the merchants of the Mysterie into an awkward situation. If they were going to capitalize on their investment in Chancellor's voyage, they realized that they needed a royal charter, or an Act of Parliament, to formally establish a company to pursue the privileges of the Muscovy trade monopoly. Letters patent had been duly prepared in 1553, before the ships had departed, but Edward had not signed the document—possibly because he was too ill, possibly because Dudley was too distracted by the succession plot to follow through on the paperwork.[27]

Now the Mysterie organizers had to petition Mary and Philip in order to finalize the charter. It was far from certain that the monarchs would agree to a new charter, given Philip's likely interest in defending the terms of the Treaty of Tordesillas. But, in a sign that Spain was not particularly interested in northern territories, Mary and Philip gave their assent. Accordingly, on February 26, 1555, a charter was granted for a new company: the Company of Merchant Adventurers for the Discovery of Regions, Dominions, Islands, and

Places Unknown. By dropping the word "mysterie," which harked back to the days of the medieval guilds, the merchants could present themselves as a forward-looking commercial enterprise. Also, by commissioning a seal featuring a ship whose prow pointed to the east—very definitely not to the west—they could make it abundantly clear that they did not seek to challenge Spain.

The Company of Merchant Adventurers (not to be confused with the Merchant Adventurers that still held the exclusive rights for cloth exports to Antwerp) was given a monopoly of trade with Muscovy and with all lands "northwards, north-eastwards or northwestwards"—a vast expanse of the world. The monopoly meant that only members of the company could trade in the designated regions. Any interlopers—people who dared to enter those regions without the company's "licence, agreement, and consent"—would risk the forfeiture of their ships and goods.[28]

On a daily basis, the company, empowered as "one body and perpetual fellowship," was to be administered by one or two governors, four "consuls" or deputy governors, and twenty-four "assistants" or directors. Sebastian Cabot was granted the honorary title of governor-for-life, and he continued to serve as a kind of father figure to the emerging generation of overseas venturers until his death in 1557.

Investors flocked to buy shares. In all, 201 people invested in the new company—199 men and two women, widows who probably inherited their stake from their merchant husbands.[29] The merchants were dominant, and they included not only the principal doers—Sir George Barne and William Garrard—but also Sir Andrew Judde and his son-in-law, Thomas Smythe; Thomas Gresham and his uncle, Sir John; Lionel Duckett, Gresham's business partner, and Thomas Lok, a Gresham family associate; and Sir John Yorke, who had helped conduct the revaluation of the coinage just a few years earlier.

Among the noblemen on the list of investors were Henry FitzAlan, the Earl of Arundel, who was lord steward of the royal household; John Russell, Earl of Bedford, who was lord keeper of the privy seal;

William Howard, baron Howard of Effingham, who was lord high admiral; and William Paulet, Marquis of Winchester, who was lord high treasurer. Henry Sidney and William Cecil were also investors. Although they had been close to John Dudley and supported Lady Jane Grey's succession, they had saved themselves and their positions through political cunning. Sidney won Philip's affection to such a degree that the future Spanish king agreed to become godfather to his son, who was dutifully named Philip. Cecil had chosen to stay in England and try to win favor, rather than follow many other committed Protestants and flee the country. He even took Spanish lessons.[30]

With the charter in hand, the Company of Merchant Adventurers began preparations for the next venture — a return visit to Muscovy. In Willoughby's absence, Richard Chancellor, who had proved himself as navigator, captain, merchant, and diplomat, was named pilot general of the fleet.[31] Queen Mary and King Philip supplied a letter — in Greek, Polish, and Italian versions — to the tsar.[32] Richard Eden prepared another dossier, with information translated from a variety of sources, including Peter Martyr's *Decades of the New World,* the first history of Spain and Portugal's exploits in the New World. Eden's was a seminal work, introducing several words into the English language, including "China" — although "Cathay" continued to be the preferred word for several years.[33] For the merchants' benefit, it featured a section on the duchy of Muscovy, although some of this information was unreliable and even fanciful. One story tells of a Muscovite who fell into an eight-foot pool of honey and rescued himself by grabbing hold of the loins of a passing bear.[34]

The Company of Merchant Adventurers, by now often known more simply as the Muscovy or Russia Company, prepared a new set of articles of instructions.[35] Hoping to develop a long-term, sustainable commercial enterprise in Russia, the company sent a number of young merchants to serve as "Agents, Factors and Attorneys general." These commercial representatives were invested with substantial authority to operate on the company's behalf. In particular, they were to establish factories—that is, offices and warehouses where the factors and agents would operate, not facilities for the manufacture of goods.

If the company focused on new business in Russia, it was careful to remind Richard Chancellor that the goal of finding a northern route to the East was not to be abandoned. He and his men were to confer with any "learned or well travailed persons" they might encounter to determine if there really was a passage from Russia to Cathay, either overland or by sea. Neither should Willoughby be forgotten. If Chancellor and his crew gained any credible information of the whereabouts of Willoughby and his crew, they were to go there and "refresh and relieve" their compatriots.

The final instruction (number twenty-three) echoed and elaborated on one of Cabot's original ordinances: "It is not possible to write and indict such prescribed orders, rules and commissions" for all situations because conditions "change or shift." The company, therefore, put its faith in its people, trusting them to work on its behalf, taking whatever actions and decisions they deemed to be "good and beneficial." They were not only to keep the "honor, good name, fame, credit and estimation" of the company but also to consider the "public benefit of this realm" of England.[36]

IN MAY 1555, Chancellor set sail once more, this time with two ships, the *Edward Bonaventure* and a newly constructed vessel, the *Philip and Mary*. The ships arrived safely at Wardhouse, and there the *Philip and Mary* ended the outbound leg of its journey, as intended. Its goods were exchanged and some merchants were dropped off to take up residence in the growing port, with the goal of establishing a commercial presence for the trading of English cloth for fish, fur, timber, and other goods.[37] Chancellor's ship, the *Edward Bonaventure*, continued east through the White Sea and then south to the mouth of the Dvina River, where the crew set up a warehouse on a small island across from a monastery of St. Nicholas.[38] They named it Rose Island, a place fragrant with "roses damaske and red, of violets and wild rosemarie," as a later visitor described it.[39]

Not long after arriving there, Chancellor received—it is not clear exactly when or how—some disturbing news: Willoughby's ships had been discovered by Russian fishermen at a location they had certainly passed on their voyage. The vessels lay at the mouth of a river the Russians knew as the Arzina, probably today's Varzina River, which flows through the Kola Peninsula of northwestern Russia and empties into the Barents Sea some two hundred miles east of the Wardhouse. All the men had perished.[40]

The news of Willoughby's fate reached England, possibly from the crew members of the *Edward Bonaventure,* which had also briefly returned home in the fall of 1555.[41] Before long, word spread throughout Europe. Giovanni Michiel, the Venetian ambassador to England, supplied some gruesome details, reporting that the English mariners told strange stories about the "mode" in which Willoughby's crew had been discovered. They had, it seems, been frozen alive. Some were "seated in the act of writing, pen still in hand and the paper before them; others at table, platters in hand and spoon in mouth; others opening a locker, and others in various postures, like statues, as if they had been adjusted and placed in those attitudes." Dogs, too, were found frozen, rock solid.[42] When Chancellor learned the tragic news, he sent one of his men to inspect the ships, confirm the findings, and retrieve the valuable merchandise and Willoughby's precious logbook.*

The story of this first English business foray into Russia was told by George Killingworth, who was one of the factors named in the royal charter. From Rose Island, Chancellor, Killingworth, and the rest of the English commercial party were soon exposed to the

---

* Eleanora Goodwin posits that the burning of sea coal on Willoughby's ship produced carbon monoxide that suffocated the men and dogs aboard. See "The Fate of Sir Hugh Willoughby," *Geographical Journal* 152, no. 2 (1986): 243–47.

realities of doing business in an environment very different from one they knew in western Europe. To begin with, it was not like Antwerp, a trading city with a commercial infrastructure that enabled an expeditious exchange of goods to and from ships and waterfront warehouses. Their goods had to be off-loaded from the English ships and onto local barges for transport—sailing when there was wind, towed when there wasn't—to the upriver trading centers, the first of which was Colmogro, now Kholmogori, a journey of some seventy miles. This was a busy commercial outpost, with wooden houses and plenty of drinking, where Russians, Tatars, and other regional merchants came to trade in such commodities as fish and fur. From there, the English party traveled another seven hundred miles farther upriver on to Vologda, a major trading town in western Russia that they reached in mid-September.[43]

At Vologda, Killingworth and his fellow merchants did what salesmen have always done in trade fairs and marketplaces—they "laid their wares" out for all to see. One local Muscovite made an offer to buy all of Killingworth's supply of broadcloths at twelve rubles each. But the Englishman was reluctant to jump at the first deal, not least because he had no basis for evaluating the bid. What was a ruble worth in exchange for an English pound? What—and how much—would other merchants be willing to trade for the prized English cloth? Sebastian Cabot had supplied no ordinance to cover pricing and sales techniques. As a result, Killingworth and his fellow merchants chose to bide their time and "sold very little" in this first sales session.[44]

Foreigners were not unknown in the trading cities of Russia.[45] Nevertheless, Killingworth struck a particularly memorable figure. As Henry Lane, his friend and fellow factor reported, Killingworth sported a thick, "yellow-colored" beard, "in length five foot and two inches."[46]

Eventually, the Englishmen realized that if they were to establish themselves as traders in Muscovy, they would have to develop a regular presence in the capital city of Moscow, the seat of government, which lay another 550 miles inland from Vologda. Accordingly, Chancellor,

Killingworth, and three others left their associates—notably Richard Judde, Sir Andrew's son—and set off on the journey to Moscow with commodities for sale and a gift of sugar for the tsar. The snow soon became so deep that they had to turn back, abandon their carts, leave behind the sugar, and take to horseback. Continuing on, they passed through market towns along the route to Moscow and got a sense of the products available for trade: plenty of furs—including sable, mink, beaver, and fox—and a variety of other valuable commodities, such as salmon, seal oil, sea salt, feathers, flax, tallow, and hemp.[47]

Chancellor's delegation reached Moscow in early October 1555. Once again, the English were cordially received: the tsar ensured that they were housed near the Kremlin and took the time to dine with them.[48] When Killingworth stepped forward to drink a toast, his five-foot beard fell across the tsar's table. Intrigued, Ivan took the beard in his hand and displayed it to the man sitting with him—Macarius, the Metropolitan of Moscow, the leading figure in the Russian Orthodox Church, considered to be "God's spiritual officer."[49] Macarius, who himself possessed a fine beard, proclaimed that Killingworth's was "God's gift."[50]

During their time in Moscow, the English merchants negotiated trading terms with imperial officials and eventually hammered out a trade agreement. They also came to understand that the capital city, while important for nurturing high-level political relationships, was not a commercial center. Prices were high and few goods were available for trade. So Chancellor and Killingworth determined that Colmogro would be the best place to set up the first English factory. There, goods were plentiful, prices were lower, and Moscow was still within reach.

In July 1556, Chancellor set sail for England, leaving Killingworth to nurture this embryonic Muscovy trade. His ships, the *Philip and Mary,* which had returned to Russia once again, and the *Edward Bonaventure,* were laden with a rich supply of valuable commodities—including wax and tallow, furs and felt—that were reckoned to be worth some £20,000.[51] Also, they carried a special Russian guest: Osep Napea, the first Russian ambassador to England, who bore gifts of sable to present to the English monarchs.

The expedition that had begun with so much promise ended in disaster. On the way home, Chancellor picked up the two long-lost Willoughby ships—the *Bona Esperanza* and *Bona Confidentia*. These, however, were soon shipwrecked in treacherous seas. Then, as Chancellor approached home, he suffered a final blow. Putting into Pitsligo Bay, near Aberdeen on the northeast coast of Scotland, the *Edward Bonaventure* was beset by "outrageous tempests, and extreme storms." The flagship was ripped from her moorings and driven onto the rocks "where she broke and split in pieces."[52] In a final act of bravery, Chancellor saved the Ambassador Napea from the roiling waters, but sacrificed his own life in the rescue. One of his sons perished, too. The *Edward Bonaventure* was wrecked and all the goods lost—most of them not to the sea but to plunder "by the rude and ravenous people of the Country." Virtually everything of value—including Chancellor's notes, records, and accounts—was "rifled, spoiled and carried away."[53]

Chancellor had been, as Clement Adams put it, the "great hope" for the company, and he had accomplished much of what they had asked of him—even if he had not found the passage to Cathay. But he lost everything in doing so. Great reward, it seemed, could not be attained without great risk, and success seemed often to arrive riddled with failure.

For the merchants, however, the shipwreck, though unquestionably a setback, was one from which they could recover. The good news was that Osep Napea was alive, and they dispatched some Muscovy Company officials, including the translator Robert Best, to escort him to London. There the Russian ambassador was feted by the merchants, who dressed up for the occasion, "riding in velvet coats and chains of gold."[54] They paid all his costs during his stay in England.

Yet, even for the merchants, there was some sadness amid the joy. Muscovy may have come closer to home, but Cathay and the East remained strangely, frustratingly, beyond reach.

5

———⫸◈⫷———

AN ELUSIVE REALM

ON SATURDAY, JANUARY 14, 1559, a young woman who would transform England's place in the world was conveyed through the streets
of London in a satin-lined litter, attended by four barons and
announced by trumpet fanfares. Just twenty-five years old, Elizabeth
Tudor progressed slowly, responding to the exultations of enormous
cheering crowds. It was, wrote one observer, a "wonderful spectacle"
featuring a "noble hearted princess" presenting herself to "her most
loving people."[1] The following day—the date that John Dee, her
favorite astrologer, had assured was auspicious—Elizabeth was
crowned queen of England, Ireland, and France.

But the grandeur of her title and the magnificence of her coronation belied the reality of Elizabeth's pitiful inheritance and England's
perilous situation. The crown was still deeply in debt, the cloth trade
continued to falter, the problems of unemployment and wealth disparity still plagued the realm, and people across the land were riven
by religious division. Above all, Elizabeth's position as queen was
under threat almost as soon as she was anointed in Westminster

Abbey: in England, she faced a contested succession; in France, she counted few supporters for her claim to the throne there; and in Ireland, she possessed limited sovereignty.

Elizabeth's father, Henry VIII, had never intended Elizabeth to be queen. In the 1530s, he had declared her, the daughter of Anne Boleyn, a bastard and debarred her succession to the throne. Although she was reinstated in the 1540s, the stain of illegitimacy remained with her. When her half-sister, Mary, acceded to the crown in 1553, Elizabeth had to tread carefully because conspiracy theorists sought to implicate her in every plot to overthrow the Catholic queen. She even suffered a brief incarceration in the Tower of London. But when Mary died unexpectedly at the age of forty-two, Elizabeth knew that it was her time—at last. She had survived. Evidently, her succession was meant to be. When she heard the news that she was to be queen, she was walking in the grounds of Hatfield House, her country mansion. She is supposed to have sunk to her knees by an old oak tree and whispered a prayer: *"A domino factum est et mirabile in oculis nostris"* (It is the Lord's doing and it is marvelous in our eyes).[2]

Complications quickly arose, however. Elizabeth was approached by Philip, Mary's husband and king of Spain, with an offer of marriage. Philip had held the title of King of England *jure uxoris*—by right of marriage to Mary. With her death, he lost the title and his claim to succession, but he had no desire to lose his influence in England. The English Channel was a lifeline to Spain's dominions in the Low Countries. With France controlling the coast on the south side, he needed to preserve his relationship with England to ensure safe passage for his ships. But Elizabeth dithered, time went by, circumstances changed, and the political union did not take place. As a result, Spain could no longer count on England for unfettered access to the Low Countries, and England could no longer count on Spain as an ally.

While she was being courted by the Spanish, Elizabeth was confronted by the French and Scots. Another Mary—Elizabeth's cousin

Mary, Queen of Scots—believed she was the rightful successor to the English throne. Aged just sixteen, Mary was Henry VIII's great-niece, and she had acceded to the Scottish throne on the death of her father, King James V of Scotland, when she was six days old. But with a French mother, she was raised in the French court, and in 1558, just prior to Elizabeth's accession to the throne in England, she married Francis, heir to the French throne. The following year, when he became king as Francis II, she became queen of France.

Mary was a zealous Catholic, and like most Catholics across Europe, she never accepted that Elizabeth's mother had been lawfully married to Henry VIII. In a bid to assert her own claim to the English crown, she added the heraldic symbol of England—three golden, blue-tongued lions—to her coat-of-arms, along with those of Scotland and France.[3] It was a brazen act of cultural appropriation.

So, almost immediately upon her accession, Elizabeth found herself in a power struggle with the major powers of Europe. A map tells the story of her plight. Soon after her coronation, Elizabeth came into possession of an atlas that had been commissioned by Mary as a gift to Philip. In the beautifully illustrated book of maps, created by Diogo Homem, a gifted Portuguese cartographer, the countries of the world are marked with the flag of the crown that claimed possession of them. Philip's coat of arms is stamped over the very heart of England as if the proud island nation were nothing more than an outlying province of the great empire of Spain.

The atlas has survived to this day, but the coat of arms—with its turreted castle and rampant lion—has been scratched out. Historians have speculated that Elizabeth herself was responsible for this, as a petulant act of iconoclastic defiance.[4] This is certainly possible. The young queen reviled Spain's apparent assumption that it could rule the world. Her father, Henry VIII, had proclaimed England an empire in an Act of Parliament in 1533, the year Elizabeth was born. The monarch was *rex imperator*, king-emperor.

But Elizabeth could not be an emperor without an empire over which to rule, and just a year before she became queen England had lost its last slice of sovereign territory beyond the British Isles—the port of Calais on the coast of France.

FOR CENTURIES, CALAIS had been England's commercial gateway to the European continent—the only trading center for its principal export: raw wool. But English monarchs had long laid claim to much more French territory, having once held sway over a sprawling continental empire that stretched from the Pyrenees on the France-Spain border to the ancient Roman wall that marked the England-Scotland border. In a series of conflicts now remembered as the Hundred Years' War, England was forced to retreat from France and, by 1453, the country's only foothold in France was Calais, its wool staple.

Calais was more than just a coastal port and a staple for wool exports. It was also a strategic base, allowing England to safeguard the trade route between London and Antwerp. Its territory encompassed the surrounding area, covering 120 square miles comprising marsh and farmland and embracing several villages. This became known as the Pale—a word derived from the Latin phrase for "stake," specifically a marker that delineates an area of land with a protected perimeter. There was a castle, but the center of Calais life was the market square and, in particular, the Staple Inn, an imposing building where the Staplers held sway. Here, merchants from Europe's clothmaking capitals flocked to purchase English wool. And even as the raw wool trade faded in the 1550s, some English merchants continued to make a handsome living there. One of these was Sir Andrew Judde, who became Mayor of the Staple after helping to found the Mysterie.[5]

The importance of Calais as one of England's key links to the rich consumer markets of Europe was recognized across the continent. As Giovanni Michiel, a Venetian ambassador to England, put it, Calais was "the key and principal entrance to England's dominions." Without Calais, he said, the English would have "no outlet" from their country, "nor access to other countries, at least none so easy, so short and so secure." Indeed, he suggested, evidently overlooking the enduring value of Antwerp, Calais was so essential that if the English were to lose control of it, "they would not only be shut out of the continent, but also from the commerce and intercourse of the world."[6]

Throughout Sir Andrew Judde's mayoralty, reports circulated that the French were preparing to recapture Calais. These were dismissed as idle talk. Then, on the first of January 1558, the rumored invasion came. A French army attacked Calais. In a belated move, Queen Mary made a desperate attempt to defend the "chief jewel of the realm."[7] London merchants dispatched a relief force of five hundred men, while the Staplers, led by Judde, sent another hundred.[8] But it was too little, too late. Within a week, the city had fallen to the French. Henry Machyn, a merchant and diarist, recorded that it was "the heaviest tidings to London and to England that ever was heard of."[9] For Andrew Judde, the news was devastating. Eight months later he was dead. Mary, too, was overcome by grief at the loss. Already suffering from stomach cancer, she succumbed some ten months later. "When I am opened," she is supposed to have lamented, "you will find Calais lying in my heart."[10]

The loss of Calais, given its role as the staple for raw wool, was also a serious blow to England's economy and the personal fortunes of some prominent merchants. One of Elizabeth's first acts as queen was to dispatch emissaries to demand the return of Calais from France. But the best deal they could get was an agreement from the French to return the city after eight years—so long as Elizabeth did not start a war in the meantime. For the merchants, whose business was interrupted, this was deeply disappointing. They needed a new staple immediately and soon negotiated a move to Bruges, a Flemish town a few miles west along the coast from Antwerp. By 1561, the Staplers had secured a new charter and established a staple there.

Elizabeth was not satisfied with this partial solution, and Cecil, who was now Elizabeth's Principal Secretary, supported her contention that Calais must be won back. "Calais must be had," he wrote, "for the honor of the realm, surety of the seas and trade of merchandise."[11] In September 1562, Sir Thomas Smith was brought back from the political wilderness and named England's ambassador in Paris with the express task of negotiating a return of Calais through diplomacy. At about the same time, Elizabeth was presented with a highly risky proposal for regaining sovereign control of Calais by military means. A group of French Protestants—known as Huguenots—sought her support in a quest to overthrow France's Catholic rulers by force and take possession of the country. They appealed to Elizabeth, as the standard-bearer of the Protestant cause in Europe. She agreed to support them, on one condition: England would have Calais.

The enterprise was a huge gamble. The terms of the deal struck with the French clearly specified that Calais would be returned after eight years only if Elizabeth refrained from starting a war. So if she joined now with the Huguenots, her forces would have to win a decisive victory. If they lost, Calais would also be lost, and probably forever.[12]

Elizabeth decided to take the chance, securing the financial support of two London merchants, Sir Thomas Gresham and Lionel Duckett.[13] In October 1562, a six-thousand-strong English military force, led by Ambrose Dudley, son of John Dudley, was dispatched to Le Havre on France's northern coast to join the fight alongside the Huguenots. But as the English prepared for battle, Elizabeth fell gravely ill with smallpox, perhaps from the strain of making such a difficult decision. With the patient nursing of Mary Sidney, Sir Henry's wife and the Dudley brothers' devoted sister, Elizabeth pulled through, although her skin was pockmarked for life.

As she recovered, however, her hopes of recovering Calais faded. After seven months, the campaign to regain Calais fell apart. In April 1563, the Huguenots agreed to a truce with the French crown. Dudley had to abandon the effort, and Smith was obliged to sign Calais away. But that did not stop Elizabeth from using the title of Queen of England, Ireland, and France.*

IF THE LOSS of Calais was not painful enough, Elizabeth soon faced an even greater challenge to her imperial status, a crisis that threatened to strip her of the royal title: Queen of Ireland. An Irish chieftain, Shane O'Neill, one of the most powerful and unpredictable Gaelic warlords, was leading a violent uprising against English rule, and threatening to collaborate with France and Spain to mount an invasion of England—just fifty miles across the Irish Sea.

Elizabeth's relationship with O'Neill and the Irish had been rocky from almost the start of her reign. In 1559, just as Elizabeth assumed her throne, O'Neill had come to power in Ulster, in the northeast of the island, where the O'Neills were one of the dominant clans. Three years older than Elizabeth, O'Neill rejected everything English. Nicknamed "The Proud," he spoke in Gaelic and wrote in Latin, but reportedly refused "to writhe his mouth" around the "clattering English" tongue.[14]

Nevertheless, at the outset of Elizabeth's reign, he sought good relations. He petitioned Elizabeth, promising her that he would achieve peace in Ireland by bringing the "rude, uncivil, and disobedient people" of Ulster in check and forcing them to become "faithful, obedient, and true subjects" to the queen. He would also "subdue traitors" and "overcome rebels" and rid Ireland of the queen's enemies.[15]

O'Neill's declarations of loyalty did not hold for long, and soon enough he was waging war with rival clans: terrorizing the countryside and burning villages in an effort to maintain his authority over Ulster. By June 1561, Elizabeth's Lord Deputy, or viceroy, issued a proclamation, denouncing O'Neill as a "rebel and a traitor."[16]

In the face of this recalcitrant clan chief, Elizabeth had taken a dignified diplomatic approach, inviting O'Neill to visit her in London.

---

* English monarchs would continue to maintain a nominal claim to the French crown until 1801.

She always preferred conciliation to confrontation. O'Neill agreed in principle, but demanded the queen loan him three thousand pounds to make the trip—money her advisers were sure she would never see again. This became the critical issue, with O'Neill letting it be known that "nothing hinders his own repair to her presence but the lack of money." Eventually, Elizabeth released funds for O'Neill's visit, and by November 1561 he was reported to be "ready to embark."[17]

By the first week of January 1562, O'Neill was in London, protected by a bodyguard largely composed of mercenaries known as gallowglasses—from the Gaelic, meaning "foreign warriors." These fearsome fighters, whose heritage was Scottish, had settled in Ireland and won a reputation for devilish deeds on the battlefield. According to the celebrated chronicler William Camden, they marched through the streets of London "armed with hatchets, all bareheaded, their hair flowing in locks upon their shoulders." They caused "as much staring and gaping as if they had come from China or America."[18]

On January 6, O'Neill signed a document of submission, after prostrating himself before the queen. Henceforward, he was to be considered "a good and natural subject."[19] But once he got back to Ireland, O'Neill reneged on the deal, claiming that he had been coerced to sign the document. "They kept me there until I had agreed to things so far against my honour and profit that I would never perform them while I live," he said. "Ulster is mine and shall be mine."[20] For the next four years, O'Neill was in open rebellion, threatening the Pale—the isolated enclave of English settlers built around Dublin and modeled on Calais.

IN 1565, SEEKING a different approach, Elizabeth appointed Sir Henry Sidney as her Lord Deputy in Ireland. Then in his mid-thirties, he had tried to avoid the assignment, regarding the place as a wasteland with an intractable problem—the division and antipathy of the two main communities: the Celtic Irish and the Old English.

The Celtic Irish were Gaelic-speakers, with their own distinctive culture. They dominated the north and west, living as members of clans, including the O'Neills, the O'Donnells, and the O'Connors. Theirs was a pastoral, aristocratic society, and to the English the seminomadic Irish—they practiced "booleying," taking cattle to upland pastures during the summer—seemed alien, even barbarian.

The Old English, by contrast, were descendants of the Norman knights who had crossed the Irish Sea in the twelfth century at the behest of Pope Adrian IV, the first and only Englishman to be anointed Pope. Ireland was declared a "lordship," and over the years the invader-settlers established towns under the command of powerful feudal magnates such as the earls of Kildare, Desmond, and Ormond. But they struggled to assert their authority on the land and constantly fought with the Celtic Irish. Many gradually adapted and adopted Irish ways. "Lord, how quickly doth that country alter men's natures," remarked Edmund Spenser, the English poet.[21]

In his position as Lord Deputy, Sidney presided from Ireland's largest city, Dublin, which lay at the center of the Pale. He soon came to the conclusion that nothing could be accomplished in Ireland while Shane O'Neill was alive. In a letter to Robert Dudley, his brother-in-law, Sidney described Ireland in the bleakest terms. The Pale was "spoiled daily" by attack, he wrote, and the place had fallen into "utter poverty."[22] Elizabeth had been reluctant to use force against O'Neill, not least because of the costs of waging war. But she changed her mind when Sidney warned her that if she did not take some kind of decisive action, she could well "lose Ireland as her sister lost Calais."[23] That Elizabeth could not afford to let happen.

So, in the summer of 1566, a military force was dispatched to subdue O'Neill, a company that numbered a young headstrong captain named Humphrey Gilbert. He was well-known to Elizabeth. As a boy, Gilbert had been presented to Elizabeth by his great-aunt, Katherine Ashley, who had served Elizabeth as governess and who had become a kind of surrogate mother to the queen.[24] He had entered Elizabeth's service when she was a twenty-one-year-old princess and he was a teenager. Elizabeth soon "took a particular liking" to Gilbert. Tall, handsome, and well-educated, having studied at Eton and Oxford, he was the very model of the virile young gentleman that the queen favored at court.[25] He went on to prove his mettle in the abortive military effort to reclaim Calais, earning praise from his commander that there was "not a vallianter man that liveth."[26]

Gilbert returned to England from France in 1563 in search of fresh opportunities, bold projects that befitted his motto, *Quod non?* Why not? In the fall of 1565, he sought a commission from Elizabeth to lead a new quest to find the Northwest Passage to Cathay.[27] He had no naval experience, however, and assumed that his proposal would be scorned, even ridiculed. To win over his skeptics, Gilbert wrote an elaborate treatise entitled "Discourse of a Discoverie for a New Passage to Cataia." Addressed to his brother, it presented his rationale for the initiative.[28] "You might justly have charged me with an unsettled head if I had at any time taken in hand to discover Utopia or any such country feigned by imagination," he wrote. "But Cathay is none such: it is a country, well known to be described and set forth by all modern geographers."[29]

Gilbert completed his "Discourse" at the end of June 1566, but before it could be published he was summoned to serve in Ireland and obliged to postpone his plans to search for the Northwest Passage to Cathay. By November, however, after the English army had failed to bring down Shane O'Neill, Gilbert was back in England renewing his proposals for a voyage to Cathay. In December, he petitioned Elizabeth, asking to be granted a "captainship" of any new lands he might discover in his expedition of discovery.[30] This she could not immediately do because his proposal might conflict with the rights of the Muscovy Company, which had recently been confirmed by Act of Parliament.[31] For this reason, the proposals were sent to the two governors, William Garrard, one of the principal doers of the Mysterie, and his protégé, Rowland Heyward. But after swift reflection, they decided they did "mislike wholly" Gilbert's proposal, which they deemed to be derogatory to the company's privileges.[32] Although their business activity was largely in Muscovy, the governors asserted that the company had "from the beginning of the first attempt" intended to pursue the "discovery of Cathay" and insisted that they "were determined to do so again, either by the north-east or by the north-west."[33]

With the Muscovy Company opposed, Elizabeth rejected Gilbert's petition. But the young courtier seemed unperturbed. He set aside his plans for reaching Cathay and began discussions with some of his West Country friends about a new scheme: establishing a colony in Ireland.

AS WELL AS being strategically important, Ireland was a potential source of significant revenue for English investors and the English crown largely thanks to its chief asset: land. While much of its 32,500 square miles consisted of bogs and swamps, there was plenty of fertile farmland, rich coastal waters, and thick forests. Also, Ireland boasted a thriving, if underdeveloped, economy — although the Spanish were the biggest beneficiaries, thanks to the trade in fish. According to Sidney, some six hundred Spanish ships were said to visit Ireland annually, taking advantage of the abundant fishing grounds. In Munster, in the south, Spanish fishermen took to sheltering in the coves and havens of the crenellated coastline, and constructed makeshift camps for drying and salting their catch, much as they did off the coast of Newfoundland. The Spaniards so valued the Irish fishery that Charles V, Philip II's father, offered to pay a thousand pounds annually for exclusive rights to fish in Irish waters.[34]

Gilbert worked with several collaborators on the colonization scheme, including his uncle, Arthur Champernowne, and William Winter, one of Elizabeth's senior naval officials. Together, they drew up plans for a corporation, following the model of the shareholding approach pioneered by the Mysterie, which was growing in popularity among leading merchants. And as he had with his proposal for a voyage to Cathay, Gilbert sought to bring the queen into the enterprise. He requested a £20,000 loan, an army of fifteen hundred men, and the use of the *Phoenix,* a royal ship under Winter's command. With such support, Gilbert and his associates promised they would not only establish a colony of four thousand English settlers in Ulster but also oust Shane O'Neill.[35]

The timing was good. The idea of an English colony was being widely discussed among Elizabeth's advisers in the mid-1560s, and one of these was Sir Thomas Smith, author of the *Discourse of the Commonweal* and Elizabeth's ambassador in Paris. In a letter to William Cecil, he reasoned that if England wished to conquer Ireland, it "needeth nothing more than to have colonies." Such settlements, he wrote, would serve "to augment our tongue, our laws, and our religion in that Isle." These three elements, Smith believed, were the "true bands" of a commonwealth, the very bands by which the Romans had "conquered and kept" their empire for such a long time.[36] Sidney, too, recognized the potential of colonization. In the mid-1550s, as an emissary in Madrid, representing Queen Mary and King Philip, he had seen how Spain's New World settlements enabled it to realize enormous wealth—albeit through authoritarian, violent, and ultimately unsustainable means.

Elizabeth was eventually persuaded to support the idea of an Irish colony. In July 1567, she wrote to Sidney, instructing that two villages on Ulster's northeast coast were to be colonized. She recommended "our servant Humfrey Gilbert" as the negotiator.[37] With Elizabeth's blessing, Gilbert voyaged to Ireland to advance the colonization scheme. But soon after his arrival, he discovered that the principal Irish thorn in Elizabeth's side had been plucked out. Shane O'Neill and his supporters had been defeated in a conflict with one of his rivals for supremacy in Ulster, the O'Donnells. He then sought an alliance with the MacDonnells, another of his longtime enemies. At first, they seemed willing to shelter him. But they soon fell upon him, slit his throat, chopped him into chunks, and cut off his head. Later, they had his head delivered—"pickled in a pipkin"—to Henry Sidney, who had it impaled and displayed on the gates of Dublin Castle.[38]

With O'Neill out of the way, Elizabeth was less inclined to supply Gilbert and his associates with the soldiers, ships, and cash that they needed to build a colony. And without her active support, they seem to have lost their enthusiasm for an Ulster settlement. But although the project faded, Gilbert did not give up on Ireland.[39] He began to consider the potential for yet another settlement, this time in Munster, in the south of the island, where there was a thriving fishing industry. With his fellow investors—including Richard Grenville, his cousin, and Sir Warham St. Leger, son of a former Lord Deputy of Ireland—he sought rights to the lands and havens stretching along the southern coast.

In February 1569, Gilbert petitioned Sidney, outlining the proposed terms of a new corporation that would establish a colony centered on Baltimore, a fishing port on the south coast.[40] Some three thousand people would be recruited. They would enjoy the right to all fishing—free of customs duties—and the liberty to grant land "to such Englishman as shall inhabit there."[41]

The enterprise attracted great interest from London merchants. According to one observer, "a company of thirty of the richest of the London merchants" had "made an agreement with the queen that they will conquer a certain part of the country [Ireland], the lordship of which shall belong to them on payment of a tribute."[42] But, in the end, Elizabeth declined to provide the £10,000 loan Gilbert needed to launch the colony. Without royal funding, the risks of establishing a colony were too great, even for a group of gentleman investors. Once again, Gilbert's colonial ambitions foundered on Elizabeth's unwillingness to invest ever more royal resources in this seemingly impossible place.[43]

But even if Gilbert and his associates had received royal approval for the Munster plantation, it might have run into serious trouble. When rumors spread that Gilbert's corporation would simply seize land in Munster to establish its proposed plantation, both communities—the Gaelic Irish and the Old English—temporarily set aside their differences and rose up in protest. One of the Old English feudal lords declared a holy war against the intruders he characterized as "Hugnottes"—a term that lumped all Protestants, including French Huguenots, into one reviled category.[44] This faith-fueled Irish rebellion erupted just as a group of powerful earls—men who, in effect, ruled the north of England—led a violent but ultimately futile insurrection to overthrow Elizabeth and install Mary, Queen of Scots, in her place.

In an effort to restore peace in Ireland, Henry Sidney dispatched Humphrey Gilbert, who was now a colonel, to subdue the rebels. Gilbert was given only five hundred men to counter an Irish force that numbered as many as four thousand soldiers. Perhaps because of the daunting odds, Gilbert was merciless in warfare, winning a brutal victory in less than six weeks. As he remarked to Sidney, he "refused to parley or to make peace with any rebels." Whenever he demanded the surrender of a castle or fort and the Irish resisted, he took it by force, "however many lives...it cost," and he did not flinch from "putting man, woman, and child...to the sword."[45]

Thomas Churchyard, a courtier-poet who accompanied Gilbert, reported that the colonel ordered "that the heads of all those...which were killed in the day, should be cut off from their bodies and brought to the place where he camped at night." There, the severed heads were to be "laid on the ground by each side of the way leading to his own tent." As a result, any visitor to Gilbert's tent had to "pass through a lane of heads." Understandably, this spread "great terror" among the Irish, and those who came to negotiate or supplicate with the colonel had no choice but to behold the lifeless expressions of "their dead fathers, brothers, children, kinsfolk and friends."[46]

This behavior was so dreadful, and the picture it evoked so graphic, that it became the defining expression of Gilbert's character, even though it was far more extreme than any action he took before or after. Perhaps responding to criticism, Gilbert tried to justify his actions. "No conquered nation will ever yield willingly obedience for love," he told Sidney, "but rather for fear."[47] The queen, we can assume, agreed. In Dublin, on January 1, 1570, Sidney knighted Gilbert for his services to England.

SOON AFTER THE knighting ceremony, Gilbert returned to England, his vision of a commercial Irish settlement unrealized, but the failure of his colonial ambitions did not mark the end of England's efforts to reassert Elizabeth's sovereignty in Ireland. Indeed, this goal rose to the top of the Privy Council's agenda in February 1570, the month after Gilbert returned to England. Quite unexpectedly, Pope Pius V issued a bull, or papal edict, declaring Elizabeth to be a heretic and demanding that Catholic subjects reject her as their rightful queen.[48] It was more than an excommunication — it was, in effect, a Christian fatwa. From that point onwards, Elizabeth lived in fear of attack, and even assassination; Cecil and the Privy Council were constantly on the lookout for plots against her. They were right to do so. The following year, Cecil did uncover yet another plot — this time led by a Florentine banker, Roberto Ridolfi — to put Mary, Queen of Scots, on the throne. As Philip II, the man who had once proposed marriage to Elizabeth, put it, "If I provide some help, it would be easy for [Ridolfi's associates] to kill or capture Elizabeth and place the Scottish queen at liberty and in possession of the throne."[49]

With the threat level so high, it was imperative to address the unresolved issue of Ireland because it was seen as a back door to England that could easily be opened for an attack, insurrection, assassination attempt, or major military invasion. Once again, Cecil and the Privy Council considered the idea of creating colonies as the best way to guard that vulnerable back entrance.

Now the man who had previously expressed deep concerns about the state and proposed ways to save the English commonwealth stepped forward to put his ideas into practice and, ideally, to make his fortune: Sir Thomas Smith.

As a first step, he prepared a petition on behalf of himself and his son, also Thomas, asking for a royal grant of lands in the Ards Peninsula on the northeast coast of Ireland. There they would conquer the Irish in order to make them "civil" and to ensure the area was populated by "natural Englishmen born." Smith, knowing Elizabeth's parsimoniousness, pledged to personally bear the costs of the mission, and in November 1571 he received letters patent from the queen. He was granted 360,000 acres of land, about 560 square miles, in the Great and Little Ards region.[50]

Of course, neither Smith nor his son actually had the resources to cover the costs, but they presumed they could raise funds from rich families. To that end, they published a promotional pamphlet. Smith explained to his fellow privy councillors that they would only be able to raise money through "persuasion" in one of two forms, speaking or writing—and he had concluded that "writing goes further."[51]

Quite unlike anything that had been published before, the pamphlet combined cogent arguments for colonization with an appeal for subscription to the proposed settlement in Ards. It was, in effect, the first dedicated marketing brochure for an English corporate venture. Smith reassured would-be adventurers—the investors—that settlement could indeed be achieved in Ireland without great effort, expense, or danger, and with assured profit and prestige. And planters—the colonists, who would live in Ireland—could expect to reap a greater benefit by going it alone, "without the Queen's pay."[52]

Smith made a particular appeal to those who had suffered as a result of the dissolution of the monasteries. Although the raid on church property had been a boon to those who were able to buy land from the crown at reasonable prices, it had been a disaster for many others, both those with means and those without. The poor lost their social safety net. The wealthy lost a convenient occupation for their younger sons, who received little if any inheritance under the rule of primogeniture.* For years, these junior members of the family had been "thrust into abbeys, there to live (an idle life)" as clergymen. With the monasteries destroyed, many scions of great dynasties faced a bleak future with fewer opportunities.

Smith passionately believed that, as planters in Ireland, these young men could take their place in the world. He urged them to "employ two or three years of [their] youth" in what was the "most honorable service than can be in our times done for England." Their reward would be "thanks, estimation, and a profitable inheritance" and, above all, "to be the patron & first founder of a family in that country, which in time to come, with God's favor, may spring up to great authority." And what a place they could expect to own, he exclaimed: "a land that floweth with milk and honey."

Unlike Sidney, who wanted to create an English community of farmer-settlers, Smith realized that, given the frequency of raids by Irish clans, a colony would have to start out as a military operation. Some of the colonists would be "footmen"—household servants from aristocratic families or conventional soldiers (without a horse). If they came furnished with the necessary accoutrements, they would be required to commit ten pounds for victuals and other necessaries for the first year. Those with a horse would need twenty pounds. Smith also stipulated that any adventurer who did not wish to go to Ireland himself could underwrite a footman or horseman, with the appropriate sum, in his stead.

The potential benefits sounded appealing. Each footman would receive one "plowland," or 255 acres, of arable ground, with an additional forty-five acres of pasture and meadow. A horseman would get two plowlands and ninety acres of pasture or meadow. "I believe," Smith wrote, "you would call that in Essex a good manor." Footmen

---

* According to the rule of primogeniture, the firstborn son inherited a family's main estate.

and horsemen alike would be bound to pay a penny sterling for every acre, though the payments would not start until the fourth year, in 1576—by which time, Smith assured his readers, the colony would be profitable and self-sustaining. "How say you now," Smith asked, harking back to the days of Sir Thomas More, "have I not set forth to you another *Eutopia?*"*

In one respect, Smith's piece of colonial promotion proved very successful: by May 1572, only six months after being granted approval, the required number of colonists—around eight hundred—had assembled with Thomas, Smith's son, at Liverpool, the port on the northwest coast of England that looked towards Ireland. Most were soldier-farmers, travelling on their own account. Smith also attracted a few of England's notable magnates to invest, including William Cecil, who ventured more than three hundred pounds, and Sir John Thynne, Thomas Gresham's brother-in-law and the lord of the manor of Longleat—one of England's great estates.[53]

In another respect, Smith's pamphlet was a disaster. "I could well have wished rather some abstinence had been used," wrote Sir William Fitzwilliam, Sidney's successor as Lord Deputy. It was read by the Irish whose lands were to be affected—that is, seized—for the new settlement. He suggested that the "rumours spread both by talk and show of printed writing" made the prospect of success all the more difficult.[54]

Faced with objections and complaints, the sailing of the colonists was delayed. Everyone waited for Elizabeth's blessing to embark. As time dragged on, some of the planters began to desert the enterprise, and when at last the voyage set off, arriving in Ireland at the end of August 1572, the original eight hundred had dwindled to a motley band of one hundred. Undermanned and underfunded, young Thomas and his men faced an uphill battle, made all the more difficult by the resistance of the Irish. Sir Thomas had anticipated peaceable

---

* Note the spelling; "Eutopia" ("good place") is a clever pun on "utopia" ("no place").

relations, but his son wrote to Cecil not long after landing that one of the lords "would not part with one foot of the land," and that he had withdrawn his men from the Ards, away from danger.[55]

After this, things went from bad to worse. In October 1573, the younger Smith was murdered by "Irishmen of his own household, whom he much trusted"—clearly without cause.[56] His body was boiled up and fed to a pack of dogs.[57] Sir Thomas, devastated, withdrew from court and retreated to his Essex country estate. But within a few months, he put together a plan for a second wave of settlers, to be led by his brother, George, a cloth merchant and member of the Worshipful Company of Drapers. By this time, however, he was not the only one with colonial ambitions in Ireland. Walter Devereux, the first Earl of Essex, had embarked on the creation of another Irish settlement in Ulster. And he had something that Gilbert and Smith had failed to extract from Elizabeth—her money.

The Essex Colony was to be thoroughly military in character and organized along feudal lines, complete with castles and forts, incorporated towns, new laws, and the authority to wage war with the Irish—in effect, to carry on where Gilbert left off.[58] Smith, for his second attempt, while facing up to the reality of Irish hostility, did not embrace the totalitarianism of Devereux's plan. He envisaged a capital city to be named Elizabetha, after the queen.[59] A military commander would govern the plantation, but only until it could achieve enough "quietness" that residents could safely work in the fields and merchants could travel without danger "to fairs and markets within the territories of the colony."[60] Remarkably, Cecil and John Thynne again invested in Smith's venture, and Sir John Berkeley, a gentleman-courtier, plowed a thousand pounds into the enterprise.[61]

In the end, neither colony succeeded. Smith's settlers reached Ireland in August of 1574, but they were repelled and forced out of the Ards area. Essex's scheme also failed to take hold, and he was reduced to blaming the planters for his colony's demise. They were "weakhearted men," he wrote, who were too enamored of "the delicacies of

England."[62] Elizabeth was unimpressed. In the space of two years, she had spent £46,000 on Essex's plantation.[63] By contrast, her revenues from Ireland over the previous fifteen years amounted to a paltry £19,000.[64] She wrote to Essex to say that she was "relinquishing the Ulster project."[65]

Elizabeth's campaign to reassert her sovereignty as queen of Ireland had been a resounding failure. For Sir Thomas, there was to be no third chance. His health failed, and he fell into a long and painful decline, finally dying in August 1577. His tomb in the church in Theydon Mount near Hill Hall, his Essex mansion, features a full-figure effigy, resting almost jauntily on his left elbow. It belies the reality of a man who, though he achieved much, left the world with his greatest ideas unproved.

In a dispiriting final act, Smith's brother and nephews eventually bartered some of his land holdings in Ireland for "an annual rent of a boar and a hogshead of claret."[66]

PART II

ENTERPRISE

1574–1604

6

———— ❖ ————

THE LAST GREAT CHALLENGE
OF THE AGE

IN DECEMBER 1574, with Calais a fond memory and Ireland a fading hope, a rough-hewn seaman from the north of England named Martin Frobisher paid a visit to Muscovy House, which served as the company's headquarters on Seething Lane in the London parish of All Hallows Barking. A "fair and large" building, it stood near the Tower of London and close by the Old Wool Quay, the wharf where England's greatest medieval export had traditionally been loaded onto ships for export to foreign lands.[1]

The purpose of Frobisher's visit was to hand-deliver an important letter from the Privy Council. In it, the royal advisers called on the governors of the Muscovy Company to mount an expedition for "the discovery of the country of Cathay by sea." This, they said, "would be to England a matter of great commodity" — that is, of great advantage or benefit. If, however, they chose not to mount such a venture, the privy councillors requested that the Muscovy Company grant their license to others who were "desirous now to attempt the same" — namely the deliverer of the letter, Martin Frobisher.[2]

Of course, this was not the first time that an advocate of the Northwest Passage to Cathay had sought support from the Privy Council and rights from the Muscovy Company. Nearly ten years earlier, Humphrey Gilbert had sought approval for essentially the same westward voyage, but the leaders of the Muscovy Company had quashed his proposal because they wished to protect their commercial rights to the territory.

Frobisher, however, enjoyed the full support of the Privy Council. So even though the Muscovy Company held the monopoly to trade in the north, secured by both a royal charter and an Act of Parliament, they could not so easily brush him aside. His letter delivered, the court, or ruling body, of the company — which comprised two governors, four "consuls," and twenty-four assistants — met to consider his proposal. After their review, they requested a further meeting with Frobisher so that "they might determine what were mete to be done."[3]

Frobisher duly made his way once again to the great house on Seething Lane. There he met with the members of a subcommittee composed of four men who possessed vast experience of financing, organizing, and leading pioneering overseas voyages: George Barne, William Towerson, Stephen Borough, and Michael Lok.[4] Barne was the son of the late Sir George, who had been one of the Mysterie's principal doers. A leading member of the Worshipful Company of Haberdashers, he was a hugely influential figure in London's merchant community and would follow in his father's footsteps as Lord Mayor of London. His marriage to Anne, the daughter of Sir William Garrard, another of the principal doers, had united two great mercantile dynasties.[5] His brother-in-law was Sir Francis Walsingham, one of the leading privy councillors, which further enhanced his standing and influence.*

---

* 1562, Walsingham married Anne Carleill (née Barne), George's sister, after her first husband, Alexander Carleill, died. She died just two years later, in 1564.

William Towerson, like Barne, was a merchant—a leading member of the Worshipful Company of Skinners. But unlike Barne and most London merchants, he had practical experience of the open ocean. Not only had he financed three expeditions to Africa's Gold Coast in the 1550s, he had led them, too. His first, in 1555, was his most successful: he traded cloth and other commodities, returning to England with about fifty ivory tusks and 127 pounds of gold. Also, Towerson had the distinction of being one of the first English travel writers, carefully documenting what he saw during his voyages. He liked to jot down key words spoken by local people. "I learned some of their language," he wrote, in a lengthy report on his first voyage to Guinea, on the Gold Coast: "Dasse, Dassee," for example, meant "I thank you"; "foco, foco" was "cloth"; and, most important, "sheke" was the word for "gold."[6] But in 1557, after his third voyage, Towerson gave up life on the high seas and settled down, trading on his own account and importing furs—the stock in trade of Skinners—as well as silk tapestries, feathers, and carpets from the Low Countries.[7]

The third member of the subcommittee was Stephen Borough. He had been one of the youngest founding members of the Mysterie— in his twenties at the time. Now, at fifty, he was arguably the Muscovy Company's most knowledgeable mariner. He had served on the first of the Cabot-inspired ventures—the training voyage of the *Aucher* to the Levant in 1550—and he had been master on Richard Chancellor's ship, the *Edward Bonaventure,* on the 1553 voyage to Cathay. Then, in 1556, he made another attempt to navigate the Northeast Passage, and although he was forced to turn back, he nevertheless sailed well beyond the White Sea—the farthest east that any English voyager had traveled at that time.[8]

And, finally, there was Michael Lok.

Lok, forty-three years old, sprang from a long and distinguished line of London merchants—members of the Worshipful Company of Mercers. In the fifteenth century, his great-grandfather had been Sheriff of London, the Lord Mayor's deputy who was responsible for collecting taxes and enforcing the law. Lok's father, who also became Sheriff and was one of the Gresham family's business associates, served as Henry VIII's personal mercer and "agent beyond the seas," supplying the court revels with jewels, silk, and other mercery ware. In the mid-1530s, when Elizabeth was still a toddler-princess, he was commissioned to acquire velvet and satin cloth for her dresses.[9]

As was typical of young men of his position, Lok attended grammar school until he was thirteen years old. But his life then took a dramatically different turn. He was sent to the Low Countries and France so that he could, as he later recalled, "learn those languages" and "know the world."[10] He spent fifteen years travelling, "passing through almost all the countries of Christianity." During this time, he captained "a great ship" of a thousand tons — larger than anything in Elizabeth's fleet at the time — sailing her to the shores of the Levantine countries that lay at the western end of the Silk Road.[11] He endeavored to learn about "all matters appertaining to the traffique of merchants" in the "commonwealths" that he visited on his travels.[12] This experience abroad gave Lok an apprenticeship in international affairs — very different from the practice increasingly favored by some of the great merchants, who sent their children to Oxford or Cambridge and then expected them to attend one of the Inns of Court in London.

Lok's extended sojourn outside England during the 1550s was almost certainly due to his religion. He was a staunch Protestant — his sister-in-law was a close associate of John Knox, the Scottish cleric and one of the leading Protestants of his day. For this reason, he had little desire to be in England during the reign of "Bloody" Mary, who earned her sobriquet after authorizing the burning of nearly three hundred Protestants as heretics. With Elizabeth's accession in 1558, Lok returned to England and resumed his activities as a mercer, following in the footsteps of his brothers, who had remained in England and built up a business as overseas merchants. Thomas Lok, the eldest, who inherited their father's estate in 1550, had been a founding member of the Muscovy Company.[13] He was also a co-investor, along with Sir George Barne and Sir John Yorke, in an expedition to Africa's Gold Coast that was captained by John Lok, another of the brothers.[14] In 1571, Michael became the London agent of the Muscovy Company — in effect, the general manager, with responsibility for arranging the exchange of goods between Russia and England.[15] As he put it, he had "the chief charge" of the company's business.[16]

Despite the considerable experience and knowledge possessed by these four men — Barne, Towerson, Borough, and Lok — Frobisher had no reason to be overawed by them. He, too, was vastly experienced and was, almost certainly, well-known to them all. Born in Altofts, a village near Wakefield in Yorkshire, in 1535 or 1536, he was sent to London to be raised in the household of his uncle, Sir John Yorke, when he was thirteen or fourteen years old.[17] The move, which took place after the death of his mother, was prompted by the "lack of good schools" near his childhood home.[18] But for any young, aspiring merchant, the move to Sir John's household was a remarkable opportunity. As Sheriff of London and a senior official in the royal mint, Yorke was well-connected with the great courtiers — he was a personal friend of John Dudley — and the leading merchants.[19]

Yorke soon realized that his burly nephew was, as one contemporary noted, a lad "of great spirit and bold courage, and natural hardness of body," better suited to a life of adventure than to a mercantile career.[20] In 1553 he arranged for the young Frobisher, still a teenager, to join the expedition to Africa's Gold Coast that he was cosponsoring with several investors in the Mysterie — including Sir George Barne, the elder.

Yorke's assessment of his nephew was spot-on. Frobisher survived his first voyage to Guinea, even though most of the crew — including the captain — perished in the African sun. The following year he joined a return trip led by John Lok. Soon after reaching the Gold Coast, Captain Lok sought to strike a commercial deal, but the local African king demanded a pledge of good faith from the English before trading could begin: namely, a member of the ship's crew would be required to stay in their village, as security against shady dealing. Frobisher, not yet twenty, volunteered and was duly delivered into the custody of the chief. It was not long, however, before things went awry. The African traders fired off some ordnance and the English, assuming trouble was at hand, hastened away. Lok left Frobisher behind, seemingly without so much as a backward glance, for he did not return or make any effort to rescue his young charge.

The Africans eventually handed Frobisher over to the Portuguese, who transported him to the formidable fortress of São Jorge da Mina, Portugal's commercial outpost in West Africa. There, according to Frobisher's later testimony, he was imprisoned for nine months, although he soon proved useful to his captors. He was routinely dispatched into the forests to barter for "goats, poultry, and other victuals" with local African tribesmen, because the Portuguese "durst not, for peril of their lives, do that."[21] Frobisher survived that experience, and the Portuguese eventually sent him back to England, after a brief incarceration in a Lisbon jail.

Over the next twenty years, Frobisher continued—with great gusto—on the path his uncle had determined for him. He took part in countless voyages, even committing acts of piracy for which he spent more time in jail.[22] No imprisonment lasted long, however, and he seems to have earned the endorsement of a number of England's most influential figures, including William Cecil. As Michael Lok noted, Frobisher had "the good liking" not only of Cecil but also "others of her Majesty's honorable Privy Council."[23] Almost certainly, this approval was associated with his work as a government spy and privateer—a kind of licensed pirate. In a classic case of poacher-turned-gamekeeper, he was hired to seek out pirates and smugglers of prohibited goods in the English Channel.

But it was during the days Frobisher spent in the jail in Lisbon that he first dreamed of reaching Cathay via the Northwest Passage. Apparently, one of his fellow prisoners, a Portuguese sailor, revealed that he had "passed" through the icy seaway and shared with Frobisher the secrets of the route.[24] For the next few years, as he later told one of his officers, he discussed the idea with "his private friends" and he had made "many offers" to "sundry merchants of our country" to make the northwest attempt.[25] Despite his persistence, however, Frobisher failed to spark much interest among London's business elite. As a result, as George Best, the son of the Muscovy Company's translator and the official chronicler of the voyages, noted, Frobisher grew weary of merchants, who demanded "sure, certain, and present gains." They were careful and conservative, willing to take a risk—but not recklessly so. Given the failure of the attempts to reach Cathay by the northeast route, this is not surprising.

Frobisher did not give up, however. Navigating the Northwest Passage was seen—especially for the English—as the last great challenge of the age. Frobisher understood it as "the only thing of the world that was left yet undone, whereby a notable mind might be made famous and fortunate." So, in late 1574, tired of being spurned by merchants, he at last turned "to the court (from whence, as from the foundation of our commonwealth, all good causes have their chief increase and maintenance)." There, he "laid open to many great estates and learned men, the plot and sum of his devise."

He could not have picked a better time to make his pitch. There was growing alarm at the scale of the Iberian trade with China. This commercial activity had grown significantly since 1565, when the Spanish established a base in the Philippines, named for Philip II. Now, they were regularly transporting silver across the Pacific from mines in South America and trading the precious metal for silks, spices, and other luxury goods from Chinese merchants.

Yet the privy councillors, respectful of Elizabeth's wishes, had no desire to undermine England's political or mercantile relations with the Spanish. Only a few months before Frobisher presented his proposal, they had rejected a petition by a group led by Sir Richard

Grenville, which they believed might have caused just such a diplomatic rift with Spain. Grenville, supported by his cousin Sir Humphrey Gilbert, proposed to sail into Spanish waters and through the southwest passage—the Magellan Straits—to the Spice Islands, which would have certainly riled Spain. Frobisher's route through the Northwest Passage was less likely to raise objections from either the Spanish or the Portuguese, since neither had shown much commercial interest in northern lands or northern routes to the East. This evidently appealed to Cecil and his fellow councillors, and so they had dispatched Frobisher to the grand mansion on Seething Lane to seek the formal approval of the Muscovy Company.

The Muscovy Company's committee did not share the Privy Council's enthusiasm for Frobisher's project. As one of the members reported, they heard "no good evidence" for a Northwest Passage. And given that "they themselves with their very great charges already had discovered more than half the way to Cathay by the north-eastward"—a reference to overland explorations of Persia made by their associate, Anthony Jenkinson, in the late 1550s and early 1560s—and given that they "purposed to do the rest so soon as they might have good advice," they rejected Frobisher's petition.[26]

Sir Rowland Heyward, one of the two governors of the Muscovy Company, was charged with relaying the news to Cecil. Eight years earlier, he had been one of the merchants who informed Cecil that the company would not approve Gilbert's petition to seek the Northwest Passage. In that instance, the privy councillors had chosen not to take a confrontational approach and contest the company's decisions. This time, however, they refused to accept the verdict of the recalcitrant merchants. They issued an ultimatum, demanding that the Muscovy Company do one of two things: either they should press ahead with their own mission or permit someone else to make the attempt. Under intense political pressure, the Muscovy Company had little choice but to back down. In early February 1575, as a result of "diverse considerations," they granted Frobisher a license to pursue his venture.[27]

What were these "diverse considerations"? Frobisher later credited the influence of Ambrose Dudley, the Earl of Warwick, and a member of the Privy Council since 1573, who had always been interested in developing new markets.[28] Dudley's twenty-seven-year-old wife, Anne, the Countess of Warwick, may also have put in a good word for Frobisher. As one of Elizabeth's favorite ladies-in-waiting, whom one contemporary characterized as "more beloved and in greater favour with the Queen than any other woman in the kingdom," she was a trusted conduit to Elizabeth for those with petitions and requests for royal patronage.[29] Richard Willes, an Oxford geographer, would later dedicate a section about the Northwest Passage in his book *History of Travayle* to the countess.[30]

Another influence on the Muscovy Company was Michael Lok. He had initially rejected Frobisher's proposal, but after reflecting on his "duty towards my country" and "the great benefit" that might arise from an English northwest trade route, he changed his mind. He "did so entirely join with" Frobisher that he proceeded to persuade other Muscovy merchants to think again. "Through my friendship with the company," Lok wrote, "I obtained of them a privilege and license" for Frobisher to make his attempt.[31]

What changed Lok's mind? The most obvious factor, he admitted, was "the great hope" of finding that the "English seas open into the seas of East India." Also, he realized that, even if ships did not reach China, they might encounter "new found lands" along the way that could be "full of people and full of such commodities and merchandise," just as Richard Chancellor had found in Muscovy.[32] Finally, Lok had faith in Frobisher. He had enjoyed a "former acquaintance with him" and knew of his "courage," a very necessary trait for making an attempt on the Northwest Passage.[33]

Lok's change of heart had opened a fissure at the top of the

Muscovy Company. One governor, Rowland Heyward, remained skeptical of the arguments for a Northwest Passage, but the other governor, Lionel Duckett, was more receptive to different perspectives. Sir Thomas Gresham's business partner, and a long-standing investor in maritime ventures, Duckett became one of the first merchants to support the Frobisher venture, with a twenty-five-pound pledge.

In all, some eighteen people put money into the venture, including Sir Thomas Gresham, Sir William Burde, William Bonde, and Thomas Randolph, a former ambassador to Muscovy.[34] Also, Anthony Jenkinson, who had long been an advocate for the northeast route to Cathay, contributed twenty-five-pounds. Among the privy councillors who invested funds were the Dudley brothers: Ambrose, who contributed fifty pounds, and Robert, Earl of Leicester. Two of the privy councillors who invested were also members of the company: William Cecil and Francis Walsingham, who clearly disagreed with the negative opinion of the venture held by his brother-in-law, George Barne.

Lok, as the leading advocate for the Frobisher venture, became its chief organizer. The plan was to dispatch the expedition in the spring of 1575. As the English had learned through years of experience in sailing to Russia, it was unwise to depart on a northerly voyage any later than June. Unfortunately, Lok missed the window "for lack of sufficient money," and the voyage was postponed until the following year.[35]

THROUGHOUT THE REST of that year, 1575, and in the first few months of 1576, Lok and his business associates gathered at Crosby Hall, a palatial residence in the northeast part of the City owned by William Bonde, one of the eighteen initial investors in the venture. Bonde, an original Mysterie member, was among the most influential London merchants, having built a trading empire in Spain, the Baltic, and the Low Countries.[36]

Crosby Hall stood near Bishopsgate, one of the stone-arched entrances in the Roman wall that still surrounded the city. Originally built in the 1460s by Sir John Crosby, a wool merchant and mayor of London, the grand structure towered over neighboring mansions and the parish church, St. Helen's. According to John Stow, it was a "very large and beautiful" mansion, the grandest and "the highest at that time," constructed with sturdy oak and the same fine-grained sandstone used for Westminster Abbey, where English monarchs were crowned.[37] It was, quite literally, fit for a king. Indeed, after Crosby's death, Richard Plantagenet, who would become King Richard III, took up residence there. In 1523, a few years after publishing *Utopia,* Thomas More acquired the place. By the time Lok and his fellow investors met there, Bonde had enhanced the grandeur of the house by adding a mighty fortress-style turret.[38]

In those months, Lok, Bonde, Gresham, and William Burde, one of the royal tax collectors in the city, regularly met there to plan the voyage. Their first priority was to attract more investment. The four had committed £400—nearly half the sum pledged by the eighteen investors. But the total, £875, was a paltry amount compared to the £6,000 raised for the Mystcrie's voyage to Cathay. It is likely that they spent time speaking with prospective investors at the Royal Exchange, the magnificent bourse built by Gresham and opened four years earlier by Elizabeth I. Here, among the colonnades, merchants could go about their business and, if they so pleased, purchase goods from the luxury boutiques that adorned the upper floor and looked down over the courtyard.[39]

Cecil, Elizabeth's closest adviser and the prime mover behind the Privy Council's support for the venture, kept a watchful eye on the preparations and insisted that "a convenient person" be put in charge. The chief investors carefully considered "who should take charge of the money," who should take care of the "provision and furniture of the ships" and who should be entrusted "with the ships at sea."[40] After some discussion, Edmund Hogan, one of Lok's nephews, was charged with collecting subscriptions from new investors, beyond the original eighteen. He was a trusted businessman, recognized, at about this time, as one of "the wisest and best merchants in London."[41] In the 1540s, he had served in the household of Thomas Gresham, after whom he named his son, and he rose through the ranks of the Mercers, serving on its governing body in 1570.

But Hogan, despite his talents, struggled to attract further investors. Throughout 1575, as Lok observed, he "took pains" and "received such money as he could get," but it was not enough. Lok came to the conclusion that the problem was not Hogan, but, surprisingly, Martin Frobisher himself. As Lok later recalled, the major stumbling block was who should "take charge" of the expedition. Frobisher may have proposed the idea and he may have attracted the support of the privy councillors—and through them Elizabeth herself—but there was the sensitive matter of his checkered career. As a result, he was thought to have "very little credit" in England, and this, Lok believed, was why Hogan had been unable to raise enough money to sail in 1575 and why most of the potential investors continued to hold back. The venture was risky enough; they did not want to have to worry about its leadership.

Lok could not remove Frobisher from the expedition. He could, however, reassure the investors by bringing in new talent. So he enlisted William Borough, younger brother of Stephen, to recruit some reliable seamen for the voyage. This Borough did effectively, although he did not have sufficient belief in the venture to invest his own money. On Borough's recommendation, Lok hired Christopher Hall as master and Nicholas Chancellor, the surviving son of Richard Chancellor, as "merchant & purser." Then Lok, perhaps following the by now standard practice of the Muscovy Company, made a canny move. He drew up instructions specifying that Frobisher "should not command nor carry the ships" without the consent of the other senior officers, who were known to be "trusty men." As Lok recalled, "This did satisfy most of the venturers."[42]

But even if the expedition to Cathay was to be a modest expedition in scale, Lok and his associates were determined to take care in its preparation. They were fortunate that they could draw on a great deal of expertise. London was then on the cusp of becoming one of Europe's preeminent centers of science, a veritable "jewel house," with expert practitioners in a range of disciplines, including astronomy, natural history, mathematics, medicine, and shipbuilding.[43] To construct the flagship, Lok commissioned none other than Matthew Baker, the queen's own shipwright, who worked from the new royal docks at Chatham on the Medway, a tributary of the Thames. In his mid-thirties, Baker, the son of Henry VIII's shipbuilder, was the rising star of England's shipbuilding industry. There is a rare contemporary portrait of Baker that is quite unlike the formal portraits of the great and the good posing in an artist's studio. It depicts the shipwright hard at work, bending over a green-topped wooden table strewn with various instruments and a large sketch of the hull of a ship. Born in 1530, he was closely linked to the search for new markets, having joined the voyage of the *Aucher* to the Levant in 1550 when he was about twenty years old. This trip to the eastern Mediterranean, with stops in Genoa and Venice, the home ports of Columbus and Cabot respectively, made an enduring impression on the young shipwright. Years later, when he compiled the first English treatise on ship design — *Fragments of Ancient English Shipwrightry* — his drawings manifested the influence of Italian boatbuilders, who were the pioneers of oceangoing ship design.

Lok may have piqued Baker's interest in the job with his vision of a great merchant ship. In the end, Lok only had enough money to pay Baker to build a thirty-ton bark, the *Gabriel*, and a pinnace.* A second bark, the *Michael,* also thirty tons, was bought from two of the canny investors. But Baker and Lok did not skimp on the materials or

---

* A pinnace was a small, shallow-draft sailboat, sometimes with oars. It was used for navigating close to the coast, communicating between ships in a fleet, and investigating inland waterways.

craftsmanship, and the *Gabriel* was constructed to the highest specifications of the day. Baker placed great emphasis on the importance of arithmetic and geometry, which he considered to be "the two supporting pillars of every art." He was the first English shipwright to build a vessel based on plans created on the drafting table.[44]

Just as Lok engaged England's best-known shipwright, he also sought the expertise of the country's most illustrious maker of marine instruments: Humfrey Cole. Like Baker, Cole was one of a new breed of practitioners who applied mathematical principles picked up during the course of their work—rather than at university. Gabriel Harvey, one of Sir Thomas Smith's protégés, later argued that anyone who condemned expert artisans or industrious practitioners—such as "Humfrey Cole, a Mathematical Mechanician," or Matthew Baker the shipwright, or any other "cunning or subtile Empirique"—because they were "Unlectured in Schools, or Unlettered in Books," must be seen as foolish.[45] Harvey's point was that it was possible to be a superb practitioner without a formal university education.

Cole was a northerner—like Frobisher—who had trained as a goldsmith and then secured a job at the Royal Mint. By the 1570s, he was developing a reputation as a maker of precision instruments, which he produced at his workshop near St. Paul's Cathedral. For Lok, he made, or supplied, an *Armilla Tolomaei,* a celestial globe that was left blank for plotting the constellations, and a blank terrestrial globe for plotting new lands or geographical features that might be discovered. Two other instruments, a *Sphera Nautica* and a *Compassum Meridianum,* enabled the navigator to determine the variation between true and magnetic North, and a *Holometrum Geometrum* was a device for charting the features of a coastline.[46]

The mission's account books—meticulously kept by Lok—show the amounts the investors spent on the essential items for the voyage. Although a goodly sum, just over fifty pounds, went towards the purchase of marine instruments, the largest amount by far was spent on victuals—£387, fourteen shillings, and ten pence. At this time, the practice of victualling was well developed, thanks to the work of Edward Baeshe, a naval administrator. During his tenure as the surveyor-general of victuals for the Royal Navy—he was the first to hold this office, created in 1550, as England began its search for new markets—Baeshe established the process for supplying the navy with food and equipment. In particular, he formalized standards for rations: a gallon of beer and a pound of biscuit (or bread, when in port) every day, two pounds of beef on "flesh" days, and a quarter portion of stockfish (or four herrings), a quarter pound of butter, and half a pound of cheese on "fish" days.[47]

Lok would have been familiar with the allocation of victuals because as agent of the Muscovy Company he regularly sent sailors on long voyages. But it was Nicholas Chancellor, as purser, who was in day-to-day charge of procuring and preparing the provisions—and for this role he had served a long apprenticeship. He had grown up with the Muscovy Company, and after his father's untimely death in 1556 he was "kept at writing school long" and acquired an understanding of algorithms and the "keeping of books of reckonings."[48]

The accounts of the voyage show there was a significant outlay on beer: five tons came from the queen's own stocks. Chancellor also purchased three hogsheads—about 160 gallons—of aqua vitae, a distilled wine. The record is sketchy on what foodstuffs were bought for the expedition, but they would have included enough beef or pork for four days per week, stockfish for three days, as well as ship's biscuit (every day), peas (four days), and cheese and butter (three days)—amounts that were typical on later expeditions.[49]

Also, Lok and company invested in the general welfare of the sailors. Although the basic living conditions were spartan—only Frobisher had his own cabin and well-upholstered bed—the company hired a French surgeon to look after the crew's health, providing him with a large chest filled with some exotic medicines supplied by a London apothecary. There was *ambra grisi oriental,* which, according to one modern expert, was "a wax-like substance from the sperm whale's intestine found floating in the Indian ocean" and used as a stimulant. There were several laxatives—such as *myrobboralia chebue bellerichi*—and a remedy for diarrhea—*boli oriental*. For the treatment of venereal disease, there was *argenti viti*—quicksilver or mercury, administered as an ointment. Another strange drug was *castorum,* which was taken from the anal glands of beavers and used to counter the rancorous odor from gangrenous limbs.[50]

As Edmund Hogan wooed investors and Nicholas Chancellor gathered the victuals, Lok considered the navigational requirements of the voyage itself. He realized that Frobisher and Hall, the second-in-command, did not have sufficient understanding of the latest navigational thinking. For all of Frobisher's conviction and persuasive bluster, it had been obvious during his meeting with the Muscovy Company that he did not have a clear understanding of the route his ships would take. This would need to be addressed, and Lok knew just the man to help.

In May 1576, with about two weeks to go before the planned departure, John Dee, the queen's astrologer and longtime cosmographer for the Muscovy Company, had approached Lok, "desiring to know of the reasons" for their enterprise. When he learned what was planned, Dee offered his services. Lok accepted the offer and invited him to his house, along with Frobisher, Hall, and William Borough.[51] There, as Lok recalled, "I laid before [them] my books and authors, my cards [charts] and instruments, and my notes thereof made in writing." These he had assembled over a period of twenty years, spending around five hundred pounds—a significant financial commitment.[52]

In the days before departure, Dee met with Frobisher and Hall at Muscovy House and put them through a crash course "on geometry and cosmography" and the Northwest Passage. During his tutorials, he referred his pupils to a "great map universal," which had been purchased for the expedition's library of books and charts for one pound, six shillings, and eight pence: this was the world map of his old friend

Gerard Mercator, published seven years earlier. Also, he provided them with Abraham Ortelius's *Theatrum Orbis Terrarum,* or "The Theatre of the Lands of the World," the world's first recognizably modern atlas, which had been published in 1570.*

With this intense tutoring from Dee, as well as the benefit of pioneering marine technology, boatbuilding, and medical knowledge, Frobisher was the best prepared captain that England had ever put to sea—despite the budgetary constraints. Yet for all their preparation and planning, Frobisher and his crew of thirty-four were still venturing into the unknown as they weighed anchor from Ratcliffe, in a protected loop of the Thames, on June 7, 1576.

---

* This atlas may have inspired the name of a new theatre: The Globe. See Neil MacGregor, *Shakespeare's Restless World* (London: Allen Lane, 2013), 14–17.

7

―――•((●))•―――

THE SUPPOSED STRAIT

THE NEXT DAY, after anchoring overnight at Deptford, Frobisher and his fleet sailed on down the Thames. After a few hours, they reached Greenwich, where Elizabeth was holding court. Although she had not personally invested in the voyage, she took an active interest, allowed the involvement of William Cecil, Francis Walsingham, and other privy councillors in the venture, and even expressed her encouragement to the ships as they passed by. "We shot off our ordnance and made the best show we could," recorded Christopher Hall, the master of the *Gabriel*. The queen "commended it, and bade us farewell, shaking her hand at us out of the window."[1]

Frobisher's fleet made its way up the east coast of England, reaching the Shetland Islands two weeks after leaving Greenwich. There, one hundred and fifty miles off the northeast coast of Scotland, they tarried for "one tide to refresh their water" and to stop a leak in the *Michael*.[2] Also, Frobisher took the time to write a letter to the man who had so feverishly tutored him in the weeks before sailing, John Dee. He gratefully referenced Dee's "friendly Instructions: which when we use we do remember you, and hold ourselves bound to you as your poor disciples, not able to be Scholars."[3] This was a humble admission for an experienced mariner who had successfully sailed down the African coast and throughout the waters of the Narrow Seas. But as he left the coast of Scotland, he knew he needed all the help he could get. He was not the first European to venture west through the North Atlantic. But he might as well have been. Although Viking warriors had first rowed their way across the ocean five hundred years earlier, establishing colonies in Greenland and Newfoundland—which they called Vinland— they left no detailed charts of their voyages.

In mid-July, after sailing west from the Shetland Islands for two weeks, a lookout caught sight of a jagged, glinting mass on the horizon. "We had sight of the land of Friseland," Christopher Hall noted in his logbook. It rose "like pinnacles of steeples, and all covered with snow." Frobisher ordered a landing craft to be prepared, and with four men he "rowed to the shore to get on land, but the land lying full of ice, they could not get on land, and so they came aboard again."[4]

This was a crushing disappointment. Just a month into the voyage, Frobisher believed he had found the island of Friseland, which was shown on the maps of Mercator and Ortelius. This would have made a fantastic acquisition for England, if only he could have reached the shore to make the claim. As it turned out, however, Friseland was nothing more than a figment of a Venetian mapmaker's imagination. Even the greatest mapmakers relied on a rich concoction of hearsay, dubious hydrography, and cartographical hunches when it came to the northern Atlantic. But Nicolò Zeno was not a great mapmaker. He was a fraudster. The map he published in 1558, which showed a group of islands that he claimed had been discovered by his ancestors, Nicolò and Antonio Zeno, in the 1390s, was a hoax. It was intended to provide Venice with a claim to all of North America—just as England had made a claim for Newfoundland, based on John Cabot's voyage of 1497. It certainly hoodwinked the greatest cartographers of the day. Although he never realized this, what Frobisher had actually sighted was the southern tip of Greenland—which had been populated by Arctic peoples for thousands of years.[5]

The fleet sailed onwards and soon encountered heavy weather. As the storm raged, the ships of the fleet became separated from one another. The smallest vessel, the pinnace, with four crewmen, was "swallowed up" by the sea and sank to the bottom of the icy waters. One of the two barks, the *Michael,* came through the storm, apparently unscathed. Matthew Kindersley, the ship's captain and also one of the original eighteen investors, sought the advice of his "mariners and comrades" about the best course of action. It seemed that they were the only survivors, and so Kindersley's men, fearing for their lives, demanded that they turn back for England. He acceded to their wishes and the *Michael* returned home, reaching London at the beginning of September. Lok was told that Frobisher and the flagship had been "cast away."[6] The news must have been devastating for him. After all that expense and effort, he faced the prospect of losing a substantial part of his fortune and achieving nothing—no route to Cathay, no gold or silver, not even any trade of the kind found in Muscovy.

As it turned out, Frobisher's flagship had not, in fact, gone down. It had come through the storm, albeit badly damaged: the "extreme foul weather" had sheared off the top mast and blown it overboard. But Frobisher was not Kindersley, and whatever his crew thought, he had no intention of abandoning his quest to achieve the one great thing still "undone" in this world. As George Best reported, Frobisher had "determined and resolved with himself" to prove the existence of the Northwest Passage "or else never to return again." His words echoed those of Richard Chancellor more than twenty years earlier.[7]

Frobisher continued to head northwest, and in late July "he had sight of a high land," and he named the promontory "Queene Elizabeth's Forland," the first piece of the American continent to be named after an English monarch. (It is now known as Resolution Island, which lies off the southern coast of Baffin Island, some five hundred miles west of Greenland.) Once again, however, Frobisher was frustrated in his attempt formally to claim the land, because a surging current, drifting icebergs, and howling winds prevented a landing. He pressed ahead, and the next day the land opened to reveal a wide strait—an ocean passageway between two bodies of land—and he "conceived no small hope" that this was what he had come to find: the Northwest Passage.[8]

Frobisher sailed the *Gabriel* about sixty leagues west into the strait—about two hundred miles. On the starboard side of the ship was Asia, or so Frobisher believed. The land on the port side was, he assumed, America. He took the liberty of naming the passage after himself—following the precedent set by Magellan, who had named an equivalent strait that provided passage round the southern tip of the American continent. Also, in a striking gesture of comradeship, he named some of the islands in the strait after members of the crew—Hall's Island, after the master of the *Gabriel;* Burcher's Island, after the fleet's carpenter; and Thomas Williams Island, after another mariner. For a while, at least, these humble English sailors could enjoy a kind of immortality on the other side of the world.

On one of the islands, Frobisher went ashore and soon found evidence of human habitation, including a recent fire where the embers still seethed. He climbed the highest hill and, from the summit, caught sight of several men "in small boats made of leather" in the distant waters. When it looked as if they were heading towards the ship's boat, which they had hauled up on shore, he and his eight companions hurried down the hill, ready to defend themselves and their landing craft. But the local people—the Inuit—seemed to have had no malicious intent, and the two groups were soon sharing food and exchanging goods. "They came aboard" the ship, wrote Best, and brought "salmon and raw flesh and fish," a welcome change of diet for the Englishmen after weeks of living on biscuit, stockfish, and salted beef. They exchanged the skins of seals and polar bears—gifts that were highly prized in England. The English had a store of fine cloth, which the investors had supplied in order to test the market for the country's premier commodity. But the Inuit were far more interested in the manufactured items that the sailors had to offer—"bells, looking-glasses, and other toys."[9]

Over the next few days, Frobisher's sailors continued to engage with the Inuit and "began more easily to trust them." Conversation, however, was not easy. "They spake," reported Christopher Hall, "but we understood them not," and so the strangers relied largely on gestures to communicate with each other.[10] But Hall did his best to understand them, and, like Towerson many years before, he drew up a list of key words:

Argoteyt—hand.
Accaskay—ship.
Callagay—a pair of breeches.
Mutchater—the head.
Yacketrone—the little finger.[11]

In the course of the "conversation," Frobisher gained what he deemed a far more significant piece of information. As he understood it, the passage "through the Straits into the West Sea" was not far away. One of the natives "made signs that in two days' rowing" Frobisher could be there. What's more, the Inuit seemed to suggest that he could show Frobisher the way, apparently promising that he would go ashore, get his kayak, and then act as their pilot.[12]

Frobisher, not wishing to lose his guide to Cathay, sent a party of five men to accompany the Inuit. But as the men's craft approached the land, it drifted out of sight. For several hours, Frobisher was left wondering what had happened, and when neither the navvies nor the native returned, he feared the worst. As Lok recorded, Frobisher "judged they were taken and kept by force."[13]

The loss of the five men and the ship's boat put the whole expedition in jeopardy. Frobisher had vowed to achieve his goal or die in the attempt—and, if the Inuit were right, he was tantalizingly close: the western opening of the Northwest Passage into the Pacific Ocean was just a couple of days away. But now he had to face the reality of his situation. He had just one bark, no pinnace, no ship's boat, and scarcely enough men to "conduct back his bark again" to England—and those men were exhausted.[14]

Frobisher opted to return to England, but he did not dare go home without proof of his achievements and determined there was only one import that would be genuinely convincing to the investors back at home: an Inuit. Accordingly, he "wrought a pretty policy" in order to "deceive the deceivers," luring one curious Inuit, who was circling the *Gabriel,* by throwing a bell towards him so that it fell just short and into the water. He then rang "a louder bell," and this enticed the man to paddle even closer to the bark, and as Frobisher leaned out to hand him the bell, he "caught the man fast, and plucked him with main force—boat and all—into his bark and out of the sea." Once aboard, the Inuit resisted so fiercely that he "bit his tongue in twain." For Frobisher, the man was "a sufficient witness" of his voyage "towards the unknown parts of the world."[15]

As well as the Inuit, Frobisher and his men gathered a few items of interest to take home with them and to support their claim that they had reached a distant, exotic land. Among these was an odd-looking piece of rock picked up by Robert Garrard, one of the mariners. Frobisher thought it looked like a piece of sea coal, and although this bituminous rock is sometimes mistaken for gold because it can have a shine and variegated glitter, he considered it "a thing of no account." He kept it as a "novelty...in respect of the place from whence it came." But it was not, he thought, a precious souvenir.[16]

Finally, in late August, the *Gabriel* sailed from the newly named Frobisher Strait, reached the Scottish coast a month later, and came into the Thames in early October. Michael Lok, who had feared for his investment, jubilantly reported that Frobisher and the crew of the *Gabriel* were "joyfully received with the great admiration of the people."[17] For the triumphant entry into the Thames, Lok had acquired an ornamental globe, and Frobisher had this mounted on the bowsprit of his flagship.[18]

When Frobisher reached the dock "with his strange man of Cataye, and his great rumor of the passage to Cathay, he was called to the court and greatly embraced and liked of the best."[19] The Inuit caused a sensation. He was only the fifth recorded Native American to reach England—and few people had seen the last one, a king from Brazil, brought to the court of Henry VIII in the 1530s.[20] Described by Best as Frobisher's "new pray" and "strange Infidel," the Inuit was, according to Lok, "such a wonder unto the whole city and to the rest of the realm that heard of it."[21] He was noted for his "very broad face," his "very fat and full body," and his little eyes and beard. His "long hanging" hair was "coal black" and tied in a knot. His complexion was "dark [and] sallow," Lok reported, "much like the tawny Moors, or rather the Tatar nation, whereof I think he was."[22]

Lok may have hoped to generate publicity by parading the man before the court, but the captive was clearly miserable—his countenance, noted Lok, was "sullen or churlish and sharp"—and he was probably in pain, given the wound to his tongue.[23] Within days of reaching London, the man was dead, and he was buried in the churchyard at St. Olave's, close to Muscovy House.[24]

AS INTRIGUING AS the Inuit was to Londoners, the investors focused on Frobisher's claim that he had entered the eastern end of the waterway to Cathay and christened it Frobisher's Strait. Convinced that he was telling the truth, Lok and his fellow merchants moved fast to secure legal protection and thereby safeguard their investment. Towards the end of 1576, a royal charter was drafted for a new company, to be called the Company of Cathay. This left no doubt as to the ultimate goal of the merchants and their fellow investors. After more than two decades of missteps, Lok and his associates were determined to reach the land of the Great Khan.

It was an audacious move. While they had been given permission to conduct a voyage, Lok and his associates were now proposing to establish a commercial organization that would threaten the monopoly rights of the Muscovy Company. But the audacity was typical of the new company's leading members—Gresham, Burde, Bond, Duckett—who had built extensive mercantile operations outside England. According to some "articles of grant" that were drafted—and required the queen's signature if they were to become effective—the investors were to have the "power and authority" to choose a governor, two consuls, and twelve assistants.[25] The provision for a single governor is significant. Clearly, the Company of Cathay did not want the kind of internal conflicts that were causing strife at the Muscovy Company, which had two governors.

Michael Lok was named the first governor for life and Frobisher received the exalted designation of "High Admiral of all seas and waters, countries, lands, and isles, as well as of Cathay as of all other countries and places of new discovery." In addition to their extravagant titles, Lok and Frobisher were to be granted one percent "of all the wares, goods, and merchandise that shall be brought into England or other countries."

The draft charter defined the mercantile mission of the Company of Cathay, providing it with the monopoly "to seek, discover, and find whatsoever seas, waters, isles, lands, regions, countries, provinces, and other places whatsoever.... which before this time, and before the late voyage of discovery made by Martin Frobisher to the northwestwards hath been unknown, or not commonly frequented, by the subjects of our realm of England for trade of merchandise."

After some deliberation, the articles of the charter were "fully agreed" by the Company of Cathay.[26] Cecil, who reviewed the document, jotted down the names of a number of the company's members, including Gresham, Bond, Burde, Duckett, William Winter, Edmund Hogan (who was elected treasurer), Thomas Randolph—and two other interesting participants: Anthony Jenkinson, who had pioneered the overland route towards Cathay, and Sir Humphrey Gilbert.[27]

Gilbert had been an enthusiastic supporter of the first voyage, collaborating with Michael Lok, who described him as "a great good willer to this like enterprise." Lok knew about Gilbert's "diverse good discourses in the favour" of the Northwest Passage—namely, *A Discourse of a Discoverie for a New Passage to Cataia*—and worked with him to get the unpublished manuscript into print. It was hoped that the treatise would make prospective investors "see many good causes to move them to like well therof."[28] In the end, however, Gilbert's tract was not published until April 1576—too late for it to have any real impact on the financing of the first voyage.

Now, ahead of the second voyage, potential investors had the opportunity to read Gilbert's discourse and reflect on the broader vision of the Company of Cathay. In the treatise, Gilbert asserted that Cathay was no "Utopia, or any country fained by imagination," but rather "a country, well known to be described and set forth by all modern geographers." He argued that "the passage thereunto, by the Northwest from us, through a sea which lies on the northside of Labrador, [was] mentioned and proved, by no small number of the most expert, and best learned amongst them."[29]

To provide visual support for his written arguments, Gilbert prepared "a rough draft of a universal Map." Today, it looks rudimentary, a mere sketch. But in the 1570s, it was groundbreaking—the first map of the world to be published in England. Strikingly, it showed an open channel separating the northern coast of the "island" of America and a landmass labeled "Anian."[30] In doing so, Gilbert was lending credence to the idea that there was a "strait of Anian," a Northwest Passage that had first appeared on maps in the early 1560s and that can be traced back to Marco Polo.*

---

* The word "Anian" came from Marco Polo's *Travels*. In one version, the Venetian referred to the Gulf of Kienan, which is "so great, and inhabited by so many people, that it seems like a world in itself." Its southern side "borders the province of Manzi,

If England could successfully navigate this strait or passage, Gilbert argued, she could find "a far better vent" for its cloth than "yet this realm ever had."[31] At the same time, he contended, she would have access to countries beyond the jurisdiction of Spain and Portugal "where there is to be found [a] great abundance of gold, silver, precious stones, cloth of gold, silks [and] all manner of spices."

But Gilbert was not just concerned with navigating the Northwest Passage. He proposed that the English should start "inhabiting for our staple some convenient place of America...where it shall seem best for the shortening of the voyage." In effect, he was proposing a new Calais—but one established along the Northwest Passage. This would be a stepping-stone en route to Cathay. It was bold thinking. But Gilbert envisioned more than a trading outpost. As he explained, "We might inhabit some part of those countries, and settle there such needy people of our country, which now trouble the commonwealth, and through want here at home, are enforced to commit outrageous offences, whereby they are daily consumed with the gallows."

This argument for a colony—as a trading post and a place to rid England of the vagrants and vagabonds of society—had been drafted before Gilbert went to Ireland. Now, in the light of Frobisher's discoveries, it took on new relevance. Gilbert's participation in the Company of Cathay suggests that he thought this new corporation could help him see some of his ideas come to fruition.

IN AN EFFORT to build momentum behind the planned second voyage, Lok and his associates worked closely with the Privy Council, which had Elizabeth's support. The queen let it be known that she would lend her royal ship, the *Ayde*, to serve as flagship for the second voyage—a significant sign of her support and increased interest. The council also dispatched letters to the Council of the North—the

---

and on the other side with Anin and Coloman": see Polo, *The Most Noble and Famous Travels of Marco Polo*, 240.

queen's administrative assembly that implemented royal policy and, among other things, oversaw merchants in York, Newcastle, and Hull—and to the Mayor of Bristol. These urged them to make an investment, since the next Frobisher voyage "will be beneficial both to the whole realm and particularly to such as are venturers."[32]

Meanwhile, Lok commissioned a Dutch painter, Cornelius Ketel, to create portraits of some of the key figures associated with the enterprise—not only Frobisher, the Inuit, and Lok himself but also the *Gabriel,* probably the first English ship to be honored in this way.[33] These paintings were presumably intended to hang someday in the company's hall, although the investors had not yet acquired a corporate headquarters.

The Inuit was already dead by the time Ketel worked on the portraits, but Lok showed striking foresight by hiring a Dutch engraver to prepare a wax death mask, and it was this that Ketel used to paint several pictures of the man in his Arctic garb. Although Ketel's portraits of the Inuit have not survived, such was the man's celebrity that other images of him were produced, probably derived from Ketel's work. One of these shows the man wearing his warm hooded suit, complete with kayak paddle, bow, and two arrows. In the background, Frobisher is depicted at the moment when he, leaning over the edge of the *Gabriel,* grabbed the Inuit and plucked him out of the water, kayak and all.[34]

Of the Ketel portraits, only Frobisher's has survived the rigors of time. It shows a giant broad-chested man standing in front of a globe and bearing a pistol and sword. Beneath his silk and linen, the subject seems to convey a simmering anger, a hint of danger. Frobisher was not a man to be trifled with. As the investors came to realize, he was just the kind of person needed to lead another perilous mission into the unknown. The concerns about his character, which had put off investors before the first voyage, were apparently allayed by his triumphant return.

These various marketing efforts, as clever as they were, did not raise the entire amount needed. At the end of March 1577, a special commission, established by the Privy Council to oversee the preparation of a second voyage, met to consider the feasibility and finances of the venture. Lok was a member of this commission, along with Sir William Winter, Winter's brother George, Anthony Jenkinson, Edmund Hogan, and Thomas Randolph. They had some good news to report: after completing interviews with Frobisher and his crew, they sent a note to William Cecil and his fellow privy councillors, informing them that "the supposed Strait" was, as far as they could tell, "a truth, and therefore a thing worthy, in our opinions, to be followed."[35]

There was also some bad news. Only forty-five men and women had agreed to subscribe and become, in effect, inaugural members of the Cathay Company. There were some significant subscribers. The queen was the single largest investor, contributing five hundred pounds—followed by Lok (three hundred pounds), Gresham (two hundred pounds), and William Bond's son (two hundred pounds), his father having died on the eve of the first voyage. Among the courtiers were the Dudley brothers, Ambrose and Robert, their sister, Mary Sidney—Sir Henry's wife and Elizabeth's loyal lady-in-waiting—and her son Philip. Also, Sir James Croft, closely associated with Irish colonization and now controller of Elizabeth's household, pledged fifty pounds to the venture.[36]

All told, these investors pledged £3,225—scarcely enough to cover the estimated cost of £4,500 for a second voyage to Frobisher Strait. The project seemed in danger of foundering for lack of funds until a startling new piece of information came to light that completely changed the nature of the enterprise.

8

———◆———

TRESOR TROUVEE

IT WAS THE ordinary stone picked up by Robert Garrard—and deemed insignificant by Frobisher—that caused a sensation that March of 1577. About the size of a small loaf of bread, and black in color, it turned out to be something much more than a curio, a worthless souvenir from an icy, barren land. This fragment of the New World seemed to contain the most precious metal known to man: gold.

Garrard had not made it back to England the previous October—he was one of the five mariners taken by the Inuits. But Frobisher kept the friable stone, which could easily be broken into chunks, and gave a piece to Michael Lok as a gesture of respect for his support and recognition of his investment.[1] After all, there was not much else to give him—no gold or silver, no spices or silks, no exotic goods, and no letter of greeting from the Great Khan of Cathay, along the lines of the letter that Richard Chancellor had brought back from Ivan Vasilivich, Tsar of Muscovy. Yes, there was the astonishing news that Frobisher had discovered the entrance to the Northwest Passage, but this would not immediately provide a financial return on Lok's considerable personal investment of £738 — nearly half the total venture cost of around £1,600.

Then, according to George Best's possibly fabricated account, a certain gentlewoman — "one of the adventurers wives" — threw a piece of the stone into a fire. It burned for some time and then, after it was "taken forth and quenched in a little vinegar," it "glistered with a bright Marquesset of gold." Lok now began to fixate on the possibility that the stone contained gold and that Frobisher might have stumbled upon an unexpected source of wealth. So, even as he worked with his fellow investors to prepare for and promote a second voyage in search of the Northwest Passage, he secretly pursued his own assay of the lump of ore.

An assay — from the Old French for "a trial" — is a complex process that combines art and science and was still being developed in the sixteenth century. Precious metals — including gold and silver — are typically embedded in rock and earth. They are rarely found in a pure state. The purpose of the assay, therefore, is to separate the precious metals and render them into a pure condition, with the goal of determining the percentage of gold or silver in the ore. The most common approach was to burn the ore in a furnace, often in combination with other materials, until the precious metal melted out. There was no standard procedure, and results could vary widely depending on many factors, including heat, duration, additives, and the skill of the assayer.

Lok sent some of his ore to William Williams, one of the assay masters at the Tower of London and one of England's leading metallurgists.[2] The assay came back negative. The stone, Williams said, was an iron compound of some kind — a pyrite, otherwise known as fool's gold. Lok, reluctant to accept Williams's findings, took samples to two other experts. They both confirmed Williams's view that the rock was worthless. Lok refused to accept these tests as conclusive, either. So, like a hypochondriac seeking a doctor who will confirm his imagined ailment, he looked for an assayer who would give him the analysis he wanted.[3]

He soon found one: Giovanni Baptista Agnello, a Venetian goldsmith living in London, who was considered an expert in alchemy and metallurgy.[4] He examined Lok's sample and, after three days of tests, reported that he had managed to extract "a very little powder of gold" from the ore. But Lok, finally hearing what he wanted to hear, now seemed unable to accept it. Why was it that Agnello had found gold when three other skilled assayers had found none? Agnello replied, in his native Italian, easily understood by the well-traveled Lok, *"Bisogna sapere adulare la natura"* (You have to know how to flatter nature).[5] Was Agnello dissembling? And, if so, to what end?

Lok met with Agnello several more times, and during these conversations the Venetian surprised Lok by pestering him for information on where the ore came from. He even suggested that the two of them might form some kind of enterprise to mine the ore and benefit from the proceeds for their "own use." Lok finally divulged that the ore came from "the new land discovered by Mr. Frobisher" and that the Cathay Company held the commercial rights to the place. In other words, there could be no private dealing—which was always a concern in such joint-stock ventures. Lok told Agnello about the law of, as they spelled it, *tresor trouvee*—found treasure—which meant that such riches that belonged to the realm could not be taken without permission and license from the queen.

Even so, as he rejected Agnello's proposals, Lok was not yet ready to reveal his secret assaying activities. In late January 1577, he dined with Frobisher, who said he was "desirous to know what was found in the stone." Lok prevaricated. He said that he had given samples to three or four assayers, and that one of them had found a bit of tin and a trace of silver, which pleased Frobisher. Lok did not mention Agnello or the grains of gold.[6]

Over time, this dissembling seems to have weighed on Lok's mind. Although he was the principal organizer of the venture, he was now acting on his own, contrary to the joint-stock principle. Also, by contravening the rule of secrecy surrounding the venture, he was taking a potentially fatal risk. As Bernardino de Mendoza, the Spanish ambassador, later reported to Philip, the Frobisher venture was so hush-hush that if anyone "should divulge anything about it, he should be punished with death."[7]

Three days after his dinner with Frobisher, Lok sent a letter to Elizabeth, briefing her on his activities.[8] He did not provide sufficient detail to satisfy Sir Francis Walsingham, the queen's principal secretary and member of the Privy Council, who read the letter first. Walsingham was one of the advocates of—and investors in—the Frobisher voyage and he immediately sensed something was not quite right about Lok's written account. This is not surprising, given Walsingham's background, expertise, and interests. Born around 1530, he was the son of a prominent lawyer and, like William Cecil, his mentor, he was educated at Cambridge and Gray's Inn. He and his family were zealous Protestants and, soon after Mary's accession, he had, like Lok, fled abroad. He had lived in the Swiss city of Basel, one of the great centers of Protestantism, and studied at the university. Later, he enrolled at the university in Padua, one of the oldest in Europe, where he studied civil law. After returning to England following Elizabeth's accession, he became a Member of Parliament and entered service at court, working for Cecil and, for a time, alongside Sir Thomas Smith as one of the two ambassadors to France.[9]

Walsingham's reputation as a rising star was solidified in 1573, when he became Secretary of State, once again working with Sir Thomas Smith. In this role, he became, in effect, the queen's "spymaster" and chief of her "secret service," assembling an extensive network of agents who were positioned in foreign courts and who gathered and relayed intelligence back to London.[10] So when Lok came to discuss the matter with Walsingham, he found himself dealing with a man accustomed to investigation and interrogation and on the lookout for duplicity or scheming. Walsingham accused Lok of not revealing the entire story of the ore in his note to Elizabeth. Realizing he was on weak ground, Lok quickly confessed, admitting everything about Agnello and the assay. Walsingham was unimpressed by what Lok had to say and dismissed it all as an "alchemist matter"—in other words, worthless. Even so, he crumbled the ore sample into three or four pieces, explaining that he would distribute them among "diverse men to make proofs."[11]

There followed a protracted series of investigations, conversations, and negotiations among the investors, courtiers, and assayers. It all came to a head on March 28, when the commission appointed by the Privy Council met at the house of Sir William Winter, surveyor of the navy. After the meeting, Winter took Lok aside and asked to meet privately with him the next day. Described by Cecil as a "man to be cherished," Winter was a figure to be reckoned with.[12] A founding member of the Muscovy Company, his long experience in a wide range of commercial ventures—from Africa's Gold Coast to Ireland—made him a highly competent head of the Privy Council's commission.

When they met the following morning, Winter revealed to Lok that he knew all about Agnello, the ore, and the gold. It seems that Agnello had violated his own pledge of secrecy and disclosed his work—almost certainly to Cecil, who held secret meetings with the Venetian, and unquestionably to Sir John Berkeley, an enthusiastic investor in overseas enterprises who had been among Sir Thomas Smith's staunchest supporters in the Irish colonial venture.[13] Eventually, word reached Winter, who, with Berkeley, resolved to engage yet another assayer. They chose Jonas—also known as Christopher—Schütz, who was in England on temporary leave from his master, the Duke of Saxony. Described as "a Saxon metallurgist"—that is, among the most knowledgeable in the world—he also had experience with England's fledgling mining industry.[14]

Winter explained to Lok that Schütz had duly conducted his tests and had done more than just confirm Agnello's assay results. He pointed to a golden lump glittering on his windowsill and told him that, according to Schütz, the ore was much richer than they had imagined—a "far greater treasure than was known."[15] Schütz estimated there were four ounces of gold in every hundred pounds of ore. In financial terms, that meant each ton was worth some £240. And, with ore this rich on the surface of the earth, there was possibly much more gold that could be mined underground. It also meant that, as Winter explained, this venture was far too great for them to pursue solely as a company. It was now a matter of national importance. The queen had to be informed and involved.

ONCE THE NEWS broke, the Frobisher venture was swiftly transformed from a quest for the Northwest Passage into a hunt for gold, with the hope that the mineral wealth of England's new Arctic region could be exploited for the enrichment of the voyage's investors and the good of the realm. Lok's financial worries swiftly evaporated, as London was gripped by gold fever and new investors pledged money. In the six weeks between the news of gold and Frobisher's departure, nearly £2,000 was pledged, taking the total to £5,150—more than enough to cover the costs of the second voyage.[16] Courtiers were the biggest enthusiasts, contributing two-thirds of the new capital, compared with one-third in the first voyage. Robert Dudley, the Earl of Leicester, tripled his investment—from fifty pounds to one hundred and fifty. Even more striking was the about-face of Walsingham. He set aside his skepticism and quadrupled his investment, pledging two hundred pounds.[17]

Among the merchants, who were usually more cautious than courtiers with their money, Lionel Duckett and Thomas Gresham remained enthusiastic, even as the priorities of the venture shifted away from the search for Cathay. That may be partly because they, along with Winter and several of the courtiers, were already knowledgeable and significant supporters of England's nascent gold and silver mining industry. For them, it was another extraction project. It did not seem like a shot in the dark.

Both Duckett and Winter had been involved in English mining ventures. Duckett served as the governor of the Company of the Mines Royal, which had been incorporated in 1568 for the discovery of precious metals, namely gold and silver, and Winter acted as his assistant governor.[18] A "mine royal" was one that contained gold or silver and as such was automatically considered the possession of the crown, regardless of who owned the land. Other leading investors included Robert Dudley, William Cecil, and Thomas "Customer" Smythe — all members of the Muscovy Company.

These three — Dudley, Cecil, and Smythe — were also prominent supporters of England's other major mining company, the Mineral and Battery Works, which was licensed by Elizabeth to mine lesser minerals, those with more practical, often industrial, uses — notably "calamine stone."[19] Better known today as zinc oxide, calamine is a necessary element for making latten — a brass-like alloy used in the manufacture of wool cards, machines with bent wire teeth for carding, or untangling, wool before it is spun and woven into cloth. Wool cards, essential to England's most vital trade, had long been imported.[20] Now, it was hoped, wool producers would be able to have a local supply. England would be self-sufficient — just as Sir Thomas Smith had advocated in his *A Discourse of the Commonweal*.

A striking feature of these emerging English mining companies was their reliance on merchants and metallurgists from the German states of the Holy Roman Empire. In both organizations, the patents — as opposed to the shares — were held jointly by one Englishman and one German. Letters patent for the Mines Royal were granted to Thomas Thurland and Daniel Höchstetter.[21] Letters patent for the Mineral and Battery Works were granted to William Humfrey, assay master at the Royal Mint in London, and Jonas Schütz, the metallurgist employed to carry out the assay on Lok's ore.[22]

The English had long boasted a thriving tin industry in the southwest — the desire for tin had attracted the Romans to England, the most northerly outpost of its empire, more than fifteen hundred years earlier—but they lagged the German states when it came to the mining of other metals. Ever since the mid-900s A.D., with the accidental discovery of the great silver mine of Rammelsberg in the Harz mountains of Saxony, German miners had won renown across Europe. Legend has it that the mine was discovered after a Teutonic knight tied his steed to a tree while hunting for deer. As he pursued his quarry on foot, the horse pawed the ground, struck its hooves against a rock, and exposed a shiny vein of silver.[23] The disgorging of silver that ensued produced the fortunes of, among others, the Fugger family, who rivaled the Medici in their wealth.

Over the years, Germans became master miners, leaders in the emerging science of metallurgy. In 1556, Georgius Agricola, a Saxon like Jonas Schütz and Europe's leading expert, published *De Re Metallica,* one of the first great manuals on "the art of mining."[24] The work is filled with advice on a range of practical matters, such as the best place to "obtain a mine" and the most effective way to recognize the natural signs of a vein beneath the surface—such as a patch of herbage on which no frost has formed. Agricola also tackled some philosophical controversies, in particular the issue of whether mineral wealth such as gold was inherently evil. He contended that it wasn't—precious metals were essential to the creation of tools needed by physicians, architects, painters, merchants, and artists in a good civilization.[25]

With German help, the English mining companies saw some early success. In 1565, soon after the founding of the Mineral and Battery Works, German miners established a blast furnace in Keswick, in the heart of the ancient Lake District in the north of England. The following year, as the company engaged in an accelerated program of surveying, prospecting, smelting, and assaying ores, some encouraging discoveries were made. By June 1566, calamine had been found in Somerset, a traditional tin-mining district.[26] A month later, a copper mine was discovered in the Newlands valley in the Lake District that was said to be "the best in England."[27] The German miners dubbed it *Gottesgab*—God's gift. Over time, this was corrupted into English as Goldscope mine.[28] While calamine was essential to the cloth industry, copper ore was valuable because, among other things, it sometimes contains small amounts of gold and silver.

But by 1577, as Frobisher prepared for his second voyage, England's mining companies had not discovered a gold or silver mine that would transform the fortunes of the investors and the country—as the discoveries in the New World had done for Spain.

THE STORY OF Spanish New World wealth loomed large in the minds of English investors. Spain, after all, had no tradition of mining whatsoever. And yet, in the half century after Columbus's first voyage, Spanish conquistadors had explored the West Indies for precious metals and found enough alluvial gold, first in Hispaniola and then in the surrounding islands, to persuade them to search the mainland. In 1518, Hernán Cortés, who first went to the West Indies in 1504, started to subjugate the Aztec empire in what is now Mexico, pillaging their stores of treasure. Francisco Pizarro pushed southwards into the land of the Incas, largely with the goal of finding gold, and after garroting Atahualpa, the Incan emperor, in 1533, claimed sovereignty over that territory for Spain.[29]

To capitalize on the rich trove of precious metals they found in Mexico and South America, the Spanish established settlements and organized their newly claimed territory into three governmental regions, each ruled by a viceroy. New Spain lay to the north, basically what is now Mexico; New Granada comprised the northern area of South America; while Peru was delineated as the vast area embracing the Andean mountain range.[30]

By the 1540s, New World metals constituted an important source of revenue for Spain. But the Spanish spectacularly hit the jackpot in 1545 when they stumbled across the silver mountain of Potosí, which sits on a cold arid plateau in the Andes, more than 12,000 feet above sea level. There are many stories about how the Spanish became aware of the *cerro rico*—the rich mountain—of Potosí, in what was then called Peru, now modern-day Bolivia. One features a native, who, while trying to recapture a bolting llama, fell or tripped on a silver-gleaming outcropping of rock—four-legged creatures seem to take a starring role in these tales.[31] Another story, perhaps more likely, tells of a man called Diego Gualpa who scaled the red-tinted peak looking for the location of a shrine in the hope of looting precious relics. Near the bracing summit, a bluster of wind thrust him to the ground. He seized at a rock and found he was gripping a lump of silver ore.[32]

These eureka stories may all be apocryphal. It seems most likely that Incans had long known about the silver mountain. They had already established mining operations at a place called Porco, some twenty miles southwest of Potosí. They had even developed a smelting method that was, in effect, a small-scale, wind-driven blast furnace—the *guayra,* derived from the Quecha word for "wind"—which they set up on mountain ridges.[33] In 1549, Pedro de Cieza de León, who wrote a history of Peru, reported that at night there were so many of these furnaces burning "all over the countryside and hillsides that they look like decorative lights. And when the wind blows hard, much silver is extracted. When the wind falls, they can extract none. And so, just as the wind is useful for sailing on the sea, so it is here, for obtaining silver."[34]

It was at Porco that Spanish mine operators first heard about Potosí, however it may have been discovered. What they found was an extraordinary vein, measuring some three hundred feet long and thirteen feet wide, containing ore of 50 percent purity. As the news spread, a silver rush began.[35] Within months, a mining camp had formed around the base of the mountain, and before long some twenty-five hundred dwellings had been erected, housing 14,000 people.[36] The landscape was barren, the climate chilly, yet by 1550 Potosí was a sixteenth-century boomtown.[37] Fortunes were quickly accumulated, and mine owners and merchants, as well as some individual miners, became avaricious consumers of luxuries from Europe and the East, including English-made hats and woolen coats—proof that new markets could be created and become profitable.[38] It was the irresistible temptation of this magical city of treasure that had prompted John Dudley to ask Sebastian Cabot to prepare plans for a raid on the silver-rich viceroyalty of Peru, although nothing came of it.

Potosí became an important node in a global network of trade in precious metals, largely controlled by Spain. The most visible—and vulnerable—element of this vast commercial enterprise was Spain's treasure fleet, which operated under the jurisdiction of La Casa de la Contratación and which maintained a relatively regular schedule of two outbound sailings of armed convoys—one to the mainland of South America, and the other to New Spain, or Mexico. As many as sixty merchant ships traveled together in a fleet, and they were accompanied by several warships and additional smaller craft, which facilitated transport and communication among the ships and patrolled the waters in search of pirates and privateers.[39]

The main ships were sturdily built and heavily armed galleons—one hundred feet long, with three or four masts, a capacity of five hundred to six hundred tons, and as many as three dozen cannon. They were well-suited for carrying large cargoes of supplies and treasure over long distances. As a comparison, Elizabeth's *Ayde,* which Frobisher was using for transporting what he thought was a hoard of gold, had a capacity of just two hundred tons.

The New Spain fleet sailed from Seville in the spring, bound for Veracruz, east of what is now Mexico City on the coast of the Gulf of Mexico. In the summer, another fleet sailed from Seville to Cartagena, on the northern coast of modern-day Colombia, and stopped there. The main purpose of the stopover was to send word overland to Spanish functionaries in Panama City, on the Pacific coast of the isthmus, and to begin transport of the silver from Panama City to Nombre de Dios, on the Atlantic coast, for collection.[40]

Meanwhile, transport from the mines had to be organized so the silver would reach Panama City in time to coincide with the arrival of the ships at Nombre de Dios. From Potosí, silver bars would be loaded onto llama packs for the trek overland to the coast—a journey that could take six months—where they were loaded onto coastal vessels for the voyage northwards to Panama City. The silver was then off-loaded and taken by mule train or riverboat across the isthmus to the port of Nombre de Dios—a distance, as the crow flies, of some forty miles—where the big ships waited after the journey from Cartagena. One such llama train, which departed Potosí in March 1549, consisted of two thousand llamas bearing 7,771 bars of silver. It was accompanied by a thousand Incans, whose role was primarily to protect the silver from attack by bandits operating from their hideouts in the surrounding hills.[41]

When the silver at last reached Nombre de Dios, a great fair was held, where some of the silver was traded for goods, which were transported back to the mining operations in Mexico and Peru again by mule, ship, and llama. The homeward-bound Spanish convoys stopped at Havana in Cuba, where a large shipyard had been established, and supplies were plentiful and, to the delight of the sailors, the climate was mild.[42] They then sailed together north along the coast of Florida, riding the Gulf Stream and prevailing winds. Here, they were more exposed to natural hazards—the waters were dangerous, the weather was variable, and the storms were fierce and frequent. Also, they were vulnerable to attack from privateers, hostile ships darting out from coastal harbors.

The precious metal trade quickly expanded beyond the Atlantic trade routes into India and China, initially conducted by the Portuguese. The Chinese had an "extraordinary preference" for silver over gold.[43]Although they had mines of their own and had developed advanced expertise in metallurgy and smelting, they regarded mining as bad for the earth and as a source of human corruption. Indeed, it was banned in 1078, and China became what has been called a "receptacle" country, preferring to let others engage in the nasty work of mining but more than willing to buy the product.[44]

Eventually, the Spanish pioneered the Pacific crossing from South America to the Far East, trading much of the silver in the Philippines. Spain's silver ships would depart from Acapulco on Mexico's west coast and sail across the Pacific to the great bay of Manila—a distance of around nine thousand miles as the crow flies. There, they would meet merchants from China and use their American silver to buy a range of goods that Spanish consumers desired, including silks, beautifully crafted Ming porcelain, and custom-made furniture.[45]

This trade became an important part of the global trading system, fueling Spain's imperial ambitions. Its most striking symbol was the *peso de ocho reales*—the piece of eight. This large silver coin, about one and a half inches wide, was first minted at Potosí in the 1570s.[46] It became the first global currency, beloved of princes and pirates.

For Michael Lok and his fellow investors, including Elizabeth, Spain's global activity in precious metals was an ever-present reminder of the power—and potential—to be had from mining a rich seam of gold or silver. They dearly wanted to find their own.

IN MAY 1577, as Martin Frobisher prepared to depart on his second voyage, he received some specific instructions, probably drafted by William Cecil. According to these, the fleet was to proceed to Hall's Island and, after finding a good harbor, repair to "the place where the mineral ore was had which you brought hither the last year." There he was to set the miners to work.[47] It was a sign of the changed priorities of the voyage that Frobisher commanded a crew of 120 men that included several miners and gold finers. They were under the supervision of Jonas Schütz, the assayer, who was funded by William Winter and Michael Lok and given the title "chief master of the mines."[48]

While the workers gathered ore and loaded it on to the *Ayde,* Frobisher was to proceed farther into the strait, search for more mines, try to locate and recover the five mariners lost on the previous trip, and continue far enough into the passage to be certain that he had reached the South Sea. Once he had attempted—and ideally achieved—these goals, he was to return to Hall's Island to evaluate the progress of the mining operations. Also, he was to consider implementing the idea of settlement propounded by Sir Humphrey Gilbert. This would mean leaving some men behind to stay over the winter so that they might "observe the nature of the air and state of the country, and what time of the year the Strait is most free from ice."[49]

Although the goals of the voyage were ambitious, the investors were realistic about the chances of success. One instruction noted that if Frobisher failed to find the gold he was looking for, he was to send the *Ayde* home and "proceed towards the discovering of Cathay" with the two barks.[50]

On May 26, 1577, the fleet departed Blackwall, another of the little shipbuilding villages on the banks of the Thames. Frobisher commanded the *Ayde*, while Edward Fenton, his second-in-command who had seen service in Ireland under Sir Henry Sidney, took the helm of the *Gabriel*. After a two-month voyage, the fleet arrived at Hall's Island, where the rock that started it all had been picked up. But try as they might, they could not find anything "so big as a walnut."[51] So they sailed on to the neighboring island, which Frobisher named after the Countess of Warwick, the wife of his chief sponsor, Ambrose Dudley, and an investor in her own right.[52]

There the men found a "good store of the ore," and after washing it, gold was "plainly to be seen."[53] Leading by example, Frobisher, alongside five miners, pitched into the work of digging the ore. Soon, a "few gentlemen and soldiers" joined them. It was not normal practice for gentlemen to dirty their hands with the manual tasks of such a venture, but Frobisher was no typical gentleman. Indeed, George Best, who had been hired to write an account of the voyage, gives the admiral and his fellow commanders a hearty "commendation" for their "great willingness" and "courageous stomachs" to take on such backbreaking, tedious work.

The mining went on for nearly three weeks, during which time almost two hundred tons of rock were loaded aboard ship. Finally, on August 20, with the weather turning nasty, Frobisher determined that the work was done: the ships' holds were filled and it "was a good time to leave." By then the men were physically exhausted. Some of them were badly injured — their "bellies broken" and their "legs made lame." But there was a sense of achievement and, as they departed the island, Frobisher ordered the firing of a farewell volley "in honor of the right Honorable Lady Anne, Countess of Warwick."[54]

The fleet returned to England, carrying not only the ore but also three Inuits: a man, a woman, and her baby. As before, there was great anticipation as the ships sailed along the Thames. Had gold been found? Had Frobisher finally navigated through the Northwest Passage? In his diary for Tuesday, September 24, Francis Walsingham, one of the biggest investors, wrote, "Captaine Furbusher arrived at the Court, being returned from Cathay."[55] Walsingham clearly harbored hopes that the sought-for destination had been reached at last.

Frobisher made his way to Windsor. There he was "courteously entertained and heartily welcomed of many noblemen."[56] Elizabeth gave a great show of support, and "because that place and country, hath never heretofore been discovered, and therefore had no special name, by which it may be called and known, her Majesty named it very properly *Meta Incognita,* as a mark and bounds utterly hitherto unknown."[57]

The name *Meta Incognita* — literally, "unknown limit" — did not necessarily indicate that Elizabeth wanted to take possession of this distant land. And yet, in November, a couple of months after Frobisher's homecoming, she received a visit from her favorite astrologer, John Dee, urging her to do just that. He came with a sheaf of documents he hoped would make her think differently about Meta Incognita as an extension of what he termed the "Brytish Impire." As he noted in his diary, he bestowed upon her the "title to Greenland, Estotiland and Friseland," which he contended were Arctic lands that fell within her realm.[58] Greenland was well-known, and it may have surprised Elizabeth that she could claim this territory. Friseland was supposedly an island—and Frobisher named its ice-topped mountains on what was actually the southern tip of Greenland after his navigational tutor: Dee's Pinnacles. Estotiland, believed to lie far to the west of Friseland, was almost certainly modern-day Baffin Island.

It is not clear how Elizabeth reacted to Dee's argument. But, the Cathay Company seems to have been inclined towards settlement. In Frobisher's second voyage, a small group of "condemned men" were taken along on what seemed like a suicidal mission: they were to overwinter in the Arctic. In the end, they got no farther than Harwich, on England's east coast, where they were off-loaded to cut costs.[59] With a third voyage under consideration, however, the directors of the Cathay Company took the idea more seriously, partly because they had received secret intelligence that the French might be eyeing the territory for themselves. As Frobisher learned, the French king had armed twelve ships "to pass to the same new country, to take possession of the straits and to fortify the mines there."[60]

Accordingly, the company instructed Frobisher to assemble a colonial party of one hundred men. The task fell to Edward Fenton, Frobisher's second-in-command, who assembled a community of carpenters, bakers, tentmakers, coopers, and smiths—ordinary artisans who were given the honor of establishing England's first colony in the New World. In a sign that this was a serious investment, Lok ordered 10,000 bricks for the construction of a permanent fort, as well as the component parts of a prefabricated building that would provide temporary lodgings for the settlers.[61] Also, victuals were ordered for an eighteen-month stay, even though resupply vessels were expected to return within a year. Drawing up his provisional list, Fenton calculated that he would need 15,600 pounds of beef, 5,200 pounds of bacon, and 1,200 pounds of pork, as well as beer, bread, fish, cheese, and peas.[62]

The colonial venture was still subsidiary to the main purpose of the third voyage: the hunt for gold. Soon after Frobisher's return from the second voyage, Walsingham and his fellow investors heard the crushing news that the fast route to Cathay lay undiscovered. But they remained excited by the mountains of ore that Frobisher had extracted from the New World, and the curious black stone was treated very differently than it had been after the first voyage. There was none of the casual passing around of souvenir rocks, no tossing them into the fire. The *Ayde* and the *Gabriel* put in at Bristol, where the rock was transferred to the castle and locked away. Four men were entrusted with keys, including Frobisher and Lok. The *Michael* had proceeded to London and off-loaded its ore at the residence of Sir William Winter, on St. Katherine's Hill, just east of the Tower of London, where a furnace was being prepared for the testing of the ore.

The news generated huge excitement. Philip Sidney, son of Sir Henry and one of the main investors in the Frobisher voyages, sent off a letter to his friend Hubert Languet, a French Protestant considered to be "one of the most learned men of the day."[63] He reported that Frobisher had "given it as his decided opinion that the island is so productive in metals, as to seem very far to surpass the country of Peru."[64] In other words, better than Spain.

In his reply to Sidney, Languet eloquently warned of the dangers of the treasure hunt. England, he wrote, had "stumbled on that gift of nature, of all others the most fatal and hurtful to mankind, which nevertheless nearly all men desire with so insane a longing, that it is the most powerful of all motives to them to incur risk." Languet reminded Sidney of the problem of land enclosure, which had been abused as a result of avarice. "And now I fear England will be tempted by the thirst for gold." [65]

England was indeed tempted, and sorely so. Now began an assaying frenzy—with the queen watching and waiting for word. Jonas Schütz, who had conducted assays on the first piece of rock and had sailed with the second voyage, began working with the furnace at Winter's house in the first week of October. Within a month he had preliminary results, which he said were positive. But even so he argued that he would need bigger and better furnaces to make a more definitive judgment.

Several assayers were drawn into the proceedings—not only Schütz but also Agnello and another German metallurgist, Dr. Burchard Kranich (sometimes known as Dr. Burcott), who also happened to be personal physician to the queen. [66] The assayers bickered with each other and accused each other of tampering with the ore and with the results. There was, however, some agreement that a new furnace was needed for smelting the ore—a blast furnace of the kind only available in England's mining districts, far from London.

After much searching, Lok and Frobisher identified what they considered to be a suitable existing mill to establish a larger furnace, at Dartford on the Thames estuary. [67] At the start of 1578, the Privy Council's Commission approved construction of the new works, and Frobisher and Lok traveled to Dartford with a mason and carpenter who drew up plans for the new house, mills, and furnaces. But it soon became clear that construction could not be completed before the departure of a third voyage, planning for which was already underway. They decided, therefore, to conduct preliminary tests on ten tons of the ore, using the existing blast furnace owned and operated by the Company of Mines Royal, in Keswick, three hundred miles north of London. [68]

The activity culminated in a report made by the Commission to William Cecil in March 1578. It stated that the "sundry proofs and trials made of the north-weste ore" showed that the "richness of that earth is like to fall out to a good reckoning" and that, therefore, a third voyage should be taken in hand to gather more ore and send one hundred men to inhabit those parts of the world.[69]

SOON ENOUGH, A third voyage was organized, and this was the grandest of the three, with Elizabeth once again as the lead investor. The total amount pledged was £6,952 — more than the amount raised for the first two voyages combined.[70] The fleet consisted of fifteen ships, with Elizabeth's ship *Ayde* sailing for a second time as flagship. The mission was to proceed directly to the most promising ore site — the Countess of Warwick Island — where as much ore as possible was to be loaded and returned for smelting.

Frobisher set off at the end of May 1578, the ships churning towards what the English hoped would prove to be its own version of the fabled *cerro rico* of Potosí. And it was because of that perceived intention that Spain paid much closer attention this time. In April, prior to Frobisher's departure, Bernardino de Mendoza, the Spanish ambassador, had informed Philip II that the Englishman was commanding the expedition "on the Queen's behalf." She had, he revealed, "expressed herself very warmly as to the great importance of the undertaking for the welfare of her realm." He also noted that "the number of men for colonization has been increased" and that "a quantity of easily erected wooden houses and other necessaries are being taken." Mendoza had tried, without success, to get a copy of the chart that the Frobisher crew would employ — but he did manage to get his hands on a piece of ore, which he sent to the king.[71]

The route was a familiar one for Frobisher, and in mid-June he reached a familiar location: Friseland, or what he thought was Friseland. Previously, he had struggled to step ashore. This time, however, he made a successful landing, took possession of the island, and discovered, in the process, "a goodly harbor for the ships." Also, perhaps with Dee's words about a "Brytish Impire" in the back of his mind,

Frobisher named this territory West England.[72] It was the first foreign land to be named after the country.

Continuing on, Frobisher endured another eventful expedition, and after five months, returned to England with news of successes and setbacks. He did not manage to navigate through the Northwest Passage to the Pacific Ocean. Nor did he establish a settlement—the plan had been abandoned, largely because part of the prefabricated wooden house the expedition had taken along had been lost when one of the barks carrying the structure sank after a collision with an iceberg.

Yet the new land was now scattered with English names—evidence that Elizabeth's people were starting to summon the self-belief to imagine an empire. A map, drawn by James Beare, master of one of Frobisher's ships, shows the scale of England's burgeoning territory. In addition to West England, it includes, among many landmarks, Cape Walsingham, Hatton's Headland, Lok's Land, and Winter's Furnace, where much of the mining took place. There is even a Charing Cross, a familiar London landmark, and a fond reminder of home. Of course, Frobisher's Strait is marked, and it leads west, with Beare noting "the way trending to Cathai."

With this, the investors could live in hope. But, when Frobisher docked, there was the more immediate concern of the ore—1,296 tons of it. Frobisher sent the ore to the now-completed Dartford smelting works, and the process of extracting gold was begun.[73] But what might have been a triumphant return gradually degenerated into a three-year squabble that resulted in bankruptcy and disillusionment. By the end of October 1578, the Commissioners requested that Lok provide a full account, in writing, of the "doings and proceedings in this voyage," as well as the current state of the operations at Dartford. Lok calculated that an additional six thousand pounds would be needed to meet expenses, pay the miners and sailors, and cover the cost of handling the ore. In December, with permission from the queen to collect the necessary funds, he set about trying to raise more capital from the investors. But collecting money after the completion of a venture turned out to be more difficult than doing so in advance, especially when news of the assays conducted at Dartford proved disappointing. Soon enough, Lok and Frobisher were blaming each other. Lok sought funds to cover his personal outlay. Frobisher accused him of duplicity.

Lok came to realize that he had made a terrible mistake by signing an agreement on behalf of the entire company. As it turned out, the Cathay Company was never given formal legal status. "There is no such corporation or company in law," noted William Cecil, as things started to unravel.[74] It meant that Lok was left having to take responsibility for the costs of the entire venture, and when some investors refused to pay, he was stuck with the entire obligation. He was soon suspended as treasurer of the company and found himself in serious financial difficulty. In a "humble petition" to the Privy Council's commission for the disbursement of funds to him, he warranted that he and his wife and fifteen children had been "left in a state to beg their bread henceforth except God turn the stones at Dartford into his bread again."[75] Eventually, he was sent to debtors' prison, returning several times for nonpayment of obligations. Meanwhile, Frobisher railed against the Dartford assayers, certain that his ore was the genuine article.[76]

As the Cathay Company disintegrated, the Spanish, continuing to keep track of Frobisher's activities, came to the conclusion that there was nothing much to worry about. In February 1579, Mendoza sent a letter, along with more ore samples, to Philip: "They are of but little value, as the Englishmen and assayers themselves confess, and no matter what heat is employed they cannot smelt them satisfactorily, owing to their great crudity, which is a certain sign they are not rich." The whole business, he continued, "is not thought much of now as the sailors have not been paid, and the merchants who took shares in it have failed, so that people are undeceived."[77]

Although Frobisher had come closer than anyone to discovering the Northwest Passage to Cathay, the queen and the other investors gave up on the project after further assays produced no precious metals of any significance. William Williams conducted the last assay in May 1581. It proved once and for all that the ore did not contain sufficient precious metal to make it profitable. The rock was not completely worthless, however. It was taken from Dartford and repurposed in a variety of ways — from the repairing of roads to the construction of the wall of the queen's manor house not far from the smelting works.[78]

9

⸺◈⸺

ILANDISH EMPIRE

AT THE BEGINNING of November 1577, a few weeks after the return of Frobisher's second voyage, John Dee prepared to receive an old friend at his home in the riverside village of Mortlake, ten miles up the Thames from the Tower of London. Just turned fifty, Dee had become something of a celebrity, revered across Europe as a mathematician, cosmographer, cartographer, and astrologer. He often welcomed visitors to his country residence, a fine assemblage of buildings that included a main house, gardens, a courtyard, and several outbuildings containing alchemical laboratories from which often emanated noxious fumes.[1] On one occasion, Elizabeth herself had called on Dee, to examine a mirror that he claimed could produce optical illusions.[2] The highlight of any visit was a tour of Dee's wondrous library, which outshone the collections at Oxford and Cambridge as the largest in England, containing more than three thousand volumes in some twenty-one languages on Dee's favored subjects of alchemy, astrology, history, geography, optics, and more.[3]

Dee's visitor that November was Sir Humphrey Gilbert, who had a matter of great urgency on his mind: Spain. Sir Humphrey had just finished writing a treatise entitled *A Discourse How Her Majesty May Annoy the King of Spain*.[4] This was not about mildly irritating Spain. This was about war. Back then, the word "annoy" equated to "injure," "hurt," and "harm."[5] As such, Gilbert advocated a set of bold actions that he believed Elizabeth should take in order to slice into Spain's wealth and gain a presence for England in Spain's lucrative corner of the New World.

Although there is no definitive evidence that Dee and Gilbert discussed Sir Humphrey's treatise at Mortlake, Dee was generally sympathetic to Gilbert's views. Nearly ten years earlier, when Gilbert had sought the rights to conduct a voyage in search of the Northwest Passage, it was Dee who had written a promotional tract (now lost) called *Atlanticall Discourses*— "Atlanticall" referring to "Atlantis," the word Dee preferred to "America." When Gilbert was subsequently forced to abandon that initiative, Dee had praised his thwarted efforts. He characterized Gilbert as "the Courragious Capitaine" who had been "in a great readiness, with good hope, and great causes of persuasion" and would have made the venture of discovery, if he had not been "called and employed otherwise."[6] And, just two months before Gilbert's visit, Dee had produced another tract exploring the same topic as Gilbert's — how to deal with Spain and build England's influence in the world — called *General and Rare Memorials Pertaining to the Perfect Art of Navigation*. Dee dictated this rambling screed to an amanuensis in a manic six-day explosion of ideas.

Gilbert had developed his increasingly anti-Spanish attitude over a period of several years. In 1572, he led a voluntary force in a military action to support Dutch rebels against Spanish forces in the Low Countries. That same year, 13,000 Protestants had been slain in a three-week orgy of violence that followed the assassination of Huguenot leaders on St. Bartholomew's Day in Paris — a murderous day of bloodletting, after which the French word "massacre" entered the English language.[7] In the wake of this attack, Gilbert had written to

Cecil urging Elizabeth to consider "taking revenge" against "the Papists," as loyalists of the Pope and the Catholic Church were often called. If she did not, he warned, it would surely mean "the tragical destruction of all the Protestants in Europe."[8] In 1574, Gilbert and his kinsman, Richard Grenville, petitioned Elizabeth to support a voyage of discovery into waters south of the equator, deep into Spanish-claimed territory.[9] But since Elizabeth had recently signed the Treaty of Bristol, which was intended to mend relations between the two countries, neither she nor Cecil wanted to risk provoking Philip at that time. The proposal was vetoed.

The crown's lack of enthusiasm for Gilbert's schemes may also have stemmed from reservations about his character. Sir Thomas Smith, who had known him since his Eton days, wrote to Cecil that, when it came to "handy work," Gilbert was "one of the best that I have seen," but otherwise he was "brimful of fickleness" and "overflowing with vanity." Elsewhere, Smith characterized Gilbert as having a nature "as good as any gentleman in England as soon as he is out of his storms."[10] As Gilbert had demonstrated with his brutal actions in Ireland in 1569, his moody storms could escalate into catastrophic tempests.

Snubbed by the Privy Council, Gilbert threw his support behind Lok and Frobisher, allowing his *Discourse of a Discoverie for a New Passage to Cataia* to be published and investing in the Company of Cathay. But he remained alive to other possibilities, and by the end of 1577, things had changed: Spain had unleashed its army on the Protestant Dutch. The previous November, Spanish soldiers had looted and plundered Antwerp, where England did most of its cloth trade. Around eight thousand Protestant civilians defending their city were slaughtered without mercy. The three days of violence were remembered as the "Spanish Fury."[11]

With Spain now beset by conflict across its global empire, Gilbert's treatise on how to annoy the king of Spain reflected a widening view at court that Elizabeth should no longer struggle to maintain amicable relations with Philip. Instead, she should adopt an aggressive policy towards Spain and her possessions.[12] The principal advocates of this hawkish view were Robert Dudley, Francis Walsingham, and Sir Christopher Hatton, captain of the queen's bodyguard and an increasingly influential figure at court.

These men harbored a deep antipathy towards Spain and all it stood for. Walsingham, in particular, had long practiced an uncompromising form of Protestantism. In the 1550s, during the reign of Mary and Philip, he went to live abroad rather than be subject to the Catholic monarchs. By contrast, William Cecil, while also a committed Protestant, had stayed in England during Mary's reign.

John Dee advocated a less abrasive approach than the one proposed by Humphrey Gilbert. But he was no less assertive. In *The Perfect Art of Navigation,* which he dedicated to Christopher Hatton, Dee argued that it was time for England to establish what he called a "Petty Navy Royal." This fleet of new ships would be deployed in the English Channel with the express purpose of preventing an invasion by foreign countries. Also, it would protect English merchant ships from pirates and privateers, and thereby safeguard the country's economic wealth.

Dee believed the fleet could "bring this Victorious British Monarchy" to a state of "marvellous Security" and ensure that the crown and the commonwealth could "wonderfully increase and flourish." He further suggested that it could be deployed beyond English waters and "towards New Foreign Discoveries," which would enhance "the Honorable Renown of the Ilandish Empire."[13]

It was Dee who first framed the argument for a British empire that stretched far beyond the islands of the British archipelago. In the 1540s, advisers to Henry VIII and then Edward VI developed the idea of an empire that embraced England and Scotland.[14] Sir Thomas Smith, in fact, was commissioned to develop civil law arguments for uniting these two separate kingdoms.[15] But Dee went further. As he conferred with Gilbert, he was in the process of writing the series of reports that he would deliver to Elizabeth about her title to the Atlantic territories of Greenland, Estotiland, and Friseland.[16]

Like Gilbert, Dee could see the opportunity for England. Also, he felt Gilbert's urgency to act. He often ascribed portentous political meaning to astrological and cosmographical phenomena. In 1572, when a supernova appeared, Dee foresaw a rise in the influence of female leaders in European states. Furthermore, he believed that an apocalypse was nigh and would most likely occur with the conjunction of Saturn and Jupiter in 1583. In his estimation, the New World would play an important role in the New Age that would then dawn, and Elizabeth would become the last empress, reigning over "the most Peaceable, most Rich, most Puissant, and most Flourishing Monarchy" in Christendom—but only if Philip II of Spain were subdued.[17]

IN KEEPING WITH his "handy" character, Sir Humphrey was far more practical than Dee in his proposals to Elizabeth. To make itself "strong and rich," he wrote, a country needed to make its enemies "weak and poor."[18] For England, that meant taking action against Spain in America—along the full length of the Atlantic coast, from the international fishing grounds off the coast of Newfoundland to the Spanish-controlled islands of the West Indies.

Gilbert wanted to begin annoying Philip by sending English "ships of war" to Newfoundland, where England could assert its sovereignty because of John Cabot's claim of 1497. But it was not only right that Gilbert thought was on England's side—it was might, too. While Spain's fishing fleet was large—with one hundred ships, it had twice as many as England—the English ships carried more weaponry. As a result, they were, as Anthony Parkhurst, a widely traveled merchant and one of Gilbert's advisers, noted, "lords of the harbors."[19] So much so that the ships of other nations often looked to the English for protection "against rovers or other violent intruders."[20]

Gilbert's plan was straightforward, even brazen. The English would seize all the best ships in the Newfoundland harbors, burn the rest, and impound any valuable freight. This action would have multiple benefits for England. At a stroke, it would decrease Spain's shipping capacity and increase England's. Also, it would reduce Spain's fishing catch, and since Newfoundland codfish was one of their principal and richest commodities, "everywhere vendible," Philip's revenue from customs and duties would be trimmed. And, with less cod available for sale in Spain, people would have less to eat and might starve.[21]

Gilbert offered to lead the Newfoundland enterprise, but his Irish experience taught him not to make the mistake of asking Elizabeth for a financial contribution. Instead, he suggested that, after he had successfully gained control of the fishing grounds in Newfoundland, the way would be cleared for Elizabeth to establish a colony in the area. She could deploy six thousand men in this venture and defray the costs with the revenue gained through tariffs and taxes on foreign fishing vessels.

Once all this had been accomplished, Gilbert proposed that he would then sail to the West Indies to make an even bolder, more direct strike on Spain's sources of wealth — attacking and taking possession of the island of Hispaniola. This, Gilbert argued, would not be difficult to accomplish, because there were "but few people" there. By establishing a base on the island, the English would be able to intercept the Spanish treasure fleet. Also, it would be a fine place for a settlement, because the island boasted a "great abundance of cattle," plenty of fish, and a surplus of juca root, useful for the making of bread. Gilbert believed Hispaniola offered commercial opportunities, too, such as mining and sugar harvesting.

Gilbert seems to have anticipated Elizabeth's concerns about such a venture, because he offered a less aggressive alternative. He could take the uninhabited island of Bermuda, some five hundred miles north of Hispaniola, which Spain had claimed in the early 1500s but had never settled. Named after Juan de Bermúdez, the Spanish navigator who discovered it, but sometimes known as the Isle of the Devils—because unpredictable winds, uncharted shallows, shoals, and strong currents caused frequent wrecks—Bermuda was also within striking distance of Spain's treasure fleet.

Either way, Gilbert argued that any English action in the West Indies would be disruptive for Spain. Even a small loss there would be "more grievous" to Philip "than any loss that can happen to him else where" because of Spain's reliance on the constant flow of silver from the New World into the royal coffers. Also, the action would be highly cost-effective for England. The queen, Gilbert calculated, could do more damage to Philip with an expenditure of £20,000 in the West Indies than she could with £100,000 spent on any other means of annoyance.

Gilbert, who perhaps had learned from previous rejections, was careful to acknowledge the risks involved in his schemes. He admitted that aggressive action could cause Philip to retaliate and, in doing so, jeopardize the regular, routine, and profitable business that English merchants conducted with their Spanish traders. If his armed assault resulted in such a loss of trade, Gilbert acknowledged, "then your Majesty might be hindered in shipping, and customs, to the great decay of the common weale."

Knowing this, Gilbert presented a method to avoid such a commercial disaster. All Elizabeth had to do, he suggested, was grant him a general license "to discover and inhabit some strange place," without being specific about where. With such a "cloak," the English ships could go to sea, attack, and conquer—but not appear to be doing so explicitly at the queen's behest. If the Spanish took offense, Elizabeth could disavow everything. She could even make a show of arresting Gilbert and his crew and imprisoning them somewhere on the English coast as if she were "in displeasure." There, they would languish until the whole thing had blown over. Conveniently, Gilbert's uncle, Arthur Champernowne, vice-admiral of Devon, and the man charged with coastal defense in the West Country, had many such secluded havens to secret the ships, if this scenario were to develop.

Gilbert urged Elizabeth to act quickly. "[Consider] that delay doth often times prevents the performance of good things," he wrote, "for the wings of man's life are plumed with the feathers of death."

GILBERT WAS WISE to acknowledge concerns about the potential loss of Anglo-Spanish trade. Even as he was devising his plan to annoy Philip and do harm to Spain's commercial activities, many of England's leading merchants were preparing to take quite a different approach. They wanted to get along better with their Spanish trading partners and take advantage of Spain's wealth by building stronger business ties. They had no desire to annoy. This was because the Spanish trade was vital to England. The Spanish bought English cloth and the English acquired Andalusian wines, oils for dying cloth, citrus and other fruits — and, of course, American silver.[22]

In the past, there had been ruptures in relations, which damaged trade. Back in 1568, Spanish ships bound for Antwerp and loaded with treasure for paying the occupation force in the Netherlands were beset by bad weather and attacked by French-Huguenot privateers.[23] The ships took refuge in English harbors, where some of the treasure was taken ashore and transferred to the Tower of London. The Spanish protested, but in an uncharacteristically confrontational move, William Cecil, supported by Elizabeth, did not return the treasure. Retaliating, the Spanish seized English goods. For the next five years, trade came to a standstill between the two countries. So for the English merchants who did regular business with Spain and who, in some cases, lived there for long periods, those years were lean times.

Then, in 1574, Elizabeth and Philip II signed the Treaty of Bristol, the embargo on English goods in Spain came to an end, trade relations were restored, political amends were made, and it was back to business as usual. English merchants had a long-standing, direct commercial relationship with Spain. In 1517, when Katherine of Aragon, a Spanish princess, sat on the English throne as wife of Henry VIII, a lively community of English merchants could be found living in San Lucar, the Atlantic seaport of Seville, which lies upstream on the Guadalquivir river. That year, these merchants were granted corporate privileges entitling them to "a piece of ground in the street down below the waterside" where they could build a chapel dedicated to the patron saint of England, St. George.[24]

The day-to-day livelihoods of the English merchants trading with Spain depended to an overwhelming degree on the routine, stable trade between England and the continent. Although the Bristol Treaty was in place, they wanted a more certain way to maintain, regulate, and safeguard their Anglo-Spanish business. So even as they supported Frobisher's efforts to find a fast route to Cathay and loosen Spain's grip on the New World, many of the same merchants came together with leading courtiers to found a new company. Its purpose was to promote and protect English merchants trading directly into Spanish markets, including Seville. They petitioned Elizabeth for incorporation as the Spanish Company, akin to the Muscovy Company. They were successful, and in June 1577 they were granted extensive rights and privileges and permitted to appoint governing bodies in London and Spain.[25]

Some 389 merchants were listed in the Spanish Company's letters patent. More than two-fifths came from England's outports—notably Exeter, Bristol, and Southampton. But the list was dominated by the powerful merchants of London, men who were experienced investors in international trade. These included Thomas Gresham, Thomas Smythe, Anthony Jenkinson, the pioneer of the overland route towards Cathay, and the two leaders of the Muscovy Company who had taken opposing views of Frobisher's venture: George Barne and Lionel Duckett. Strikingly, the new company included two honorary members who were renowned for their anti-Spanish views: Francis Walsingham and Robert Dudley. Both men were close to the great City merchants and depended on the income they derived from investments in overseas enterprises.

Spain kept a close eye on the state of English trade with her country. The Spanish ambassador, Bernardino de Mendoza, calculated that "the trade with Spain is of the greatest importance to the English." Indeed, he considered it "the principal source of their wealth and strength," not least because of the "vast sums of specie" — gold and silver coins — that the merchants brought from Spain. Also, it helped sustain England's merchant fleet. The English were "daily building more" ships, reported Mendoza, and becoming "almost the masters of commerce."[26]

It is hard to believe that the English shared Mendoza's view that they were masters of commerce. The country had lost Calais, retreated from Antwerp, and did not have direct access to the most prized markets of the Far East — China, India, the Spice Islands — or the New World. This is why some courtiers, including William Cecil, concluded that the conciliatory approach to Spain was best.

ELIZABETH WAS QUICK to bless the Spanish Company initiative, but despite Gilbert's plea for speed, she took her time to reach a decision on his proposal. It seems likely that she was waiting for the report that John Dee had been commissioned to write, on the legal case for territorial acquisition. Until then, England's efforts to expand overseas had been about commerce. But Gilbert was proposing something different, something altogether bolder: conquest, colonization, and the potential disruption of the international balance of power. Could it be justified?

Dee's view, though he did not directly refer to Gilbert's proposal, was yes. In his report, "Unto Your Majesty's Title Royal to the Foreign Regions and Islands," which he finished writing at the beginning of May 1578 and presented to Elizabeth soon after, he showed how she could claim title "to all the coasts and islands beginning at or about *Terra Florida,* and so along or near unto *Atlantis,* going northerly, and then to all the most northern islands great and small, and so compassing about Greenland, eastwards."[27]

He justified his conclusion on historical grounds. He reported, albeit erroneously, that one of Elizabeth's royal ancestors, King Arthur, had conquered the lands of the North Atlantic in 530. Next, some 640 years later, another of Elizabeth's direct ancestors, Lord Madoc, a Welsh prince, had "furnished himself with ships, victuals, armour, men and women sufficient" to establish a colony. Madoc had "speedily" led his people into a land then named Iaquaza, now Florida, or possibly into "some of the provinces and territories near thereabouts" such as Apalchen, Mocosa, or Norumbega. All of these places were considered "notable portions of the ancient Atlantis," which was now known, Dee wrote, as America.[28]

Dee incorporated his report in a grander work called the "Limits of the British Empire," which was never published. Elizabeth had named the land discovered by Frobisher as *Meta Incognita,* unknown limit, but, as Dee wrote in his treatise, the limits to empire were known and they put few, if any, restrictions on what England could claim.

Seven months passed before Elizabeth finally responded to Gilbert's proposal. At last, on June 11, 1578, she said yes. She granted letters patent to Gilbert, calling him her "trusty and well-beloved servant," and providing him with license to "discover . . . such remote . . . lands, countries and territories not actually possessed of any Christian prince" and to "inhabit or remain there to build and fortify."[29] Gilbert was given sweeping powers, grand and unspecific, which licensed him, in effect, to establish a new Elizabethan realm, a new England in any faraway place he might discover. He could use his discretion in selecting the "lands" and "territories" to be inhabited, choosing wherever and whichever place might "seem good." Gilbert, along with his "heirs and assigns," was empowered to "hold, occupy and enjoy" these places, with "all commodities, jurisdictions and royalties, both by sea and land." The patent allowed other subjects to travel to the new place, and Gilbert could "dispose" of all lands—as well as any cities, towns, or villages—to these people or others however he chose, so long as the methods conformed with the laws of England.[30] Also, Gilbert would have the power to establish new laws that would cover capital and criminal offenses, in both civil and marine cases. And if babies were eventually born in this remote realm, they, too, would "have and enjoy all the privileges of free denizens and persons native of England," just as if they had been born at home.[31] In return for all this, Elizabeth was to receive a fifth of all revenues from the gold and silver that might be found within the new lands.

It was a remarkable document. Who was responsible for making it happen? While Dee was influential, presenting historical arguments for Elizabeth's territorial claims, it was Walsingham who seems to have played the most influential role in the decision to grant the patent. According to Gilbert, Walsingham was his "principal patron" in the petition and was responsible for procuring Her Majesty's "favor and license" for the voyage.[32] Given Walsingham's inclination for confrontation with Spain, it is likely that Elizabeth well understood the essentially aggressive character of the enterprise, even with the various face-saving alternatives Gilbert had outlined for her. She therefore calibrated her support carefully. She chose not to contribute cash, but she did lend Gilbert one of her royal ships, although not a very large one. He would have use of the rather diminutive, one-hundred-ton, *Falcon*.

Despite the secrecy surrounding the voyage, news of it inevitably leaked out. Eight days before Gilbert received his patent, the Spanish ambassador correctly reported to Philip that the "ships which had been fitted out by Humphrey Gilbert" were going "towards the Indies." Furthermore, he noted, Elizabeth had agreed "that the way to be safe from your Majesty and to injure your prosperity" was to "rob the flotillas."[33] The French ambassador also got wind of the expedition and noted that "Sir Gilbert, a very shrewd man," was "to go on a voyage of discovery, with seven or eight ships very well armed," and that they would travel "by the southern region where there are vast lands inhabited only by savages"—just the kind of place "where empires and monarchies may be built up."[34]

WITH ELIZABETH'S BLESSING secured, Gilbert set about putting together the funding, starting with an investment of his own. As the Spanish ambassador observed, Gilbert purchased and "fully armed" four ships "with his own money."[35] Actually, some of the funds came from his wealthy and well-connected friend Henry Knollys. In return for his badly needed investment, Gilbert named Knollys as second-in-command of the venture, despite his friend's complete lack of experience in such matters.

Eventually, Gilbert assembled a syndicate of some fifty investors that included family members, close friends, and leading merchants.[36] John Gilbert, Humphrey's older brother and overseer of the Gilbert family estate, provided funds and took charge of victualling the venture.[37] Also, Adrian Gilbert, the youngest of the Gilbert brothers, invested, as did their half-brothers: Carew Ralegh and his younger brother, Walter. Another notable investor was Thomas "Customer" Smythe, who was vastly experienced as a supporter of overseas enterprises. Like many merchants, he had built a diversified portfolio, investing in the Muscovy Company, the new Spanish Company, and now Gilbert's colonizing enterprise.

As Gilbert went about raising money, organizing a fleet, and recruiting personnel, those outside his inner circle could only guess at his true intentions for the voyage. He assembled an impressive fleet of eleven ships that he "furnished with 500 choice soldiers and sailors" and victualled for a year.[38] With such a large contingent of vessels and men, he could confront a Spanish convoy of silver ships or war vessels. On the other hand, he could also travel a great distance to a far-off land and found a colony. Perhaps Gilbert wanted, as he had outlined in his *Discourse,* to do a bit of both. *Quid non?*

Even so, the venture was more military in character than colonial.

Gilbert had recruited not only skilled mariners—such as the talented Portuguese pilot Simão Fernandes who was in Walsingham's employ—but also some former pirates to serve as crew. He rigged his ships in a "warlike manner," carrying a total of 120 cannons. *Anne Aucher,* the flagship captained by Gilbert and named after his wife, was the most heavily armed, with twenty-nine cannons. The *Hope of Greenway,* captained by Carew Ralegh and named after the Gilbert family seat in Devon, was fitted with twenty-two cannons.

Gilbert's fleet set sail from Dartmouth on September 25, 1578, with great fanfare. Almost immediately, it ran into trouble. Gilbert's ship was blown completely off course, and traveled eastwards—in effect, backwards—to the Isle of Wight rather than westwards towards Newfoundland, and all the ships had to return to port, re-assemble, and wait for a favorable wind. With this setback, tensions rose. Gilbert and Knollys feuded and the bad blood between them boiled over as they waited restlessly in port. Knollys quitted himself of Gilbert's command and took charge of three of the ships. Gilbert wrote to Walsingham that Knollys had "forsaken" his company.[39]

It was not until mid-November that Gilbert, now commanding a fleet reduced in size, departed a second time, and it was, once again, a disaster. Little is known of what Gilbert's ships actually did, but one thing is certain: they did not get close to Newfoundland, let alone the West Indies. One ship sprang a leak and returned to England. Others put in at Irish ports for revictualling and sailed no farther. Young Walter Ralegh, who captained the queen's ship *Falcon,* seems to have sailed off to do some privateering in the West Indies, becoming entangled in a sea fight with a Spanish vessel.[40]

Three months later, the grand venture was over. Gilbert, hardly chastened or discouraged, started to make preparations for another expedition. But he was not going anywhere. The Privy Council warned that they would revoke his license for another voyage unless he gave "sureties for good behavior." They sent instructions to sheriffs, vice-admirals, and justices of the peace in Devon ordering them to prevent Gilbert and his company, including Walter Ralegh, from leaving port. What is more, they enjoined Gilbert "to meddle no further" in overseas enterprises "without express order from their Lordships."[41]

Clearly, Sir Humphrey had annoyed many people, but most of them were English, not Spanish. Now his practical abilities, along with his character, came into question. And the inexplicable collapse of Gilbert's venture came just as the disappointing results of the latest Frobisher assays were coming to light. Gilbert went silent, just as Frobisher had.

Perhaps, after all, England was not capable of creating its own "Ilandish" empire.

10

———«()»———

NOVA ALBION

IN SEPTEMBER 1580, a three-masted galleon, riding exceptionally low in the water, sailed into the English Channel. As the ship, the *Golden Hind,* neared land, her captain—a short, stout man—barked out a question to some fishermen as they scudded by.

"Is the queen alive?"

The captain, Francis Drake, had not set eyes on his home coastline for nearly three years. During that time, he had sailed around the world, completing the first circumnavigation by an English captain and the first since the sole surviving ship of Magellan's fleet returned to Spain in 1522. After such a long time away, Drake knew it was entirely possible that Elizabeth had died or lost the throne.

It would not have been the first time an English mariner had come home from a voyage to find a new monarch on the throne. In 1509, when Sebastian Cabot returned to England, Henry VII had died and, with him, royal interest in voyages of discovery. Likewise, in 1554, Richard Chancellor returned from Muscovy to find Edward dead and Mary wearing the crown—and preparing to marry Philip of Spain.

By now, Elizabeth might well have died of illness, or been assassinated or overthrown, and replaced by Mary, Queen of Scots, her closest rival. If she had lost power, then Drake could assume that her principal courtiers had lost power, too. It was her most vehemently anti-Spanish courtiers—Francis Walsingham, Robert Dudley, Christopher Hatton, and William Winter—who had sponsored his voyage.[1]

Drake was not only concerned about the queen's fate, however. He was also concerned about the fate of the immense cargo that weighed down his ship and made it sit so low in the water: an astonishing haul of treasure that he had looted from Spanish ships and ports in the New World—gold ingots, bars of silver, pearls, emeralds, and other precious stones. The plundered cargo was worth a fortune, but if someone other than Elizabeth occupied the English throne, then Drake could be in trouble.

The fishermen allayed the first of Drake's fears. Elizabeth, they replied, was indeed alive.

But although the *Golden Hind* proceeded towards Plymouth harbor, Drake did not dare unload the cargo. He knew too well the reaction that it would provoke from Spain—one far more vehement than the protest at Elizabeth's seizure of the Spanish treasure ships a decade earlier that had led to a five-year cessation of Anglo-Spanish trade. There was no telling what this disgorging of Spain's stolen wealth onto an English quayside might provoke. Seeking advice, Drake quickly dispatched a messenger to court, where he was to get instructions from Sir Christopher Hatton—one of his patrons and the man after whom he had named his flagship: Hatton's coat of arms was a hind *trippant*—a trotting deer.

ABOUT FORTY YEARS old, Francis Drake, a daring and accomplished seaman, had been waging a personal battle against Spain for more than a decade. Born in Tavistock in Devon around 1540, he was wind-blown and ruddy-cheeked, with scars from battle wounds on his face (an arrow) and his leg (a bullet). Although a West Country man through and through, Drake had learned seamanship nearer to London. In 1549 his father, Edmund, a clothworker and recent convert to Protestantism, fled Devon to escape a Catholic uprising against King Edward VI and his reforms.[2]

The family settled in Gillingham on the Medway, a tributary of the Thames, and there the young Drake was apprenticed to a local shipmaster. For the next few years he learned the ways of the sea, working aboard vessels that transported goods along the Thames and across the Channel to France and the Low Countries. As a teenager he may have heard about, perhaps even witnessed, Richard Chancellor's celebrated return from Muscovy in 1554. He may well have been in contact with ships or crewmen carrying exotic cargoes from Antwerp, the Canary Islands, or Africa — the Gold Coast and the Barbary Coast.

In his twenties, Drake returned to Devon and introduced himself to his distant kinsmen, John and William Hawkins, merchants who were well-known as pioneers of England's slave trade. In 1567, they hired Drake for their third slaving venture, a particularly risky voyage because the Hawkins brothers intended to sail "beyond the line" — which meant they would not only cross the equator but also the invisible Tordesillas line that would bring them into Spanish-controlled waters.

John Hawkins commanded a fleet of five ships and Drake captained one of them. They headed for Africa's Gold Coast, where they loaded around five hundred Africans into the miserably cramped holds of their ships. Then, they sailed west, crossed the Tordesillas line, and reached the Spanish-occupied islands of the West Indies. They engaged in some profitable trading there and were preparing to sail home when an early August storm whipped up a frothing, violent sea. Hawkins did not wish to jeopardize his cargo — which he valued at an astonishing £1.8 million — so the fleet took refuge on the island of San Juan de Ulúa, near the Mexican port of Veracruz.[3] Once in the harbor, Hawkins sought to buy victuals for the journey home and secured permissions from the Spanish to do so. Then, to his surprise and alarm, the great treasure fleet sailed into harbor. For two days, all was quiet as Hawkins traded for supplies. But then, with no warning, the Spanish attacked.[4] Most of Hawkins's men who were doing business ashore were slain "without mercy." In the sea battle, Hawkins lost all but two of his ships and most of the cargo.[5] Drake, captaining the *Judith*, managed to slip away without engaging in battle. Hawkins followed in his wake in the *Minion*. Both made it home. The catastrophe at San Juan de Ulúa left Drake burning for revenge against the Spanish.

WHEN DRAKE'S MESSENGER arrived at court, he informed Christopher Hatton of the sea captain's safe return and the huge bounty in the hold of the *Golden Hind*. Until then, the investors had received only patchy reports of Drake's activities during the three years he had been at sea. One report came back with John Winter, Drake's vice-admiral and nephew of Sir William, who was forced to return after his ship separated from the fleet in a storm near the islands of Tierra del Fuego. Also, a few sporadic notices of Drake's activity had been included in the official protests made to Spanish viceroys by victims of his plundering in the Pacific. But the news was unreliable and out of date by the time it reached England.

Delighted by what Drake's messenger had to say, Hatton sent him back with orders for Drake to make his way to London. Before long, the news had swept through the court, and while awaiting Drake's arrival Elizabeth's inner circle debated what should be done with the spoils. Not surprisingly, William Cecil and the doves among the privy councillors argued that the treasure should be returned to its rightful owners. But Francis Walsingham spoke for the hawks who wanted to keep the treasure, rebuff the protests of the Spanish, and divide up the spoils. These included Hatton, Robert Dudley, John Hawkins—who had invested five hundred pounds in the voyage—and the Winter brothers, Sir William and George, who together had invested £1,250.[6] On both sides, there was frustration, anger, and resentment among

Elizabeth's councillors. As Mendoza, the Spanish ambassador, noted, "The Councillors who are not concerned in the enterprise have become jealous that the others should enjoy the profit."[7]

As news spread about Drake's treasure, Cecil called an emergency meeting of the Privy Council, but only five councillors — all close to Cecil — attended. They drafted a letter ordering that the treasure be sent to the Tower of London for safekeeping. But for the letter to be official, three more signatures were needed: those of Walsingham, Leicester, and Hatton. These three, as investors in the Drake voyage, refused to sign until they had spoken with the queen.[8]

All eyes turned to Elizabeth. The final decision was to rest with her. As she considered her next step, she met with Drake, who had arrived from Plymouth. According to Mendoza, the queen and the captain spent six hours together, Drake regaling Elizabeth with accounts of his extraordinary adventures. Much of what he had to say was classified, and Elizabeth quickly realized that it had so much value to England that she ordered anyone who knew anything about the voyage to keep silent, under pain of death.[9]

Drake had returned with something even more valuable than the glittering cargo: knowledge of the New World. He brought the queen three new pieces of information — three secrets — that could significantly change England's position in the world.

WHEN DRAKE SET sail in December 1577, his destination had not been publicly disclosed. It was said that even Cecil, Elizabeth's trusted adviser, was in the dark about the purpose of the voyage. Ostensibly, it was a commercial venture to the Mediterranean port of Alexandria, the ancient trading center at the western end of the great Silk Road. But Drake's actual mission was far more ambitious: he was to sail for the southern tip of South America and seek any commercial and colonial opportunities he could find. Although the Spanish and Portuguese had a dominant presence throughout much of South America, there was a large expanse of land below 30 degrees south—the northern border of present-day Uruguay—that the Spanish had not colonized.

Drake sailed south with his fleet of five ships, reached the Magellan Strait in late August 1578, and navigated through it in just sixteen days—less than half the time it took the great Portuguese navigator himself to make it through.[10] He then explored the islands of the region. On one of the islands—which Francis Fletcher, the fleet's chaplain and official chronicler of the voyage, called the "utmost" of them—Drake erected a stone engraved with Elizabeth's name and the date. For a few moments, the captain lay prostrate on the sand, overcome by the gravity of his achievement: no European had ever ventured so far south. Meanwhile, members of his crew, in search of food and other supplies, slaughtered some three thousand of the flightless birds they found nesting on the islands—*pen gwynns,* or "white heads," as the Welshmen on board called them.[11]

Drake dubbed these the Elizabeth Islands, and his exploration of them yielded important cosmographical and navigational information. Many cartographers of the day believed there was a great southern landmass, *Terra Australis,* that connected to South America and extended towards the underside of the world. In an attempt to locate this land, Drake sailed south through the constellation of islands known as Tierra del Fuego and reached open ocean—with no sign of a connected continent. This made it clear to him not only that *Terra Australis,* if it existed, was not connected to South America but also that it was possible to sail around the tip of South America—instead of passing through the tricky Magellan Strait—and into the Pacific. Although this route was longer than going through the Strait, it might be a welcome alternative because it would enable English ships to avoid the treacherous conditions of the Magellan Strait and, just as important, stay well beyond the reach of Spain. It is still known as Drake's Passage.

This finding was Drake's first secret.

Once Drake had completed his reconnaissance of the far extent of

South America, he had intended to return to England, passing once again through the Magellan Strait, this time west to east. But he ran into ferocious winds and chose to steer north instead, along the west coast of South America. As he went, he plundered Spain's unprotected colonial ports, whose inhabitants were incredulous that an English vessel had reached the southern part of the Pacific Ocean.

Off the coast of Panama, Drake encountered a Spanish treasure ship, *Nuestra Señora de la Concepción*, known colloquially as *Cacafuego*, or "shitfire." Almost certainly, it was on its way from Peru to Panama City, where it would transfer its cargo of silver for transport across the isthmus to Nombre de Dios, to be picked up by the treasure fleet. In an act of rampant opportunism, Drake captured the ship and its treasure, including eighty pounds of gold, twenty-six silver ingots, and several chests of silver *reales*. It took six days to transfer the hoard from the *Cacafuego* to the *Golden Hind*.[12]

Because of his plundering—the Spanish called it piracy and christened him El Draque, the "dragon"—Drake assumed the Spanish would soon come after him. So he decided to continue sailing north, along the west coast of New Spain (Mexico) and North America. He may have been hoping to locate the mouth of the Strait of Anian—the northern channel described by Sir Humphrey Gilbert in his *Discourse* of 1576, that was believed to be the western entry to the Northwest Passage. This would provide the quickest way home to England and was the discovery that Cabot, Frobisher, and Gilbert had hoped to make during their voyages.

Drake avoided Spanish ships as he traveled north but eventually ran into a different torment: the weather. According to contemporary accounts, Drake and his crew encountered the "most vile, thick, and stinking fogs" as well as "gusts of winds" of "such extremity and violence" that they could not fight against them.[13] The crew was "grievously pinched" with the cold and complained about the "extremity thereof." The farther they sailed, the colder it got.[14]

How far north Drake traveled is unknown. He may have reached about 48 degrees north, in the vicinity of present-day Seattle.[15] At any rate, after spending several weeks in the area, the crewmen were "utterly discouraged" by the cold, and Drake came to the conclusion that "either there is no passage at all through these Northern coasts (which is most likely) or if there be, that yet it is unnavigable."[16]

Drake's fleet reversed direction. For the next twelve days, they coasted south until they came upon "a convenient and fit harbor" at roughly 38 degrees north, in the vicinity of present-day San Francisco.[17] Here, Drake and his crew tarried for five weeks. While there, they had many encounters with the local Indians—members of the coastal Miwok people—who seemed to believe that the English were visiting deities. "Nothing could persuade them, nor remove that opinion, which they had conceived of us, that we should be Gods," remarked Fletcher.[18] A local king went so far as to swear allegiance to Drake, as Elizabeth's ambassador—at least, that is how the English interpreted the ceremony. Apparently, the king offered to grant Drake the "right and title to the whole land" and even "become his subjects." The Indians sang, set a crown on Drake's head, and honored him "by the name of *Hioh*."[19]

Drake had no experience of such people or such situations. He did not want to cause offense, nor did he want to forego whatever "honor and profit it might be to our country." So, in the name of her Majesty, Drake "took the scepter, crown, and dignity of the said country into his hands" with the wish that "the riches and treasure thereof might so conveniently be transported to the enriching" of Her Majesty's "kingdom at home."[20]

Then, to leave his mark and establish "her Majesty's right and title" to the land, Drake had a plate fashioned from brass or lead and engraved with his name, the queen's name, and the date and year of their arrival. He attached to the plate a sixpence piece—showing Elizabeth's face and coat of arms—and nailed it "upon a fair great post" for all to see.[21]

Drake bestowed a name on the land that he believed the Indians

had given him and that he had claimed for Elizabeth: Nova Albion, or
New England. The land's "white banks and cliffs" were reminiscent
of the cliffs of England's south coast, while the word "Albion," deriving from the Latin for "white," was the ancient name for England.[22]

This, then, was the second secret that Drake conveyed to Elizabeth: he had gained for England a toehold on the western shore of the
American continent, a little bit of empire.

Towards the end of July, Drake left Nova Albion behind, conclud-
ing that the only way home was across the Pacific—the route taken
by *Victoria*, Magellan's ship, sixty years earlier. But, unlike Magellan,
Drake had the benefit of navigating with charts snatched from vessels of the Spanish silver fleet plying the route between Mexico and
the Philippines. After sixty-eight days out of sight of land, they
reached an island called Ternate, in a group of islands called the
Moluku—better known as the Moluccas. These were the fabled
Spice Islands, offering the goods that had been the object of English
dreams and ventures for more than eighty years. Not quite Cathay,
perhaps, but fantastically rich with potential.

Drake arrived at an opportune moment for England. Relations
between the local people and the Portuguese, who had first established
a trading presence in the islands in 1511, had turned sour. As a result,
Drake received word from the local sultan that he would be "wondrous
glad" to welcome the Englishman. Drake sent the sultan a velvet cloak
as a token of goodwill and evidence of the fine merchandise the English
were prepared to offer in trade. In return, the sultan sent Drake six
tons of cloves, as well as rice, chickens, and sugar cane.[23]

With a bond established, Drake was able to negotiate a trade
agreement with the sultan. He agreed to support the ruler in his conflict with the Portuguese in return for the monopoly of the spice
trade. As evidence of his good faith, Drake gave the Sultan a coat
of armor, a helmet, and a gold ring set with precious stones. For the
first time, the English believed they had an ally—commercial and
political—in the East Indies.

This was the last one of Drake's three secrets. Not only had he located a new passage around the Spanish and claimed a new realm for Albion, he had forged a trade deal in the Spice Islands.

BACK IN ENGLAND, Drake's treasure haul was anything but a secret. To keep it safe, some of it was dispatched to the Tower of London. The rest was placed under lock and key at Trematon castle in Saltash near Plymouth, where it was guarded by forty soldiers. All told, the officially registered treasure amounted to some £126,000, approximately half the queen's annual revenue.[24]

Meanwhile, Elizabeth continued to ponder what to do with the booty. Should she side with Cecil or Walsingham? There was no doubt that her instinct was to keep the treasure and resist the increasingly threatening demands of the Spanish for its return. In an attempt to ease the tension, Elizabeth tried to downplay the significance of Drake's treasure haul, calling for a rumor to be spread that he "had not brought much money" back with him.[25] But the evidence to the contrary was plain for all to see. Drake was reportedly "squandering more money than any man in England."[26] No wonder: Elizabeth had allowed him £10,000 for his personal use.[27]

Also, in a calculated act of defiance, Elizabeth took every opportunity to be seen with Drake. "The Queen frequently has him in her cabinet, and never goes out in public without speaking to him," reported Mendoza, before adding that she "often" took to "walking with him in the garden." By contrast, she refused to meet Mendoza and hear Philip II's protests.[28]

On April 4, 1581, six months after Drake had returned home, Elizabeth finally came to a decision about the disposition of the treasure. At Deptford, where the *Golden Hind* was moored, she dined with Drake. She teased him by drawing a gilded sword and threatening to cut off his head for his audacious deeds. Then she asked the ambassador of France—no friend to Spain—to take the sword and knight

Drake. This single action represented a decisive moment that set Elizabeth on a new collision course with Philip. She had, in essence, endorsed Drake's hostile action against Spain.[29]

The Spanish, however, persisted in their efforts to recover the stolen goods. Mendoza continued to seek an audience with Elizabeth to register his protest, but she snubbed him time and time again. He warned the Spanish Company merchants that Spain would seize their ships and property in Seville if Drake's plunder were not returned. Hearing this, the merchants sent a delegation, led by John Marshe, governor of the Spanish Company, to meet with Walsingham. But even though he was a member of the company, Walsingham could not be persuaded to exert influence on the queen to change her mind. He advised the merchants to "do very little trade" with Spain that year.[30] Later, when they continued to press their case, he told them that, if they did suffer losses at the hands of the Spanish, there was "plenty here to pay for it."[31]

As Mendoza issued threats, the Privy Council attempted to buy him off, or so he claimed: "They resolved to delay matters and tempt me by saying that, if I softened my tone towards Drake's voyage I might count upon for myself, or for any other person I might appoint, 50,000 crowns profit." Mendoza, of course, refused. On another occasion, Drake himself vainly sought to woo Cecil, Lord Burghley, who was urging the queen to compromise. "He offered to Burghley ten bars of fine gold worth 300 crowns each," noted Mendoza. But Cecil reportedly refused the golden gift, "saying that he did not know how his conscience would allow him to accept a present from Drake, who had stolen all he had."[32]

In October 1581, a year after Drake's return, Mendoza at last got his audience with Elizabeth. He tried flattering her, saying she was "so beautiful, that even lions would crouch before her." He tried threatening her, warning that, if the treasure was not returned, Philip would seize all English goods in his dominions and use the takings "to reimburse" his subjects.[33]

Elizabeth, however, stood resolute: the treasure would not be returned.

DRAKE'S DAZZLING ACHIEVEMENT unleashed a torrent of activity in England, even more intense than the gold fever that erupted after Frobisher's first voyage. Leading merchants and courtiers scrambled to organize a follow-up to Drake's venture and capitalize on the trade deal he made in the Spice Islands. "There is hardly an Englishman who is not talking of undertaking the voyage, so encouraged are they by Drake's return," Mendoza observed.[34]

As early as January 1581, four months after Drake's return, there were reports that Elizabeth had authorized a new voyage for him. He would command a fleet of ten ships this time, bound for the Moluccas and possibly Nova Albion. The terms of a "project of corporation" were drawn up, and the queen was asked to grant the new group privileges similar to those enjoyed by the Muscovy Company. Drake was to become the governor of the company and receive a tenth of its profits. The crown was to receive a fifth of the profits of any gold and silver mines that he discovered in the new territories.[35] Drake promised investors a return of seven pounds for every pound invested. This was such an alluring offer and had "so great an influence over Englishmen," Mendoza noted, "that everybody wants to have a share in the expedition."[36]

In the end, Drake's voyage did not take place. The threat of war loomed over England, and his services were needed closer to home. In April 1581, the same month that Drake received his knighthood, Philip had been crowned king of Portugal—adding to the title he already held as king of Spain—after defeating a rival claimant for the Portuguese throne. Drake may have "encompassed" the world by his seafaring exploits, but Philip II's empire really did encompass the world: all the lands once divided between the two monarchies under the terms of the Treaty of Tordesillas now fell within Philip's domain. At a stroke, he became the most powerful man in history—more exalted, even, than Alexander the Great. Accordingly, Philip embraced Alexander's motto as his own: *Non Sufficit Orbis* — the world is not enough.[37]

Now Spain became even more jealously protective of its claims to overseas territories. In the wake of Drake's triumph, Mendoza urged Philip to order that any foreign ship entering the Spanish or Portuguese territory "should be sent to the bottom" and that "not a soul on board" should be "allowed to live." Mendoza asserted that such aggressive action was "the only way to prevent the English and French from going to those parts to plunder."[38]

Also, Mendoza tried to persuade Philip to seize English goods in Spain, but this proved unworkable because, despite the tension between the two countries, Anglo-Spanish trade was booming. In February 1582, the merchants of the Spanish Company told Mendoza they had "never been received so well in Spain as during the last eighteen months." This surge in trade with the English, Mendoza wrote, had "given rise to an impression" among Spain's home traders that business with England was essential to their commercial success. This, in turn, had the effect of swelling the "pride and insolence" of the English.[39]

As evidence for this, Mendoza pointed to preparations for yet another English expedition. Through his spy network, he learned that a fleet of ships was to sail for the Moluccas. And he took the fact that the ships were "being manned with a large number of all sorts of artificers," such as carpenters and bricklayers, as "an indication of their intention to colonise."[40]

Mendoza's information was accurate. Preparations for an expedition to the Spice Islands were underway. The new venture was backed by many of the courtiers and merchants who had supported Drake, as well as some of the leading merchants of the Muscovy Company — notably George Barne. Drake himself put six hundred pounds into the venture. Initially, it was to be led by Martin Frobisher, who was busily restoring his reputation. In the end, however, Edward Fenton, who had been second-in-command on Frobisher's third voyage, was given the task of leading the fleet.

In May 1582, Fenton departed England, intending to sail to the Spice Islands via Brazil and Africa's Cape of Good Hope—the traditional route of Portuguese traders. His crew included John Drake, Francis's cousin, as well as several merchants. As the fleet approached Africa, Fenton declared that he wanted to occupy and fortify St. Helena, an island in the mid-Atlantic, where he would be crowned king and where they would lie in wait for the Portuguese fleet carrying riches from Brazil.[41] Was he thinking of Drake's coronation in Nova Albion? Fenton, after all, had been set to become the first leader of an English colony in the New World—until the prefabricated building that was to shelter the settlers was lost in an Arctic storm.

But in the end Fenton's ships did not stop at St. Helena. Instead, they continued on to South America, where the crew broke into squabbling factions. John Drake sailed away with his followers, never to be seen again in England. Fenton ran into Spanish warships guarding the entrance to the Magellan Strait to prevent another English passage. He turned around, returned home, and wrote to William Cecil that he was "sorry to advertise...the bad success of 'our voyage.'" He blamed contrary winds and disagreements among his crew; but mostly, he said, the failure was caused by Spain. His "honest proceedings" had all been "overthrown" by the King of Spain. "Such wrongs," he said, were "not to be put up with."[42]

As the English pursued efforts to build on Drake's success, Mendoza did what he could to learn the exact details of the great circumnavigation, dispatching spies to Plymouth with instructions "to discover the particulars from the men who went on the voyage."[43] He managed to uncover two of Drake's secrets: one, that Tierra del Fuego "was not [a] continent but only very large islands" with "open sea" beyond them; and two, that the English had struck a deal with the sultan of Ternate.[44]

He did not, however, uncover the third secret, of Drake's landing at Nova Albion. This, it seems, was the most closely guarded secret of all, the one the English most wanted to keep from the Spanish: the idea that a New England could be established in America.

11

⥤◈⥢

TO HEAVEN BY SEA

SIR HUMPHREY GILBERT may have been temporarily silenced, but he had not given up. In 1583, as Fenton was limping home, his dreams of emulating the great Sir Francis Drake in tatters, Gilbert was in Cawsand Bay, a protected haven near the entrance to Plymouth harbor, readying a fleet for his most ambitious venture of all—one that would establish a network of great colonies in northern America. Gilbert would not be crowned, as Drake had claimed to be in Nova Albion, nor would he be proclaimed king, as Fenton had hoped to be. But he would be the next best thing, a governor with power over a vast territory, ruling in the name of Queen Elizabeth.

Gilbert still held the letters patent, issued by Elizabeth in 1578, which gave him license to "discover, search and find out" new territories, and he was determined to do just that before the patent expired in 1584. He drafted a statement that amounted to a founding constitution for his imagined American domain. Gilbert and his wife, Anne, along with their sons and daughters, would hold dynastic and commercial rights to the lands. All merchants who did business in regions he controlled would have to pay him hefty customs duties on their trading activities.[1]

The colony would not be entirely nostalgic and feudal, however. Indeed, it would have a strikingly forward-looking and democratic feature that seems remarkably modern. As governor, Gilbert would be advised by a group of colonists who would be "chosen by the consent of the people"—that is, elected. This was a radical departure from the Privy Council, whose members were chosen on the basis of social status and royal favoritism.[2]

Gilbert's imperial vision was going to be costly to realize, but his finances were in a parlous state after his last abortive enterprise to "annoy" the king of Spain. In his first effort to capitalize on his royal patent, he had frittered away his wife's inheritance and, as he confided to Walsingham, had been forced to sell her "clothes from her back." Also, he had suffered enduring damage to his reputation, complaining he was "subject to daily arrests, executions, and outlawries."[3]

But by the terms of his license, Gilbert held an incredibly desirable asset that was potentially more valuable than any treasure or trade. That asset was land. In England, land was precious because it was scarce. In the New World, land was unknowably plentiful, but it was no less valuable for all that. For the younger sons of great families, such as Sir Humphrey, who could not inherit the family estate, the abundance of land offered an opportunity to claim an exalted place in the world that was denied them in England.

The letters patent did not set territorial limits, and given that Dee had confirmed England's right to empire, Gilbert could consider all of America as his own property, and he did just that. In May 1582, he attracted his first major investor—Philip Sidney, Walsingham's son-in-law and grandson of John Dudley. Gilbert, rather arbitrarily it would seem, assigned Sidney 3 million acres, an area about the size of Yorkshire or Jamaica.[4]

Then, Gilbert managed to attract another set of investors who pictured a colony devoted to a very different purpose: a haven for

Catholics. In mid-July, Bernardino de Mendoza, the Spanish ambassador, reported that Walsingham had "secretly" approached two "Catholic gentlemen" about Gilbert's venture.[5] Almost certainly, these two gentlemen were Sir George Peckham and Sir Thomas Gerrard. The two men bought into the arrangement, committing unspecified sums of money in Gilbert's expedition.[6]

Given Gilbert's track record, particularly his ferocious slaying of Catholics in Ireland, his willingness to deal with Catholic investors seems out of character. On the other hand, Gilbert knew Peckham: they had been co-investors in a planned expedition through the Magellan Strait in the mid-1570s, and Peckham had some involvement in Gilbert's 1578 venture.[7] Also, through Peckham, Gilbert may have known Gerrard, since Peckham's daughter married Gerrard's son. Gerrard, who also hailed from a renowned Catholic family, had previously flirted with the idea of overseas colonization. In March 1570, he had petitioned Elizabeth for rights to develop a part of the Ards peninsula in Ireland that eventually went to Sir Thomas Smith.[8]

According to Mendoza, Peckham and Gerrard were "spendthrift gentlemen," facing ruin.[9] This may have been another reason that the prospect of a great deal of land, along with the freedom to act on that land as they pleased, was attractive to them. Certainly, life was not easy for Catholics in England at this time. Although Peckham was a moderate Catholic, and was knighted by Elizabeth in the year that she was excommunicated by the Pope, he had, by 1580, become more outspoken, even doing a stint in prison for sheltering the renowned Jesuit Edmund Campion, who had secretly come to England.[10] Gerrard had also spent some time in prison for his participation in a plot to free Mary, Queen of Scots, who was living in England under a kind of house arrest having long before fled her homeland after a Protestant coup d'état.[11]

When Elizabeth had first come to the throne, she endeavored to take a tolerant approach in religious matters—a *via media,* or middle way. She herself was Protestant, but she did not abandon the crucifix in her chapel, despite opposition from her advisers.[12] After 1570, when the Pope excommunicated her, Elizabeth became the target of many Catholic plots, and she got much tougher on Catholic practices. There were no persecutions or bloodlettings in England to rival the St. Bartholomew's Day massacre in Paris in 1572, but there were new prohibitions and tougher laws. In 1581, the English Parliament passed a bill authorizing a fine of twenty pounds per month to be levied on people who refused to attend English church services—a hefty amount and certainly enough, over time, to ruin a Catholic of modest means.[13]

Elizabeth and her councillors had little interest in expelling Catholic recusants, as they were called. Instead, they preferred to keep them at home, where they could monitor their movements, and, through fines, reduce their ability to organize any action of their own. If Catholics were ousted or banished from the country, so the reasoning went, they might join forces with fellow Catholics in France or Spain, plan an invasion, coup, or assassination, or further torment Protestant groups in those countries.

However, the idea of sending Catholics far from England—to a distant, unpopulated place such as America—was an altogether more appealing proposition. In the New World, they would not pose a serious threat and they could follow their religion without being seen to defy the practices of the English church. Walsingham seems to have come to the conclusion that the time was right for contemplating a colony of Catholics, and that is probably why he helped smooth the path for a deal between Gilbert, Peckham, and Gerrard.

Gilbert granted the two men 1.5 million acres of land, a massive estate, about the size of the state of Connecticut or the county of Devon. As an extra incentive, he threw some islands into the deal— although they were unidentified, undiscovered, and may not have actually existed. Also he granted the Catholic colonists the freedom to trade without regulation. In return, Gilbert was to receive rental income, customs duties, and two-fifths of any gold and silver they discovered on their land. As the negotiations progressed, Gilbert doubled the land grant to 3 million acres in exchange for the Catholic colonists' pledge to supply armed ships and men for a colonial militia. Then, he granted a further 1.5 million acres to Peckham and his son, near a scoop of water that John Dee had marked on his map as Dee River, and is now known as Narragansett Bay.[14]

Peckham and Gerrard, perhaps concerned about Gilbert's past violence towards Catholics, sought some assurances from Walsingham about the details of the grant.[15] They wanted guarantees that, when the time came, their colonists, including recusants, would be permitted to leave England and travel to the new territories, as Gilbert had promised them. In return, they agreed that their colonists would not leave America, once there, and travel to any other foreign realm. Nor would they participate in any treacherous act that might cause a breach between the queen and "any other Prince." Also, they promised that one in ten of their colonists would be a person unable to "maintain themselves in England." This would help England with the problem of "idle persons."

According to Mendoza, Elizabeth accepted the terms and gave Peckham and Gerrard a "patent under the Great Seal of England to settle in Florida"—as the entire east coast of America was known. But Peckham and Gerrard's vision did not seem to inspire others, and the two men struggled to generate support from fellow Catholics. They were not helped by Mendoza, who fought a kind of rearguard action to scuttle the plan. He instructed Catholic clergymen to warn prospective colonists that the lands in the New World belonged to Spain, and if they dared travel there, "they would immediately have their throats cut."[16]

The specter of Spanish retaliation on American colonists could prove disastrous to the undertaking, so Peckham sought to confirm that England had the necessary sovereignty, turning to the expert who knew most about it: John Dee. Peckham asked Dee if their proposed estate would constitute an encroachment on Spanish rights, contrary to the Treaty of Tordesillas. Dee assured him that the lands did not fall within Spain's domain. Peckham rewarded Dee with five thousand acres in the New World, a tiny sliver of his millions.[17]

EVEN WITH FINANCIAL support from Sidney, Peckham, and Gerrard, Gilbert needed to attract a broader group of investors to raise the full amount of capital required to found a colony in the New World. To do this, he embarked on a far-reaching marketing campaign. He had seen the value of promotional literature when his *A Discourse of a Discovery of a New Passage to Catai* was published to help promote Frobisher's voyages. So when a young former Oxford don named Richard Hakluyt stepped forward, perhaps on Walsingham's recommendation, and suggested he might write just such a pamphlet, Gilbert gratefully accepted the offer.[18]

Hakluyt was beginning to establish a reputation as a powerful advocate of English overseas endeavor. He first came to public notice with the appearance of a report, completed in 1580, that made a compelling case for England's taking possession of the Strait of Magellan—although no such audacious move took place. After gathering information from John Winter, Francis Drake's second-in-command on the voyage around the world, Hakluyt wrote that "the Strait of Magellan is the gate of entry into the treasure of both the East and the West Indies, and whosoever is Lord of this Strait may account himself Lord also of the West Indies."[19]

But Hakluyt had been in the thrall of travelers' tales, voyages of discovery, and explorers since he was a schoolboy. When he was about sixteen, he paid a visit to his cousin, also named Richard. The elder Hakluyt was a lawyer, but his real passion was for maps and geography. There, lying on the table in his study, were "certain bookes of cosmography with an universal map," Hakluyt remembered, years later. Seeing his young cousin's interest, the elder Hakluyt picked up his "wand" and pointed out the "seas, gulfs, bays, straits, capes, rivers,

empires, kingdoms, dukedoms, and territories of each part." He identified the commodities available in each place, the needs of the people
there, and talked about the "traffic and intercourse of merchants" supplying them.[20]

All of this made such an impression on the young Richard that he
resolved to study geography when he went on to university. Indeed,
soon after, Hakluyt went up to Oxford, where he read widely on the
subject and, thanks to scholarships from two livery companies—the
Skinners and the Clothworkers—gained an understanding of merchants and the commercial impulse. After taking his master of arts
degree, he embarked on a series of lectures, presenting to his audi-
ences a variety of "Maps, Globes, Spheres, and other instruments of
this Art," much to the "singular pleasure, and general contentment"
of his listeners.[21]

Now, ahead of Gilbert's intended voyage, Hakluyt began putting
together a compendium of narratives, maps, and other information
that traced the story of English exploration. Published in May 1582 as
*Divers Voyages Touching the Discovery of America and the Islands Adja-
cent,* it was dedicated to Philip Sidney.[22] But if Hakluyt's immediate
goal was to promote Gilbert's venture, his larger goal was to ignite a
whole new spirit of adventure for overseas enterprise. He marveled
"not a little" that, since the discovery of America by Christopher
Columbus, the Spanish and Portuguese had accomplished "great
conquests and plantings" in the New World. By contrast, during the
same period, "we of England" had not had "the grace to set fast footing in such fertile and temperate places." This was puzzling to Hakluyt and, in his eyes, a national failing.[23]

He was an optimist, however, and believed that the time was right
for England to take her fair share in those parts of America and other
regions that were "as yet undiscovered." He argued that the pur-
ported motive of the Spaniards and the Portuguese for their ventures
of exploration and colonization—to convert and bring salvation to

the heathens—had been exposed for what it was: a false and cynical cover-up for their real intentions. All the Spanish and Portuguese really wanted, Hakluyt proclaimed, was "the goods and riches" of the New World.

Hakluyt asserted England's historical right, based on John Cabot's claim of 1497, to inhabit the vast American territory from modern-day Florida to 67 degrees north (roughly the northern border of modern Canada). He argued that England's need to expand had become an urgent one because the prisons were full to bursting, and such "superfluous people" could be sent to inhabit the "temperate and fertile parts of America."[24] He exhorted that the effort would take grit and determination—and, frankly, a change of attitude. "If there were in us that desire to advance the honor of our country which ought to be in every good man," he wrote, the English would have long ago taken advantage "of those lands which, of equity and right, appertain to us."[25]

To put together *Divers Voyages,* Hakluyt was fortunate to have access to Michael Lok's extensive collection of maps, historical documents, and other items pertaining to the Frobisher voyages, including a sketch of *Meta Incognita* and the Northwest Passage. In return, Hakluyt went out of his way to praise the merchant, who was still trying to rebuild his reputation after the Frobisher debacle. Hakluyt lauded Lok for his expertise in languages and cosmography, asserting that he was a man capable of doing "his country good" and that he deserved a "good reputation and better fortune."[26]

Hakluyt's work was well received. Walsingham personally thanked him, praising the young scholar for shedding "much light for the discovery of the Western parts yet unknown." In a letter, he urged Hakluyt to continue his efforts, since this would not only be for the young man's "own good" but also bring "public benefit of this Realm." He signed the letter "your loving friend."[27]

It seems that *Divers Voyages* did have the desired effect and stimulated investment in Gilbert's colonial venture. In November 1582, a few months after its publication, Gilbert was able to launch a new corporation with the self-aggrandizing name "the Merchant Adventurers with Humphrey Gilbert." The entity was to have a governor, treasurer, agent, and secretary—all four senior officials chosen by Gilbert—and eight assistants or directors chosen by the members. It was to be headquartered in the port of Southampton, where Gilbert had concentrated his fund-raising efforts and where he promised to establish an exclusive staple for the American trade. This was a calculated snub to London's merchants—specifically those from the Muscovy Company who had previously prevented Gilbert from pursuing his American dream.

For Southampton's merchants, the draw was land, just as it was for Sidney, Peckham, and Gerrard. Under the terms of Gilbert's offer, those who put in money, but did not go themselves, were to receive one thousand acres if they sent five men and two thousand acres if they sent ten. Those who went but did not invest cash were to be granted a piece of land according to the equipment they brought with them. For example, the man who came furnished with a "sword dagger and arquebuse" would be granted 120 acres. The adventurer who went himself, recruited others to join him, and bore all expenses, got the best deal. If he brought five men, he would be granted 2,000 acres of land. If he could put together a company of ten, he would receive 4,000 acres.[28] To avoid the kind of trouble Michael Lok had got himself into, Gilbert promised to reward investors who delivered their funds up front, in advance of the sailing, with an additional eleven hundred acres.

Just as Gilbert casually dispensed land he knew nothing about, the crown also made an extravagant pledge. The queen, according to a report by Mendoza, promised to dispatch 10,000 people, at the government's expense, to conquer the new land and inhabit the plantation, just as soon as Gilbert had landed and fortified a suitable place.[29] If

Mendoza's information was correct—and it may not have been—this would have been Elizabeth's biggest commitment to any overseas expedition.

Nearly fifty people from Southampton invested in Gilbert's venture—cloth merchants as well as the middling sort, including bakers, brewers, and a tailor. Walsingham also invested, putting in a relatively modest fifty pounds. To beef up the list of associates, Gilbert granted free trade rights to those who had invested in his first voyage, including Thomas Smythe, and to a number of "grave and honorable personages," including Cecil, the Dudley brothers, and Sir Christopher Hatton.[30]

Although the number of investors sounds impressive, most of the financial commitments were small, with many investments of just five to fifteen pounds. In total, Gilbert raised no more than a thousand pounds. As a result, he had to turn to his relatives for extra funds. Walter Ralegh, Sir Humphrey's half-brother, contributed the *Bark Raleigh,* an investment worth upward of two thousand pounds. So, while the rhetoric was lofty, enthusiasm ran high, and the venture had friends in high places, the truth was that it was underfunded— which is never a propitious way to begin.[31]

EVEN WITH LIMITED funds, Gilbert managed to assemble a fleet of five ships and recruit a company of 260 men. There was just one final hurdle to overcome: Elizabeth's blessing for him to make the journey. She had denied Ralegh permission to participate in the voyage, even though he had contributed his ship. Also, initially, she had refused Gilbert's request to sail because he was not, as she delicately put it, "of good hap by sea"—which had certainly been demonstrated in his previous voyage.[32] Elizabeth only relented and allowed Sir Humphrey to sail after Ralegh pleaded with her on behalf of his half-brother. As Gilbert prepared to embark, Ralegh wrote to him from Richmond, where Elizabeth was holding court, saying that the queen wished him "as great good hap and safety to your ship as if herself were there in person," enclosing a gift from her: a pendant bearing "an anchor guided by a Lady."[33]

The fleet of the Merchant Adventurers with Humphrey Gilbert set sail from Plymouth on June 11, 1583. Gilbert owned the *Swallow* and the tiny *Squirrel.* The bark *Raleigh* was the fleet's largest vessel at two hundred tons. The *Delight,* the admiral of the fleet, was captained by William Winter, son of Sir William, surveyor of the navy. The *Golden Hind* — no doubt named in honor of Drake's famous ship — was captained by its owner, Edward Hayes. He was an enthusiastic supporter of overseas expansion, had subscribed to Gilbert's 1578 voyage, was well known to Cecil and his circle, and had agreed to write an account of the voyage.[34] On board were men with the wide range of skills needed for the founding of a colony — including shipwrights, masons, carpenters, and smiths, as well as "mineral men" and refiners.[35]

Gilbert had originally intended to sail south and then proceed north to Newfoundland. But because they were getting a late start and facing contrary winds, they decided to set sail to Newfoundland first. They set off, but after two days at sea, many members of the *Raleigh* crew were "infected with a contagious disease," and the ship turned back for Plymouth. This was a severe blow, but Gilbert kept on.[36]

En route, the ships encountered bad weather, temporarily separated, but managed to rendezvous in Newfoundland at the beginning of August. They gathered at the entrance to St. John's harbor, where, by Hayes's count, thirty-six fishing vessels "of all nations" were at work. Although Gilbert's little group of ships looked relatively modest in comparison to the vast fishing fleet, he prepared to implement the plan of conquest he had laid out in his treatise, *A Discourse How Her Majesty May Meet with and Annoy the King of Spain.* He "made ready" to fight any of the ships that might resist him. But confrontation turned out to be unnecessary. The captains of the English fishing fleet came aboard Gilbert's ships, and when he presented them with his commission from Elizabeth they agreed to support him.

Gilbert went ashore and read his commission aloud to the fisher-men. He declared that he thereby "took possession" of St. John's Harbor and all lands within two hundred leagues of it, in every direc-tion, in the name of the queen. He further explained that the fisher-men would henceforward be governed by three new laws. First, all "public exercise" of religion had to conform with the practices of the Church of England; second, anyone who acted against Elizabeth's right of possession would be prosecuted as if it were a case of high treason; and third, any person uttering words "to the dishonor of her Majesty" would have his ears cut off, his ship seized, and his goods confiscated. Gilbert then laid out the new financial arrangement that would be enforced in Her Majesty's territory. The fishermen would have to pay a tax for the right to fish along the Newfoundland coast. Also, they would have to pay rent on the plots of land they used for camping and processing fish—even though they had been occupy-ing and using them free of charge for years.[37]

To complete the act of taking possession, Gilbert and his men erected "a pillar of wood," engraved in lead with the English coat of arms, much as Drake had done four years earlier on the west coast of America. Now, with Gilbert's claim of Newfoundland and Drake's claim of Nova Albion, Elizabeth could claim sovereignty on both sides of America.

Although Gilbert and Drake's claims may seem spurious, they were consistent with the widely accepted rules of territorial ownership at the time. These derived from the work of Justinian, the sixth-century Byzantine emperor who vainly sought to restore the fragmented Roman empire to its former greatness. Justinian defined four ways in which one nation could claim sovereignty over another. The first was the physical occupation of land not already under the jurisdic-tion of another state. In this, Gilbert's claim to Newfoundland could not be challenged. He had set foot on the territory and no one, no European at least, had prior claim to it. The second was a right of "prescription," meaning that the claimant has held possession of the place for an extended period of time, even if it has not been occupied. Here again, Gilbert was within his rights if one accepted that Newfoundland had been discovered and claimed by John Cabot nearly a century earlier. The third way of achieving dominion was through the acquisition of a territory by means of a treaty with the current holder of the land. There was no such holder of Newfoundland that Gilbert knew of or might recognize as such. The fourth path to dominion was through "subjugation," which meant that one nation could take land belonging to another state through conquest. Again, this did not apply to Gilbert's claim to Newfoundland. He had encountered no resistance and conquered nothing.[38]

After laying claim to Newfoundland (and evidently taking no account of the rights or views of the native people of the place), Gilbert set about learning as much as possible about the region. Some of his men searched for commodities, others drew "plats" or maps of the harbors and roadsteads. One of the mineral men — a Saxon metallurgist — came across a piece of ore that looked as if it contained silver, and in the mountains they discovered what they thought could be traces of iron, lead, and copper.[39]

These were promising finds, and after a month in Newfoundland, Gilbert told Hayes that he was ready to sail home. However, he had a duty to his investors to explore farther south. Many of Gilbert's crew, however, felt no such obligation. They did not mutiny, but some plotted to steal a ship and sail home, others hid in the woods hoping to gain passage aboard some other vessel, and some developed a sudden sickness. In the end, Gilbert agreed to leave the *Swallow* in Newfoundland to take on provisions and ferry the disaffected and diseased back to England.

Gilbert departed St. John's on August 20 and headed south with three ships — the *Delight,* the *Golden Hind,* and his favorite, the *Squirrel.* Nine days later, they encountered a storm of "rain and thick mist." The *Delight* ran aground, broke apart, and the crew was cast overboard, though some were able to clamber aboard their pinnace. They eventually made their way back to Newfoundland, keeping themselves alive thanks to "no better sustenance then their own urine."[40]

Disheartened by the loss of the *Delight* and with winter coming on, Gilbert and Hayes decided to return to England. Although Gilbert had not identified a suitable location for his colony, he remained optimistic that one could eventually be found. He even expressed confidence to Hayes that Elizabeth would loan him £10,000 for a voyage the following year and he would be able to carry out his grand plan. Although he had lost all his documents, much to his distress, he knew he would be able to draw on Hayes's written account when preparing a new petition.

But Gilbert did not get the chance. On September 9, the ships ran into another storm. The *Squirrel*, overloaded with equipment, was top-heavy and unstable.[41] Gilbert's officers entreated him to come aboard the *Golden Hind,* but he refused. As the little vessel churned alongside the *Golden Hind,* Hayes saw Gilbert sitting on deck reading a book, which some have suggested was Sir Thomas More's *Utopia.* Gilbert called out to Hayes, "We are as near to heaven by sea as by land!"—perhaps paraphrasing More's comment that the "way to heaven out of all places is of like length and distance." That night, the lights on the *Squirrel* flickered out and the ship and its commander were "devoured and swallowed up of the Sea," never to be seen again.[42]

"The first great English pioneer of the West," observed Sir Winston Churchill in his history of the English-speaking peoples, "had gone to his death."[43]

12

—◆—

WESTERN PLANTING

WITH GILBERT LOST, what would become of his patent?

The sorry news of Sir Humphrey's demise catalyzed a flurry of activity. George Peckham expressed his desire to claim the land that Gilbert had granted to his father and enlisted some big names to support him — Frobisher, Hawkins, and Drake. But his venture went nowhere.[1] Then Christopher Carleill, grandson of Sir George Barne and stepson of Walsingham, put out his own tract arguing for the development of "the hithermost parts of America." The land, he said, was "bigger than all Europe," and since "the larger part [bent] Northward," the local people "shall have wonderful great use of our said English Clothes." At first, leading merchants of the Muscovy Company, which had fallen on lean times, showed some interest. But they would only invest on one condition: he had to secure letters patent from the queen.[2]

As was her wont, Elizabeth took her time to reach a decision. When, in March 1584, she finally issued new letters patent, they did not go to Peckham, Carleill, or the Muscovy Company. Instead, they went to Sir Humphrey's half-brother and Elizabeth's new favorite at court, Walter Ralegh. Seventeen years younger than Gilbert, he was now presented with a thrilling, if daunting, opportunity: to take up his brother's unfulfilled quest to establish an English presence in America. It caused envy at court, the latest evidence that Elizabeth was besotted with the dashing soldier.

Ralegh had first come to prominence in Ireland four years earlier, distinguishing himself with a mix of valor and violence while serving in an English force sent to quell a Spanish-backed uprising in the rebellious kingdom. Afterwards, he was sent to court, where he offered himself as an adviser on Irish affairs. Within a few months, he famously caught the queen's eye with a memorable display of chivalry. As a later chronicler recounted it, the queen was out walking one day when she came to a "plashy," puddly place. She hesitated and Ralegh made his move. He lay "his plush new coat on the ground, whereon the queen trod gently." She rewarded him with "many suits" as recompense for his "free and seasonable tender of so fair a footcloth."[3]

It was said Elizabeth came to love Ralegh "in preference to all others."[4] He was just the kind of "proper" man she most admired. Bursting with energy, beautiful in his "white satin doublet, all embroidered with rich pearls," he was adored by the ladies of the court. Ralegh, too, "loved a wench well," noted the antiquarian John Aubrey. The young courtier, he wrote, had once squired a queen's maid "up against a tree in a wood."

Elizabeth came to rely on Ralegh "as a kind of oracle."[5] Clever and bookish, he was "an indefatigable reader, whether by sea or land." He "carried always a trunk of books along with him."[6] Like Gilbert, Ralegh had attended Oxford, studying at Oriel College. He went on to the Middle Temple, where he picked up a smattering of law and where he almost certainly came into contact with Richard Hakluyt, the elder.

The queen showered Ralegh with gifts, patents, and benefits. When his military commission had come to an end in 1583—which brought him an annual salary of at least six hundred pounds—

Elizabeth granted Ralegh the leases of two fine estates owned by All Souls College Oxford, which he traded for ready money.[7] He was awarded not only a patent to license vintners and sell wine but also a license to export undyed woolen broadcloth, giving him a lucrative slice of England's most important industry. These were generous perquisites that became the bedrock of his wealth.

As icing for this very rich cake, Elizabeth granted Ralegh a grand residence — Durham House — situated on the north bank of the Thames and distinguished by castellated walls, turrets, a water gate onto the river, and a pleasant orchard. Built in the thirteenth century, it became the London residence of the bishops of Durham before being seized by Henry VIII in the 1530s during his assault on the church. By the early 1550s, it had been handed to John Dudley, who no doubt discussed the business of the Mysterie while he lived there.[8]

At Durham House, Ralegh established a kind of corporate head-quarters where, as Aubrey reported, his study, "a little turret," looked over the Thames, providing a "prospect which is pleasant perhaps as any in the world, and which not only refreshes the eyesight but cheers the spirits" but also "enlarges an ingenious man's thoughts."[9]

Ralegh, following the model set by his half-brother, brought together a number of expert advisers to help him plan a colonial venture. Among them was Thomas Harriot, a twenty-three-year-old mathematician and cosmographer in the John Dee mold. Although humbly born, Harriot had been well educated at St. Mary's Hall, an Oxford institution later affiliated to Oriel, Ralegh's alma mater.[10] Ralegh engaged the young scholar towards the end of 1583, even before he received the letters patent, and installed him in rooms at Durham House adjacent to his own.

Like Dee before him, Harriot was hired to prepare three men that Ralegh had recruited to lead the first mission of his grand venture, a reconnaissance voyage to America: Philip Amadas, a nineteen-year-old from solid Devon gentry stock; Arthur Barlowe, a seasoned sea captain; and Simão Fernandes, the skilled Azores-born pilot and shipmaster who had sailed with Gilbert on his first voyage. Harriot prepared a navigational manual (now lost) called *Arciton,* and he conducted classes in cosmography and other new sciences.

In late April 1584, the three men set off with two small ships in search of a suitable location for settlement while Ralegh began planning for his own version of a fully-fledged colonial enterprise in America. He realized that if he was going to mount a successful expedition, he would need royal backing that went beyond the issuing of letters patent. Although he had Elizabeth's ear, he needed to make a complete and convincing case to win her support. To help him prepare this, he turned, at Walsingham's suggestion, to the man who was emerging as England's foremost authority on America and its greatest cheerleader for colonization: Richard Hakluyt, the younger.

HAKLUYT, NOW AGED about thirty-two, had enjoyed great success with *Divers Voyages,* which was produced to promote Gilbert's final, disastrous voyage. After its publication, Hakluyt was sent to Paris, on Walsingham's recommendation. There, he served as chaplain and secretary to Sir Edward Stafford, newly appointed ambassador to France.

Even though Hakluyt had spent much of his life reading the works of great travelers, this was his first visit to a foreign country, and he got a taste of the hazards of long-distance travel. The journey from London to Paris took two weeks; the rough crossing of the English Channel alone left the party "sea-beaten" and "half dead."[11]

Hakluyt was not simply an ambassadorial assistant. He was, in effect, an operative in Walsingham's intelligence network, charged with gathering information about America. As Hakluyt himself put it, he was expected to make a "diligent inquiry of such things as may yield light unto our Western discovery." In this endeavor, he was extremely energetic. He interviewed countless New World experts, writing often about them for Walsingham. He inspected the furs of "sables, beavers, otters" brought back to France from Canada, worth five thousand crowns. He made the acquaintance of André Thevet, France's royal cosmographer, and talked with him further about the Canadian fur trade. He met with Pierre Pena, a French botanist and Henry III's physician, probably discussing the trade in herbal remedies coming from the New World. He visited an instrument maker, André Mayer, in Rouen, where he also took the opportunity to meet the merchant-explorer Étienne Bellenger, who had recently returned from a voyage to the northeast coast of America. And with Dom Antonio, the exiled pretender to the Portuguese throne, Hakluyt examined a map of the world showing the Northwest Passage.[12]

Hakluyt passed the useful information back to Walsingham, who, it seems, was often playing a double game when it came to overseas ventures: he wanted to help the country, yes, but he also wanted to enrich himself and those close to him. He had used his influence to help his son-in-law, Philip Sidney, gain an estate of 3 million acres in Sir Humphrey Gilbert's fiefdom. Also, he had pushed his stepson Carleill's project. But when that enterprise foundered, he threw his support behind Ralegh's venture, encouraging him to draw on Hakluyt's expertise.

When summoned to London, Hakluyt did not hesitate. He wrote to Walsingham that he was ready to fly from France to England "with the wings of Pegasus." By July 1584, after just nine months in Paris, Hakluyt was back in England, and for the next two months, he labored intensively on the report, burning the midnight oil.[13] The result was the first great English treatise on colonization: *A Particuler Discourse Concerninge the Greate Necessitie and Manifolde Commodyties That Are Like to Growe to This Realme of Englande by the Westerne Discoueries Lately Attempted, Written in the Yere 1584, by Richarde Hackluyt of Oxforde*. Today, it is known as the *Discourse of Western Planting*.

In the first week of October, Hakluyt presented the treatise to Elizabeth. Although only a handful of copies were made—and it was never published in Hakluyt's lifetime—it delivered on its promise to present the case for colonization in the New World.* In some ways, the rationale for overseas expansion—the problems facing England—had not changed since the dark days of 1549, when Sir Thomas Smith wrote his *Discourse*. English trade had become "beggarly" and even "dangerous," Hakluyt wrote. In Spain, English merchants risked being seized and interrogated by the Inquisition. In the Mediterranean, pirates patrolled the North African, or Barbary, Coast. Doing business in Turkey, which controlled the western end of the Silk Road, was expensive. The Muscovy market, which had begun with so much hope, was now, after the death of Ivan in March 1584, full of uncertainty.[14]

Hakluyt's proposed solution to England's chronic problems was different than it had been in Smith's day, when merchants had dreamed of Cathay. Now, Hakluyt argued, they should look to America. All the commodities of the Old World were available there—including fruits, wine grapes, flowers, fish, metals, furs, oil, sassafras, spices and drugs, and timber for furniture, weapons, and ships. And colonization would ease social problems. Planting colonies in America would require workers aplenty: shipbuilders, farmers, trappers, stoneworkers, fishermen, traders. Cottage industries—the knitting of woolen goods, for instance—could occupy women, children, the old, and the lame. Increased prosperity of one would benefit the commonwealth of all.

Not only would American colonization benefit England directly, it would reduce Spain's dominance. In America, the English would be able to find good havens from which their ships could attack the Spanish treasure fleet. Given that the Indians of the region "do mortally hate the Spaniard," they were sure to join the English in opposing the Iberian rulers. And the English would be able to get rich from mining and, as they surpassed Spain in wealth, make Philip a "laughing stock of the world."

---

* The *Discourse of Western Planting* was first published in Cambridge, Massachusetts, by the Maine Historical Society, 1877.

America was, therefore, the solution to many of England's commercial, social, and political problems. But time was of the essence. Like Frobisher, Dee, and Gilbert before him, Hakluyt urged Elizabeth to make haste, lest England "come too late and a day after the fair." Other nations had designs on America, and procrastination could mean England losing out to "enemies and doubtful friends."

ON SEPTEMBER 15, just as Hakluyt was finishing up his *Discourse on Western Planting*, Amadas and Barlowe returned from their reconnaissance voyage. They brought home glowing reports of the land they had discovered in the New World and had claimed for England, since it was "not inhabited by any Christian Prince or Christian people." Also, as Frobisher had done, they brought home living proof of their discovery: two Indians, Manteo and Wanchese, who could testify to the "singular great commodities" of the new land.[15] But unlike the Inuits captured forcibly by Frobisher, the two native Americans seem to have been brought to England without coercion. They were presented at Elizabeth's court, where onlookers gawped with a sense of wonder. One German aristocrat, on a tour of England, described the Indians as having a "countenance and stature like white Moors." He marveled that, although "their usual habit was a mantle of rudely tanned skins of wild animals, no shirts, and a pelt before their privy parts," they were "clad in brown taffeta" for the court visit.[16]

Barlowe presented Ralegh with a written account of the five-month expedition. After a two-month Atlantic crossing, the voyagers had sailed along the Florida coast until they came to the Outer Banks, a scattering of islands protected by natural sandbanks, and found a sheltered river entrance. They landed on Haterask, an island with "many goodly woods," plenty of game, and "the highest, and reddest Cedars in the world." Here, Barlowe reported, "the earth bringeth forth all things in abundance, as in the first creation, without toil or labour." They claimed possession of the land in the name of Queen Elizabeth.[17]

A few days later, they had encountered some local people and, using sign language, asked them for the name of the country. "Win-gandacoia," was the word the English wrote down. Then, one of the Indians came aboard the flagship. The English "gave him a shirt, a hat, and some other things, and made him taste of our wine, and our meat, which he liked very well." Soon enough, trading began, the English exchanging metal tools and utensils for the Indians' deer skins and buffalo hides. With an undertone of disbelief, Barlowe reported that they traded "our tin dish for twenty skins, worth twenty Crownes, or twenty Nobles."[18] (A noble, the higher value coin, was worth about one-third of a pound.) In these dealings with the Indians, Barlowe wrote, "we found the people most gentle, lov-ing, and faithful, void of all guile, and treason, and such as lived after the manner of the golden age."[19]

After a while, Barlowe and a party of men had sailed north until they reached an island called Roanoke, just off the coast of what is now North Carolina. It looked promising as a location for a settle-ment, with its "fertile ground" and "goodly cedars" and other "sweet woods," as well as grapes, flax, and other commodities.[20] Not only this, but it was tucked far enough inland so as to be out of view of passing Spanish ships and yet close enough to the ocean to launch raids on the Spanish treasure fleets.

Reading this encouraging reconnaissance report, Ralegh was moved to act quickly in order to protect his claim, and so, as he had recently been elected as an MP for Devonshire, he decided to try to garner parliamentary support for his enterprise. In December 1584, a bill was read in the House of Commons to confirm Ralegh's letters patent to colonize America. This—the first piece of legislation regarding Amer-ica to appear in Parliament—was reviewed by a committee of MPs that included some of the most experienced advocates of overseas expansion in England: Francis Walsingham, Christopher Hatton, Philip Sidney, Richard Grenville, and Francis Drake. They approved it without altering a single word.[21] In the end, however, the bill was not put before the House of Lords—because it was unlikely to win support there — and so Ralegh's rights were not enshrined in an Act of Parliament. But the bill nevertheless served to mobilize the support of England's ruling elite behind a colony in America.

AS RALEGH SOUGHT to win the support of Elizabeth and his fellow parliamentarians — we don't know if she read Hakluyt's elaborate *Discourse* — he set about organizing the practical business of a transatlantic voyage. For the Amadas and Barlowe reconnaissance voyage, he had come to rely on Thomas Harriot as a kind of project manager, whose responsibilities included not only tutoring the mariners but also maintaining the accounts, developing maps, and advising on shipping.

Now he asked Harriot to take on an altogether more complex task. If Ralegh's venture was to succeed, it was imperative for his colonists to be able to communicate with the local people. So Harriot's assignment was to learn Algonquian, the Indians' native tongue and the language spoken by tribes inhabiting America's eastern seaboard from modern-day South Carolina all the way to Massachusetts. At the same time, he was to instruct Manteo and Wanchese in English, so that the two men could eventually serve as interpreters.[22]

In this endeavor, Harriot meticulously studied the mechanics of Manteo's and Wanchese's speech — the sounds their vocal cords produced, the shapes their lips formed, the ways their tongues moved. He then devised an orthography — a "universal alphabet" — composed of thirty-six symbols representing sounds common to the English and Algonquian languages. These symbols formed a strange-looking cursive script that drew on cossic, or algebraic, numerals.[23]

While Harriot closeted himself with the Indians in the sumptuous surroundings of Durham House, Ralegh undertook to raise the substantial funds needed to supply the voyage and the plantation. He did so with the help of William Sanderson, a rich merchant and leading member of the Worshipful Company of Fishmongers who had recently married Ralegh's niece.[24] The MPs who had supported Ralegh's bill, who were among the enthusiastic backers of overseas enterprise, seemed the likeliest investors. For them, it was not just about anti-Spanish patriotism—it was also about profit.

Walsingham, for example, held the position of Secretary of State, which brought him an annual income of one hundred pounds. To build out his fortune, he relied on other remunerative *douceurs,* activities, and investments. From 1574 to 1582, he was granted exclusive licenses to export more than 200,000 pieces of broadcloth, or kerseys. In effect, he controlled nearly half of England's export trade in unfinished cloth of the finer quality. Also, he seems to have inherited a stake in the Muscovy Company held by his wife's deceased first husband, Alexander Carleill, father of Christopher: by 1568, he was one of the company's most eminent members, becoming an "assistant," or director. And he profited handsomely from Drake's voyage round the world.[25]

Not all of his business dealings were successful, however. As a director of the Spanish Company, he suffered, not least because of his own political machinations, putting the crown's interests before his own. And his investments in Frobisher's and Gilbert's voyages turned sour. But Walsingham accepted the risks and rewards involved and invested in the Ralegh Colony. As George Peckham noted in his *True Report,* which he dedicated to Sir Francis: "Nothing ventured, nothing have."[26]

AS THE DAY of departure approached for Ralegh's fleet, the queen, too, upped her stake in the colonial venture. She had already invested in him indirectly—granting him monopoly rights over portions of England's cloth and wine industries, the profits from which went to help fund his American enterprise. Now she lent him one of her royal ships, the *Tiger,* and ordered the Master of Ordnance of the Tower of London—Ambrose Dudley, Frobisher's great champion—to release an allotment of gunpowder worth four hundred pounds, a valuable commodity often in short supply.

Elizabeth expressed her support in symbolic ways as well. She knighted Ralegh and granted him permission to bestow her name, or at least her epithet, the Virgin Queen, to his claimed territories: *Vir-*

ginia. Soon enough, Sir Walter was referring to himself as lord and governor of Virginia. This drew the scorn of many envious courtiers who derided Ralegh as a jumped-up paragon of the nouveaux riche. As one of them put it, Ralegh was "the hated man of the world, in Court, city and country."[27]

So Elizabeth had given Ralegh a flagship, a knighthood, gunpowder, and a rich stream of revenues. But there was one thing she was not prepared to grant her favorite: permission to leave the country and lead the expedition. With his brother, Sir Humphrey, she had allowed herself to be persuaded to change her mind, letting the headstrong adventurer lead the ultimately fatal voyage to Newfoundland, against her better judgment. But with Ralegh, she was not ready to do this. She simply could not bear to be without her "Water" or to risk losing him, as she had lost Gilbert.

Ralegh acquiesced. What choice did he have? To act in his stead as commander, he turned to Sir Richard Grenville, a kinsman and keen colonialist, who had considerable experience in Ireland and extensive knowledge—albeit through books—of the New World. He had been one of the MPs who had so enthusiastically supported Ralegh's attempt to get parliamentary ratification of his letters patent. Grenville's family had deep roots in the military affairs of England. His grandfather, also Sir Richard, had been Marshal of Calais, responsible for the colony's defense, in the 1530s and early 1540s. His father had been master of the *Mary Rose,* Henry VIII's flagship and the *Titanic* of its day, which sank spectacularly before the king's eyes as it departed Portsmouth to wage battle against French warships. In the early 1570s, Grenville collaborated with Humphrey Gilbert in one of his many unrealized schemes, a project to colonize the great southern continent—*Terra Australis*—beyond the Magellan Straits. So when Ralegh approached him about leading the Roanoke venture, Grenville pounced on the offer.[28]

On April 9, 1585, Grenville's fleet, led by the flagship *Tiger,* weighed anchor at Plymouth. The four vessels carried six hundred men—three hundred soldiers and three hundred other passengers with a variety of skills deemed necessary to establish a colony in the strange and foreign land of Virginia. One of these was a gentleman artist named John White. It was Richard Hakluyt, the elder, who had suggested that "a skillful painter" be sent to America to produce a visual record of the new land. The Spanish were known to do this "in all their discoveries," he said, in order to provide "descriptions of all beasts, birds, fishes, trees, towns" and other features of the New World.[29] Ralegh selected White, a watercolorist who had gained recognition nearly a decade earlier for his depiction of scenes of the Frobisher voyages. These included a drawing of a violent skirmish between Frobisher's men and Inuit archers and a finely detailed sketch of a woman and her baby — the child riding on the mother's back, peeking out from within the hood of her fur parka.[30]

Thomas Harriot was also among the passengers, with a commission to write a report on the commercial potential of the American settlement. He was accompanied by the two Indians he had tutored (and been tutored by), Manteo and Wanchese. Harriot had made good progress in mastering Algonquian. Much to Ralegh's amusement, he had even learned that Wingandacoia was not the Indian name for the land they hoped to inhabit, it was actually a phrase meaning "What fine clothes you're wearing!"[31]

It was a good omen, perhaps. The thing the native people noticed, above all, was the voyagers' fine garments of cloth — the very commodity for which England's merchants hoped America would prove a new market.

AFTER A STORMY but successful voyage across the Atlantic, Grenville suffered a serious setback as the fleet approached Roanoke. The *Tiger,* sailing through the shallow sandbanks, struck bottom. For two hours, Simão Fernandes, the pilot, fought desperately to save the ship. The mariners frantically off-loaded some of the vessel's stores into the sea to lighten its load. As one colonist later reminisced in a letter to Walsingham, "we were all in extreme hazard of being cast away."[32] The action worked and they finally managed to beach the hulking vessel, but there was a price to pay: a significant proportion of their provisions was spoiled by the salt water. This meant there would not be sufficient food and other supplies to establish a colony with all the prospective settlers. As a result, most of them were sent back to England—just 107 men were left behind to establish a settlement. Grenville stayed for two months to help Ralph Lane, a soldier with extensive experience in Ireland, who had been appointed governor of the colony.

While lodgings were constructed, John White and Thomas Harriot got down to work, travelling with the colonial leaders on an exploratory mission to the mainland across Pamlico Sound. Not far inland, they came to the native village of Pomeiooc, and there White began painting. He employed a watercolor technique that was then in vogue among gentleman-artists, known as limning—"a kind of gentle painting," as one contemporary called it. Generally, he began by sketching his subject on paper in black lead. Then, having mixed his colors in mussel shells, using rare pigments from apothecaries, he applied the paint with brushes made from the finest squirrel hair, starting with wide brushes for the background colors and graduating to finer brushes and deeper colors as he built up the scene. For added effect, he created a powder by grinding gold into a dust, thickening it with honey, and then applying it sparingly for highlights.[33]

At Pomeiooc, White found a well-kept village containing eighteen buildings arranged in a circular formation, with a communal fire roaring at its heart. It was encompassed by a palisade formed of tree branches ten or twelve feet high, embedded in the ground and sharpened at the tip—obviously prepared for protection against attack. Farther along, the Grenville party encountered another village, Secotan, with a wide boulevard running through its center. Seemingly more agricultural, it was bounded by fields of corn, or maize, one patch with plants ripe and ready for harvesting, another with green corn, and a third with corn just "newly sprung."

In addition to landscapes, White produced several portraits, including one of Wingina, a local chief, or *werowance*—meaning "he who is rich." The chief looks benign, with his graying hair tied in a knot and adorned with feathers. He wears a swatch of fringed cloth around his waist, a necklace, and an impressive status symbol—a large square copper plate hanging from his neck. Other images depicted a mother and daughter, the child holding an Elizabethan doll, evidently a gift from one of the colonists; a medicine man identified as "the flyer," who is shown hovering above the ground; and a squatting man and woman sharing a meal of hulled corn, which looks like popcorn, laid out neatly on a wooden platter. Also, White captured family gatherings, religious ceremonies, burial rituals, fishing, and farming.[34]

White's paintings were not intended as works of art, although that is what they have become. They were visual marketing designed to stimulate interest from prospective investors and settlers. It was hoped that they would reassure would-be English colonists and quell their fears about making a life in America. White went to great lengths to portray the Indian culture as friendly, charming, and even familiar. Indeed, some of the Indians are presented in poses similar to those found in the costume books then popular in Europe.[35] The chief crooks his elbow to rest the back of his wrist on his hip, looking almost like a gentleman waiting for his carriage. One of the chief's wives hooks her left foot around her right and lays her palms upon her shoulders, covering her breasts, as a shy teenager might. All in all, White presents an idyllic image of Virginia. The people are well-fed and even-tempered—they appear as if they would be delighted to welcome English settlers into their communities, offer them a home-cooked meal, and support them in their battle against the Spanish empire.

While White painted his exquisite watercolors, Thomas Harriot prepared his report on the commercial potential of the new land.[36] He searched for what he called "merchantable commodities," and he found many: "grass silk," sassafras, deer skins, otter fur, iron ore, copper, some silver, pearls, medicinal plants, and dyes for the clothmaking industry. Also, he looked for staple goods that could sustain a colony, year after year, and found maize, beans, peas, pumpkins, and a variety of wild animals for meat: rabbits, squirrels, bears, "wolfish dogs," and "lions," by which he meant panthers, pumas, and cougars.

Above all, Harriot embarked on an ethnographical study of the Algonquian peoples. Were they people that Ralegh, his fellow investors, and Englishmen could do business with? The answer was, in a word, yes. "They, in respect of troubling our inhabiting and planting, are not to be feared," he reported. "They shall have cause both to fear and love us that shall inhabit with them." They dressed simply and were naked but for "loose mantles" and skirts or "aprons" made from deer skin. They lived in small villages, of typically about ten houses — although Harriot did see one with thirty. So scattered were the communities that the most powerful ruler controlled no more than eighteen villages and could only amass an army of around eight hundred warriors. For all their apparent simplicity, however, Harriot noticed that "in those things they do, they show excellence of wit," and he believed they could become good neighbors and trading partners.

GRENVILLE LEFT ROANOKE in August 1585, promising to return by the following Easter with fresh supplies. He got back to England in mid-October, and presented Ralegh with, among other things, an album of White's paintings that provided the English people with their first view of America. They had read the detailed accounts of Frobisher's voyages. They had seen the Inuits and Indians brought back from *Meta Incognita* and Virginia. But they had never seen the country with their own eyes. Looking at White's watercolors would be the closest most of them would come to doing so.

It soon became apparent, however, that the Roanoke Colony did not match the idyllic environment portrayed by White. Grenville had brought with him two letters from Ralph Lane, one addressed to Walsingham, the other to Philip Sidney. They presented very different views of Roanoke: the opportunity and the challenge.

To Walsingham, Lane described "Her Majesty's new kingdom" as a "vast and huge" territory that was "by Nature fortified" and blessed with many "rare and...singular commodities." He pledged that he and his men would rather "lose our lives" than lose possession of so "noble a kingdom." He showered praise on Ralegh and his "most worthy endeavor" to make a "conquest" of Virginia.[37] In his letter to Sidney, by contrast, Lane complained about the "unruliness" of the men and suggested that the colony was in trouble. Later, he concluded that only if England discovered "a good Mine" or a "passage to the Southsea" could her countrymen ever expect to successfully inhabit this part of the world.[38] The lure of gold and Cathay continued to loom large in the minds of England's colonists.

One incident of unruliness involved Philip Amadas, the hotheaded twenty-one-year-old who co-led the reconnaissance mission with Barlowe the year before. He razed an Indian village to the ground after suspecting a native warrior of stealing a silver cup. This was not a solitary act of violence, and Wingina, the local chief who struck such a graceful pose in one of White's paintings, started to lose patience with the English colonists—especially after they began to make ever greater demands for food.

The colonists managed to survive the winter, but the situation gradually grew desperate. As supplies dwindled, they engaged in a battle that left the inhabitants of an entire Indian village, including Wingina, dead. By now, relations between the Indians and the English had slumped to a new low. The only salvation for the settlers would be fresh supplies from England. They anxiously awaited Grenville's return, and at the beginning of June 1586, as if in answer to their prayers, they spotted a fleet on the horizon. It was not Grenville's, as they hoped. Nor was it Spanish, as they feared. Instead, the fleet was commanded by Sir Francis Drake.

WHILE LANE AND his fellow colonists had been busy battling to survive in the New World, England had begun battling with Spain in the first of a series of conflicts that amounted to an undeclared war. Drake was at the forefront of England's campaign. In September 1585, he commanded a massive fleet—twenty-five ships (two supplied by the queen) and two thousand three hundred men—to wreak havoc in Spanish territories in the New World.[39] It was, in effect, a terror campaign, with Drake and his men, including Martin Frobisher and Christopher Carleill, burning, spoiling, and looting Spanish settlements on their way from Santo Domingo to Hispaniola, Cartagena, and Cuba.

Drake had then proceeded north and reached St. Augustine, the Spanish outpost in Florida, in May 1586. The English believed that the purpose of the fort there was to "keep all other nations from inhabiting any part of all that coast."[40] So Drake sacked the town, destroyed the fort, and took whatever equipment he could find that might be useful to the settlers in Roanoke. He then went in search of his countrymen.

When he arrived at Roanoke, Drake found a colony that was much smaller than he had expected—and suffering great distress. He offered Lane one of his smaller ships, the *Francis,* as well as men, and enough supplies to tide the colonists over until Grenville returned. But when a storm hit the coast and scattered Drake's fleet, the *Francis* disappeared over the horizon and with it the hopes of those colonists who wanted to stay in Virginia. At last, the entire company abandoned Roanoke and boarded Drake's vessels to return home.

Just days after the settlers sailed for England, a small supply ship that Ralegh had organized arrived at Roanoke. Finding no English in residence, it turned around and headed home. Soon after, Grenville arrived, with his larger relief expedition. When he, too, found the settlement abandoned, he made an inexplicable decision. He did not disembark his entire company of three hundred to four hundred, nor did he take them all home again. Instead, he left behind just fifteen men provisioned for two years, a tiny squad of Englishmen settled on a scrap of island that Walter Ralegh—some four thousand miles away—dreamed would one day be the seat of a great empire.[41]

13

━━◉━━

PRINCIPAL NAVIGATIONS

WHEN THE BEDRAGGLED Roanoke colonists arrived back in England at the end of July 1586, after just one year in Ralegh's Virginia, they found England in a state of high tension as a result of the undeclared war with Spain. Sir Francis Drake's tormenting of Spanish colonies had provoked outrage across the Iberian Peninsula. "Monstrous robbery" is the way Mendoza—who was now stationed in Paris, having been expelled from London for plotting to overthrow Elizabeth— characterized Drake's actions.[1]

But El Draque was not the only marauding English sea captain harassing the Spanish. Elizabeth issued hundreds of letters of marque, or reprisal, permitting profit-hungry merchants to use their privately owned ships to capture Spanish vessels and seize their goods, ostensibly in recompense for losses of goods or shipping that they themselves had suffered at the hands of the Spanish or Portuguese. These privateers— or "voluntaries" as they were called at the time—often exceeded their commission and essentially waged an incessant, warlike campaign of harassment up and down the Spanish coast and across the Atlantic.[2]

Soon after Elizabeth let loose this de facto navy, Philip retaliated by declaring a prohibition on any voyage to the West Indies that did not originate from the Spanish port of Seville. The ban was virtually unenforceable, and the privateering activity grew so rampant that Mendoza could scarcely keep track of it all. In November, he wrote an extensive report to Philip explaining how difficult it was to gather intelligence about what was going on in England. He had tried to "tempt" or bribe "merchants of all nations" to supply him with information, but they were too afraid. Nor could any of his spies sneak into English ports because the "arrival of a man, or even of a fly" who was not known in the neighborhood would be noticed. As Mendoza melodramatically put it, any foreigner who set foot on English soil "drags the hangman's rope after him."[3]

For Walter Ralegh, the intensifying conflict had become all-consuming, and he was now one of the busiest men in England, scarcely able to take the time to fully assess the consequences of his failed colony. In the year that Ralph Lane and his fellow settlers had been away, Ralegh had taken on three hugely powerful positions: lord lieutenant of Cornwall, vice-admiral of the West, and lord warden of the Stannaries—the Cornish tin mines.[4] The first two positions put Ralegh in charge of heading up the defense of the counties in the southwest. In effect, he was Elizabeth's personal envoy in those regions, responsible for mobilizing soldiers and sailors in the event of an invasion. Cornwall was a place of particular vulnerability for England. It was virtually a land apart, where the Celtic language was still spoken, and where its misty moorlands and hundreds of smugglers' coves could provide sanctuary for an invading Spanish force. But Ralegh's offices did not just hand him new responsibilities; they also handed him new opportunities to increase his personal wealth. As vice-admiral and lord lieutenant, he could extract profits from the privateering exploits of England's sailors. As head of the Stannaries, he could extract a slice of one of the country's most valuable industries.

While fulfilling these responsibilities, Ralegh seized the chance to do something that his beloved half-brother, Humphrey Gilbert, had tried and failed to do: establish a colony in Ireland. A few months before the Roanoke colonists returned, John Perrot, the Lord Deputy of Ireland, wrote to William Cecil and the rest of the Privy Council warning of the "great preparation . . . by the Spanish King against this realm." In his opinion, Spain's invading force was "likely to be bent against Munster"—and particularly its towns and cities, "which in truth are very weak."[5]

To prevent Munster falling into Spanish hands, the Privy Council, with Cecil and Walsingham taking the lead, drew up plans for attracting prospective colonists, especially from "the younger houses of English gentlemen" who might profit from the opportunity to create dynastic estates in Munster.[6] As in Gilbert's day, the Privy Council's rationale was that an Ireland populated by loyal Englishmen would be less likely to join forces with Spain than would the hostile native population, who might be eager to "shake off the English government."[7] In June 1586, as the Roanoke colonists were preparing to abandon Virginia, Ralegh was granted letters patent giving him and his associates the title to lands in the counties of Cork and Wexford. Under the terms of the grant, no investor was to be given more than one land unit, or seignory, of 12,000 acres. But Ralegh was always the exception. By February 1587, he laid claim to 42,000 acres.[8]

With these activities commanding so much of his attention, Ralegh's commitment to Roanoke might well have faltered. It did not help that some of the returning settlers made accusations about mismanagement, overselling, and unmet expectations. Some of the gentleman travelers railed that the colonial lifestyle, under Ralph Lane's strict military rule, was far harder than they had been led to expect. Others, who had hoped to create homes on their vast American estates, claimed they instead had been financially ruined by the experience. Thomas Harvey, for example, who had gone along as the cape merchant—the official authorized to buy and sell goods within a settlement—was left "poor and unable to pay" his obligations in England. He had invested "the greatest part of his own wealth," and borrowed additional funds, to buy commodities for trade. In a polite understatement, he said the voyage had not fallen out "so prosperous as was expected."[9]

This disaffection risked undermining Ralegh's position at court, where there was no shortage of people who would celebrate his misfortune. But his trusted allies assured him that Virginia remained a land of opportunity and advised him to ignore the complaints. Thomas Harriot, for one, expressed disdain for the gentlemen's accusations. As he later wrote, some of the settlers were nothing more than gold seekers, who "had little or no care of any other thing but to pamper their bellies." They had led sheltered, comfortable lives, having enjoyed "a nice bringing up only in cities or towns" and had "never . . . seen the world before." In America, they found neither cities nor "fair houses," nor any of "their old accustomed dainty food, nor any soft beds of down or feathers."[10]

For his part, Ralph Lane acknowledged there had been difficulties, but he argued that these were largely to do with the chosen location: Roanoke was a small island, affording little room to expand the colony, while the lack of a deep-water harbor limited access by larger ships. He was convinced that the area to the north, now Chesapeake Bay, would offer a better location for a settlement and port. He also believed that copper and even gold might be found inland and that the Pacific Ocean might not be far away.[11]

Given the negatives, Ralegh might well have considered walking away from the Virginia project, but the greatest advocate of overseas enterprise reminded him why he shouldn't. In February 1587, Richard Hakluyt's latest publication appeared at the book stalls in St. Paul's Churchyard. It was a reissue of Peter Martyr's classic work *Decades of the New World,* which Richard Eden had translated thirty years earlier as the Mysterie prepared to launch its second voyage to Muscovy.

In a powerful dedicatory letter, Hakluyt made an impassioned plea for Ralegh to continue the glorious enterprise: "Reveal to us the courts of China and the unknown straits which still lie hid," Hakluyt urged. "Throw back the portals which have been closed since the world's beginning at the dawn of time. There yet remain for you new lands, ample realms, unknown peoples." Hakluyt insisted that these lands were just waiting "to be discovered and subdued, quickly and easily." This was something that Ralegh could achieve, especially given the support he enjoyed from Elizabeth, whom Hakluyt described as the "Empress—as even the Spaniard himself admits—of the Ocean."

Not afraid to speak his mind, Hakluyt reminded Ralegh that he had made a commitment to keep going—no matter what. Indeed, Ralegh had sworn, in letters to Hakluyt, "that no terrors, no personal losses or misfortunes could or would ever tear" him from "the sweet embraces" of Virginia, "that fairest of nymphs." Such grand poesy was out of character for Hakluyt, and it reveals not only his great passion for the enterprise but also his great fear that the American initiative might be abandoned.

As for the naysayers, Hakluyt, echoing Harriot, encouraged Ralegh to dismiss them and the disgruntled ex-planters: "Let them go where they deserve, foolish drones, mindful only of their bellies and gullets."[12]

HAKLUYT'S APPEAL DID not fall on deaf ears. In fact, by the time his book was published, Ralegh had already entered into an agreement to form a new corporation to open up the New World: the Governor and Assistants of the Cittie of Raleigh in Virginia. But if this demonstrated that Ralegh did not lack for commitment, his choice of governor showed a peculiar lack of judgment.

Ralegh picked John White, the watercolorist from the first Roanoke settlement, as leader of the second colony. A little older than Ralegh, White had no experience as a soldier, sailor, or leader. Perhaps Ralegh's choice shows just how distracted he was. Perhaps it was his only practical option: with England on a war footing and with the rewards of privateering so great, there may have been few people willing to accept the dubious burden of leading a colony into an uncertain future. Perhaps, also, the testimony of disgruntled colonists had convinced prospective adventurers to stay at home. It is certainly noteworthy that the new colonists did not include any young men from illustrious families.

The whole enterprise was quite different from those that had been planned before. The 150 people who signed up to join Ralegh's venture were mostly artisans, small landowners, lesser merchants—the middling sort. Among them, for the first time, were seventeen women and nine children. The City of Raleigh was to be a real community, not a fortress colony. But like the gentlemen on the first voyage, these people were going to Virginia with hopes of making their fortune. Each colonist was to be granted five hundred acres of land, no matter how much money he or she invested in the venture. This would constitute a sizable estate in England—even if it was dwarfed by the millions of acres Humphrey Gilbert had promised his associates. Also, White's twelve "assistants" in the new corporation were offered an additional incentive: a coat of arms. To be an armigerous person or family—one entitled to bear heraldic arms—was a sign of distinction and status. By going to the New World, these people would be moving up in society.

The fleet set sail from Portsmouth towards the end of April 1587, with three vessels: a ship called the *Lion,* as well as a pinnace and a "flie boate"—a smaller, shallow-draft boat.[13] Also on board were two Indians, one of whom was Manteo, who had returned with Drake the previous year. For nearly two weeks, they beat against the wind, trying to clear the Lizard—the southern-drooping peninsula of Cornwall—and endured a difficult journey across the Atlantic. The weather was bad, and as conditions worsened, so did relations between White and his chief pilot, Simão Fernandes, the Azorean navigator who had first participated in Humphrey Gilbert's abortive voyage eight years earlier. By late July, the fleet, having scattered during the crossing, regrouped on the coast, south of Roanoke. White then made ready to sail to the island, hoping to pick up Grenville's fifteen men and continue to the "Bay of Chesapeake," which Ralph Lane had identified as the preferred location for a colony. But Fernandes objected to the plan and refused to take the colonists any farther than Roanoke. It was a mutinous defiance. Yet, astonishingly, White backed down, meekly accepting his subordinate's objections.

At the Roanoke site, they found abandoned houses but no settlers, "nor any sign that they had been there, saving only we found the bones of one of those fifteen, which the Savages had slain long before."[14] The English soon learned, from Indians who lived on the island of Croatoan, that Grenville's men had been attacked by Indians and skirmished with them; most escaped in a boat and were never seen again.

After a month on Roanoke, Fernandes prepared to return to England. But he was delayed for nearly a week after a dispute erupted over which of the colonists should return with him to arrange for the next resupply. Most of the colonists wanted White to go back. They believed that he would be able to wield the greatest influence with Ralegh. But White wanted to stay on. As governor, he felt responsible for the colonists, and was concerned that he would suffer "great discredit" if he returned prematurely. Nor did he wish to part from his new granddaughter, Virginia Dare. The daughter of Elenora White and Ananias Dare, she was the first English baby to be born on North American soil. Also, White worried about the safety of his "stuff and goods" while he was gone. Eventually, however, the colonists convinced him that he, and he alone, could best represent their interests in England. To reassure him, they gave their bond that they would look after his possessions and that should anything be damaged, they would make it good.

White finally succumbed to "their extreme intreating" and, at the end of August, set sail. After a brutal Atlantic crossing, he reached England in early November. He soon met with Ralegh, and his appeals, we must assume, propelled Ralegh to supply a stopgap resupply mission — a single pinnace to sail immediately. It was to be followed by a larger expedition, once again overseen by Grenville.[15]

UNFORTUNATELY FOR WHITE and the colonists, England's relationship with Spain was deteriorating rapidly, even as preparations for the pinnace were put in place. And once again, Francis Drake was at the center of the dispute. Earlier in the year, Elizabeth, in an act she would later regret, had signed the death warrant for Mary, Queen of Scots, who had been linked to yet another assassination plot. After Mary's execution, Drake was dispatched to deliver a preemptive strike against Spain, knowing that Philip was preparing to invade England. As Hakluyt put it, "Her Majesty being informed of a mighty preparation by sea begun in Spain for the invasion of England, by good advice of her grave and prudent Counsel thought it expedient to prevent the same."[16]

En route, Drake learned from a passing vessel that "there was a great store of warlike provision" being readied in Cádiz, a port on the southern coast of Spain, not far from the Strait of Gibraltar. Drake proceeded, with "all speed possible," and over the course of two nights he destroyed a hundred ships, including a "new ship of an extraordinary hugeness in burthen above 1,200 tons," which belonged to the high admiral of Spain.[17]

Drake memorably called his raid the "singeing of the King of Spain's beard." It demanded swift retaliation, and Philip ordered his admiral, Álvaro de Bazán, first marquis of Santa Cruz de Mudela — known as Santa Cruz — to assemble the great Armada's ships in Lisbon and make sail for England. But this was no easy task: Drake had destroyed so many ships, and so many others were scattered in various ports, that Santa Cruz could not quickly get the fleet together. Towards the end of 1587, Philip repeated his orders, to no effect. The Armada was still not ready. As preparations dragged on, the Spanish lost all hope of surprise. It had become the "worst-kept secret in Europe."[18]

Facing the prospect of imminent invasion, Elizabeth placed a stay of shipping in English ports. This prevented Ralegh from sending even a pinnace with resupplies for the Roanoke colonists. But in early April 1588, five months after White's return, Sir Richard Grenville finally got permission to deploy, as he saw fit, any ships that would not be involved in England's defense. In late April, White finally sailed from England with two small vessels carrying supplies and prospective settlers, seven men and four women.

If they left with great hope, this soon faded when they discovered that the captain appointed by Grenville was far more interested in fortune-hunting than in ferrying the colonists across the ocean to America. Once again, White, showing his weakness as a leader, was unable to assert his authority on board. As their ships got into scrapes, some of the mariners were killed or wounded. White, as he revealed, was "wounded twice in the head, once with a sword, and another time with a pike, and hurt also in the side of the buttock with a shot."[19] The damaged vessels limped back to England, arriving home after just four weeks at sea.

THEN, AT LAST, came the event that Elizabeth and England had feared for years: the invasion of the Armada. For the best part of ten years, Philip had been planning a great naval force. Now, from his seat in El Escorial, his magnificent palace forty-five miles northwest of Madrid, that was built with the profits of his American empire, he finally sent instructions for the invasion of England. In May, the mighty fleet of 130 ships, 18,000 soldiers, and 7,000 sailors departed Lisbon and made its way to the Bay of Biscay.[20]

England was prepared—as prepared as she could be. Her navy was a motley assemblage of thirty-four royal ships and 160 other vessels, including privateers owned by merchants and courtiers looking to capture Spanish prizes while doing their duty for queen and country. Among the leaders of the fleet were some of the pioneers of England's overseas expansion. The flagship, the *Ark Royal,* was commissioned by Ralegh and given as a gift to Elizabeth. The *Revenge* was captained by Drake. The *Triumph,* the biggest ship in the English fleet, was commanded by Martin Frobisher.

Battle was joined on July 20, and for the next nine days, the English ships harried and hustled the Spanish fleet. Eventually, the Armada reached Calais, where it moored, awaiting the arrival of a massive Spanish invasion force stationed in the Low Countries. But overnight, the English sent fire ships to disperse the fleet. Amid the chaos caused by these hellburners, the Spanish ships broke their moorings and scattered across the Channel. On July 29, at Gravelines, a little port east of Calais, the Spanish turned to fight the English but were beaten. Across England, church bells rang out, celebrating the achievement of defeating the Armada.

After the battle of Gravelines, Philip's ships fled north, chased by the English, who pursued them all the way to the Firth of Forth, the wide estuary that leads to Edinburgh, Scotland's capital. The Spanish intended to sail round the Shetland Islands, where Frobisher had long ago rested on his way to *Meta Incognita,* and south along the west coast of Ireland in order to avoid Elizabeth's rampant naval forces. But as they reached the Atlantic, they were scattered by fierce storms, which England's propagandists remembered as a "Protestant wind," sure proof that God was on the side of Good Queen Bess, as Elizabeth had come to be known.

Over the next three months, the Spanish fleet was destroyed and many of the sailors lucky enough to scramble ashore on the Irish coast were brutally murdered by local people. The Irish may have been fellow Catholics, but they did not want to be stopped from going after the rewards within the wrecked ships. The Spanish had been dispatched to conquer England and had brought with them precious ornaments of gold and silver to show off Spain's imperial glory. One of these was a salamander, or "winged lizard," that had been fashioned from gold mined in Mexico and set with rubies from India—a testimony to Spain's far-flung empire. The jewel traveled aboard the *Girona,* a seven-hundred-ton galleass carrying thirteen hundred men, including an array of Spanish nobles. When the fleeing ship hit the rocks not far from the Giant's Causeway off the coast of northern Ireland in violent storms, the salamander sank to the bottom of the sea.[21]

What was a tragedy for Spain was a triumph for England and provided Elizabeth with an opportunity to proclaim her imperial status. As the Spanish ships were wrecked or struggled home, her loyal vice-admiral, Sir Francis Drake, who had performed a crucial part in the victory, commissioned a portrait that presented the queen as an empress with global reach. Sitting resplendent on her golden throne, she rests her right hand on a globe, with her fingers spanning the east and west coasts of America. Above the globe is an imperial crown. Behind her, two windows capture memorable scenes from the sea battle. This painting—now known as the "Armada" portrait—left no one in any doubt about the message Drake wished to convey. The queen, having vanquished the most powerful emperor on earth, was herself an empress, an imperial ruler with territories in the New World.[22] At last, John Dee's vision, it seemed, was coming true.

In addition to the painting, Drake ordered a commemorative medal to be struck, commissioning Michael Mercator, grandson of the great cosmographer, for the job.[23] On the front, the silver medallion depicts the Old World: Europe, Africa and Asia, China, and dreamed-of Cathay. On the opposite side is the New World, with all the key places in Elizabeth's embryonic empire: the Elizabeth Islands lie to the south; Nova Albion is etched in bold lettering across northern America; and Virginia, the newest colony, also appears. As if to gloat, the words "N. Hispania," marking Spain's much larger territory, are engraved in a tiny font. Drake's circumnavigational route is traced by a fine dotted line. With this medal, ordinary Elizabethans could hold the world in their hands, just as Elizabeth herself did.

THE ARMADA ARTWORKS—the portrait of Elizabeth and the silver medal—were silent heralds of a new, self-confident, more assertive country contemplating its imperial future. But it was Richard Hakluyt, the preacher and American proselytizer, who gave voice to this new mood in his masterwork, *The principal navigations, voyages, traffiques and discoveries of the English Nation, made by Sea or over-land, to the remote and farthest quarters of the Earth, at any time within the compass of the 1500 yeeres.* It begins with the travels of ancient Britons to the Holy Land and continues right through to the "last most renowned English Navigation round about the whole Globe of the Earth," namely the second English-led circumnavigation made by Thomas Cavendish, completed in September 1588.

The first edition of the *Principal Navigations* was entered into the Stationers' Register on September 1, 1589, under warrant from Sir Francis Walsingham, who was the guiding spirit behind the project. There was no mistaking that this was an endeavor of national importance, the magnum opus that Hakluyt had been working towards since his time in Paris, after the publication of *Divers Voyages.* There, he had constantly heard and read stories about "other nations miraculously extolled for their discoveries and notable enterprises by sea." But he heard nothing other than derision for England and its "sluggish security" and condemnation of its "continual neglect" of overseas expansion. When Hakluyt realized that no one was going to step forward to speak up for the "industrious labors, and painful travels" of his countrymen—who had, by that time, ventured throughout the world and circumnavigated it—he resolved to take on the task of celebrating their accomplishments.[24]

Hakluyt did not wish to produce one of those "weary volumes" in which the material is simply "ramassed" (summarized from others) or "hurled together." So, from the late 1570s onwards, he was constantly in search of original, primary material: making visits, picking up scraps of information, and engaging in conversations that pertained to his great subject. He wanted the protagonists to speak for themselves, and he endeavored to transcribe his interviews with them "word for word."[25] Hakluyt collaborated with Thomas Harriot to interview a Spanish soldier captured by Drake at St. Augustine. He corresponded with Walter Ralegh and Richard Grenville and interviewed Martin Frobisher. He rode from London to Norfolk to interview Thomas Butts, a well-to-do young man who had been grievously emaciated during a voyage in the 1530s.[26] Also, as part of his research, he collected or inspected countless materials from travelers, including ships' logs, firsthand accounts, personal diaries and letters, official reports, maps and rutters (mariner's handbooks), drawings, treatises, ordinances, catalogs, and poems.[27]

It was a labor of love, "a burden," as Hakluyt called it, because "these voyages lay so dispersed, scattered, and hidden in several hucksters' hands." He wondered how he had managed "to endure the delays, curiosity, and backwardness" of the people from whom he collected the original documents.[28] But he was justly proud of the result. Until the publication of *Principal Navigations,* only sixteen accounts of English voyages had been printed. Hakluyt offered readers sixty-four accounts.[29] Perhaps the most sensational story in *Principal Navigations* was the one that was almost omitted. Its inclusion testifies to Hakluyt's determination to provide the most up-to-date account. In the course of his research, he had pieced together the story of Drake's circumnavigation from the recollections of members of the crew. Walsingham did not want him to publish the story, however, because parts of it were still considered secret, particularly the claim to Nova Albion. To make sure nothing leaked out, Walsingham had the whole book vetted by Dr. John James, the Keeper of the State Papers Office, who served as censor and who was scrupulous in removing sensitive material.[30] It was only after the first printing of *Principal Navigations* that Walsingham relented and allowed the inclusion of the Drake narrative. Hakluyt trimmed the story of "the famous voyage" to 10,000 words and had it hastily inserted into unsold copies. The pages were unnumbered.[31]

When it came to packaging all this information, Hakluyt was as innovative as he had been while collecting it. *Principal Navigations* is adorned with some advanced bibliographic features, including a table of contents, shoulder notes and marginal notes that provide useful signposts to the contents of each page, and an index. For the gentleman reader—and prospective investor—this became the bible and the encyclopedia of travel literature.

We do not know how many copies of *Principal Navigations* were printed, distributed, or sold. But it was a transformative publication. This, remember, was a time when there were no daily newspapers and no public libraries. Information was distributed through broadsheets, pamphlets, and sermons delivered from the pulpit. English itself was still a language in development, evolving from a tongue long considered marginal and inferior to Latin and Greek. It was not until the following year—sometime in 1590—that William Shakespeare's first play, *Henry VI Part II*, probably had its first performance.[32]

Hakluyt's collection of stories gave England a new way to think about itself—no longer as a sluggish and neglectful nation but as a bold seafaring people whose brave navigators, sent out by forward-thinking merchants and courtiers, were able to voyage across the oceans and venture to new lands. "In this most famous and peerless government of her most excellent Majesty," Hakluyt wrote in the dedicatory epistle to Walsingham, "her subjects through the special assistance, and blessing of God, in searching the most opposite corners and quarters of the world, and to speak plainly, in compassing the vast globe of the earth more than once, have excelled all the nations and people of the earth."[33]

RICHARD HAKLUYT'S *PRINCIPAL* Navigations was not just a paean to a newly confident England, it was also a pragmatic marketing publication for promoting the next voyage across the Atlantic. And for the first time, Hakluyt was an investor, putting his money where his mouth was. Around the time of publication, he joined a syndicate that had been formed to organize yet another expedition to establish contact with the Roanoke Colony, a group led by Thomas Smythe, the thirty-one-year-old grandson of Sir Andrew Judde and the second son of Customer Smythe.

This group agreed to invest in Ralegh's faltering Roanoke project "for the inhabiting and planting of our people in Virginia."[34] Under the terms of the agreement, Ralegh was to remain lord governor, but the syndicate was to form an alliance with the existing colonists, led by John White. It was an intriguing group that included William Sanderson, Ralegh's business manager; John Gerard, an expert in plants and plant-based medicines who served as superintendent of the garden at William Cecil's London residence; and Thomas Hood, a Cambridge mathematician who may well have been recruited to perform the role played by Harriot (who was no longer available, having moved to Ralegh's estates in Ireland).[35]

The syndicate seems never to have launched a voyage to Roanoke, perhaps because, in February 1590, the Privy Council once again issued an order forbidding merchant ships from leaving English ports. But John White was not to be deterred. He learned that a cloth merchant, John Watts, wanted to sponsor a privateering expedition to the Caribbean. White urged Ralegh to approach Elizabeth and persuade her to grant Watts a special dispensation to transport him and a new contingent of settlers to Roanoke.

This was arranged, but things did not turn out as White had hoped. When he prepared to board one of the ships with his group of colonists, Watts—or, more likely, one of his captains—refused to transport any settlers or supplies. White was obliged to board alone with "not so much as a boy to attend upon me."[36] The fleet finally departed in March, but as White must have feared, it did not speed across towards the American coast. Instead, the ships engaged in a series of privateering escapades.

It was not until mid-August that White finally reached Virginia. He had promised his daughter that he would return as quickly as possible. In the end, it had taken him three years to get back to Roanoke. As he looked across the island, he spotted a column of smoke rising "near the place where I left our Colony in the year 1587." This gave him "good hope" that the settlers were alive and looking forward to seeing him.[37]

White stepped ashore and walked to the site of the Roanoke encampment. There, he discovered, "curiously carved" into a tree trunk, the "fair Roman letters CRO." It was, wrote White, "a secret token" that he knew the settlers would use "to signify the place" where they might be found. This discovery further heartened him, because it indicated that he might find the colonists on the neighboring island of Croatoan, "the place where Manteo was born."

Also, it was clear to White that the move had been voluntary. The colonists had agreed to carve "a Cross †," if their removal had been in distress. White found no such mark. He was further encouraged when he found the complete word "CROATOAN" carved into one of the posts of the fort. Although the houses had been "taken down" and abandoned, there were no signs of battle or struggle, no bones or graves, no indicators that the settlers had suffered a cruel end. But White was less delighted when he came across several chests containing his belongings, "spoiled and broken." His books were "torn from the covers" and his armor "almost eaten through with rust." Just as he had feared, his "goods and stuff" had been ruined.[38]

White resolved to go on to Croatoan, but after a series of mishaps and the onset of bad weather, he decided to make for one of the islands in the West Indies, winter over, and then return to Virginia. That plan did not work either, and White was obliged to return to England, where he arrived in October, after a dispiriting six-month expedition. After so much hopeful planning, his valiant effort to reunite with his family in Roanoke had failed.

It was to be White's last voyage to Virginia. He would never return to Roanoke. He would never see his granddaughter again. Some years later, when he was living on Ralegh's estate in Ireland, he sent Hakluyt a mournful account of his final Roanoke voyage.[39] He wrote that he had no choice but to "leave off" his endeavor—but wished to God that his wealth had been "answerable" to his will.[40]

Like so many other Englishmen, White had invested everything and lost it all in his American dream.

14

THE OLD EAST AND THE NEW WEST

AS HOPES OF ever resurrecting the Roanoke Colony faded, there followed a long hiatus in England's expeditions to the New World. It was not until 1598, five years after receiving John White's regretful letter, that Richard Hakluyt, by now in his late forties, made a renewed effort to rekindle England's dreams of expansion. He brought out the first volume of a revised, greatly expanded, three-volume edition of his masterwork, *Principal Navigations,* first published almost a decade earlier.

Hakluyt believed the massive new work was necessary because England had not fulfilled the destiny that he foresaw when the original came out in 1589: to conquer land, find new markets for cloth, and spread the gospel across America. He knew that England had been distracted from pursuing that great quest, and for a number of reasons. Many of the great merchants, who were the masterminds of the earliest overseas enterprises, had switched their attention to the lucrative business of privateering. Meanwhile, the Spanish war had hindered overseas trade, dampened domestic demand for goods and services, and created widespread unemployment. Also, the weather—including the hottest summer of the century, 1593—had wreaked havoc, and bubonic plague returned to London, decimating the population in the true sense of the word: in one year alone, one-tenth of the capital's population died from the pestilence and other diseases.[1]

But the most devastating factor that brought England's overseas expansion to a shuddering halt was the sudden loss of the first generation of New World leaders. In April 1590, just after publication of Hakluyt's first edition of his *Principal Navigations,* Sir Francis Walsingham died at his London home, the former Muscovy House. This longtime champion of New World development was just fifty-eight years old. In 1591, he was followed to the grave by Thomas "Customer" Smythe, Sir Richard Grenville, and Sir Christopher Hatton. In 1594, Sir Martin Frobisher, knighted during the Armada, suffered a mortal leg wound while fighting alongside the French against the Spanish. The war then took Sir Francis Drake, who was buried at sea off the coast of Panama. And, on August 4, 1598, William Cecil, Lord Burghley, the standard-bearer of the old order, died at Cecil House, his London home along the Strand.

Then, soon after Cecil's death, came the news that proclaimed that an era had indeed come to an end: Philip II, king of Spain, at last succumbed to the terrible illness that had kept him in excruciating pain for months. Elizabeth did not mourn the passing of her former brother-in-law, onetime suitor, and longtime adversary. With his death, it was possible that peace negotiations might begin and the protracted Anglo-Spanish war might end.

FOR HAKLUYT, THIS seemed to be a time of new possibilities, an opportune moment to release the first of what would be three volumes of his expanded *Principal Navigations.* When all three were released, the final one appearing in 1600, the new edition constituted a monumental achievement: a two-thousand page trove of more than a hundred accounts, testimonies, and commentaries on English activities of exploration, discovery, and settlement, as well as many additional narratives on foreign initiatives.[2]

In the dedicatory epistle to the first volume, Hakluyt honored an old stalwart of the sea war with Spain: Charles Howard, the lord admiral who had commanded the navy against the Armada. But Hakluyt chose to dedicate the second volume to Sir Robert Cecil, son of Sir William. In doing so, he signaled his belief that England was on the cusp of a new beginning. Still only thirty-six years old, Cecil was, nevertheless, uniquely influential and, Hakluyt knew, a progressive when it came to English overseas activity. In the wake of his father's death, people whispered about the continuation of England as "Regnum Cecilianum," Cecil's kingdom.[3] It was striking testimony to the young man's astonishing rise to power. Unlike Elizabeth's other favorites at court, Cecil was physically unprepossessing: small, hunchbacked, with an awkward walk. It was said that a negligent nurse dropped him as a child, although it is more likely that he suffered from inherited scoliosis.[4] Elizabeth called him "my pigmy," but he had a giant intellect and she knew his value as an administrator and adviser. Not only was he clever, he was formidably conscientious. If he owed his spectacular ascent to his father—he was a privy councillor at the age of twenty-eight—he earned the queen's affection through diligence and dedication. He had the energy and drive that was so characteristic of second sons in England at this time. His elder brother, Thomas, had inherited Lord Burghley's title and glorious estate near Stamford in Lincolnshire, and Robert knew he would have to follow in his father's footsteps, building his own fortune through bureaucratic brilliance.

Hakluyt may have first met Cecil in Paris in the early 1580s, when the future royal adviser studied at the Sorbonne, as part of a broad education that included time at Cambridge and Gray's Inn, his father's beloved institutions. There, Cecil was hosted by Sir Edward Stafford, the ambassador and Hakluyt's employer at the time. Later, Hakluyt expressed "no small joy" that Cecil knew so much about

"Indian Navigations," referring to America as well as Asia.[5] In his dedicatory epistle in *Principal Navigations*, Hakluyt acknowledged Cecil's role in the book's publication—a sure sign that the young courtier, like his father before him, was eager to lead a second generation of English expansionists.

As always, the search for new cloth markets remained one of Hakluyt's chief concerns. "Because our chief desire is to find out ample vent of our woollen cloth, the natural commodity of this our Realm," Hakluyt argued, "the fittest places, which in all my readings and observations I find for that purpose, are the manifold Islands of Japan, & the Northern parts of China, & the regions of the Tartars." In winter, he reported, these lands were "as cold as Flanders," the capital of Europe's clothmaking industry.[6]

Given his great knowledge of England's efforts to establish trade in Asia, Hakluyt was called to advise the Privy Council on "why the English Merchants may trade into the East Indies, especially to such rich kingdoms and dominions as are not subject to the king of Spain & Portugal." He noted that although some lands were off-limits under the terms of the Treaty of Tordesillas, most of the world was open to English mercantile development: in particular, "the most mighty & wealthy Empire of China" and "the rich and & innumerable islands of Malucos and the Spicerie."[7] The longing for Cathay had not subsided.

There were complications, however. Philip's death, while promising to the cause of peace, had unleashed a new disruptive force for the English: the Dutch. In the mid-1580s, they had turned for help to Elizabeth, inviting her to become queen of their dominions. She had rejected their appeals, although she lent them military support.[8] Now, the Dutch, still waging a long war of independence against Spain, saw an opportunity to assert themselves on the global stage. Sensing Spain's waning interest in fighting them, they launched the first of a series of voyages to the Spice Islands. They sent some forty ships to trade in Asian ports in the last five years of the century.[9] In 1598 alone, they dispatched twenty-two ships. When, in July 1599, one of those ships returned with a particularly spectacular haul of spices, the English merchants sat up and took notice.[10] It seemed that just as the Spanish threat was abating the Dutch were making a bid to supplant Spain as the major commercial power.

Two months later, sixty English merchants met urgently to discuss the idea of a direct venture to the distant market they had long coveted: the Spice Islands of the East Indies. It was twenty-five years since Sir Francis Drake had cut a deal with the local ruler of Ternate, one of the Moluccas, but there had been no successful follow-up. Now, belatedly, London's merchants were looking to capitalize on that earlier success. Before long, more than one hundred investors had pledged around £30,000 in support of the proposed East India venture. Even though the English economy was in the doldrums, this was the largest sum ever invested in a single English expedition, and it showed not only the enthusiasm for the venture but also the sheer quantity of liquid capital available for high-risk investment, which largely came from the spoils of war.[11] More than a quarter of the capital came from merchants who had made their fortune from privateering, when profits soared as high as £200,000 per year.[12]

These London merchants drafted a petition to Elizabeth that sought royal support for a voyage "for the honour of our native Country and for the advancement of the trade of merchandise within this Realm of England."[13] The petition stated that "divers merchants" of England, "being informed that the Dutchmen prepare a new voyage...were stirred up with no less affection to advance the trade of their native country than the Dutch merchants were to benefit their commonwealth." They requested to be "incorporated into a company," since the East India trade, "being so far remote from hence, cannot be traded but in a joint and a united stock."[14]

But no sooner had these merchants put together plans for a new overseas trading company than they had to put them on hold because peace negotiations with Spain had reached a sensitive stage and the Privy Council was reluctant to do anything that might cause the

Spanish to walk away from the table. The merchants agreed to postpone their preparations "for this year."[15]

As good as their word, the adventurers reconvened on September 23, 1600, after a hiatus that had lasted a year and did not produce a peace agreement. The directors were, for the most part, members of the new generation of venturers—men like Robert Cecil. The star of this new generation was a scion of the Judde-Smythe family: Thomas Smythe. Ten years earlier, he had led the syndicate—which included Richard Hakluyt—that acquired the rights to the City of Raleigh in Virginia. After the debacle of John White's voyage to rescue the Roanoke colonists, Smythe occupied himself in other ways. Following the death of his father, Customer Smythe, he inherited the lucrative tax-collecting contract for the Port of London, the foundation of his wealth. Also, he joined the Levant Company—the entity formed by the merger of the Turkey Company, which his father had cofounded, and the Venice Company.

In the 1590s, Smythe became a civic figure, following in the footsteps of his grandfather, who had served as Lord Mayor. He was elected to the House of Commons in 1597, representing Aylesbury, a market town north of London, and two years later he joined the ranks of London's governing elite, becoming an alderman in London and master of one of his livery companies, the Worshipful Company of Haberdashers.[16] As the new century dawned, he was elected governor of both the Muscovy Company and the Levant Company.[17] It was a stellar ascent. And there was yet another honor to come his way. In October 1600, when the general court of the new East India Company met at Founders Hall, "a proper house" along Lothbury, not far from the Guildhall, the shareholders elected Smythe as their first governor.[18]

Even with all this capital and commercial know-how, the merchants still faced one major obstacle: the aging queen. They needed her to sign the letters patent that would give them permission to conduct England's business in the Far East. Eventually, on December 31, 1600, the queen duly completed the paperwork, and the East India

Company, under the governorship of Thomas Smythe, came into being. The merchants were granted the right to "set forth one, or more voyages, with a convenient number of ships and pinnaces, by way of traffic and merchandise to the East-Indies." They promised to do so "at their own adventures, costs and charges" and "for the honour of this our realm of England," the "increase of our navigation," and the "advancement of trade of merchandise" from England.[19]

Now that they had royal approval, Smythe and his fellow directors moved quickly to launch the first voyage. Hakluyt was hired to brief the senior commanders of the voyage on the best places to find pepper, cloves, and a host of other spices.[20] Thus prepared, five ships, loaded with five hundred men and victuals for twenty months, and led by James Lancaster, a renowned English captain, set sail for the East Indies in February 1601.[21]

TWO HUNDRED AND thirteen people subscribed to the East India Company venture in 1600. But one man was notable by his absence: Sir Walter Ralegh. This was strange because, like many of the other backers, he had reaped rich rewards from his bold enterprises beyond England's shores. In 1592, he and his associates hit the jackpot when their privateering fleet captured a Portuguese vessel, *Madre de Dios*, which carried jewels, spices, silks, calicoes (cotton cloth), ivory, porcelain, and other luxury commodities worth around half a million pounds, the single biggest prize of that privateering era.[22]

But Ralegh had also suffered his share of failures. In the mid-1590s, he sailed to South America in search of El Dorado, a fabled kingdom of gold that was said to be located deep in the Amazon jungle. He did not find it. It may have been this setback, together with the gradual ending of the privateering war, that caused Ralegh to ignore the East India venture and revive his interest in the Roanoke settlement. Under the terms of his letters patent, he could still lay claim to his title as lord and governor of Virginia.

Ralegh's patent gave him enormous power and scope in the New

World. He had the right to hold and occupy the lands he discovered and to dispose of them as he saw fit. Also, he could "expulse, repel and resist" any person or group who tried to trespass on his territory in America. In other words, without his say-so, no one could settle within two hundred leagues—about six hundred miles—of any colony that he founded in the first six years of holding the patent. In effect, that gave him a huge, twelve-hundred-mile holding along the American coast from Florida in the south to modern-day Maine in the north, as well as across to what is now Kentucky to the west.

This had the potential to become an enormous imperial domain; but, to claim it, Ralegh had to prove that the Roanoke Colony was still thriving. If, on the other hand, the colonists were dead, his patent would have no value. As it happens, there were plenty of experts who believed the Roanoke colonists were alive and well, even if White had not found them at their original location. In 1597, John Gerard, the herbalist and Roanoke investor, maintained that there was every reason to think that English people were still living in Virginia unless "untimely death by murdering, or pestilence, corrupt air, bloody fluxes, or some other mortal sickness" had finished them off.[23]

Hakluyt, Ralegh's old friend, also asserted that the Roanoke settlers were still alive "for ought we know."[24] And he again expressed his great enthusiasm for America. "There is under our noses the great & ample country of Virginia," he wrote, "the inland whereof is found of late to be so sweet and wholesome a clime, so rich and abundant in silver mines, so apt and capable of all commodities, which Italy, Spain, and France can afford." Hakluyt expressed the hope that Elizabeth would, after securing "a good & godly peace," transport "one or two thousand people" to Virginia, since he knew others who would "willingly at their own charges become Adventurers in good numbers with their bodies and goods." If Elizabeth did this, she would "by God's assistance, in short space, work many great and unlooked for effects, increase her dominions, enrich her coffers, and reduce many Pagans to the faith of Christ."[25]

With such widespread belief in the survival of the Roanoke colonists, Ralegh revived his interest in America. Starting in 1600, he dispatched three expeditions to Virginia in as many years in an effort to make contact with them. In the final expedition, undertaken in 1602, Ralegh's men saw nothing of the settlers, although they had been prevented from landing at Roanoke by stormy weather. All they brought home was a cargo of herbs and flora, including the leaves and bark of the tree that was becoming extremely fashionable throughout Europe: sassafras.[26]

IN MARCH 1602, as Ralegh contemplated the fate of his colonists, a young, enterprising man emerged whose goal—implicit if not explicit—seems to have been to test Ralegh's claim to Virginia. Bartholomew Gosnold, aged about thirty, came from an old Suffolk family of well-to-do landed gentry with connections to some of the pioneers of the New World ventures. His father, a lawyer, had been an adviser to Lady Dorothy Stafford, a friend to the queen and mother of Edward Stafford, who had been Hakluyt's employer in Paris.

Educated at Cambridge and, like Ralegh, at the Middle Temple, Gosnold turned his hand to privateering, and made £1,625—a significant sum—on one adventure in the late 1590s. Also, he gained further wealth from his marriage to Mary Golding, a granddaughter of Sir Andrew Judde, of Mysterie fame. Through marriage, Gosnold was related to George Barne, another Mysterie investor and former Lord Mayor of London, and thus to Barne's nephew, Christopher Carleill, who had tried unsuccessfully to secure Humphrey Gilbert's patent.[27]

The organizational structure and financial backing of Gosnold's enterprise remain murky. No joint stock company was established for the voyage, nor did the queen involve herself. It is likely that Gosnold attracted support from his remarkable network of influential friends and relations and invested some of the money he had won in prizes during the privateering war. Henry Wriothesley, third Earl of Southampton and Shakespeare's sponsor, may have been a contributor to, or at least an important inspiration for, Gosnold. A later chronicler wrote that "he largely contributed to the furnishing out of a ship to be commanded by Captain Bartholomew Gosnold."[28]

The venture, undertaken without Ralegh's knowledge, seems to have been an all-purpose reconnaissance, settlement, and commercial mission: to explore the largely unknown northern coast, look for a passage to China, evaluate the commercial prospects, find a suitable location for a trading post, leave some settlers behind there, and collect a variety of commodities to bring back to England—in particular, the sassafras tree, whose leaves and bark were becoming renowned throughout Europe for their medicinal properties.

Gosnold set his sights on the area well north of Ralegh's Roanoke—a region then known as Norumbega, essentially what is now New England. In choosing this destination, almost completely unexplored by the English at this time, Gosnold may have been following the star of Giovanni de Verrazzano, a Florentine explorer who led the first comprehensive investigation of the northern American coast in 1524.

Verrazzano was not only an accomplished mariner, he was also a skilled chronicler. Nearly eighty years after his voyage, his celebrated account remained the only substantive report on the north stretch of American coast, from what is now Cape Fear in North Carolina all the way north to New York harbor (the Verrazano Narrows and the bridge that spans them are named after him) and beyond to the great bays of the Gulf of Maine. He reached as far north as the "land that in times past was discovered by the Britons, which is in fifty degrees"—a reference to John Cabot and his claim to Newfoundland, whose northern extent falls along 51 degrees north latitude.

Verrazzano made the area sound even more alluring than Thomas Harriot had done with his portrait of Virginia. The people were "courteous and gentle," Verrazzano wrote, adding that the place was shaded with trees as "delectable to behold as is possible to imagine," with "good and wholesome air," and a profusion of flowers. In the most elegiac passage of the account, Verrazzano described one of their stopping places—the bay now known as Narragansett in the state of Rhode Island. It was "very fertile and beautiful, full of tall spreading trees" and blessed with a harbor in which "any large fleet could ride safely...without fear of tempest or other dangers." Verrazzano and his mariners took sanctuary there from the rough seas, christening the place *Refugio*.[29]

Gosnold may have been alerted to Verrazzano's travels by Richard Hakluyt, who lived in the village of Wetheringsett, not far from the Gosnold residence, and who included the Verrazzano voyage in his *Principal Navigations*. Certainly Gosnold knew about Verrazzano's account. In a letter to his father, Anthony, he mentioned Verrazzano's narrative in Hakluyt's work, noting that it contained useful information about America.[30]

GOSNOLD, COMMANDING A single ship, the *Concord,* and thirty-two men, including mariners, adventurers, and twelve who had committed to staying on as settlers, set sail from Falmouth on March 26, 1602.[31] The *Concord* made land early on the morning of May 14, somewhere along the middle coast of Maine. It is not clear if Gosnold was intentionally trying to avoid infringing Ralegh's rights, but he had in fact landed beyond the two-hundred-league perimeter of the Roanoke domain.

Gosnold was the first Englishman to reach those shores on an expedition of discovery and trade, but he was hardly the first European to do so. Soon after arriving, a group of Indians appeared in a shallop, a small, shallow-draft boat rigged with mast and sail—clearly not a native vessel. They approached the *Concord,* hoving themselves boldly aboard. In the shallop, the English could see an iron grapple and a large copper kettle. Even more striking, one of the Indians was dressed in European attire: a waistcoat, breeches, hose, shoes, and a hat.

The Indians could speak "divers Christian words"—some in English, some in other languages. Gosnold's men delighted in the Indians' ability to speak and mimic. One of them tossed out the playful sentence "How now sirrah, are you so saucy with my Tobacco?" to an Indian, who immediately shot back the entire sentence, as if he had long been a "scholar in the language." Thanks to the Indians' facility with language, the English were able to learn that the foreign-made goods, such as the waistcoat, had been acquired through trade with "Basks"—that is, people of the Basque region at the border between France and Spain who had long frequented the waters around New-foundland.[32] The English probably did not realize how extensive the Indian-European trading network was at the time. Indians acted as middlemen in a sophisticated trading economy that linked the American hinterland, and its great supply of furs and timber, with the coast, and its fish and stream of exotic commodities coming from Europe.[33]

The Gosnold party caught so many cod, herring, and mackerel that John Brereton, the official scribe of the voyage, became "persuaded that in the months of March, April, and May, there is upon this coast, better fishing, and in as great plenty, as in Newfoundland." Compared to the "far off" Newfoundland banks, where waters were forty or fifty fathoms, the fishing grounds lay close to shore and in waters just seven fathoms (forty-two feet) deep.[34]

Sailing south, the *Concord* and her crew, always on the lookout for trading opportunities, continued engaging with Indians. They partook of tobacco, a variety they found more pleasant than that available in England, though they did not seem to consider it as a marketable commodity. In exchange for deer skins and the furs of beaver, marten, otter, and wildcat, they traded the small objects they had brought for the purpose: knives, mirrors, bells, and beads. As other Europeans had learned, the Indians prized most what they did not have—manufactured goods of glass and metal. Particularly popular were points, little tubes of tin used to finish the end of a strip of cloth or leather, like the aglet encasing the tip of a modern shoelace.[35] Points were cheap to buy in England and took up little space in the ship's hold, and the differential in value between a small quantity of points and an animal pelt was substantial.

Coasting still farther southwards, the *Concord* lost sight of land for some days until Gosnold's men spotted a headland they first took to be an island because it was separated from the mainland by a "shole-hope"—a shallow haven—and a capacious sound. There, they caught so many fish that they named the land Cape Cod.

They traveled on until they hailed a group of "fair isles." They named one of these islands Martha's Vineyard, possibly in honor of Gosnold's mother-in-law, Martha Golding. In this area, they decided to establish their trading post and settlement, choosing another of these islands, which they named Elizabeth's Isle (probably the modern-day Cuttyhunk). The island was uninhabited, and offered a good anchorage, a source of fresh water, easy access to the mainland, rich fishing, and plenty of crabs and shellfish.

Gosnold and his crew set about their operations, constructing a house and rudimentary fort. They planted wheat, barley, oats, and peas in the "fat and lusty soil," and then watched, amazed, as the tendrils sprang up nine inches in two weeks. Every so often, Indians of the Micmac tribe came to visit and trade with them. They noticed that these visitors possessed seemingly large amounts of copper, which was used to create jewelry, arrowheads, and eating utensils, including drinking cups and plates. Gosnold wondered if copper mines were close to the island. The Indians seemed to confirm this, although the Englishmen did not go in search of them.[36]

From this site, Gosnold's men applied themselves to the gathering of sassafras. The tree—which grows to between twenty and forty feet in height, and has broad leaves and cinnamon-colored berries— was plentiful on the island. In this work, which continued over a number of days, the Indians sometimes lent a hand. They also dined with the English, drinking beer and eating dried codfish. They did not, however, fancy the strong mustard their hosts used to improve the taste of the fish. "It was a sport to behold their faces made being bitten therewith," wrote one of Gosnold's men.[37]

By the middle of June, Gosnold's crew had packed the hold of the

Concord with sassafras, cedar logs, furs, and skins—the commodities they considered most valuable in the European markets. Gosnold hoped this would be the first of many consignments from his new trading post in Norumbega. But when it came to depart, the men who had signed up to stay behind to manage the trading post began to have second thoughts. Perhaps the fear that they would be left stranded, like the colonists at Roanoke, weighed on their minds. Also, as Gosnold realized, there were not sufficient supplies if the settlers were to survive the six months of winter. In the end, Gosnold's little trading post was abandoned and the entire party sailed home, arriving in Exmouth in late July after a brisk five-week passage.[38]

IN AUGUST, RALEGH caught wind of Gosnold's voyage, and he was furious at what he saw as an infringement of his American rights. He had traveled to the port town of Weymouth, on the southwest coast, not far from Exmouth, where Gosnold had put in with the *Concord*. He was planning to meet with Samuel Mace, who had just returned from his voyage to southern Virginia in search of the Roanoke colonists and whose ship's hold was also full of sassafras. While there, Ralegh appears to have bumped into Bartholomew Gilbert (no relation of Sir Humphrey), who was Gosnold's second-in-command and who may have told him about the sassafras brought in from Norumbega.[39]

Outraged by this breach of his monopoly, Ralegh had the *Concord* detained, tried to track down the sassafras that had already been unloaded, and fired off an urgent message to Robert Cecil asking him to secure a letter of seizure from the lord admiral because his patent stated "that all ships & goods are confiscate that shall trade" in America without his license. He contended that sassafras was selling for as much as twenty shillings a pound, and that the Gosnold shipment would flood the market, suppress prices, and reduce his profits. Before discovering Gosnold's sassafras, Ralegh had calculated that his own sassafras would be worth up to ten times its cost—such was the demand.[40]

Sassafras was *the* plant of the moment. There was a vast apothecary of decoctions, lineaments, and herbal admixtures made from the sassafras tree that was administered as a cure for almost everything. With the added cachet of the exotic, a New World remedy favored by Indians, it became widely accepted as a cure-all after its inclusion in a book, published in English in 1577, called *Joyfull Newes out of the newe Founde Worlde wherein is declared the rare and singular vertues of diverse and sundrie hearbes, trees, oyles, plants and stones.* This tome, written by Nicholas Monardes, a Spanish physician, and translated into English by John Frampton, a Bristol merchant, revealed how sassafras bark from Florida could "dissolve obstructions in the body" and thereby "engender good humors."[41] In his *Discourse of Western Planting* of 1584, Hakluyt mentioned sassafras as a promising commodity, while Thomas Harriot, in his *Brief and True Report of the Newfound Land of Virginia*, reported that the Indians called sassafras *Winauk* and used it "for the cure of diseases."[42] Over the years, people came to rely on sassafras as a cure for stomach ache, coughs and colds, diarrhea, nosebleeds, indigestion, scurvy, syphilis, and as a way to increase menstrual flow and thus encourage pregnancy.[43]

These medicinal properties made sassafras a reliably marketable commodity. But if there was a surfeit of sassafras for sale, then its price, and possibly its allure, would fall. It is not clear how the dispute resolved itself. Ralegh may have been able to impound some of Gosnold's shipment and sell it on his own behalf. Also, he seems to have made arrangements with a German merchant to export an unspecified amount for sale across Europe. This was an early instance of the re-export of English New World goods to the European market.[44]

In any case, Ralegh took no further punitive action against Bartholomew Gosnold. In fact, they evidently came to an amicable solution to the patent infringement, since Brereton's published account of the voyage was subsequently dedicated to Ralegh. In capital letters, the subtitle assures the reader that the voyage to northern Virginia had been undertaken "by the permission of the honourable knight, Sir Walter Ralegh."

As the first published narrative of an English voyage to the northern part of America since Verrazzano's account, Brereton's little book *A Briefe and True Relation of the Discoverie of the North Part of Virginia* proved a popular hit. Brereton's prose, while not as lyrical as Verrazzano's or as rigorous as Harriot's, painted a pleasing picture of this virtually unknown stretch of territory, making it sound ideal for a colony: the friendly Indians, lovely trees, copious fruits and plants, abundant fish—all this, and the "goodness of the Climate," which was neither as hot as that of the West Indies nor as cold as that of Newfoundland. "We found our health and strength all the while we remained there," Brereton wrote. Far from suffering any disease or sickness, the adventurers returned home "much fatter and in better health than when we went out of England."[45]

GOSNOLD'S VOYAGE SPARKED new interest in the north of America, and before long, another expedition was dispatched, paid for by Bristol merchants who had been advised by Richard Hakluyt. But this venture was overshadowed by the death of Elizabeth I on March 24, 1603. The last of the Tudors, she was the first queen of America, giving her name to Virginia, claiming sovereignty over Nova Albion.

Always, she had been wary of committing herself too visibly to the cause of empire. But she had found discreet ways to fund imperial dreamers such as Walter Ralegh—diverting customs revenues from the cloth and mining industries and crown revenues from landed estates. And in the wake of the victory over the Armada, she had gladly posed with her possessive hand stretched wide over the American continent depicted on a globe.

With Elizabeth's passing, the champions of overseas expansion lost one of their staunchest, if sometimes mercurial, supporters. Nobody knew whether her successor would continue her imperial project. But James I, the Protestant son of the Catholic Mary, Queen of Scots, was known to be keen to strike a peace deal with Spain. And so for one person, the omens were not good: Sir Walter Ralegh.

If Ralegh had been one of Elizabeth's greatest favorites, he was one of the new monarch's least. Ralegh's was the embodiment of an archaic, anti-Spanish way of doing things — the last of the old generation of merchants and courtiers who had defined themselves by their virulent opposition to the Iberian superpower. Now, the times were changing, and James did everything he could to marginalize the lord and governor of Virginia.

Ralegh stoically endured one ignominy after another. He was replaced as Captain of the Guard, stripped of his monopoly in the wine trade, and booted out of Durham House, his beloved residence of twenty years. Then, while joining James in Windsor for a hunt — in an effort to maintain his relationship with the crown — he was detained for questioning. A few days later, he was sent to the Tower, and eventually found guilty of involvement in a couple of intertwining plots against the king, including a scheme to replace him with Arbella Stuart, a great-great-granddaughter of Henry VII.[46]

Ralegh had already lost almost everything. With this imprisonment, he forfeited perhaps his most valuable asset of all: his claim to America. Under the terms of the original letters patent, the king could withdraw Ralegh's title to the lands of Virginia if he committed "any act of unjust or unlawfull hostility."[47] His conviction for high treason meant that as long as he was in prison he would be denied the right to his lands in Virginia. Also, it meant that for the first time in more than a quarter century America was up for grabs.

PART III

COMMONWEALTH

1604–1621

John Dee

John Dudley

Martin Waldseemüller's map of the world, 1507

Thomas Smith's treatise of 1549

A group of "grave" merchants and advisors initiated England's first attempt to pioneer overseas commercial markets for its chief export, cloth, and to strengthen its commonwealth.

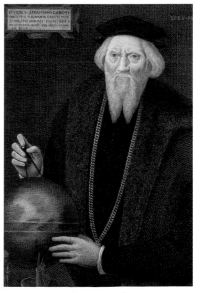

Sebastian Cabot

Martin Frobisher

Three well-organized and well-funded voyages, 1576–78, sought an American settlement site and a northern route to the riches of Cathay.

Anne Dudley

William Cecil

Matthew Baker (right)

Frobisher's map showing the Northwest Passage, 1578

Michael Lok's accounts, 1576

The English hoped to find new sources of wealth to rival Spain's incredibly lucrative silver mining operations in Mexico and Peru.

Silver mining at Potosí

London, c. 1560

Most of the developers of England's New World ventures were based in the thriving capital and commercial center of London.

Thomas Gresham

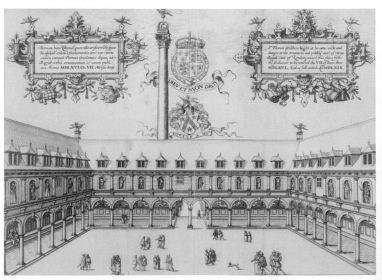

The Royal Exchange, c. 1569

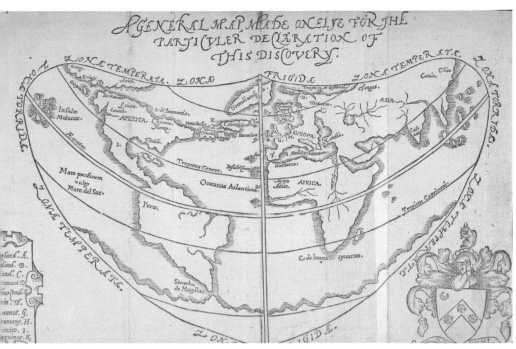

Gilbert's map of the world, 1576

Francis Walsingham

Humphrey Gilbert

As tensions between England and Spain
heightened, prominent courtiers and
adventurers dreamed of establishing an
empire in the New World.

The Roanoke Colony, established in Virginia in 1585, was the first English settlement in America. Despite repeated efforts to keep it going, a supply mission of 1590 found the colony abandoned. The fate of the "lost colonists" remains unknown.

Walter Ralegh

John White's drawings of Indians at Roanoke, 1585

Drake's circumnavigation in 1580 and the defeat of the Spanish Armada by English naval forces in 1588 boosted England's self-confidence and enhanced its standing as a force in global affairs.

Francis Drake

Elizabeth I

Philip II of Spain

The signing of a peace treaty between England and Spain after the accession of James I opened the way to English settlement at Sagadahoc, Jamestown, Plymouth, and elsewhere in America.

Treaty of London ceremony, 1604

Thomas Smythe

James I

John Smith

Pocahontas

15

———⦿———

TWO VIRGINIAS

IN MAY 1604, eleven government officials representing England and Spain convened at the resplendent Denmark House, a short boat ride up the Thames from the Tower, where Ralegh now spent his days. The purpose of the conference was to negotiate peace between the two countries, after almost two decades of undeclared war.

The move towards negotiation had begun soon after James took the throne, when a Spanish diplomat was sent to congratulate the new king. He found, perhaps to his surprise, that his mission was looked upon with favor at the English court and that he was "most amicably received." Spanish diplomats were accustomed to much worse treatment, as was the case when Elizabeth kept Bernardino de Mendoza cooling his heels during the dispute over Drake's treasure haul in the early 1580s. Pretty quickly, one thing led to another, and the Spanish and English diplomats agreed that there "was no reason why they should have an Enmity at one another" and that negotiations should begin.[1]

Denmark House, named after Anne of Denmark, James's queen consort, had been specially prepared for the event, the walls hung with

231

tapestries and greenery arranged before the windows. A fine carpet, possibly from Henry VIII's grand collection, adorned the long table where the dignitaries faced each other, dressed in somber gowns with ruffed collars, all sporting tidily trimmed beards.[2] The English delegation included Charles Howard, the Lord High Admiral, Thomas Sackville, the Earl of Dorset, and Robert Cecil.[3] After eighteen sessions, the delegates came to terms, and spelled them out in a document entitled *A Treaty of perpetual Peace and Alliance between Philip III King of Spain, and the Archduke and Archduchess Albert and Isabella on the one side, and James I King of England on the other side. Made in the Year 1604.*

The breakthrough was testimony to the fresh thinking of the two kings. James had been keen to bring an end to the debilitating and unnecessary conflict with Spain and come to a peace. Likewise, the young King Philip III of Spain, twenty-six years old and nearly five years into his reign, was just as ready to bring the war to an end. Since 1555, his country had been waging war almost continuously, fighting battles on land and sea in the Narrow Seas, the Mediterranean, France, the Netherlands, Africa, and on the Iberian Peninsula—and dealing with the constant harassment of English privateers. Only in one six-month period, from February to September 1577, had Spain *not* been prosecuting a war or conflict somewhere in the world.[4]

"Know all and everyone," the treaty announced, "that after a long and most cruel ravage of wars, by which *Christendom* has for many years been miserably afflicted," God "has powerfully extinguished the raging flame" of conflict. With the treaty, "It was and is concluded, settled and agreed, that from this day forward there be a good, sincere, true, firm and perfect friendship and confederacy, and perpetual peace" and that it should be in force "by land as by sea and fresh water."[5]

The delegates signed the document on August 18, 1604, and its thirty-six articles spelled out what is essentially a free-trade agreement. People of both kingdoms would be free to "go to, enter, sail into, import or export, buy and sell merchandise" everywhere, without any need for a license or passport.[6] No letters of marque, essentially a license for privateering, would be issued henceforward. All past infringements would be overlooked, and no party would seek restitution of any goods or valuables lost or taken to date.

The Treaty of London, as it came to be known, seemed to swing open the gates to long-closed ports and shipping lanes. However, there was something missing from the agreement: there was no mention of the enormous, largely overlapping, territories that the Spanish referred to as Florida and that the English called Virginia. In other words, the treaty avoided the tricky, unresolved, and potentially contentious issue of who had the rights to claim, inhabit, and develop America. As it later transpired, Spain's negotiators had been reluctant to raise the issue because they fully believed that England's Roanoke colonists were alive and living somewhere in Virginia and that, as they put it, the English had been "in peaceful possession" of the land "for more than thirty years."[7]

Meanwhile, in the Tower of London, the man who had been involved in almost all of England's New World initiatives for a period of twenty years—from settlement at Roanoke to gold-seeking in Guiana to colonization in Ireland to trafficking in sassafras in northern Virginia—tried to adjust to life in prison. Thanks to the relative freedom that gentlemen with no fixed term were afforded there, Ralegh kept busy, displaying his many talents as a Renaissance man. He built a smelting furnace, grew and cured tobacco, investigated methods for distilling fresh water from salt. Above all, he wrote and wrote, sitting down at his desk in the morning to make entries in his diary, compose poetry, and pen his monumental *History of the World*. Indeed, he became a kind of celebrity tourist attraction. Passersby sometimes caught sight of the famous Sir Walter as he exercised his six-foot frame along the crest of a Tower wall.[8]

IN RALEGH'S ABSENCE, a young man named George Waymouth declared his intentions to be one of the next generation of New World pioneers.

Waymouth was no Ralegh in status, style, or worldview. He came from a seafaring and fishing family that had long lived in Cockington, Devon, not far from the coast. George's grandfather, William, had accumulated enough wealth to leave his son, also William, a half share in a ship, the *Lyon,* worth some fifty pounds. The younger William expanded his activities, acquiring a number of vessels for plying the waters of the Newfoundland fishery, progressing to the purchase of larger ships and, finally, to shipbuilding. Also, he had invested in overseas ventures, ploughing money into Sir Humphrey Gilbert's mission to "annoy" Spain in 1578. George, described as a navigator, probably learned the skills of his profession, and gained his passion for adventure, on his father's vessels.[9]

Although he was no courtier, Waymouth managed to secure an audience with King James, who was only a few months into his reign and as yet had no track record of sponsoring or rejecting proposals for overseas ventures. No one knew what James really thought about his lands in the New World and perhaps he had not yet formed an opinion on them. But, apparently to encourage the king, Waymouth presented him with an elaborate, leather-bound volume called *The Jewell of Artes,* a title that provided little clue as to its actual contents. The young seaman and would-be adventurer wrote that his book was intended for anyone who wanted to undertake the "discovery of any strange countries." It was essentially a handbook filled with instructions and advice about how to create a fortified town in a wilderness setting.[10]

No previous English book had contained this kind of practical detail. Humphrey Gilbert's plans had focused on how millions of acres of land might be divided, leased, and turned into profitable estates. Richard Hakluyt had put forward the intellectual arguments and emotional pleas, selecting stirring narratives for the delectation of his stay-at-home readers. By contrast, Waymouth's *Jewell* delivered the how-to, contained in a beautifully designed volume fit for a king. The brown calf cover is decorated with a field of hand-tooled gold flowerets and emblazoned with King James's coat of arms. The text is handwritten, in English, by a single scrivener in a looping, flowing font.[11] The book contains many illustrations—"demonstrations" as Waymouth calls them—including engineering drawings, colored diagrams, functional volvelles, and cut-paper pop-ups of the kind more commonly found in a modern children's book.

The production of such an elaborately lettered, copiously illustrated, and richly bound book must have been time-consuming and expensive. It was obvious that Waymouth fervently wanted to enlist James's support for a New World venture and sought to convince him that he was the right man to lead it. In this regard, Waymouth carried some baggage. Although he was in his early twenties, this was not his first attempt to gain support for an overseas expedition. In July 1601, he had sought to revive the search for the Northwest Passage, petitioning the East India Company for sponsorship.

Remarkably, given the magnitude of Waymouth's proposal and his youth and relative inexperience, the general court of the East India Company gave serious consideration, forming a six-man committee "for the Northwest passage," led by John Watts, the merchant-privateer who had collaborated with Ralegh and who financed the ship that took John White back to Roanoke on his last fateful expedition.[12] It took some time to hammer out the deal. To start with, the East India Company had to gain the permission of the Muscovy Company, which still held monopoly rights to the territory. Eventually, after much negotiation, the two companies agreed to collaborate on Waymouth's venture. Then the East India Company drove a hard bargain. They agreed to invest three thousand pounds to purchase and outfit two pinnaces and to provide one hundred pounds for Waymouth's "instruments and other necessaries." But they would pay the handsome sum of £500 if, and only if, he successfully discovered the passage. If he failed to do so, he would get "nothing for his pains and travail."[13]

He failed. Waymouth's two-ship fleet departed London on May 2,

1602, provisioned for sixteen months. In mid-September, however, the ships returned to England. It seems that Waymouth, like other commanders before him, had suffered a mutiny and been forced to turn back. Nevertheless, he expressed his belief that the passage was there.[14] The East India Company even considered making another attempt, but at last came to the conclusion that they should focus their energy on the conventional, well-established route to the East Indies—around the southern tip of Africa, not through the Northwest Passage.

After that crushing blow, Waymouth, still young and full of ideas, turned his attention to colonization and to the *Jewell of Artes*. For all the book's ornate flourishes, the actual content is rather rudimentary. Readers were told that the leaders of colonial voyages needed technical knowledge of navigational instruments and a good grasp of shipbuilding, as well as an understanding of the art of surveying so that they can "make choice of the most fit and commodious place" to settle—a discipline not mentioned by other advocates. Devoting much of the book to the "practice of fortification," he recommended specific types of guns that had a dual purpose: effective on ships against "rovers" and other attackers and yet easily taken ashore to protect a fort.

Waymouth went on to address the creation of entire towns and how to lay out settlements with "fair and large" streets, sturdy foundations, and protective ditches and bulwarks. His designs look a bit like mandalas—a square, a cogged wheel, a rosette, a circle. Within the walls, he depicted neat villages of regular housing blocks, some with straight streets, some with curved. One plan looks like a formal garden, another like a maze. Each of these cozy habitations bristles with ordnance, cannon aimed in every direction.[15]

GEORGE WAYMOUTH COULD not persuade James to fund his proposed venture, but his appearance at court may have led to his introduction to a potential sponsor: Sir Thomas Arundell. Aged about forty-five and the scion of a noble family with a long history of military and political service, Arundell was attracted by the idea of an American refuge for English Catholics—in effect, reviving the plans first developed by George Peckham and Thomas Gerrard with Humphrey Gilbert. His interest came after James authorized a tightening of anti-Catholic legislation, including new restrictions on the sale of certain books and the creation of a revised catechism.[16]

But Waymouth did not rely on just one or two main sponsors. Like Gilbert before him, he presented his case to other investors—in particular, the merchants of Devon. They valued the proposed American plantation for a different purpose: fishing. These backers included William Parker, a Plymouth trader and privateer, and possibly John Gilbert, Humphrey's eldest son, who lived near Dartmouth.[17] Perhaps it was Gosnold's report of abundant fishing grounds close to shore—untroubled by many, if any, competitors from other countries—that led Parker and others to conclude that fishing outposts could be established to manage the catch and process fish all year round. Such settlements would be purpose-built and could quickly begin producing revenue, just as the fishing fleets of Iceland and Newfoundland had done for decades. The fishing trade, while not glamorous, was reliable and the demand was steady. People had to eat, and the English were devoted to their stockfish.

It is not clear how much money Waymouth raised from these different investors, with their contrasting aspirations—as a Catholic refuge and as a fishermen's outpost. But by the time he sailed out of Dartmouth on the last day of March 1605, he no longer had the support of Arundell, who seems to have bowed out of the venture. Commanding a single ship, the *Archangell,* with twenty-eight men, Waymouth led what was in effect a reconnaissance voyage, much like Gosnold's to Norumbega.[18]

Six weeks later, the *Archangell* reached Monhegan Island, one of the jewels of the Maine coast—a craggy mound of rock, topped with scrub and fir, set in the sea well out from the mainland but still within its sight, with an anchorage that opens to the southwest providing shelter from northeast storms. Unlike Gosnold, who had sailed south to Cape Cod and the Massachusetts islands, Waymouth lingered in Maine, exploring the islands and the coastal inlets, and venturing on foot, tracking along a great river, probably the St. George, whose mouth lies just north of Monhegan.

During the course of the expedition, Waymouth and his crew engaged with the local Indians, probably members of the Eastern Abenaki tribe, one of the Algonquian people. The relationship developed in a familiar pattern. At first, the wary Indians kept their distance. They appeared on an islet adjacent to the ship and made gestures. Eventually they came aboard ship. Trading began. Then they smoked tobacco—the Indians sometimes used a lobster claw as a pipe—and took meals together. There was singing and dancing, and eventually Englishmen and Indians had sleepovers, in camp or aboard ship.

Over time, this increased familiarity led to easier relations, and the more the English observed the Indians the more impressed they became, admiring their abilities and attributes. They especially marveled at the Indians' canoes. According to James Rosier, a young Cambridge-educated Catholic convert who was hired to write the official account of the voyage, the boats defied belief.[19] They were made "without any iron," consisting instead "of the bark of a birch tree, strengthened within with ribs and hoops of wood, in so good fashion, with such excellent ingenious art, as they are able to bear seven or eight persons, far exceeding any in the Indies."[20] Birch trees of the requisite circumference to build such a canoe—a single sheet of bark formed the hull—grew plentifully in Maine, but not much farther south. As such, Rosier was reporting on a highly specialized, localized craft.[21]

Another "especial thing," Rosier wrote, "is their manner of killing the whale, which they call *Powdawe*." He described how the English watched as a whale, twelve fathoms long—a daunting seventy-two feet, if his estimation was correct—surfaced and cleared its blow-hole. The Abenakis set out in a flotilla of boats and skewered the whale using a harpoon-like weapon, a sharpened bone fastened to a long rope, made from twisted tree bark. They let out the line as the whale plunged, and when it resurfaced "with their arrows they shoot him to death," Rosier wrote.[22] He took time to make these observations because he knew investors would be interested in the potential for whaling, which was growing in importance as a commercial activity for European merchants, especially after the Dutch got involved in the trade in the late 1590s.[23] Whale blubber was particularly prized by cloth manufacturers, since it produced train oil, which was used in the finishing process.

Rosier proved to be an astute choice as chronicler. He went beyond the recounting of noteworthy events, choosing to make observations of commercial and ethnographical value, as Thomas Harriot had before him. He paid particular attention to the Indian language. When he went ashore with Waymouth and two Abenakis to spend some time fishing with a net, he began asking the Indians to tell him their words for various items. Rosier would point to something, ask for the Indian word, and then write it down, employing, as Harriot had done, a phonetic system of his own devising. The Indians found this so intriguing that they began to fetch things—everything from fish to fruits—just to watch as Rosier wrote down their words.

The bond that seems to have developed between Waymouth's men and the Indians—at least as the English understood it—might have provided the foundation for a future peaceful English settlement. But then Waymouth committed an act of betrayal that shocked the local people and soured relations. One evening in early June, Waymouth's men brought a platter of peas ashore to share with several Abenakis. One of the Indians, suspecting treachery, walked away. At that moment, the mariners "suddenly laid hands" on two others, grabbed hold of the "long hair on their heads," and wrestled them aboard ship, along with their bows, arrows, and canoes.[24]

It seems that the kidnapping—a total of five Indians were ultimately seized—had been one of the primary goals of the reconnaissance mission all along. As Rosier later noted, the capture of Indians was "a matter of great importance for the full accomplishment of our voyage." He insisted, however, that after this violent encounter the Abenakis received "kind usage" from the English and, once aboard ship, concluded that no further harm would befall them. They never seemed "discontented with us," Rosier wrote, but rather were "tractable, loving, & willing by their best means to satisfy us in anything we demand of them."[25]

Whether this is how the kidnapped Indians actually felt and behaved is impossible to say, but it is certain that the Indian who avoided the kidnapping, and those who heard about it, had a different view. News of the event traveled quickly through the region and, as it spread, the details were exaggerated. A party of French explorers was travelling through Maine that July and met an Indian named Anassou. He told them about a fishing vessel that had lain off the coast and how the men aboard had killed five Indians "under cover of friendship." From Annasou's description, the French concluded that the ship must have been English and its position squares with Rosier's accounts of the location of the *Archangel*.[26] The memory of this incident of calculated violence against Indians lingered and affected relations between northern Indians and Europeans for years to come.

Waymouth arrived in England in July and Rosier's account, *A True Relation of the most prosperous voyage made this present yeere 1605 by Captain George Waymouth, in the Discovery of the land of Virginia,* appeared soon after, probably before the end of the year.[27] The little book does not contain the standard dedication, which authors and their sponsors typically inserted to acknowledge, praise, and flatter their investors and royal patrons. Instead, the account begins with a preface titled "To the Reader." In this, Rosier mentions Arundell—now first Baron Arundell of Wardour—and the "honourable gentlemen" and "merchants of good sufficiency and judgment" who had undertaken the project at their own expense. Also, he mentions that the investors had been "encouraged" by "the gracious favor" of His Majesty as well as "divers Lords" of the Privy Council. In other words, the Waymouth venture had been a private undertaking with informal support from James and his advisers.

Whether the timing was right or the writing particularly enticing, the book captured the English imagination and created great excitement about potential plantations in north Virginia. Rosier was effusive about the new land, claiming that the St. George river was superior even to the Loire, Seine, and Bordeaux rivers in France — although he stopped short of favoring the American river over "our river of Thames," which he hailed as "England's richest treasure."[28]

Nothing, however, proved more compelling than the living proof: the Indians themselves, whom Rosier identified and described as Tahánedo, a *sagamo,* or commander; Amóret, Skicowáros, and Maneddo, all gentlemen; and Sassacomoit, a servant. All five survived the voyage and once in England were treated like visiting dignitaries. Two of them, Tahánedo and Amóret, were sent to the country residence of Sir John Popham. The three others, Skicowáros, Maneddo, and Sassacomoit, went to Plymouth, where they were welcomed by Sir Ferdinando Gorges and his family: his wife, Ann, and their two sons, John and Robert, aged about twelve and ten, respectively.[29]

THERE ARE A few clues in Ferdinando Gorges's history that perhaps explain why he took such a keen interest in the three American Indians. As commander of the Plymouth fort, he spent much of his time monitoring the ships and mariners in the city's vital harbor, including those returning from far-off lands. Now that England was formally at peace with Spain, Gorges had plenty of time on his hands to consider projects beyond his day-to-day military duties. He was well-connected, since his family was related by marriage to many of the prominent Devonshire families, including the Gilberts, Raleghs, and Champernownes. Also, several members of his extended family had participated in a variety of overseas ventures: one cousin had sailed with Grenville on the first Roanoke voyage; another had been with Walter Ralegh on his search for the golden city of El Dorado in Guiana.[30]

Born around 1568, Gorges was a second son, with no great reputation or fortune to his name, so perhaps he saw an opportunity for a signal achievement in his connection with the Indians. His elder brother inherited the family estates, while he received a relatively modest manor house, a gold chain, and one hundred pounds. In 1587, at the age of about nineteen, Gorges began a career as a gentleman-volunteer soldier fighting in France and the Netherlands. In 1591, he was knighted on the battlefield at the French cathedral city of Rouen by the Earl of Essex, but although Gorges had acquitted himself with valor, this honor was not exceptional: he was one of twenty-four men that Essex bestowed with a knighthood, largely to motivate them rather than to reward them for their bravery.[31] In 1595, Gorges succeeded Sir Francis Drake as captain of Plymouth Fort, where his primary responsibility was to keep the fort and its garrison ready to defend England, particularly against the Spanish. It was an important position, although not a glorious one. Gorges was constantly dealing with tedious administrative matters, struggling to keep cordial relations between the crown and the town, and scratching together enough money to pay for soldiers' salaries and repairs to the crumbling castle.

It would not have been surprising if Gorges had merely hosted Waymouth's Indians for a few days until they could be sent to London for an audience with the king or shipped back to America. It was normal practice for foreign visitors and dignitaries to be housed by leading courtiers and wealthy merchants. But Gorges became fascinated by the three Abenakis, noting with particular interest that they displayed "great civility," well beyond the "rudeness" of the common people of England. This was a strikingly progressive view. Although Thomas Harriot had done much to help the English understand that Indians came from organized societies, spoke complex languages, had political and social networks, and were skilled in various crafts and disciplines, the English nevertheless continued to regard them as primitive people, calling them country men, wild men, naturals, savages, salvages, and heathens.

The Abenakis stayed on with Gorges. He questioned them extensively and learned a great deal from them—about the people and geography of the New World, about the potential for trade and sustainable settlements, all of which he recorded, along with material supplied by Rosier, in a brief document called *The description of the Countrey of Mawooshen*.[32] Above all, the Indians ignited his passion for colonial enterprise in the New World. Reflecting on this many years later, he observed that the arrival of the five Indians had to "be acknowledged" as an event of divine providence that ultimately gave "life to all our Plantations."[33]

While Skicowáros, Maneddo, and Sassacomoit lodged with Gorges and his family, Tahánedo and Amóret lived in Sir John Popham's household. It is not clear how the two Abenakis fared there, because Popham was a hardheaded pragmatist, quite different from Gorges, who was an impassioned dreamer. A large, heavyset man described by one chronicler rather bluntly as "ugly," Popham, in his seventies, had fashioned a notable career as a barrister, member of Parliament, and later as Lord Chief Justice, one of the top judges in the country.[34] He had presided over the trial of Sir Walter Ralegh, and condemned him to a traitor's execution: to be hanged almost to the point of death, then castrated and disemboweled while still conscious, then beheaded and chopped into four pieces. It was only through the clemency of James that Ralegh was spared this ghastly execution and sent to the Tower.

It may have been the arrival of the Abenakis from Maine that further opened Popham's eyes to the opportunities for colonization across the Atlantic. He had already shown interest in colonial activities, receiving a grant of land in Ireland in the mid-1580s. But he was not so much interested in increasing his own already substantial wealth as countering the scourge of poverty and idleness in England. Popham knew that, with the ratifying of the Treaty of London, large numbers of English soldiers fighting abroad would be released from duty and would flood back into England. He feared that this influx of "infinite numbers" of discharged soldiers would lead to greater unemployment throughout the land—and a rise in idleness, vagrancy, and thievery. As a result, there could be rebellion. The very state of England might even be threatened.[35]

Popham, nearing the end of his life, decided to take bold action to prevent the crisis that he foresaw and secure his legacy. He knew that he would need royal approval for any colonial initiative, and so in early 1606 he contacted Sir Walter Cope, who was Robert Cecil's right-hand man and also famous across Europe for his fascination with New World affairs. Cope had been collecting exotic novelties for years and displayed them in a "cabinet of curiosities"—actually an entire room—filled with natural wonders, such as the horn of a rhinoceros, feathered headdresses, Virginian fireflies, and a Native American canoe.[36]

Popham presented his plan to Cope and explained that his great aim was to do some social good by establishing a colony in north Virginia. Unlike Gilbert, Popham had the funds to support his mission. He pledged the fantastic sum of five hundred pounds per year for a period of five years to the American venture, the largest commitment in England by a single individual to such an enterprise at that time. Cope soon took Popham's petition to his boss, Robert Cecil. Popham simply sought permission to call a meeting with merchants and other "undertakers" to discuss the American plantation, which suggests that he hoped the venture would also be a profit-maker in the long run. After conferring with the merchants, Popham would then develop a more detailed plan and present a formal proposal to the Privy Council.[37]

Popham was not the only one thinking about American colonization at this time. The idea of a plantation in Virginia seems to have been in the air. The release of Rosier's narrative coincided with a flurry of proposals for new expeditions. Indeed, talk of America was so widespread that it entered the popular imagination: Ben Jonson, Shakespeare's friend and rival, cowrote a popular stage play, *Eastward Hoe,* that lampooned speculators and their dreams of making a fast buck in Virginia. Its characters claimed there was so much gold to be had there that it was used for making chamber pots, and so much venison — one of the preferred viands of the wealthy — that it was eaten like mutton.[38]

JAMES ACCEPTED POPHAM's proposal and signed a new charter — now known simply as the Virginia Charter, or, the First Charter for Virginia — on April 10, 1606. The charter provided investors with the same kind of authority granted to Gilbert and Ralegh: namely, to inhabit, plant, and create a colony in the territory defined as "that part of America commonly called Virginia" as well as any other parts of America "not now actually possessed by any Christian prince or people."[39] The chartered region ranged from 34 degrees north — South Carolina's location today — to 45 degrees north — where Maine is today: in other words, between the northern limit of New Spain and the southern limit of New France.

The charter made provision for two colonies, each with its own seal. The so-called First Colony was to encompass the region between the 34th and 41st parallel north, the Second Colony the region from the 38th to the 45th parallel north. Although this created an overlap, the charter specified that whichever company managed to establish the first settlement would be able to choose their preferred location. The other colony would not be permitted to make a plantation within one hundred miles of the first one. Once established, each colony would be entitled to claim the land around it, stretching fifty miles to the north and south, one hundred miles inland to the west, and to all islands within one hundred miles out to sea.

By creating two companies, the architects of the charter were making a compromise between the two groups of investors: the merchants and courtiers of London and the men of the western outports of Plymouth, Bristol, and Exeter. For more than one hundred years, since John Cabot and his son Sebastian set off from Bristol, the merchants and seafarers from the West had pioneered the route across the Atlantic. It was not until the 1550s, and the collapse of the cloth market, that London's merchants had begun the search for new markets that eventually led them to support expeditions to Muscovy, the Levant, and the Northwest Passage.

Now the two groups were brought together—under the auspices of Robert Cecil—in an uneasy alliance that reflected their quite different interests. The London, or First Colony, investors wanted a permanent base in the same latitudes as the lands of the Mediterranean, where they could produce dyes for the cloth industry and access the other products of this region: wines, currants, sugars, spices, silks, and other luxury commodities. The Second Colony merchants sought a permanent location to conduct a year-round trade in fish, fur, timber for shipbuilding, and the train oil—derived from whale and seal blubber—used in the cloth industry. After peace with Spain, it had been expected that a busy trade with the Iberian Peninsula and the rest of the Mediterranean, accessed through the Straits of Gibraltar, would recommence. In 1605, a new charter for the Spanish Company was drawn up, and more than 550 merchants from London, Bristol, Exeter, Plymouth, and various other towns and ports were listed as members.[40] But in 1606 this collapsed, dashing the hopes of merchants ready to renew their trade with the Mediterranean. It meant that the plans for a colony in Virginia took on a new importance.[41]

Considering the great number of listed investors in the charters of the Spanish and other companies, it is striking how few names are registered in the Virginia Company charter: just eight, and none of those were great merchants or great courtiers. The First Colony was chartered to Richard Hakluyt, a clear reward for his advocacy of Virginia over so many years, as well as to George Somers, a privateer, and two soldiers, Sir Thomas Gates and Edward Maria Wingfield. The Second Colony was chartered to Raleigh Gilbert, Sir Humphrey's son, along with George Popham and Thomas Hanham, Sir John's nephew and grandson respectively, and William Parker, the privateer, former mayor of Plymouth, and investor in Waymouth's 1605 colonial expedition. These men, however, were not the real organizers, the actual owners, of the enterprise. Seven months later the names of the true architects of the Virginia Company were unveiled. In November, James issued "articles, instructions and orders" for establishing "the good order and government" of the two colonies, and with these, he created a royal council, comprising fourteen "trusty and wellbeloved" gentlemen, who would take charge of governing Virginia in his name.[42]

The King's Council of Virginia, as it was called, represented a major change in the way colonial enterprises were to be run. Elizabeth had approached foreign ventures in a cautious way. She articulated no clear strategy, preferring to support individuals and their private enterprises rather than proactively pushing forward her own vision. Now James signaled his intention to do things differently. With a royal council, the Virginia Company and its colonial enterprise was transformed into a national endeavor, one with direct association to the king—and its members were the new leaders in society. These included Sir Walter Cope, representing Sir Robert Cecil, and Sir Francis Popham, representing his father, who was suffering from painful kidney stones and in no fit state to attend regular meetings. There were several royal servants, including Sir Ferdinando Gorges, Thomas West, the solitary nobleman as third Baron De La Warr, and Sir William Waad, who commanded the Tower of London. Also, among the merchants, there were three leading members of the East India Company: William Romney, John Eldred, and Sir Thomas Smythe.

Smythe's appointment to the King's Council capped a remarkable transformation in his personal fortunes. For the best part of two years, he had languished in prison, having been erroneously accused of taking part in an attempt to overthrow Elizabeth. He only won his freedom after Elizabeth's death in March 1603, and two months later, he was knighted by James, ironically in the Tower where he had spent so much of his time. Thereafter, he was restored to the governorship of the East India Company and was further reinstated into the commercial and political life of England with his appointment as special ambassador to Russia. He spent ten months there and returned home in triumph, having secured new trading privileges for the Muscovy Company. He arrived back in England amid this renewed excitement about Virginia.

Whatever Smythe's capabilities, the King's Council and its composition did not sit well with the merchants of Plymouth and others of the Second Colony group. They had assumed that they would be granted "free and reasonable" terms similar to those that had been held by "a certain particular gent" — meaning Walter Ralegh. Instead, they found themselves under the direction of a royal council dominated by London merchants and courtiers who had little knowledge of their "proceedings."[43] What's more, all council business was to be conducted from London, which, at the very least, was an inconvenience for the Plymouth contingent. One seasoned transatlantic adventurer later quipped that there was "near as much trouble, but much more danger, to sail from London to Plymouth, than from Plymouth to New England." In other words, making the trip from the West Country to London by ship was almost as daunting as crossing the Atlantic.[44]

The simmering rivalry between the London and Plymouth investors was about to reach boiling point as the two companies prepared to launch their separate colonies. They knew only too well that whoever got to Virginia first would have first-mover advantage. The London investors, richer and more established, might have been expected to get off to the faster start. But it was John Popham, the feared Lord Chief Justice, and Ferdinando Gorges, his ally on the King's Council, who got their ships out of the harbor first.

16

————))((◉)) ————

A PUBLIC PLANTATION

THE PLYMOUTH COMPANY, first off the mark, was the first to run into trouble.

Popham and Gorges each had agreed to sponsor, organize, and fund one ship that would sail separately, rendezvous on the coast of Maine, and proceed together in search of a suitable location for the proposed plantation.

To serve as captain of his ship, the *Richard,* Gorges selected Henry Challons, a man he described as "a gentleman of a good family, industrious, and of fair condition," which sounds rather like the characterization of Hugh Willoughby, who was more gentleman than sailor.[1] Gorges gave explicit instructions to Challons and the ship's master, Nicholas Hind, to sail a northerly route to Cape Breton (Nova Scotia) and then follow the coast south. Gorges sent along two of the Indians who had lived with him, Sassacomoit and Maneddo. They were to guide Challons when they approached the mainland. Gorges had complete faith in the Indians as "exact Pilots" who knew the coast well.[2]

But Challons did not follow his instructions. The *Richard* departed

Plymouth in mid-August 1606, with thirty-one men aboard, and was soon hit by a powerful storm, which forced Challons to sail south towards the West Indies: Spanish territory.[3] By early November, they had reached the Florida channel, and from there they intended to head north to their original destination.

But then they ran into unpredictable turbulence of a different kind. They came upon a fleet of eleven Spanish merchant vessels, heavily armed. Not expecting any problems—because England and Spain were now at peace, having signed the Treaty of London the year before—Challons stayed his course through the fleet, hoisting the English flag to let the Spanish know his country of origin. But, quite unexpectedly, one of the Spanish ships fired a shot at the *Richard*. Thinking the Spanish must have misunderstood his intentions or were unaware of the peace, Challons maneuvered the *Richard* within hailing distance of the admiral's ship. He identified himself, explained his mission of plantation, and even brought out his commission for the admiral to inspect—as if he were showing a driver's license to a skeptical police officer.[4]

According to the later testimony of Nicholas Hind, this did nothing to change the behavior of the Spanish. They fired two more shots at the *Richard,* this time damaging her "through and through," then boarded the ship with drawn rapiers, stabbed and wounded Sassacomoit, and "abused and beat every man in the ship."[5] All the crew members were taken prisoner and dispersed among the Spanish ships, which continued on their way to Spain. Challons, Hind, and the *Richard,* along with all its goods and possessions, ended up in Seville, where the men were imprisoned. A few of the English crew were lucky enough to have been placed aboard a ship that lost its way and ended up in France. There they were set free and returned to England, where their testimony led to frantic diplomatic efforts to get Challons's remaining crew members released and the *Richard* and her contents returned.

That proved to be not so easy. As it turned out, Challons had not only sailed off course, he had sailed into murky legal waters. This is exactly where the terms of the Treaty of London were vague and open to interpretation. The treaty called for free commerce and allowed ships to enter the other's ports—even warships could seek haven if forced by weather or emergency. Also, the treaty made null and void all letters of marque that sanctioned piracy and plundering. But it did not enshrine the rights of the English to trade in the West Indies. Nor did it settle the respective claims of the two countries to Virginia.

In Seville, Challons was interrogated but eventually released into the custody of two English merchants. The captain then began a long legal wrangle to have his men freed. Some of these sailors were forced to testify before La Casa de Contratación, which reviewed the case. But when the president of La Casa could "find no cause of offense" on their part, he changed tack and grilled them about Virginia—and, in particular, the commodities available in that part of the New World.[6] Clearly, the Spanish still mistrusted England's intentions in America and they wanted to learn what knowledge the English seafarers had about the place.

Back in London, Gorges, Popham, and Robert Cecil found themselves dragged into the whirlpool of charges and countercharges about the *Richard* incident. Even James became embroiled in the diplomatic spat. Gorges tried to put a sarcastic twist on the situation, writing that the Plymouth Company's colonial effort had been foiled by "our good friends the Spaniards." He argued that they were probably worried that the English, under the terms of the peace treaty, would enjoy too much liberty of the seas. He entreated Cecil to help with the case.[7]

As Cecil and his counselors debated the issues, it was evident that there was great uncertainty about who was in the right and who was in the wrong. Did the *Richard* have the right to pass through Spanish-controlled waters? Did the Spanish ships have any right to seize the ship and take Challons's crew into custody? To get to an answer, Cecil commissioned one of his secretaries, the lawyer Levinus Munck, to set out the options. Munck argued that, on the one hand, it might be best to leave the Challons prisoners "to their fortune"—that is, to do nothing—because pursuing the case might "stir up some greater inconveniences." On the other hand, he reasoned, an argument could be made that the Challons ship had been going towards a location, North Virginia, whose ownership was "disputable" under the treaty. If that argument were accepted, then the Spanish, while perhaps entitled to stop the *Richard,* had no right to attack it or molest its crew.[8]

As the councillors weighed the arguments, English merchants, especially those doing business in or with Spain, urged them to take a stand on the matter. In February 1607, Nevill Davis, a merchant who lived in Seville and who acted as translator for Challons's captured seamen, wrote to Sir John Popham, warning that the Spanish would continue "to prevent us from going" to Virginia "by any means they can." This was a deeply disturbing prospect to Davis because he hoped that it was precisely in these "remote and unknown places" that England would find a "safer and [more] profitable trade" than they had with Spain. The Treaty of London was supposed to have boosted trade. But, Davis complained, English merchants had been impeded, suffering molestations and onerous tax impositions, and they were facing a cumulative loss of about £80,000. And, as had been the case fifty years before, the main issue was the collapsing market for cloth. "All our woolen commodities," Nevill wrote, were "in no estimation here" because the Spanish not only made plenty of their own cloth but also their products were better suited to the hot climate than English woolens. He closed his letter with a sentence that could have been written half a century earlier: "It is requisite," Nevill declared, that "we seek other places for the venting of our cloth."[9]

FORTUNATELY, THE PLYMOUTH Company's second ship—the one organized by Popham—did not encounter any difficulties. Captained by Thomas Hanham, Popham's grandson and one of the eight original investors listed in the Virginia charter, it sailed in September 1606, a month after the departure of the *Richard*. The crew included Tahánedo and probably Amóret, the two Indians who had been living with Popham and who were taken as guides and interpreters.[10]

Of course, when Hanham set out, he knew nothing of Challons's troubles, and the party fully expected to rendezvous with the *Richard* on the north coast of Virginia in a matter of weeks. Hanham and company made their way across the Atlantic in good time, waited at the agreed meeting place, and when the *Richard* did not turn up, went in search of potential settlement sites. Early in 1607, having dropped off the crew and the Indians, Hanham arrived back in England and delivered his report to Popham. Despite the troubles with the *Richard,* Hanham's findings were so precise and encouraging that, according to Gorges's later testimony, the Lord Chief Justice waxed "confident of the business" such that "every man of any worth … was willing to join in the charge for sending over a competent number of people to lay the ground of a hopeful plantation."[11]

As Popham and Gorges raised the funds for a fully-fledged colonial voyage, they realized that they faced the pressure of time. The leaders of the rival London Company had finally dispatched their ships, and barring some kind of mishap of the kind that befell Challons, they were likely to be the first to establish a colony in Virginia. Worse than this, however, was the potential threat from France, who had long been active fur traders in North America. In a letter to Cecil, Gorges feared that England's neighbors—meaning France—could enter the country and "thereby make themselves great." He explained that the French were already "in hand with the natives"—in other words, trading with them.[12]

In the urgency to get the expedition underway, Popham selected leaders with blood ties rather than with talent and relevant experience. George, his 56-year-old nephew, was chosen to lead the colony and to serve as captain of the ship *Gift of God*. Gorges did not think much of the choice, later characterizing George as "old," large, and "unwieldy"—a man "fearful to offend" and unwilling to contest

anyone who opposed him.[13] Clearly, these were less than ideal qualities for the governor of a colony. But Sir John was the driving force
behind the Plymouth Company and Gorges could not really object.

As commander of the second ship, the *Mary and John,* Popham
named Raleigh Gilbert, second son of Sir Humphrey. Although
Gorges was Raleigh's cousin, he was no kinder in his assessment of
the young man, characterizing him as "headstrong," "desirous of
supremacy," and "of small judgment." What's more, Gilbert had a
chip on his shoulder, believing that he had rightful ownership to the
original patent granted to his father, even though the patent had long
ago passed to Walter Ralegh.[14]

Despite doubts about Popham's choice of leaders, a hundred people
signed on as settlers for his colony. Little is known about them except
that they were all men and included soldiers, carpenters, a shipwright, a
chaplain, a smith, a cooper, and one or more cooks. In addition to
Popham and Gilbert, the main figures were Edward Harlow, master of
ordnance, Robert Davis, ship captain and sergeant-major, and George
Carew, whose job as "searcher" was to ensure there were no breaches
of discipline and quash any attempts at private trading.[15] Also aboard
was Skicowáros, the last of the three Indians who had stayed at Plymouth Fort, and the man whom Gorges hoped would be instrumental
in assisting the company with its trading ventures in America.

They set sail from Plymouth at the end of May 1607.[16] During the
voyage, the *Gift of God* and *Mary and John* were separated, as so often
happened on transatlantic trips. But the two ships reunited in
the first week of August, and a few days later Gilbert and George
Popham selected a plantation site on Sabino Point, which juts into
the Sagadahoc River, now the Kennebec, not far inland from the
Atlantic. The site faced north, so it had an unobstructed view of the
river and the outflow to the sea, enabling the colonists to keep an eye
out for possible attacks from Indians, the French, or Spanish. Also, it
backed onto a hill, providing some protection to the rear. A shallow
cove, with a sandy beach, lay to the east.

Finally stepping ashore, Popham and Gilbert inaugurated the colony, which became known as the Popham Colony or, more simply, Sagadahoc, after the river where it was situated. The chaplain, Richard Seymour, preached a sermon "under the spreading branches of the great trees, which afforded a grateful shelter from the August sun."[17] As was by now customary, the colony's commission was read aloud, after which George Popham was made president of the colony, and Gilbert, James Davis, Robert Davis, and Edward Harlow were named as his assistants. The next day the workers began digging the foundations for a fort, which they named St. George, after the patron saint of England. The surviving plan shows an elaborate, enclosed compound, its stone walls punctuated with gun enclosures, and its interior containing a neat array of buildings, including lodgings for the admiral and president, a chapel, buttery, bakehouse, guardhouse, and several private houses. By October, the settlers had completed the fort as well as several of the other buildings. Also, they had constructed a pinnace, the first vessel built by the English in America, and they christened it *Virginia* — as a tribute to the land and the queen.[18] While the workmen toiled, Gilbert explored the river and met and traded with local Indians. He was able to reconnect with Tahánedo, with Skicowáros serving as a go-between.

After a couple of months, the leaders sent one of the ships back to England with cargo and news of their progress, to assure Popham and Gorges that they had arrived safely and their work was underway. They loaded up the *Mary and John* with a variety of goods, mostly furs and a plant containing silken fibers (probably milkweed) that might prove useful in the weaving of cloth. They had found no sassafras, confirming that they had settled well north of the tree's natural habitat.

The vessel arrived back in Plymouth harbor in early December, and the crew learned that John Popham, chief proponent of the colony, had died the previous June, less than two weeks after the ships had sailed to the New World. Following Popham's death,

Sir Ferdinando Gorges had taken over much of the responsibility for the project, and as soon as the *Mary and John* had docked, he dispatched a hurried letter to Robert Cecil marked "late at night." The ship had arrived, Gorges wrote with a combination of feverish excitement and worried disappointment, "with great news of a fertile country, gallant rivers, stately harbors, and a people tractable." Unfortunately, there were no goods or commodities that would "satisfy the expectation of the Adventurers." But while Gorges acknowledged that this might "blemish the reputation of the design," he oozed optimism that the colonists would still be able to bring forth a variety of commodities, including timber for ships' masts, rich furs, and even grapes — "if they can keep the Frenchmen from the trade." It seems the colonists had already become viticulturists, producing a wine "much like the claret wine that comes out of France." Gorges promised to supply Cecil with further details and added a note with news of Challons, whose men were still imprisoned in Spain.[19]

Two days later, Gorges followed up his late-night missive with another letter. This time, he blamed George Popham and Raleigh Gilbert for their failure to send more promising news of the commodities in Sagadahoc. Also, he revealed that Gilbert had sent letters to his friends in England about his claim to the patent. In view of their dereliction of duty, Gorges suggested that he himself could take on even greater responsibility and, without spending much of the king's money, "bring to pass infinite things."[20]

Meanwhile, in the Sagadahoc settlement, the colonists started to suffer from the biting cold, and they had good reason to complain. They had arrived on the northeast coast during one of the coldest periods on record—a two-hundred-year span, starting around 1550, that was so brutally severe that it has become known as the "Little Ice Age." James Rosier had reported on an idyllic land, but that was in summer, not winter. He could not have known just how far the temperature could plunge and how much snow could fall.

As the weather grew colder, Gilbert and Popham concluded that their stores could not support the entire complement of colonists through the winter. They sent home a large number of settlers—perhaps as many as half of the colony—and another cargo, mostly of felled trees suitable for the making of masts. On the way back, the colonists stopped at the Azores for provisions and, on the instructions of the leaders, sold the masts to pay for the supplies. As a result, when the *Gift of God* arrived in England, it carried no commodities that the backers could sell to recoup their investment.

Gorges was again compelled to report disappointing news to Cecil. "Our second ship has returned," he wrote, "but with nothing more" than the first ship had delivered.[21] There would be no financial gain, no return to the investors. This turn of events so angered Francis Popham that he, with his mother, Lady Anne Popham, filed a suit in the Admiralty Court against the master of the *Gift of God* for selling the masts.[22] There was some encouraging news, however. The arriving ship also carried a letter from George Popham, addressed to King James himself, that seemed to contradict the bad news and described the rich commercial potential of the colony. "All the native inhabitants repeatedly assert that there are nutmegs, mace and cinnamon in these parts," wrote Popham, as well as "bitumen, Brazil wood, cochineal and ambergris, along with many other important and valuable things, and all very plentiful at that." Even more enticing, Popham further reported that he had been assured by the Indians that, in the "western part of this province, no more than seven days journey from our Fort St. George at Sagadahoc," there was a "sea which is extensive, wide and deep"—so large, in fact, that the Indians "have no idea how far it extends." Popham concluded, without evidence, that "this can be none other than the Southern Ocean, stretching towards the land of China which doubtless cannot be far away from this region."[23]

Unfortunately, Popham's claims about the commercial potential of the region were fabrications or, more charitably, wishful thinking. Of the commodities he mentioned, only ambergris might have been available to the colonists. The route to Cathay was also an audacious fiction, although there were two large bodies of water that lay to the west—Lake Champlain and the St. Lawrence River. The colonists who returned on the *Gift of God* brought home much less rosy reports. They told of hardship, especially the "extremity of the weather" that had "sorely pinched" them. Their clothes were thin and their diet poor. Gilbert, with his headstrong ways, had sowed division in the colony. What's more, the Indians had been far from cooperative, preferring to be "subtle and cunning" in their dealings and unwilling to reveal the sources of the wanted commodities. This should not have been surprising. It had been just two years since the Waymouth kidnapping and, even with the intervention of Skicowáros and Tahánedo, the Indians had not forgotten or forgiven the transgression.[24]

As he conveyed the news to Cecil, Gorges appealed for patience and asked for permission to put together a supply mission that he would organize himself. This he received, and he promptly sent the *Mary and John* back to Sagadahoc with fresh supplies and some significant news: John Gilbert, the eldest son of Sir Humphrey, had died and left the considerable family estate to his younger brother, Raleigh.

The news forced the young Gilbert to make a difficult decision: to stay and lead a struggling wilderness colony or go home and manage a great English estate. His decision was complicated by a number of factors. Gilbert's coleader, George Popham, perhaps succumbing to the cold, had died in February, aged about fifty-eight. Also, the colony's chief sponsor, John Popham, was dead, and this meant that further supplies could not be counted on, even with Gorges managing the venture. The colonists had not yet completed the planned colonial buildings nor realized the hoped-for commercial potential: they had found none of the exotic commodities listed by Popham, and they had failed to establish reliable trading relationships with the Indians that would guarantee them a supply of furs and other tradable goods.

Raleigh Gilbert no doubt weighed his options. Although Gorges doubted Gilbert's skills as a leader, the colony had fared reasonably well under his command. The colonists had endured the cold and harsh conditions with only one casualty — George Popham. Despite some quarrels and divisions, there had been no outright conflict, no serious threats of mutiny, no resistance of the kind that Humphrey Gilbert had faced from his Newfoundland crew. In the New World, Raleigh Gilbert had a great deal of freedom as well as unlimited, if uncertain, opportunity. He could perhaps pursue his claim, based on his father's patent of 1578, to a huge portion of America, and establish the commonwealth his father had imagined. He might one day open the route to China that Sir Humphrey had dreamed of and that George Popham had believed was not far away. Alternatively, he could return home and take his place as lord of the manor at Compton Castle, the family's darkly forbidding fortified residence in Devon. He would have land, resources, a network of the best and brightest, and all the luxuries and amenities of a courtier's life.

In the end, the lure of England was too great. Gilbert chose the safer, more conventional path. His choice made the decision for the entire community. No new leader stepped forward. The settlers did not try to persuade Gilbert to continue. They boarded the *Mary and John* and departed for England, taking with them the pinnace *Virginia*, which was the most distinctive memento of the Sagadahoc Colony.[25]

The return of the settlers and the abandonment of the colony was a bitter blow for Gorges. "The arrival of these people here in England was a wonderful discouragement to all the first undertakers," he wrote, "in so much as there was no more speech of settling any other plantation in those parts for a long time after."[26]

17

═━◉━═

FIRST COLONY

RALEIGH GILBERT'S RETREAT from Sagadahoc was a heartbreaking set-back for the merchants and courtiers of the Plymouth Company, but Ferdinando Gorges exaggerated the wider significance of the failure on England's efforts to establish a colony in the New World. This is because the London Company had already embarked on a rival colonial project, 750 miles farther south along the coast.

It was better resourced, better managed—by Sir Thomas Smythe—and better staffed than the Plymouth Company. The captain of the fleet was Christopher Newport, one of England's most experienced Atlantic sailors. He had been a prominent privateer during England's long sea war with Spain. In one escapade, he had engaged in a fierce battle with Spanish treasure ships and his right arm was "strooken off." This did not slow him down, however. In 1592, the one-armed captain commanded one of the ships that seized the *Madre de Dios,* and took charge of sailing the prized vessel into port.[1] His second-in-command was Bartholomew Gosnold, who left his mark on the landscape of North America when he named Cape

Cod and Martha's Vineyard during his only other voyage across the Atlantic four years earlier.[2]

Richard Hakluyt had expected to make the journey to the new colony, where he was to serve as chaplain, and James I gave him express permission to do so.[3] The preacher-writer had come close to joining Humphrey Gilbert on his ultimately disastrous voyage to Newfoundland in the 1580s. In the end, however, he did not step on board Gilbert's ship—and nor did he go this time. By now in his mid-fifties, he was married, well-to-do, and well-established. Perhaps he felt he had more to lose than to gain by joining a risky venture. He did, nevertheless, throw himself into the preparations for the voyage and almost certainly took a leading role in drafting some of the company's instructions to Newport and his fellow leaders.[4]

Newport's fleet of three ships—the *Susan Constant,* the *Godspeed,* and the *Discovery,* a twelve-ton pinnace—set sail from Blackwall on Saturday, December 20, 1606, with a contingent of 144 men and boys.[5] They followed the southerly route, but avoided the Spanish and the fate that had befallen Henry Challons in late 1606, and on April 26, 1607, reached the coastal headland at the entrance to what is now Chesapeake Bay, in present-day Virginia. Newport and thirty of the colonists stepped ashore and named the place Cape Henry, after James I's eldest son and heir to the throne.

The "certain orders and directions" for the settlers created by the London Company's leaders had some striking new features. Newport was put in "sole charge" of everyone on board—even the aristocrats and gentlemen—from the moment of departure to "such time as they shall fortune to land upon the coast of Virginia." Then, once the ships reached their destination, his exclusive authority was to cease and power was to be transferred to a governing body, the Council of Virginia (not to be confused with the King's Council). Thomas Smythe and the rest of the King's Council had already chosen the members of the council that would run the colony in Virginia. But their names were kept secret and placed in a sealed package that was not to be opened until the colonists reached their destination. This strategy had been developed by Smythe and the other managers of the Muscovy and East India Company ventures, who had found it helped prevent the kind of corrosive conflicts that might otherwise lead to mutiny.[6]

Once they reached Cape Henry, Newport opened the sealed package as instructed and read the list of council members. Newport himself was named, as were Gosnold and Edward Maria Wingfield, who had experience as a colonizer in Ireland. They were joined by John Martin (whose father, Richard, had served as Lord Mayor of London and governor of the Company of Mineral and Battery Works) and George Kendall, a soldier and sometime government spy. Also, the supremely self-confident John Smith, an experienced adventurer and military man, was named to the Council. Surprisingly, Gabriel Archer, who had accompanied Gosnold on his previous visit to America, was excluded. So, too, was George Percy, an aristocrat with impressive connections. His elder brother, the Earl of Northumberland, was a friend of Walter Ralegh and patron of Thomas Harriot.

The councillors now chose Wingfield as their president. His election showed a certain deference to age and status. By then in his mid-fifties, he had royal connections: his grandfather had served as lord deputy of Calais and his father was the godson of Henry VIII's sister Mary, hence his middle name "Maria." In his youth, he attended Lincoln's Inn, but thereafter pursued a military career, serving not only in Ireland but also in the Low Countries.[7]

Under his leadership, the councillors turned to the pressing matter of choosing a suitable place for the plantation. The instructions advised them to take their time, so that they could be certain that their preferred location was "the strongest, most wholesome and fertile place." Ideally, the site would be "a hundred miles from the river's mouth, and the further up the better" so as to be out of reach of enemy attack, either by sea or by land. Also, the colonists were directed to set up a lookout station at the entrance to the river, so that ample warning of an attack could be given to the settlement farther upstream.

Following these instructions, the colonists departed Cape Henry and entered the wide estuary of a river that they named the James, after the king. They then proceeded upriver, searching for a good location, and finally reached an island close to shore that was deemed to be "a very fit place for the erecting of a great city."[8] The colonists named the site James Towne.

Having done this, they divided themselves into three groups of workers—again, as instructed. The first group set about constructing a series of buildings: a fort, a storehouse for victuals, and other facilities for "public and necessary use." The second group began to farm the land, sowing seeds and planting "corn and roots." The third group was tasked with searching for minerals and a passage to the East, which the King's Council believed might run straight through the middle of the American landmass and empty into the Pacific.[9] Led by Newport, these explorers ventured deep into Indian territory, a land known as Tsenacommacah. They had several peaceful encounters with Indians, and heard encouraging stories about mineral mines. But when they returned, they found to their horror that Indians had attacked the newly built fort at Jamestown. Eleven colonists had been wounded, one mortally, and one boy was killed outright.[10]

It was an ominous start to the life of the colony.

AT THE END of July 1607, having spent less than two months in Jamestown, Christopher Newport returned to England to deliver a progress report to the King's Council. (There was no news yet from the Popham group in New England.) Newport had been warned not to "write any letter of any thing that may discourage others."[11] It was one of the lessons Thomas Smythe and the other leaders had learned from the original Roanoke Colony, whose members returned home with tales of woe and undermined efforts to attract new investors.

Newport presented the King's Council with a letter from Wingfield and his fellow councillors that glowed with enthusiasm. The colonists had settled on the bank of an exceptional river sixty miles inland, where they were "fortified well against the Indians." They enjoyed a "good store of wheat," plenty of fish, and they were convinced that Virginia "would flow with milk and honey" if—and only if—the council sent a resupply mission. This, they warned, needed to be done quickly, because the "all devouring Spaniard" was still interested in Virginia.[12]

Newport brought evidence of commercial opportunity: two tons of sassafras, which continued to be a sought-after commodity, and some clapboard—long thin planks of wood cut from oak, pine, and spruce trees and used for the walls and roofs of buildings. Also, he presented samples of an ore that he believed might contain traces of gold. But this mineral caused no great euphoria. Ever since the days of Frobisher's failed expeditions, investors had greeted claims of gold with a measure of skepticism. This time Sir Walter Cope wrote to Cecil, explaining that if they were to believe what the colonists told them, then "we are fallen upon a land that promises more than the land of promise." Instead of milk, Cope wrote, "we find pearl," and instead of honey, gold. He cautioned, however, that they should learn from experience—"the wisest schoolmistress"—and be "of Slow belief." Cope's circumspection soon proved well-founded when, the very next day, the council received the results of an assay on the ore. As Cope suspected, there were no traces of copper, never mind gold.[13]

Even so, Cecil was sufficiently encouraged to sanction a resupply mission, and he did not wish to waste time. He was rightly concerned that the Spanish were preparing to destroy Jamestown, occupy the land, and seize the riches that it had to offer. In September 1607, Pedro de Zúñiga, the Spanish ambassador, wrote to Philip III, suggesting that "it would be very advisable for Your Majesty to root out this noxious plant while it is so easy." Wait much longer, he warned, and "it will be more difficult to get them out."[14]

Smythe took charge of organizing the resupply mission. He had no intention of repeating Ralegh's administrative failures, which had undermined the Roanoke Colony. He exerted his influence with some fifty London merchants of the East India Company to raise capital for the effort, and by October—just two months after Newport's arrival in England—two ships, led once again by Newport, were ready to sail for Virginia with 120 men and supplies for the fledgling colony. Smythe's masterful management so impressed his fellow councillors that Cope suggested that Cecil should offer "a word of thanks" for the merchant's "care & diligence."[15]

NEWPORT REACHED VIRGINIA on January 2, 1608—while the Challons crew was still being held in Spain and the Popham Colony was enduring a bitterly cold winter. But if he expected to find a vibrant colony full of festive cheer, he was sorely disappointed by what he found. The colony was on the brink of collapse. The previous summer, while he was sailing back to England with promising news of Jamestown, the colonists had suffered an onslaught of "the bloody flux"—dysentery. So many fell sick and died that those who lived "were scarce able to bury the dead."[16] Bartholomew Gosnold was one of the victims of that dreadful time.

As the sickness swept the colony, the leaders bickered and the government disintegrated. "After Captain Gosnold's death," wrote George Percy, "the Council could hardly agree," and they started to divide into factions.[17] Three councillors—Kendall, Martin, and Ratcliffe—accused Wingfield of hoarding oatmeal, beef, eggs, and aqua vitae for his personal consumption and forced him from office.[18] Ratcliffe became president and then moved to strengthen his position, arresting Kendall, whom he accused of being a Spanish spy, and eventually having him executed before a firing squad.[19]

With the colonists in distress and their leaders in disarray, the controversial John Smith stepped into the breach. At twenty-seven years old, he was the youngest of the councillors, but his youth belied his vast experience. Humbly born, he left England to make his fortune. Not long after turning twenty, he was fighting as a mercenary in the Christian forces warring against the Ottoman Turks in Eastern Europe. It was during this campaign that he came of age, displaying such bravery that he was granted a coat of arms—and, with it, the status of a gentleman.

Newport disliked the cocksure Smith. On the first voyage to Jamestown, Smith's abrasive self-assurance had so enraged his fellow councillors that he was charged with mutinous activities, chained in the ship's hold, and narrowly escaped hanging. But as the colony fell into crisis, Smith, demonstrating his natural leadership, started venturing out of the fort and travelling up the James River to trade for corn with Indians. There were about thirty tribes of the Powhatan group in the eastern Virginia region, a total of some 14,000 Indians. They spoke various dialects of the Algonquian language, controlled a land known as Tsenacommacah that encompassed some eight thousand square miles, and lived in a kind of confederacy under the authority of Wahunsonacock, a great chief, whom the English knew as Powhatan.[20]

It was on one such upriver foray that Smith had the encounter that has entered into American legend. After paddling up the James River with a party of colonists, he split off with two men, in order to explore the nearby woods on foot. Within a few minutes, they were ambushed, Smith's companions were slaughtered—one had "20 or 30 arrows in him"—and he was captured. He was marched to meet the brother of Wahunsonacock, who greeted him with surprising cordiality. Smith was served "great platters of fine bread" and "more venison than ten men could devour."[21] Then he was taken to meet Wahunsonacock, who resided at Werowocomoco, the capital of the Powhatan people north of Jamestown. There, some Indians forced Smith's head onto "two great stones," and he assumed that they were about "to beat out his brains." Smith begged for his life, and just when it looked as if "no entreaty could prevail," an Indian girl, perhaps ten years old, rushed forward. She took "his head in her arms, and laid her own upon his to save him from death." The girl's name was Matoaka. But Smith would know her as Pocahontas, a pet name for a cheeky, playful child. Smith was set free and returned to Jamestown in January 1608, arriving just a few hours before Newport's ships hove into view.[22]

Newport's new settlers and fresh supplies bolstered the resolve of the survivors. With a population of around 160 people, the colony had never been so strong. To make it stronger still, Newport went in search of gold mines and a fast passage to the Pacific. He took Smith with him, despite his personal dislike of the young captain. He knew Smith had greater knowledge of the locality than anyone else.

This search proved fruitless. But the expedition did mark a new chapter in the relationship between the English and the Powhatans. Until then, the English had typically captured or cajoled Indians, transporting them back across the Atlantic in order to display them as proof of discovery and to better understand their land, their language, and their culture. Now, with Smith's help, Newport cut a deal with Wahunsonacock: Thomas Savage, a thirteen-year-old English boy, was handed over to the Powhatans in exchange for the chief's loyal servant, Namontack. The teenaged "go-between," the first of many who would be swapped, was to live with the Indian leader, learn the Algonquian language and, ultimately, become an interpreter. It was a remarkable gesture that was meant to engender trust and goodwill.[23]

In April 1608, Newport departed for England once again, accompanied by Namontack and Edward Wingfield, the deposed president. Five months later, with Newport and Wingfield gone, Smith was formally installed as president. He took a tough line with the gentlemen colonists who, he wrote, "would rather starve and rot with idleness" than do their fair share of the work.[24] He warned them, "He that will not work shall not eat." He did not want the "labour of 30 or 40 honest and industrious men" to be eaten up by "150 idle varlets."[25]

Back in London, Christopher Newport delivered to the leaders of the Virginia Company a report that Smith, a prolific writer, had prepared about the Jamestown Colony. The land was "not only exceeding pleasant for habitation," he wrote, "but also very profitable for commerce in general." This vast, rich territory was ruled by an impressive Indian "emperor" who was "richly hung with many chains of great pearls about his neck" and who wore "a great covering of *Rahaughcums*": a cloak of raccoon skins. Land, precious commodities, furs, and accommodating Indian traders—so encouraging was this testimony that the London Company arranged for Smith's pamphlet to be rushed into print under the title *A True Relation of such occurrence and accidents of noate as hath happened in Virginia since the first planting of that Colony.*[26]

To this sparkling account, Smith had appended a rough sketch map which was not published. It particularly intrigued Smythe and his associates, providing them with their first view of the James River and its tributaries. Together with the scattering of Indian villages that surrounded the triangular settlement at Jamestown, it offered tantalizing evidence of a passage to the East: Smith reported that salt water, which he surmised came from the "south sea"—the Pacific Ocean—"beateth into the river," upstream from Jamestown. Perhaps, at last, the London Company was poised to discover a new route to Cathay.

Even more sensationally, Smith suggested that members of the Roanoke Colony might still be alive. Ever since 1587, when John White left the colonists, there had been rumors that they had survived—but nothing more. Near the coastline, Smith marked a village called Pakerakanick, and wrote, "Here remain 4 men clothed that came from Roanoke to Okanahowan."[27] The English did not wish to let go of the hope that Sir Walter Ralegh's colony still existed, somewhere.

IN AUGUST 1608, Newport led a second supply mission to Jamestown, this time carrying seventy new colonists with him. He was sailing west as the Popham colonists were sailing east and home to London, having abandoned their little fort at Sagadahoc. Newport carried new instructions for the colonists to search for "the South Sea, a mine of gold" or for any of those people who had been "sent by Sir Walter Ralegh"—that is, the lost Roanoke settlers. Newport also carried a letter (now lost) from Sir Thomas Smythe that dripped with frustration. Addressing Smith and his fellow colonists, Smythe expressed his anger at being fed "with 'ifs' and 'ands,' hopes and some few proofs." He apparently warned that if the colonists did not send commodities to defray the costs of the latest supply fleet—the princely sum of two thousand pounds—they would be "banished men."

This raised the ire of Captain Smith, who fired off a reply that he himself admitted was a "rude answer." He mocked Newport's new instructions, even though it had been his report and sketch map that had encouraged the investors to get excited about a passage to Cathay. He criticized the company's efforts to resupply the colony, saying the victuals were not "worth twenty pounds." And he warned Smythe not to expect a quick return or compare Jamestown's commercial output to that of the Muscovy Company. "Though your factors there can buy as much in a week as will freight you a ship," Smith wrote, "you must not expect from us any such matter." In Jamestown, he revealed, the settlers were "scarce able" to get enough to live.[28]

When Smythe received Smith's letter and other reports, including a more detailed map of Virginia, he and the other members of the King's Council were persuaded that something more, and something different, needed to be done if Jamestown was to thrive and the company was to turn a profit. He convened a series of "solemn meetings" to discuss the way forward, inviting Richard Hakluyt and Thomas Harriot, now in his late forties and arguably England's most experienced colonist, to one of these meetings, held at the London residence of Thomas Cecil, Robert Cecil's elder brother and a leading investor.[29] They resolved to take three main actions: reshape the leadership structure, broaden the territorial domain of the colony, and increase the number of investors.

The difficulties with the leadership structure were made clear in Smith's letter. The office of Jamestown president had not been endowed with sufficient power. During Smith's tenure, the other council members broke into factions and looked for every opportunity to undermine him. One colonist later noted that "such envy, dissensions and jars were daily sown amongst them, that they choked the seeds and blasted the fruits of all men's labors."[30] Acknowledging their "error" in making the president first among equals, the members of the King's Council resolved to appoint "one *able* and *absolute Governor.*"[31]

The Smythe group also decided that the governor should preside over a larger territory. The map and report that Captain Smith sent Smythe — which was later published as *A Map of Virginia. With a Description of the Countrey, the Commodities, People, Government and Religion* — set out very clearly the opportunity for England to establish a vast colony in the New World.[32] Accordingly, Sir Edwin Sandys, a gifted parliamentary speaker, was tasked with drawing up a revised, or second, charter that would extend the London Company's territorial claims. This he did, and the resulting document, which James I signed in May 1609, significantly enlarged the territory that could be claimed by the shareholders — from 10,000 miles to more than a million square miles.[33]

This stretched from "sea to sea" — an indication that Smythe and his associates were determined to find a fast passage to the Pacific Ocean and to Cathay. Also, it stretched from Jamestown and its environs in the north to Roanoke in the south — an indication that they were committed to find the survivors of Ralegh's colony. As Smythe and the other leaders of the London Company later wrote, they believed that "some of our Nation planted by Sir Walter Ralegh" were "yet alive, within fifty miles of our fort." If they could be found, they could "open the womb and bowels of this country" — in other words, they could divulge the secrets of the land.[34]

As well as new leadership and a bolder colonial vision, Smythe and his associates sought one further reform: a new company with a wider group of investors. The colony was a costly business, and they realized that they needed to put the whole enterprise on a firmer financial footing. For this, they received royal support, enshrined in the charter, for a new corporation, the Treasurer and Company of Adventurers and Planters of the City of London for the First Colony in Virginia. Better known as the Virginia Company, this came about after a flurry of promotional activity designed to attract new investors.

One of Smythe's first moves was to invite the merchants of the Plymouth Company to join the London contingent at twenty-five dollars per share, which would bring them "all privileges and liberties" of membership. It was, in effect, a corporate merger. Smythe believed that they would be stronger together. "If we join freely together and, with one common and patient purse, maintain and perfect our foundations," he argued, then they would benefit from "a most fruitful country" that was "aboundant in rich commodities."[35] He discussed the proposal with Sir Ferdinando Gorges, but in the end the talks came to nothing. Gorges and his fellow investors were still reeling from the failure of the Sagadahoc settlement, and they seem to have had scant appetite for further costly colonial ventures.

To cast his net wider, Smythe commissioned Robert Johnson, one of his close business associates and a leading merchant of the Worshipful Company of Grocers, to write a promotional pamphlet called *Nova Britannia,* echoing the language of Drake's Nova Albion, located in similar latitudes on the other side of the American continent. This was the first part of an ambitious marketing campaign that added a new element to the promotional pitch.

Johnson urged the pamphlet's readers not to make the same mistake as their English "forefathers" had—losing "the prime and fairest proffer of the greatest wealth in the world" when they spurned Christopher Columbus's offer to discover a new route to China. "Let it not be accounted hereafter, as a prize in the hands of fools, that had not hearts to use it," he warned.[36] With his soaring rhetoric, Johnson sought to stir not only national sentiment but also religious conviction. Ever since the days of the Mysterie, merchants had paid lip service to the importance of proselytizing non-Christian peoples as a motivation for overseas ventures but they had taken little tangible action to preach the gospel and win over converts. Now, Johnson insisted that the overriding purpose of English colonial efforts was the "advancing and spreading the kingdom of God."[37] The message of *Nova Britannia* came through loud and clear. Give whatever you can give, no matter how little. By investing in Virginia, you are giving to your country, and to God.

The religious message was reinforced from the country's pulpits. In March 1609, Richard Crakanthorpe, an Oxford theologian, praised anyone who would commit to the Virginia effort. Their investment would help to bring about "a new Britain in another world" and would also ensure that the "heathen barbarians and brutish people" would learn the word of God.[38] The following month, William Symonds, another Oxford scholar, delivered a sermon before leading supporters of the Virginia enterprise. Symonds, quoting from the Bible, likened the colonists' task to that of Abraham, who was instructed to leave the land of his father and build "a great Nation."[39]

Pedro de Zúñiga, the Spanish ambassador, could barely contain his contempt for this new approach. He wrote to Philip III that the English "have actually made the ministers in their sermons dwell upon the importance of filling the world with their religion and demand that all make an effort to give what they have" to forward the cause.[40] Virginia was no longer just a commercial venture. It was becoming a crusade for Protestantism, national expansion, and social good. But the appeal to religious conviction was more than a cynical commercial ruse: Smythe and other leaders were devout men driven by their Protestant beliefs. Smythe himself had been raised in a godly household, and his first wife was the daughter of Richard Culverwell, who was closely associated with the founding of Emmanuel College,

Cambridge, the puritan academy attended by John Harvard, who gave his library to the college that later took his name.[41]

As the clergymen preached from the pulpits of London, the members of the King's Council put pressure on their friends and colleagues to support and promote the campaign. They sent letters to the Lord Mayor, aldermen, and livery companies of London, soliciting subscriptions to their colony—"an action pleasing to God and happy for this Common Wealth."[42] The Lord Mayor, in turn, entreated London's great livery companies to "deal very earnestly and effectually" with their members "to make some adventure in so good and honourable action."[43]

Smythe's dynamic marketing campaign was compelling, but investors may also have been lured by another novel feature: affordability. In the early 1550s, the Mysterie had set the share price at twenty-five pounds, which was a princely sum. Half a century later, a single share in the East India Company had gone for two hundred pounds.[44] But when setting the share price for the Virginia Company, Smythe offered a drastic reduction: an individual share could be purchased for the bargain price of twelve pounds and ten shillings. The reward would be a division of land and a division of the proceeds of the colony—after seven years. In *Nova Britannia*, Johnson confidently predicted that investors would receive "at least" five hundred acres for every share.[45]

The combination of national pride, religious conviction, appealing marketing, and low price worked. The first Virginia charter had listed eight subscribers. By contrast, the second charter listed nearly a hundred times as many: 659 individuals and fifty-six livery companies and other corporate bodies. The great livery companies—the Mercers, Clothworkers, Goldsmiths, and Haberdashers—were joined by some lesser companies such as the poulterers, fruiterers, plasterers, basketmakers, and embroiderers. Mirroring this diversity, the individual investors came from across the social spectrum: not only noblemen but also doctors, captains, brewers, and even a shoemaker.[46]

The campaign's success alarmed Zuñiga, who told the Spanish king that "there has been gotten together in 20 days a sum of money for this voyage which amazes one." He reported that fourteen "counts and barons" had pledged "40,000 ducats," that "the merchants give much more," and that "there is no poor little man, nor woman, who is not willing to subscribe something for this enterprise."[47]

It had been three years since the first colonists had arrived at Cape Henry, and the track record so far was disappointing, not to say disastrous. As one contemporary observer put it, "the plantation went rather backwards than forwards."[48] In previous years, such setbacks had doomed colonial projects. But Sir Thomas Smythe and his fellow leaders did not abandon the enterprise, as so many others had given up on their ventures in times gone by. At last, they seemed to accept that the process would be bumpy, that constant adaptation would be required, and that it would take time to establish a thriving enterprise. "Planting of countries is like planting of woods," noted Sir Francis Bacon, the country's attorney general, who was involved in drafting the second charter. "You must make account to leese [lose] almost twenty years' profit, and expect your recompense in the end."[49]

So far, Jamestown had to be counted as a failure—a graveyard of people and dreams. Now, it was time for a reset. Adopting a new attitude, the leaders listened to the advice of men with great knowledge and experience—John Smith, Richard Hakluyt, and Thomas Harriot—and rethought the mission, ditched what did not work, and considered what might work better in the future. They embraced, as it were, the processes of trial and error and incremental improvement. They were encouraged in their efforts because they had the ear of the king, the support of the City, the hearty participation of the people—and, they fervently believed, the blessing of God.

18

━━ ⟪◉⟫ ━━

A STAKE IN THE GROUND

WITH THIS EXTRAORDINARY mandate, Smythe and his colleagues organized a majestically outfitted expedition. The nine-vessel fleet was led by the *Sea Venture,* a 250-ton ship purpose-built for transporting large numbers of people to the New World. Six hundred settlers, including an unprecedented one hundred women, had taken up the challenge. Sir Thomas Gates and Sir George Somers, two of the original patentees, took command.

Gates, a diplomat and soldier whom even the Spanish regarded as "very special," having seen him fight against them in the Netherlands, was to take the role of the newly defined governor of Jamestown and to oversee the expansion of the colony beyond Jamestown. In addition, he was to search for "rich copper mines" and the "four of the English alive" — the Roanoke settlers who were supposedly living not far away, oblivious of the creation of the new colony.[1]

The fleet set sail from Falmouth at the beginning of June 1609. But, a week out of England, the *Virginia* — the pinnace constructed by colonists at Sagadahoc — was forced to return to port with its passengers.[2]

The other eight ships continued on, but towards the end of July they were hit by a hurricane that scattered the fleet. Seven vessels staggered into Jamestown in mid-August and unloaded some four hundred passengers. But there was no sign of the *Sea Venture,* the flagship. As days drifted into weeks, the colonists assumed that everyone and everything must have been lost at sea: Gates, Newport, and Somers, 150 of the settlers, the charter and instructions, and significant supplies for the colony. It was a devastating blow.

News of the disaster reached Smythe and his fellow leaders in October 1609, when a ship from Jamestown returned to England, carrying a letter from Gabriel Archer, one of the original colonists. Archer reported the "absence" of Sir Thomas Gates and warned that, given the loss of the flagship's provisions, the colonists would not be able to devote themselves to commercial activities. You "must pardon us," he wrote, "if you find not [the] return of commodit[ies] so ample as you may expect." He said the colonists would have to "seek sustenance first" and only then "labour to content you afterwards."[3]

Soon after, another ship arrived in London from Jamestown, this one with an unexpected passenger aboard: John Smith. As president of the colony, Smith had faced persistent opposition. In particular, George Percy, one of his aristocratic rivals, accused him of acting like an absolute king and exercising "sovereign rule."[4] As tension mounted, Smith was the victim of an explosion caused by a spark igniting the gunpowder pouch that he carried on his belt. As he later recorded, the blast "tore the flesh from his body and thighs, nine or ten inches square in a most pitiful manner." He was lucky to survive. To this day, the event is shrouded in mystery. Was it an accident or an assassination attempt? No one knows for sure. But, whatever the truth, Smith was forced to return to England in order to recuperate. It marked the end of his tenure as president in Jamestown. His archrival, George Percy, soon took his place.[5]

This episode confirmed the Virginia Company in its view that Jamestown was being hampered by rivalry among the colonial leaders. But Smythe and his associates were concerned above all else by the news about the *Sea Venture*. If it had sunk or been destroyed, it would be a cataclysmic loss for the colonial project. With the colony's future in the balance, the leaders turned to promotion once more, publishing *A True and Sincere declaration of the purpose and ends of the Plantation*. In a bold statement, they appealed to investors not to withdraw their support, arguing that the hurricane that struck the *Sea Venture* was an act of God. They urged them to reflect on their resolve: "Is he fit to take any action whose courage is shaken and dissolved with one storm?"[6]

With Gates out of the picture, the company announced that Sir Thomas West, third Baron De La Warr, would be sent to Jamestown to serve as "Lord Governor" and "Captain General" for life. Aged thirty-two, West was a Privy Councillor, an original member of the King's Council of Virginia, and the single biggest investor, having pledged five hundred pounds.[7] The company authorized West to govern by his "own discretion." He was to exert martial law, if necessary, and make sure the colonists were "exercised and trained up in martial manner and warlike discipline." If it transpired that Thomas Gates had survived and had managed to make his way to Jamestown, then West was to install him as lieutenant governor.[8]

Mindful of the expectations of hundreds of investors, Smythe instructed the new lord governor to focus the efforts of the settlers on commercial activity. A list of the most important commodities was drawn up.[9] It included beaver and otter skins; sassafras, worth fifty pounds per ton; pine trees, worth eighteen pounds per ton; and oak trees, which were prized for their hardwood for the making of clapboard. Also, West was, "with convenient speed," to set the colonists to work on that most reliable commercial endeavor: fishing. It was hoped any catch would offset the considerable costs of this unscheduled expedition.[10] The rivers were said to be "stored with sturgeon," whose roe—caviar—could bring as much as forty pounds per every hundred pounds of haul.[11]

In the quest for profit, the religious rationale dropped down the list of important factors for the colony's new leaders. Almost as an afterthought, West was urged to spend time on "the conversion of the natives" in order to promote "the knowledge and worship of the true God."[12]

SIR THOMAS WEST and his fleet of three ships left London for Virginia in April 1610 with 150 colonists. They reached America after a two-month crossing and weighed anchor at Point Comfort on the north bank of the James River. There, the new Lord Governor West got word that the colonists were preparing to abandon the settlement upriver at Jamestown.

The settlers had every reason to have lost hope. As West later learned, the colony had descended into a wretched condition. During the winter, the Powhatans besieged the town, preventing anyone from leaving the fort to go in search of food. As a result, supplies ran dangerously low and the colonists began "to feel the sharp prick of hunger."[13] They eventually resorted to eating anything they could catch and consume: cats, dogs, horses, rats, mice, snakes, and, finally, their fellow colonists. "Nothing was spared to maintain life," Percy recalled, and they did "those things w[hi]ch seem incredible." They dug "corpses out of graves" and proceeded "to eat them." One man was so ravenous that he slaughtered his pregnant wife, "ripped the child out of her womb," threw the baby in the river, and then "chopped the mother in pieces and salted her for his food."[14] It was Percy who gave this period the name for which it would be remembered forevermore: the "Starving Time." More than four hundred settlers died, leaving a diminished colony of about sixty survivors.

When West got the news that the colonists were planning to depart, he dispatched a small boat to alert them that he had arrived with new settlers and supplies and to urge them to stay. As the little vessel proceeded upriver, it met four ships coming downstream from the direction of Jamestown. At the helm of one of the vessels was Thomas Gates.

After they finally met each other, Gates told West the remarkable story about what had happened to him and the *Sea Venture* the summer before. On July 23, 1609, when the Gates-Somers fleet was within a few days of reaching Jamestown, the ships had encountered the "dreadful tempest" that separated them. In the definitive account of the episode, William Strachey, a well-traveled former diplomat with literary ambitions, reported that while he had encountered many dangerous gales before, this one made the ocean and sky "like an hell of darkness." It was so intense that "all that I had ever suffered gathered together, might not hold comparison with this." Such was the violence that the caulking between some of the ship's planks burst out and seawater rushed in through the open seams. In the darkness, "with candles in their hands," the crew searched for the leak. But by the time they found it, the gape was too large to be plugged. They resorted to bailing and pumping and, when this made no difference, throwing ordnance and chests of belongings overboard to lighten the load.[15]

For three days and four nights, the storm raged. Just as the passengers prepared to commit themselves "to the mercy of the sea," the admiral of the fleet, George Somers, who had lashed himself to the ship, "cried 'Land.'" Miraculously, they had come upon one of the Bermudas, an archipelago of more than one hundred islands. Long known as "The Devils Islands" for their dangerous shoals, they were "feared and avoided of all sea travelers alive, above any other place in the world."[16] At last, the storm abated and the *Sea Venture*—all 150 of its men and women alive, if traumatized—made landfall on an island they named Smith's Island, after Sir Thomas.

The place, which Sir Humphrey Gilbert had identified as a possible site for a settlement thirty years earlier, turned out to be a paradise—sumptuous in its wildlife, with birds, turtles, an abundance of fish, oysters, lobsters, crabs, and whales. The island ran with hogs, which had been left by previous voyagers for the very purpose of providing sustenance to survivors shipwrecked on the dangerous reefs.[17] The English hunted them, boasting that they could bring in "thirty, sometimes fifty boars, sows, and pigs" in a week.[18]

Some settlers found the Bermuda Islands so alluring that they argued it would be better to settle there rather than to continue on to Virginia. One of these was Stephen Hopkins, a radical Protestant who cited the Bible in his effort to question the authority of Sir Thomas Gates in a strange land. He was very nearly hanged for mutiny—but was finally pardoned. Meanwhile, Gates ordered Richard Frobisher, an experienced shipwright and possibly a kinsman of Sir Martin, to recover what material he could from the *Sea Venture,* which lay on the coral reef close to the island, and construct two pinnaces.[19]

In May 1610, after the castaways had spent ten months on the Bermuda Islands, they set sail in Frobisher's vessels, *Deliverance* and *Patience,* and sailed the seven hundred miles to Jamestown, arriving there two weeks later. When he beheld the horribly reduced condition of the settlers and the settlement, Gates must have rued the day that he decided to leave Bermuda. It did not take him long to conclude that the prospects for the settlement were hopeless and that Jamestown should be abandoned. Gates and the Jamestown colonists boarded four ships and set off for the voyage back to England. It was then, as they wended their way down the James River, that they encountered West's little boat, learned that there was a new group of settlers and fresh supplies, and decided to stay.

West and his contingent proceeded to Jamestown, arriving there in June. The first aristocrat to govern an English American colony, he took control with much pomp and circumstance, guarded by fifty red-coated soldiers wielding halberds. He then got straight down to the work of revitalizing the settlement, sending Somers back to Bermuda to collect hogs and other supplies from that wonderland. At the same time, to keep Smythe and the other investors happy, he ordered the gathering of sassafras and other commodities that could be sold for a profit in London.

Strikingly, West did not devote time or effort in a search for the lost colonists of Roanoke. Nor did he go looking for gold mines or a passage to the East. These goals, once so prominent in the minds of the men who masterminded England's ventures to America, had dropped down the priority list. For the first time, America came to be seen as a destination in its own right rather than as a source of Spanish-style mineral riches or a stopover on the way to Asia. But the quest for a fast route to Cathay was not abandoned by London's merchants. As he dispatched West to Jamestown, Smythe was busily laying the groundwork for another organization: the Northwest Passage Company.

WEST SENT GATES back to England to collect more settlers and still more supplies—and, of course, to prove he was alive and show that God was on the side of the colonists. He arrived in September 1610, having been away for more than a year. Until then, most of London thought that he had perished on the treacherous coral reefs of the Bermuda Islands. He brought with him Strachey's account of the *Sea Venture,* which appeared in a letter to Sara, Sir Thomas Smythe's wife.[20] Not published until 1612, it was nevertheless passed around as an unpublished manuscript, enthralled everyone who read it, and may even have provided Shakespeare with the inspiration for his final play, *The Tempest.*

Gates's survival and Strachey's report—especially the unexpected opportunity of Bermuda and the great needs of Jamestown—energized the investors once again. The Virginia Company's leaders sought to raise a further £30,000, which they calculated would be enough to deploy three supply convoys, whose goal was pretty much the same as it had been before: to create "a very able and strong foundation of annexing another Kingdom to this Crown."[21]

In March 1611, when the first of these convoys departed England with a contingent of three hundred settler-volunteers, there was a new man in charge: Sir Thomas Dale, a grit-hard soldier who had served with West in the Netherlands. Personally recommended by Prince Henry, he was to be Jamestown's marshal, supporting the lord governor by imposing martial law.[22] But when he arrived in May 1611, Dale found the colony in disarray once again and West nowhere to be seen. It turned out that the lord governor had sneaked out of Jamestown after suffering several bouts of ill health. Officially lord governor "for life," he had stayed barely ten months, and even then, he spent much of this time on board his ship, apparently reluctant to rub shoulders with the hoi polloi.[23]

Like so many others, Dale had been persuaded by the Virginia Company's marketing campaign. He had read the pamphlets, heard the sermons, and listened to the captains. Now he could see with his own eyes that their claims of a prosperous, thriving colony were baseless. In an act of frustration, he turned to Christopher Newport, took hold of his beard, and threatened to have him hanged for misleading him and other adventurers.[24]

Without a designated governor, Dale seized control of the colony and moved swiftly to carry out the Virginia Company's instructions that had been given to Gates and then, with modifications, to West. In imposing martial law, he drew up a set of rules with the help of Strachey, who had trained at Gray's Inn. Later published as *Lawes Divine, Morall and Martiall,* it was the first legal code in America, and it was mercilessly enforced. Major crimes—including theft—carried the death sentence. Minor crimes—such as slander—were punishable by imprisonment, whippings, hard labor on the colony's galleys, or "passing the pikes," where the guilty had to go through a row of soldiers holding weapons: they were lucky if they reached the other end alive.[25]

Tough with the colonists, Dale was tougher still with the Powhatans, exacting severe retribution for the besieging of Jamestown during the "starving time." Although he never received the army of two thousand soldiers he wanted to fight the Powhatans, he vowed to "over master the subtle-mischievous Great Powhatan," and force him to sue for peace or "leave then to our possession his country."[26]

Also, Dale set about establishing a new "principal residence and seat" for the colony beyond the falls, which lay fifty miles farther up the James River. Jamestown, by now regarded as a marshy "unwholesome" place, was to be continued only as a useful port, populated "with a convenient number of men."[27] When it was finished, the new town featured "3 streets of well framed houses, a handsome church and the foundation of a more stately one laid of brick, in length an hundred foot, and fifty foot wide, besides store houses, watch houses, and such like."[28] Dale christened the new town Henrico—in honor of fourteen-year-old prince Henry, who was starting to be recognized as "the Protector of Virginia."[29]

SOON AFTER FOUNDING Henrico, Dale took his men downriver to a fertile land, creating another settlement called Bermuda, after the now famously bountiful Bermuda Islands. As he did so, Smythe and the Virginia Company considered ways to finance the colony—and settled on an intriguing and relatively new financing vehicle: a lottery. It would be the third public lottery in England's history, the first having been launched by Elizabeth in the 1560s for raising money to pay for building royal ships and developing ports.[30] Anyone could buy a lot and get a chance to receive a prize. All the money collected would go to support the Virginia colonies.

The Virginia Company commissioned a "Lottery House," where the lots would be drawn, at the west end of St. Paul's Cathedral.[31] Thomas Smythe launched a marketing campaign, approaching companies for subscriptions and engaging Robert Johnson once again to write a new pamphlet—this one called *The Lotterys best prize, declaring the former successe and present state of Virginia's Plantation*. Published in May 1612 as *The New Life of Virginea*, it acknowledged that, like all excellent things, "the business and plantation of Virginia" had been "accompanied with manifold difficulties, crosses and disasters." Now, however, was the time for citizens throughout England to take part in an enterprise "of such consequence" for the nation. Even if they did not win a prize in the lottery, they could rest assured that their "money goeth to a public work."[32]

When the lots were drawn, Thomas Sharplisse, a tailor, emerged as the winner of the first prize—four thousand crowns "in fair plate," which "was sent to his house in a very stately manner."[33] The Virginia Company was a big winner, too. According to the Spanish ambassador, the lottery raised 60,000 ducats.[34] Indeed, the London lottery was so successful that the scheme was rolled out across the country.

But even this new funding source could not be counted on to sustain the Virginia Colony indefinitely. Dale fired off a warning to Smythe arguing that the loss of Virginia would be as bad a mistake as the state had made "since they lost the Kingdom of France" — as bad, that is, as the loss of Calais in 1558. It was a comparison calculated to resurrect painful memories for Smythe: his grandfather, Sir Andrew Judde, had been Mayor of the Calais staple when the city was captured by the French.[35]

Along with his warning, Dale sent a potential solution — a sample of an aromatic leaf that might calm Smythe's nerves: tobacco.[36] During the planting season of 1612, John Rolfe, one of the survivors of the *Sea Venture* wreck in Bermuda, had sown the seeds of the plant *Nicotiana tabacum*, which produced a leaf of the Spanish style, much milder than the bitter local leaf, *Nicotiana rustica*, favored by the Powhatans.[37] Rolfe had done so, as one colonist wrote, "partly for the love he hath a long time borne" for the habit of smoking tobacco, and partly for the purpose of finding a profitable commodity for the investors back in London.[38] At this time, the English were spending around £200,000 per year on tobacco — although most of this came from Spain's colonies.[39] Rolfe's harvest proved popular, and by 1615 thirty-two of Jamestown's fifty inhabitants were farming tobacco.[40]

The prospects of Virginia were further boosted when Dale struck a peace deal with the aging Indian leader Wahunsonacock — an agreement sealed by the marriage of his favorite daughter, Pocahontas, to John Rolfe. During the Anglo-Powhatan War, the English had taken Pocahontas hostage. She was brought to Jamestown and subsequently transferred to Henrico, where she was instructed in the Christian religion and learned English. She established a relationship with Rolfe, who had lost his wife and daughter during his stay in the Bermuda Islands. For his part, Rolfe said he was moved not by "unbridled desire for carnal affection but for the good of this plantation, for the honor of our country, for the glory of God, and for my own salvation."[41]

In England, this was spectacular news—the first Christian convert among the Indians, the first Anglo-Indian marriage, and, within a year, the first Anglo-Indian child: a boy called Thomas. Thomas Smythe and the rest of the Virginia Company, always alert to marketing opportunities, invited Pocahontas, now known as Lady Rebecca Rolfe, to visit London. Arriving in June 1616 to a rapturous welcome, she led a delegation of about a dozen Powhatans. One of the Indians, Uttamatomakkin, a senior Powhatan counselor, had been given the task of preparing a report on the salient aspects of the country of England—especially the size of its population. To that end, he carried with him a long stick on which he was to cut a notch to represent each person he saw as he traveled through the country. Very quickly, however, as the chronicler Samuel Purchas reported, Uttamatomakkin lost count of all the people he saw and "his arithmetic soon failed."[42]

The Pocahontas visit was a remarkable collision of cultures—very different from any previous visit to England by an American or New World native. During her stay, Lady Rebecca sat for a portrait, commissioned by Smythe (who commissioned one of himself, too). She is dressed as a fashionable English lady, with a tall beaver-fur hat, lace ruff, pearl earrings, and a fan of ostrich feathers.

But if her visit began promisingly, it ended tragically. In March 1617, as she prepared to cross the Atlantic and return home, she fell ill and soon succumbed to a respiratory ailment that had gone undiagnosed and untreated. She was buried at Gravesend, on the south side of the Thames estuary. For Smythe and the Virginia Company, however, her visit brought long-lasting benefits. While in London, Rolfe met with tobacco merchants looking to sell Virginian "smoke" in England, mainland Europe, and the markets of the East Indies.[43]

Smythe, governor of the East India Company, seized on this opportunity, eventually sending out tobacco-trading voyages to the markets of the Far East. The people who lived on the Cape of Good Hope, where English sailors stopped to trade, soon came to recognize "Sir Thomas Smythe's English ships."[44]

IN 1616, THE year of Pocahontas's visit, some two thousand five hundred pounds of tobacco were imported from Virginia (and Bermuda). The following year, the imports jumped to 18,839 pounds. And it spiked up again the year after that—to 49,518 pounds.[45] But even with the success of the tobacco business, the Virginia Company's venture did not match the success of the East India Company's overseas trade. In the EIC's first twelve voyages, organized between 1601 and 1612, the profit ranged from 95 percent to 234 percent.[46] By contrast, in 1616, the Virginia Company failed to pay the cash dividend it had promised to its investors. But if the colony had not realized its hoped-for potential as a source of valuable commodities, the Virginia Company could still claim ownership of vast quantities of American land. And under Dale's leadership the colony had expanded, occupying and developing a substantial amount of the territory along the James River.

A survey carried out by Rolfe counted six settlements around Jamestown: on the coast was Dale's Gift, a fishing settlement with seventeen people; farther inland was Kecoughtan, with twenty people, mainly farmers; then came Jamestown itself, with fifty people, followed by West and Sherley Hundred, named for De La Warr and his father-in-law, Sir Thomas Sherley, with twenty-five people dedicated to tobacco farming; and then, up by the falls, lay Henrico, with thirty-eight people; and Bermuda Nether Hundred, the biggest settlement, with 119 people.[47]

With this expansion, it seemed as if the colony had turned a corner. Leaders of the Virginia Company concluded that "the chief brunt and doubt of the colony is now overpast."[48] Yet there was work to be done. Farm animals outnumbered people. Rolfe counted 216 goats,

144 cattle, six horses, a "great plenty" of poultry, and so many "wild and tame" hogs, supplied from Bermuda and London, that they were "not to be numbered." Yet there were only 351 colonists, including sixty-five women and children. Rolfe reported that this was "a small number to advance so great a work." Virginia was a "country spacious and wide, capable of [housing] many hundred thousand inhabitants." If only there were "good and sufficient men," it could be transformed into a "firm and perfect Common-weale."[49]

To seize this opportunity, Smythe embarked on a new plan, which he promoted with a pamphlet entitled *A Briefe Declaration of the present state of things in Virginia*. It described how the Virginia Company would distribute lands "in our actual possession" to private individuals and groups.[50] The idea was to build on the success of the decision to privatize part of the colonial estate. In 1614, several colonists who had arrived in 1607 as indentured servants for a seven-year stint had finally achieved their freedom. Some went back to England, but some stayed, and they were rewarded with small plots of land—in effect, becoming tenant farmers. Until then, the settlers had supposedly worked together for the common good. But, inevitably, there were slackers who managed to avoid doing their fair share of the work. "Glad was that man that could slip from his labour," noted one disgruntled observer.[51] Now these tenant farmers were able to enjoy the fruits of their own labor.

Under the terms of the deal they struck with Thomas Dale, they only had to work one month a year for the colony and contribute two and a half barrels of corn for the communal storehouse. The rest of the time, they could gain all the benefits of their own private plot of land. As a result, noted one senior colonist, the colony "thrived" because there was "plenty of food, which every man by his own industry may easily, & doth, procure."[52]

By the end of 1614, there were about eighty tenant farmers in Jamestown.[53] Two years on, Smythe and his associates could see a way of expanding this experimental initiative, thereby transforming

Virginia into a land of personal opportunity. In a new offer, they announced that an adventurer—whether a stay-at-home investor or a settler—would receive fifty acres for each share in their possession. To get this allocation, they had to register their names in a book held at Sir Thomas Smythe's house along Philpot Lane in London, and they had to pay twelve pounds and ten shillings—the cost of another share.[54]

Several investors came together to pool their landholding and create vast new private plantations known as "Hundreds"—the name long given to land divisions in England and derived from the fact that they could support a hundred soldiers. Leading the way, Smythe and a group of associates established the Society of Smith's Hundred. This joint-stock group came to control more than 80,000 acres on the north bank of the James River.

As these private plantations grew in popularity, the Virginia Company authorized a major expansion of the privatization reforms. In November 1618, George Yeardley, Jamestown's new governor, was issued with some special instructions.[55] Investors who had settled in Virginia or supported the colony before 1616—known as the "ancient adventurers and planters"—were to be given one hundred acres per share, while those who arrived or started supporting the colony after 1616 were to get fifty acres per share. And, significantly, the Virginia Company introduced what became known as the "headright" system, in which those who paid for themselves—or for others—to go to Virginia would receive fifty acres for each person or "head."[56]

The success of these private plantations required the recruitment of ever more indentured servants to farm the land and produce the commodities for sale back in England. Some were sent by poor families, eager to give their children a future. Others were condemned men, released from the prisons, with their sponsors rewarded by the Virginia Company. In 1617, a condemned man, Stephen Rogers, was saved from the gallows after Thomas Smythe personally requested his release "because he is of the Mystery of the Carpenters."[57]

But the instructions to Yeardley did more than simply inaugurate the headright system—they introduced the ground rules for what was, in effect, a new commonwealth. "We have thought good to bend our present cares and consultations," Smythe and his associates wrote, "to the settling there of a laudable form of government by majestracy and just laws for the happy guiding and governing of the people." Through a separate commission, Yeardley was authorized to establish the House of Burgesses, a representative assembly for handling local issues. It included members of a new council of state, selected by the leaders in London, and burgesses who were elected by "free" inhabitants in the various towns and hundreds of Jamestown.[58]

This remarkable document became known as the Great Charter, a deliberate reference to the medieval *Magna Carta,* the four-hundred-year-old document that provided the foundation for English individual rights. As one historian noted, this House of Burgesses was "the first freely elected parliament of a self-governing people in the Western World."[59] Introduced by Smythe and his fellow merchants, it was a logical extension of the process of privatization that transformed the colony into a patchwork of private property. In the space of twelve years, the leaders of the Virginia Company had turned what had originally been a royal colony, run by the King's Council, into a thriving private enterprise.

Smythe, however, did not oversee the introduction of the Great Charter. In April 1619, he was forced out of power by Sir Edwin Sandys, who masterminded a corporate coup, seized control of the company, and became its treasurer. With his associates, Sandys, who had been acting as Smythe's assistant, accused Smythe of mismanagement. The fact was that Virginia was becoming valuable property. Tobacco and land had become the prized commodities.

At long last, English merchants had founded a colony they thought was worth fighting for.

19

⟫⊙⟪

A WEIGHTY VOYAGE

NEWS OF THE Virginia Company's search for colonists for private plantations spread far and wide. Eventually it reached a group almost
completely unconnected to the network of merchants and courtiers,
dreamers and mythologizers who had been working towards America for nearly seven decades.

In the fall of 1617, two Englishmen, Robert Cushman and John Carver,
left the Dutch coastal city of Leiden, a university town and important
hub of textile manufacture, to travel across the English Channel to London. Cushman, a wool comber about forty years old, and Carver, a
merchant aged about thirty, were acting on behalf of a group of reform-
ist English Protestants — so-called religious "separatists" — who had
been living, working, and worshipping as a congregation in Holland
for nearly a decade. In due course, they would come to be known as
Pilgrims — the name the most celebrated of the congregants, William Bradford, first gave them in his book *Of Plymouth Plantation*.[1]

The two men, both deacons of the Church of Leiden, as the
separatist group was sometimes called, had been dispatched on a

critical mission: to approach the Virginia Company of London to seek a patent that would allow the congregation to establish a plantation within the company's jurisdiction in America. It represented a big step for the religious group. To bolster their case, the two men carried with them a document called *Seven Articles which the Church of Leyden sent to the Councill of England to be considered of in respect of their judgments occasioned about their going to Virginia Anno 1618.* This document asserted the Leiden Church's "spiritual communion" with all members of the Church of England and acknowledged King James as "supreme governor."[2] It was signed by the congregation's leaders, two Cambridge men who would have commanded respect among the members of the King's Council: John Robinson, the revered pastor of the group, who had begun his career in the established church as deputy to the minister at St. Andrew's Church in Norwich;[3] and William Brewster, the elder of the separatists' congregation, who had served in Elizabeth's court in the 1580s, working on the staff of Sir William Davison, one of her secretaries of state.

Carver and Cushman felt compelled to carry the *Seven Articles* because the loyalty of the Leiden group to the crown was far from obvious. It was in 1606, when religious tensions were running high in England, that leading members of the separatist congregation had first come together in the village of Scrooby in Nottinghamshire.* Like Puritans, another group of radical Protestants, the separatists wanted to purge the Anglican Church of Catholic elements — especially the powerful bishops who, they believed, indulged in sexual licentiousness and looted the riches of the church for their own ostentatious living. But whereas the Puritans sought reforms from within the existing church, the Separatists concluded that they had no choice but to detach themselves completely from the corrupt church.

---

* Bradford says they had been together "about a year" before making their first attempt to leave England in 1607.

The Scrooby congregation renounced the church hierarchy and began worshipping privately, separately, and in secret. Such clandestine meetings, or conventicles, were illegal. The archbishop of Canterbury waged a campaign of persecution against separatist groups, imposing harsh penalties on anyone over the age of sixteen who deliberately and defiantly refused to attend an authorized church: a three-month prison sentence in the first instance; banishment from the realm for those who continued to resist; execution for those who left the country and returned without royal permission.[4]

William Bradford was just sixteen when he joined the group in Scrooby. By then, he was deeply devout and committed in his rejection of the Anglican Church. Born to a local family of tenant farmers, he was orphaned at the age of one and later suffered a grave illness that left him bedridden and housebound. According to his celebrated biographer Cotton Mather, the Puritan minister, it was this experience that probably accounted for his early and deep devotion to his religion and his willingness to cast his lot with the separatists. Through sickness, he avoided being caught up in "the vanities of youth," Mather wrote, which "made him the fitter for what he would afterwards undergo." When he was about a "Dozen Years Old," Bradford began to read scripture, and this made "great impressions upon him."[5]

According to Bradford's own account, written many years later, the Scrooby congregation was tormented, "hunted and persecuted on every side." Some of their members were "clapped into prison, and others had their houses beset and watched night and day." That is why a number of the Scrooby people at last agreed, "by joint consent," to leave Scrooby, flee England, and "go into the Low Countries."[6]

There was a precedent for their move. In the 1550s, of course, many notable Protestants became exiles during Queen Mary's reign—notably Sir Francis Walsingham. But they were not separatists. The earliest champion of separatism was Robert Browne, a member of a well-to-do family and yet another Cambridge alumnus. In 1582, he led a group of followers out of England, crossed the Channel, and settled in the Dutch city of Middelburg, south of Leiden. His adherents were often referred to as Brownists—and, over time, that epithet came to be applied in a general way to other radical Protestants.

In 1608, following Browne's example, the Scrooby separatists left everything and, risking their lives, departed England in the dead of night and sailed to Amsterdam, finally settling in Leiden. There, they were able to establish themselves, form a community, work, and hold their religious meetings in peace and without harassment. Now, in 1617, nine years later, the Leiden separatists contemplated another, even more dramatic, move in seeking permission from the Virginia Company to establish a settlement somewhere in America.

It was not that they faced religious persecution in Holland. On the contrary, the Dutch province was famed for its religious tolerance. One visitor to Amsterdam declared that, on the street where he was staying, he counted as many religions as there were houses, and "one neighbor knows not, nor cares not much, what Religion the other is."[7] For the Leiden group, the pressing problem was economic. They were simply unable to make a decent living. Although most of them had been farmers in England, they had to turn their hand to cloth manufacture, since Leiden was a clothmaking city. The eighty-six members of the English separatist community followed fifty-seven different occupations, most of them associated in some way with the weaving and making of cloth. Bradford apprenticed with a French maker of silk before setting up his own operation as a producer of fustian.[8]

With economic hardship came other problems. With no lands, estates, offices, or inheritances to pass to the next generation, many of the separatists were seeing their older children abandon their religious way of life and fall into dissolute behavior. Meanwhile, some of the younger children—those born in Holland—were taking up the habits of the Dutch, having grown up knowing nothing of England.

And there was one other concern: the prospect of war. Back in 1609, Spain and the Low Countries had signed a twelve-year truce, which brought peace to this corner of Europe. But with the truce set to end in 1621, the members of the Leiden group were anxious to find another home, another place where they could pursue their worship of God in peace.

As all of these concerns started to coalesce, the leaders of the Leiden Church began to consider the idea of a colony in the New World. They, better than most, knew it would not be easy. As Bradford wrote, it had been hard enough for them to adjust to Holland, which was a "neighbor country" to England and a "civil and rich commonwealth." Making a go of it in the New World would be almost unknowably more difficult. They knew of the famous failures, the "precedents of ill success and lamentable miseries."[9] Nevertheless, the Leiden group turned their minds to "those vast and unpeopled countries of America."[10] For all its risks, there really seemed no other place to go.

THE SEVEN ARTICLES that Cushman and Carter presented to the Virginia Company may have had some positive effect. In the end, however, it was personal contacts that unlocked the door to the Virginia Company. Although they were exiles from England, the Leiden group still had important connections in England. William Brewster had a link with Sir Edwin Sandys, one of the leaders of the Virginia Company. Edwin's brother, Samuel Sandys, held the lease to the great manor house of Scrooby, where Brewster's father had been bailiff (rent collector) and where the separatists had held their early conventicles. Thanks to this connection, Cushman and Carver were able to engage with the Virginia Company and put their case to the Privy Council.

During the negotiations, the leaders of the Virginia Company declared that they were "very desirous" for the Leiden group to "go thither" to America. Indeed, they were "willing to grant them a patent" and give them the "best furtherance they could."[11] It was a big vote of confidence for the Leiden group.

Cushman and Carver returned to the Dutch city with the encouraging news. But then no sooner had the separatists celebrated than a letter was sent with news from the Privy Council, forwarded to them by Sir John Wolstenholme, one of the leaders of the Virginia Company, and a principal investor in one of Jamestown's privately run plantations—Martin's Hundred and its central conurbation, Wolstenholme Town.[12]

The letter reiterated that the Virginia Company would do its best to forward the separatists' enterprise but requested further details about the group and their plans. Robinson and Brewster swiftly responded and made the case for their commitment and capabilities. "We are well weaned from the delicate milk of our mother country," they wrote, "and inured to the difficulties of a strange and hard land, which yet in a great part we have by patience overcome." The Leiden group, they said, was "knit together as a body" and were not like other people "whom small things can discourage, or small discontentments cause to wish themselves at home again." In short, they were not likely to follow in the footsteps of colonists in Roanoke, Sagadahoc, and Jamestown. They would not quarrel among themselves, become factionalized, or abandon the settlement when the going got tough.[13]

But the Leiden group needed more than the go-ahead from the Virginia Company—they also needed to seek the king's approval and secure from him the right to practice religion as they saw fit in America. The delicate assignment of sounding out James on this matter fell to Sir Robert Naunton, a royal official who was then in the running to be named, at age fifty, Secretary of State. Naunton had a fair amount of experience beyond England, having served in various roles in Scotland, France, and Denmark. He was known for his anti-Catholic, pro-Protestant views, and had little love for either Spain or France. He had endured a number of ups and downs in his life, including the loss of his family inheritance, and given this experience and his closeness to the king, it seemed that he might have some empathy with the separatists' situation.[14] In his presentation to the king, Naunton appears to have focused on the commercial impulse behind the venture, because James asked about the group's plans for achieving a profit. Naunton replied that the goal was to generate revenue through fishing and James remarked approvingly that this was "an honest trade" and "the apostle's own calling."[15] In the end, the king gave his blessing to the patent but he refused to issue a formal decree granting the Leiden group religious freedom in America. Even so, he assured Naunton that he would not "molest" them so long as they "carried themselves peaceably."[16]

Just as it seemed that the way had been cleared, the group encountered one more delay, caused, according to Robert Cushman, by "dissensions and factions" within the Virginia Company. This was the time when Edwin Sandys seized control of the company, forcing Sir Thomas Smythe to step aside.[17] It took several weeks for the Virginia Company to sort out its governance problems, "but at last," Bradford wrote, "after all these things and their long attendance," the long-awaited patent was granted to the Leiden group "and confirmed under the Company's seal."[18]

No copy of the patent survives, so we do not know all the details, but it was probably for land somewhere between the Delaware and Hudson rivers—although the exact location was not specified.[19] The settlers were expected to travel to Jamestown and, once there, discuss possible locations for their settlement.[20]

The patent was sealed on June 9, 1619, almost two years after the Leiden group had first approached the Virginia Company. The process had taken so long and been so tedious that many members of the Leiden group had given up and dropped out, frustrated by all the delays.

IF, AT LAST, the Leiden group had their patent, they still needed something else: capital. As they soon learned, the Virginia Company's promise of "furtherance" would not take the form of money. It could allocate land—but not ready resources. For this, the separatists would have to look elsewhere. As it turned out, there was no shortage of suitors. These included the New Netherland Company, which was planning a colony around the Hudson River. Its representatives approached the Leiden congregation with an attractive offer. The Company would supply free transport to America, an allotment of cattle, and grants of land at New Amsterdam. The settlers would, of course, also have total religious freedom.

Too often, the people who signed up to be settlers were unsuited to the life they would have to lead: aristocrats who sought excitement and adventure; soldiers with no interest in farming or homebuilding; business people who expected immediate profits; and, of course, men who found it difficult to live without women. What was needed were solid, hardworking people with practical skills, leaders who were willing to learn and share responsibility, people with a long-term commitment to make the settlement work. The Leiden separatists offered all of these qualities. They had already demonstrated their ability to live and work together as a self-contained community.

After discussing various options, the Leiden group eventually entered into negotiations with Thomas Weston, a young English merchant, who had a business connection to them. Although he was a member of the Worshipful Company of Ironmongers—one of the Great Twelve livery companies—Weston was not among the first rank of merchants. He was not rich enough to join the Merchant Adventurers, which had the exclusive right of trading of unfinished cloth to the Netherlands. The only way he could trade cloth was by paying a royalty to the Merchant Adventurers.[21] This was an unreliable source of income, however. It meant that he was always subject to the whims of the Merchant Adventurers and the vicissitudes of the market. Down on his luck, he turned his focus to the business prospects in America. Like many other business people, he had heard the news coming from Virginia about land and tobacco.

Weston had a persuasive style. According to Bradford, he had "much conference" with the Leiden leaders and assured them that he could help them. He promised to reach out to his merchant friends, raise capital, and organize everything. They would have to agree on the business terms, of course.[22]

The Leiden leaders chose to work with Weston and while they began drafting an agreement, he returned to England to begin the process of raising funds. He attracted some seventy investors, including gentlemen, merchants, and "handy craftsmen." Some contributed hefty sums and others invested modestly. The total, according to John Smith, came to seven thousand pounds, although there is no record of the actual amount and others put the figure at less than two thousand pounds.[23] If Smith's figure is correct, it is a remarkably large one. Most of the investors were Londoners, few of them separatists, and none seem to have invested in other New World ventures.[24] Clearly, the English business community was in a speculative mood and willing to take a risk on a venture with very uncertain commercial prospects.

Weston does not seem to have taken much care in the way he organized the enterprise.[25] He and his fellow investors had no long-range goals, beyond this single voyage, and they did not create a set of instructions or ordinances, as had become typical. Nor did they set aside capital for any resupply missions. Indeed, they seem to have thought the colony would be fully functioning and ready to ship saleable commodities back to England by the first return ship—a completely unrealistic expectation.

It was around this time that news filtered back from Weston that the Virginia Company had issued a second, revised patent to John Peirce, an associate of Weston's. The new patent, dated February 2, 1620, was issued on the same day that the Virginia Company passed an ordinance defining a "particular" or private plantation and providing greater autonomy to the patent holder.[26]

The Virginia Company's decision to liberalize the terms of its patents reflected the reality of the high cost of settlement. After seven decades of overseas enterprise, it had become clear that the cost-per-mariner of a trading voyage was far less than the cost-per-settler of a colonization venture. Plus, an investor was likely to realize a return more quickly and reliably on a trading voyage—even one that took two or three years—than on the trade generated by a colony. If the

Virginia Company was going to derive significant profits from licensing or franchising land rights, it needed to make the process of investing in plantations as attractive as possible.

For the Leiden group, the new patent was far preferable, since they would be free to "make orders, ordinances and constitutions" for their settlements and to draw commercial benefit from their industry on the land and from trade with Indians.[27] They accepted Weston's recommendation to operate under the new patent.

IN MARCH 1620, while the Leiden group was making final preparations for the voyage to Virginia, a new entity emerged from the reorganization of the Virginia Company. As Bradford wrote, a number of "Honourable Lords" split off from the company and obtained a large grant of land from the king "for the more northerly parts" of America. One of the lords was Sir Ferdinando Gorges, and the new group was essentially a reconfiguration of the Plymouth Company, which had long lain dormant after the failure of the Popham Colony. It would have jurisdiction over the region of America that lay between the 40th and 48th parallels, north of the Virginia Company's territory, and extended all the way from the Atlantic to the Pacific.[28] This was the land that Captain John Smith had first identified as promising territory.

After his departure from Jamestown in 1609, Smith had established himself as one of the leading advocates of England's fledgling colonies in Virginia. But if Smith hoped this would win him passage back into the favor of the Virginia Company's leaders, he was mistaken. By 1614, it was clear to him that they would not be sending him back to Jamestown, and so he set his sights on north Virginia, which had been largely ignored since Raleigh Gilbert and his fellow Popham colonists sailed away from Sagadahoc, leaving Fort St. George to crumble into the ground. He managed to raise enough money from London investors to fund a two-ship venture to the region of present-day Maine.[29] Arriving in late April of 1614, Smith and his crew of eighteen men set about fishing and fur-trading. They caught nearly 60,000 fish. While the mariners hauled in their catch, Smith went ashore with eight others and accumulated 11,000 skins, predominantly beaver, through trade with Indians. All the while, Smith observed, measured, wrote, and mapped the territory, just as he had in Virginia. And when the fishing and fur trading was done, he sailed one of the ships for England laden with a cargo he valued at fifteen hundred pounds.[30]

Back in England, Smith took the opportunity to meet with Sir Ferdinando Gorges, who had lost none of his enthusiasm for American ventures. Together, Smith and Gorges, with the support of a few of Smith's friends and earlier supporters, developed a plan for a colony that would be sustained by the catching and processing of fish.[31] In March 1615, Smith set sail once again with great hopes. These were soon dashed, however, when he was captured by French pirates and held hostage for three months on board a warship, only winning his freedom after effecting a daring escape. But if he did not establish a colony, he did manage to leave his mark on the land. In a book he wrote while in captivity, *A Description of New England,* he gave a memorable name to the region variously known as North Virginia and Norumbega. As the title makes clear, he christened the area "New England."

Smith's inspiration was Drake's Nova Albion, on the far side of the continent. As he explained: "New England is that part of America in the Ocean Sea opposite to Nova Albion in the South Sea; discovered by the most memorable Sir Francis Drake in his voyage about the world. In regard whereto this is styled New England, being in the same latitude."[32]

In his descriptions, Smith took issue with the old view, which had taken root in the wake of the failed Popham Colony, that New England was not suited to the English. Rather he suggested that the region was like home in many ways, and even better. Above all, he made an impassioned argument for its commercial promise.

As well as his resonant prose, Smith created a remarkable map of

New England that arguably surpassed his efforts with Virginia. Produced by Simon van de Passe, who completed the portraits of Pocahontas and Sir Thomas Smythe, the map carries a portrait of Smith himself along with a self-aggrandizing legend: "Admiral of New England." Beautifully groomed and confident, Smith gazes upon a bucolic landscape dotted with pleasant trees, hills, and tidy dwellings. No Indians appear, and the only wild beast looks more like a housecat than a leopard. The map is crisscrossed with loxodromes, webs of lines that seem to reduce the vastness of the ocean and connect America with England. This is a country tamed and ready for colonization.

Smith had hoped to use this marvelous book to promote his own venture. But when that failed, he approached the Leiden group, offering his services as an adviser and guide. It was his last hope of returning to the New World. But despite his vast knowledge and expertise, the separatists said "thanks, but no thanks."

They explained that it would be cheaper to buy his book than to hire him. Smith later scoffed at their "humourous ignorances" which subsequently caused them a "wonderful deal of misery" and could have been avoided if they had simply consulted with him instead of "saying my books and maps were much better cheap to teach them, than myself."[33]

BUT IF THE Leiden group said no to Smith, they said yes to a new proposal from Thomas Weston. Until the creation of the Council of New England, as the new group led by Gorges was called, they were all set on a private plantation in Virginia. But Weston sniffed a good business opportunity in this newly named area. For a start, the region, as detailed by Smith, was appealing to him, largely because "of [the] present profit to be made by the fishing that was found in that country." Also, it seems, Weston believed that the new council would offer less scrutiny of his activities. He therefore urged the Leiden group that "it was best for them to go" to New England, rather than to Jamestown as they had originally planned.[34]

As they reflected on this new opportunity, the Leiden group considered the pros and cons. On the negative side, they would not have easy access to an established community of English people who knew the ways of the place. On the positive side, however, they would not face any of the religious restrictions that the Jamestown governors might choose to enforce on them.[35]

Eventually, they reached a consensus. "The generality was swayed" towards New England, wrote Bradford, even though they did not yet have permission from the Council for New England.[36] Weston assured them he would take care of this technicality and would be able to secure the patent for them.*

As the days of summer passed in 1620, Cushman and Carver negotiated their final deal with Weston. The contract called for joint ownership of the colony for seven years. All profits would go into a common fund, from which the settlers' expenses would be paid. At the end of the seven-year period, the profits would be divided based on the number of shares held. One share cost ten pounds, purchasable with cash or provisions. Every settler over sixteen years of age received one share for the payout.[37]

Everything was agreed. Then, at the last minute, in a brazen act of brinkmanship, Weston inserted two modifications to the contract that significantly changed the nature of the settlers' commitment. First, land and houses would be included in the calculation of profit. This removed a key incentive for the settlers, who had expected to have full ownership of the homes they would build and lands they would cultivate. Second, the settlers would be required to work for the company seven days a week—not five days, as they had originally agreed—until the day they finally paid off their debt.

This caused an uproar. Some of the Leiden group threatened to withdraw if the terms were accepted, while one of Weston's major

---

* Weston did not secure the patent, known as the second Peirce Patent, until November 3, 1620, after the *Mayflower* had sailed.

investors threatened to back out if the new terms were not approved.[38] Cushman and Carver accepted the modifications, contending that it was the best deal they could get—and eventually it was signed. But several of the separatists who had agreed to go dropped out, and the final contingent of "saints"—as Bradford called them—now numbered just forty-six. To make up a reasonable community for a colony, they had to recruit many people whom they called "strangers" because they had no connection to the group. Some, like Stephen Hopkins, who had survived the Bermuda tempest and lived for a while in Jamestown, were devout Protestants, travelling with their families. Many others, however, did not necessarily have sympathy with the Leiden group's religious goals.

Finally, on September 6, 1620—seven weeks after the planned sailing date—the *Mayflower*, a "sweet" merchant ship previously used to transport wine—at last departed on what William Bradford memorialized as its "waighty voyage" for America.[39] Two months later, on November 11, 1620, the ship was brought to anchor in what is today known as Provincetown harbor.[40]

The Pilgrims settled at Plymouth under the challenging terms set by Weston and his associates. Weston himself sold his stake in the American enterprise after just a year, later serving as a member of Jamestown's House of Burgesses and embarking on a series of other ventures with various degrees of success.[41] After five years, the Pilgrims renegotiated their debt with a smaller group of the original investors, but it still proved so onerous that they did not pay it off completely until 1648.* By then, the Massachusetts Bay Colony, and its capital city of Boston, completely overshadowed the little community of Plymouth as the center of activity in New England. Eventually, in 1691, these two colonies—along with the Province of Maine, the islands of Martha's Vineyard and Nantucket, and (the

---

* The debt was further renegotiated in 1628, when a still smaller group of investors agreed to continue supporting the Pilgrims. Also, some of the separatists, including William Bradford, increased their stake.

now-Canadian provinces of) Nova Scotia and New Brunswick—merged to form the Province of Massachusetts Bay.

Although the Pilgrims survived, the colony was never particularly prosperous or profitable. What's more, Bradford felt that the community had failed in its original purpose. The Pilgrims had planned a kind of socialist endeavor, where land would be communally owned and everyone would contribute their efforts to be shared among all. They had tried hard to make a go of this "common course," as Bradford called it, hoping to prove the conceit, put forward by Plato and "other ancients," that "the taking away of property" and "bringing in community into commonwealth" would "make them happy and flourishing; as if they were wiser than God."

But instead, the plan had bred "confusion and discontent": young, unmarried men did not want to labor, without recompense, for other men and their families; the stronger and fitter men felt they should get a greater share of the benefits; the "aged and graver" men felt disrespected by being "equalized" with everyone else; and women, who had been pressed into doing chores for the whole of the community, saw their lives as "a kind of slavery."

By 1623, the experiment proved unworkable; the corn harvest was meager and they did not wish to "languish in misery" any longer. Bradford and his fellow leaders debated how they could improve the yield of their harvests. They settled on a program of private ownership and each family was assigned their own parcel of land. This approach "had good success, for it made all hands very industrious."

Bradford did not lament what he called the "corruption" of his fellow settlers, by which he meant their desire to work for their own benefit, because "all men have this corruption in them." He concluded that "God in His wisdom saw another course fitter for them."[42]

That course could well be called the American Dream.

Forgotten Founders

Today, if you look closely at a map of the world, you will find faint cartographical traces of the largely forgotten story we have told of America's pre-Pilgrim beginnings.

In northern Canada, if you zoom all the way in, you will come upon an inlet called Frobisher Bay, a body of water called the Countess of Warwick Sound, and a dot of an island called Loks Land. They remind us of the headstrong Martin Frobisher; of Anne Dudley, the wife of Frobisher's aristocratic patron; and of Michael Lok, the financial backer Frobisher unintentionally bankrupted.*

A thousand miles or so to the south, you will arrive at Popham Beach, named for Sir John Popham, originator of what could have been—had bad weather and family fortunes not intervened—the first permanent English settlement in America.

Farther south, more than six hundred miles from the coast of the

---

* Another island was named after the Countess of Warwick, but its name was later changed to Kodlunarn Island, as the native Inuit call it, and is so known today. The word "Kodlunarn" means "white man's island": Helen Wallis, "England's Search for the Northern Passages in the Sixteenth and Early Seventeenth Centuries," *Arctic*, 37, no. 4 (1984): 453–72; 464.

Carolinas, you'll spot Smith's Island, a member of the Bermuda chain, christened for Sir Thomas Smythe, the most renowned (and sometimes reviled) English businessman of his day.

And a hundred miles inland you'll locate Raleigh, the capital of North Carolina, which owes its name to the famous courtier who was just as much an entrepreneur as he was an entrancer of the English queen Elizabeth I.

Apart from Sir Walter, these names—while still there in small-font map labels—have been largely deleted from the popular history of America's beginning. Far more familiar is the name adopted by the group that so famously established the English settlement that did endure in New England, the Pilgrims, and the town they founded, Plymouth, Massachusetts.

But it was not always so. In fact, the Pilgrims did not play such a central role in the American founding narrative until some two hundred years after the first thanksgiving, when the Pilgrims who had survived the first year chose to "rejoice together," drawing on the "great store of wild turkeys" and five deer brought by the Indians, who were invited to join the great feast.[1] Only then, in the early years of the nineteenth century, was their story taken up, dusted off, and retold as America's quintessential creational myth, a fable of moral rectitude and national goodness. The commercial aspects were downplayed or suppressed and, as a result, this key aspect of the country's national character was largely erased from the picture, just as Elizabeth I had tried to scratch out the symbol of Spain from the map of England.

One of the first to champion the Pilgrims as ideal Americans was Daniel Webster, a once-revered but now largely forgotten American statesman. On December 22, 1820, he delivered an address on Forefathers' Day in Plymouth, Massachusetts, an event that had been established in 1769 to commemorate the *Mayflower* landing there. (Plymouth still celebrates the occasion.) Webster, renowned as an orator, proclaimed the importance of the Pilgrims' achievement. We stand "on the spot where the first scene of our history was laid," he declared, the place where the Pilgrims had endured "sufferings" and gone through great "labors." Driven by their "principles of civil and religious liberty," Webster boomed, they had overcome hardships and lived "under a condition of comparative equality."[2]

Webster invoked this history, not out of academic interest, but in service to a greater cause and much more immediate purpose. Now, Webster warned, the Pilgrims' heroic achievement was being undermined by a deeply divisive social institution that entrenched inequality and threatened to rip apart the United States: slavery. He attacked the "Christian states" — referring to the southern states, including Virginia, home of the original Jamestown Colony, where the practice of slavery showed that they felt "no sentiments of humanity or of justice." Webster exhorted the people of New England, as inheritors of Pilgrim values, to "extirpate and destroy" the slave trade. "It is not fit," he concluded, "that *the land of the Pilgrims* should bear the shame" of slavery any longer.

Webster's address marked the beginning of the so-called "Pilgrim Century," during which the Pilgrim narrative was established as the founding story of America.[3] It was just a few years later, in 1831, that Americans adopted the song "America" — known to schoolchildren as "My Country 'Tis of Thee" — as the unofficial, de facto anthem, for the nation:

> My country, 'tis of Thee —
> Sweet Land of Liberty —
> Of thee I sing;
> Land where my fathers died,
> *Land of the pilgrims' pride,*
> From every mountain side
> Let Freedom ring.

Many Americans (and many Britons, too) may not realize that this song of a proudly independent nation was set to the tune of "God Save the King," the national anthem of England, which had already abolished the slave trade.* Nor may many Americans realize that the lyrics imply a preference for the Pilgrims over the Puritans, who in 1628 founded the ultimately far stronger and more successful Massachusetts Bay Colony. This preference reflected the perspective of nineteenth-century northerners—the New Hampshire–born Webster was one of them—who were dominant in the wake of the North's crushing victory over the South in the Civil War that split the country apart between 1861 and 1865. They saw themselves in the Pilgrim tradition and disdained what they saw as the corruption and tolerance of the Puritan leadership.[4] Although the Pilgrims advocated the radical step of complete separation from the established church—a step too far for Puritans—they were seen as more socially moderate and mainstream: a modest citizenry who valued hard work, tolerated diversity, formed democratic institutions, and devoted themselves to family and community.

This view of the Pilgrims got a significant endorsement from a notable foreign observer, Alexis de Tocqueville, a French aristocrat who famously toured America in 1831. He passionately glorified—but in many ways completely misrepresented—the founding story. "The foundation of New England presented a novel spectacle," he wrote in *Democracy in America,* published in 1835. "Everything about it was singular and original." He characterized the Jamestown Colony as based on the "disastrous idea" that "gold and silver mines constitute the wealth of nations" and dismissed its founders as "gold-seekers" who were driven by "no noble thought."

The Pilgrims, he continued, must be praised for their soaring ideals. "What distinguished them most of all from other colonizers was the very purpose of their enterprise," he wrote. "It was by no means necessity that forced them to leave their native land. They left behind enviable social positions and secure incomes. They did not travel to

---

* The Slave Trade Act of 1807 abolished the slave trade in the British empire. Slavery itself was not abolished until 1833.

the New World in the hope of improving their situation or enhancing their wealth. They tore themselves away from the pleasures of home in obedience to a purely intellectual need. They braved the inevitable miseries of exile because they wished to ensure the victory of an idea."[5]

But de Tocqueville can be forgiven for misstating the Pilgrims' motives. This is because he did not have access to William Bradford's seminal account of the Plymouth plantation. In *Of Plymouth Plantation,* Bradford explained his people's purpose very simply. Jobs were the key concern, the number one reason on the Pilgrims' list of four motives for going to America. Bradford does not mention the pursuit of religious freedom, which the Pilgrims already enjoyed in Holland; and advancing the gospel by converting natives came last, at number four. Indeed, Bradford does not even talk about the driving force of an ideal. The Pilgrims left the Old World, he wrote, "not out of new-fangledness or other such like giddy humor," but for "weighty and solid reasons."[6]

Bradford's account, probably completed around 1650, only came to light twenty years after de Tocqueville exalted the America story. The manuscript had disappeared from a private collection in Boston in the 1760s and then, like the Pilgrims themselves, had been largely forgotten. The work, handwritten by Bradford on vellum, a fine parchment made of goat skin, had been tucked away in the library of Lambeth Palace, the official home of the bishop of London, whose diocese had once, rather bizarrely, encompassed the American colonies. Charles Deane, editor of publications for The Massachusetts Historical Society, first learned that the original manuscript might be there in February 1855. Excited, he sent a note by the first available steamer to the Reverend Joseph Hunter, a vice-president of the Society of Antiquaries of London, requesting that he look into the matter. By the middle of March, Hunter informed Deane that "There is not the slightest doubt that the manuscript is Governor Bradford's own autograph." He had a longhand copy made and this arrived in Deane's hands at the beginning of August. By April of the following year, Deane had completed his editorial work and the typeset version was privately published by The Massachusetts Historical Society, dated 1856.* That same year, Little, Brown released the first commercial edition to great acclaim.

Since then, *Of Plymouth Plantation* has been hailed as the greatest written work of the early American period.[7] In 1952, the *New York Times* reviewer of the standard modern edition lauded Bradford's work, calling it "by common consent not only a historical document of the first importance but the first 'classic' in our literature" and claiming that its "finest pages belong with the best of English or American writing of the period."[8]

Bradford's book inspired new, more popular versions of the tale. In 1858, Henry Wadsworth Longfellow, the most adulated American poet of the day, came out with *The Courtship of Miles Standish*. The long, romantic poem celebrated the Pilgrims' military leader and painted the Pilgrims in broad, pious strokes. He glorified the legend of Plymouth Rock which had been "a door-step into a world unknown" for the Pilgrims and, furthermore, served as "the corner-stone of a nation!" Longfellow celebrated the Pilgrims' fellowship with one another and praised their perseverance in pursuing an idyllic, idealistic cause in the harsh environment of the wilderness.

But Longfellow, like Webster, had more on his mind than courtship and legend-making. Although he avoided outright political pros-elytizing in his poem, antislavery sentiments reminiscent of Webster's murmured through the poem's subtext: that morality and civility were attributes of the North, the home of the Pilgrims. He described

---

* The complete, fascinating story of the discovery and initial publication of the Bradford manuscript is related by Charles Deane in his "Editorial Preface" to the 1856 edition of the typeset narrative issued by The Massachusetts Historical Society. The manuscript itself was returned to the United States in 1897 and taken into the care of the State Library of Massachusetts, where it still resides. Charles Deane, ed., *History of Plymouth Plantation by William Bradford* (Boston: The Massachusetts Historical Society, 1856), iii–xix.

the original settlers as impossibly virtuous: "patient, courageous, and strong," "modest and simple and sweet," "tender and trusting," "great of heart," "noble and generous," and "austere and grave." Only such people, northerners, could and should represent the common cause of idealism and liberty that the divided nation required, not the slave-holders of the South.[9]

Longfellow's poem ignited a fire of Pilgrim admiration in the national imagination. It became an overnight sensation, selling 25,000 copies in the United States in just two weeks and 10,000 copies on publication day in London.[10] But even as the Pilgrim narrative was being invoked in the antislavery crusade, it was freighted with yet another task: to serve as the model for that bedrock of American life, the family and household. That meant, in particular, the white, Anglo-Saxon household of New England, which, at that time, seemed under siege by industrialization, urbanization, and immigration— with concomitant waves of German and Irish immigrants flooding into the burgeoning northern cities of Boston, New York, and Phila-delphia. It raised several questions: What was America now? What did it stand for? Above all, who was an American? What had hap-pened to the founding values?

All the orations, histories, ballads, and anthems seeded the idea that the Pilgrims were the true American originals, and then a national holiday rooted it even more deeply in the national conscious-ness. The first feast of thanksgiving took place in 1621, after the Pil-grims survived the first harsh winter. They celebrated again in 1623, and it was then that they referred to the event as Thanksgiving. For the next two centuries, the holiday was re-created in various ways, at various times and various places, largely in New England.[11] Then, in 1817, New York declared a day for observance of Thanksgiving and made it an official state holiday in 1830—the first state outside New England to do so.[12]

Other states gradually followed suit. By midcentury, a country-wide campaign for Thanksgiving gathered momentum, spearheaded by Sarah Josepha Hale, who is best known as the creator of the nursery rhyme "Mary Had a Little Lamb."[13] In 1846, as editor of *Godey's*, a popular periodical of the time, she inaugurated an annual editorial to promote the virtue of the "Great American Festival" of Thanksgiving.[14] Such a holiday, Hale contended, could unite the nation and, ideally, prevent the outbreak of the civil war that was then brewing.

Thanksgiving, as described by Hale and others, provided a way to celebrate the cherished American traditions of everyday life. It could bring together disparate groups, including those of different religions, as well as city dwellers and country folk, under an umbrella of shared nationhood. Thanksgiving helped remind everyone of the Pilgrims' ideal and affirm the belief that God blessed America.[15]

In 1854, at the height of the Thanksgiving Day campaign and as the dark days of the Civil War approached, another foreign voice spoke up in favor of the Pilgrim cause. Joseph Hunter, the English antiquarian who would later confirm the authenticity of Bradford's manuscript, made a grand pronouncement: "It was the working of a few private men of an overstrained spirit of opposition to the established order of ecclesiastical affairs in Protestant England," he wrote, "which led to the colonization of New England, and, in the event, to the establishment of the United States of America as one of the great communities of the civilized world."[16]

By 1859, thirty states, including twelve in the South, had climbed aboard the Thanksgiving bandwagon—perhaps with a boost from the publication of Bradford's work and the attention it received. But the holiday could not achieve what Hale desired: to bring Americans together. In April 1861, the country descended into civil war, as Confederate forces, representing the southern states that had declared secession, fired on the Union troops representing the northern states, at Fort Sumter in Charleston. Two years later, in October of 1863, three months after the Union army rebuffed the forces of the Confederacy at Gettysburg in the conflict's bloodiest battle, President Abraham

Lincoln delivered a proclamation that reflected on the year gone by. Despite the horror of war, he said, the year had been "filled with the blessings of fruitful fields and healthful skies." Even the war's drain on the "wealth and strength" of the nation had "not arrested the plow, the shuttle, or the ship." To celebrate the good among so much bad, Lincoln invited "the whole American people" to observe, on the last Thursday of November, "a day of thanksgiving."[17]

From that year onwards, Americans faithfully observed this national holiday and the Pilgrim heritage associated with it. The Plymouth history became part of the elementary school curriculum. Textbooks examined the nascent democracy manifested in the Mayflower Compact, the brief document that laid out the governance principles the Pilgrims agreed to follow to establish a "civil body politic."[18] Children learned that all Americans were immigrants or descendants of them. Thanksgiving became the holiday of the home, a nonreligious family gathering in which all could participate, and during which, as one observer put it, "the deepest feelings of patriotism were conveyed."[19]

NOT EVERYONE, THOUGH, worshipped at the altar of the Pilgrim story or the Thanksgiving Day commemoration. Into the 1880s, the Catholic Church opposed Thanksgiving as "a Protestant rite." Many Southerners considered it a "Yankee day."[20] One of New England's beloved sons, the great intellectual Henry David Thoreau, sought in the Pilgrims the ancestral roots of his own naturalism, transcendentalism, and asceticism—but he was disappointed and disheartened that their ideals were so often "disregarded in moments of commercial greed."[21] Native Americans objected to the very underpinnings of the Pilgrim narrative, such as the characterization of the land as a "wilderness." They went so far as to condemn Thanksgiving as a "day of mourning" rather than of celebration.[22] Mark Twain, in an address to the New England Society in 1881, supported their point of view. He claimed that his true American ancestor was an Indian, scoffed at the

Pilgrims, and exhorted the society to "get up an auction and sell Plymouth Rock."[23]

The debate over the meaning of the Pilgrim legend raged on for a century. "More, perhaps, has been written about the Pilgrims than any other small group in our history," wrote the American popular historian George F. Willison in his 1945 book *Saints and Strangers*. "And yet they are still extravagantly praised for accomplishing what they never attempted or intended, and are even more foolishly abused for possessing attitudes and attributes quite foreign to them."[24]

Just a few years later, Harvard historian Samuel Eliot Morison, in his introduction to the 1952 edition of Bradford's *Of Plymouth Plantation,* shot back at Willison and even cranked the hyperbole up a notch. He wrote of the Pilgrims as "a simple people inspired by an ardent faith to a dauntless courage in danger, a resourcefulness in dealing with new problems, an impregnable fortitude in adversity that exalts and heartens one in an age of uncertainty, when courage falters and faith grows dim. It is this story, told by a great human being, that has made the Pilgrim Fathers in a sense the spiritual ancestors of all Americans, all pioneers."[25]

Today, the Pilgrim narrative is not so often invoked, not so much revered, not so widely discussed as it once was. This is partly because the story, like all powerful stories, seems less relevant in the age of globalization and evolving national identities. As one of today's popular historians, Nathaniel Philbrick, put it, "I grew up taking this myth of national origins with a grain of salt. In their wide-brimmed hats and buckled shoes, the Pilgrims were the stuff of holiday parades and bad Victorian poetry. Nothing could be more removed from the ambiguities of modern-day America, I thought, than the Pilgrims and the *Mayflower*."[26] But upon further reflection Philbrick concluded that "the story of the Pilgrims does not end with the First Thanksgiving" and so he proceeded to explore the fifty years *after* the landing and there he found much relevance in the tensions between cultures and the struggle for sustainability.

We chose to look in the opposite direction, to the seventy years that preceded the *Mayflower* voyage. In doing so, we have written what is, in effect, the prequel to the Pilgrims. Accordingly, Plymouth can be seen as a staging post on the road of discovery and development towards the United States, rather than as the starting point. After all, Plymouth was not the first sustained English settlement in America — Jamestown was. Nor was it the most successful of the period, by the measures of growth or wealth or influence — the later Massachusetts Bay Colony was.

The Plymouth story, serving as America's default founding myth, derives its power from the fact that it reflects what America wants to be, how it wants to see itself and be seen. But in its popular conception the story is misleading because there is one major feature of American life that has been often left out, ignored, overlooked, or downplayed. Commerce. Business. Enterprise.

This is what caught our attention and made us curious. Looking back, we see that business and business people played a critical role in creating and establishing the earliest American settlements, laws, and civic institutions. Even the Pilgrims, those paragons of virtue, were funded by merchants, entrepreneurs, business leaders — both great and modest — and were organized as a commercial enterprise. Without the funding and the backing of a business organization, albeit a badly managed one, the Pilgrims might never have left Leiden.

Before the Pilgrim Century, there was some recognition of the vital role of commerce in America's beginnings. None other than Thomas Jefferson looked back to the pre-Pilgrim period when writing his *Notes on the State of Virginia*. He considered the license granted to John Cabot by Henry VII as among the earliest American state papers, and he regarded Sir Walter Ralegh as the founder of the first colony, Virginia.[27] In his narrative of the creation of the Constitution, Jefferson also named Thomas Smythe (which he spelled "Smith"). According to Jefferson, it was Smythe and his associates who Ralegh

315

turned to when, having exhausted £40,000 of his own funds on his Roanoke Colony, he at last found himself "under a necessity of engaging others to adventure their money."[28] One of the founding fathers of the United States and the principal author of the Declaration of Independence saw the connection between commonwealth and commerce.

Over the years, even as the moralistic storyline prevailed, other analysts worked to fill in the gaps. In 1939, Norman Gras, the first professor of business history at Harvard Business School, compiled a series of essays on great American companies and their leaders. In his *Casebook in American Business History,* Graf listed the well-known names one might expect: John Jacob Astor, Cornelius Vanderbilt, and J. P. Morgan, among others. But who did he put first on his list? Thomas Smythe of the Virginia Company. Smythe, Gras noted, was "the first business man to have a profound effect upon America."[29]

But it is that other, more renowned, Smith—Captain John, of Pocahontas fame, and the man who named New England—who first and best articulated the driving commercial impulse, the spirit of enterprise, that created America.

"I am not so simple, to think," Smith wrote in 1616, that "any other motive than wealth will ever erect there a Commonweale."[30]

Chronology

This is a selective list of important events, publications, voyages, and colonies, most (but not all) of which are featured in the book.

1492 Christopher Columbus's first voyage to the New World. Flying the flag of the Spanish monarchs, Ferdinand and Isabella, he reaches the Bahamas, naming the island where he lands, San Salvador.

1494 The Treaty of Tordesillas, officiated by Pope Alexander VI, divides the unclaimed regions of the world between Spain and Portugal.

1497 Amerigo Vespucci makes the first of four voyages to a region he later calls *Mundus Novus,* or "New World"; John Cabot, sailing for England, reaches the New World, probably Newfoundland, and claims it for England.

1498 Vasco da Gama reaches Calicut on India's west coast, having sailed round the Cape of Good Hope, Africa. By doing so, he opens a sea trade route to India, China, and the East Indies; John Cabot makes a second voyage to New World and does not return.

1503 La Casa de la Contratación, a Spanish government body, is established to manage Spain's overseas exploration, trade, and maritime activities.

1507 Martin Waldseemüller's map of the world is the first to show a landmass marked America, naming it after Amerigo Vespucci.

1508 Sebastian Cabot, son of John, sets out on a possible, but disputed, voyage in search of the Northwest Passage.

1516 The first edition of *Utopia,* by Thomas More, is published — in Latin.

1517 John Rastell, More's brother-in-law, leads a voyage to America that ends in mutiny off the Irish coast.

1519 John Rastell's *Interlude of the Nature of the Four Elements,* featuring the first English account of America, appears in print.

1519–21 Spanish soldiers, chief among them Hernán Cortés, invade and subjugate the Aztec empire in what is now Mexico and was then called New Spain.

1519–22 The crew of Ferdinand Magellan, a Portuguese aristocrat sailing for Spain, circumnavigates the world.

1524 Giovanni Verrazzano, a Florentine, sails along the Atlantic coast of America.

1526 Sebastian Cabot, sailing for Spain, explores the east coast of South America, enters the Plate River, and hears of silver mines in the Amazon.

1534 Henry VIII, in the Act of Supremacy, declares the king of England as head of the Church of England.

1534–35 Frenchman Jacques Cartier explores Newfoundland and other parts of what is now Canada, then called New France.

1535 The first Act of Suppression is passed, paving the way for the dissolution of the monasteries and the redistribution of assets of the church into private hands.

1545 The Spanish begin silver mining operations at Potosí in what is now Bolivia.

1548 Sebastian Cabot returns to England in order to pursue his dream of a passage to Cathay — after more than thirty years in Spain.

1549 Thomas Smith writes (but does not publish) *Discourse of the common weal of this realm of England*; Kett's Rebellion, a citizen uprising, takes place near Norfolk in protest over land enclosures, wealth disparity, and other grievances.

1551 A year of crisis: the coinage is debased, cloth exports fall, and hundreds of people are killed by the so-called "sweating sickness"; Thomas More's *Utopia* is published in English for the first time.

1552 A group of merchants and courtiers meet to found The Mysterie, Company, and Fellowship of Merchant Adventurers for the Discovery of Regions, Dominions, Islands, and Places Unknown.

1553 The Mysterie sends out the first expedition in search of a Northeast Passage to Cathay, led by Sir Hugh Willoughby and Richard Chancellor; Richard Eden produces *A Treatyse of the New India,* a translation of Sebastian Munster's *Cosmographia,* dedicated to John Dudley, Duke of Northumberland.

1554 Richard Chancellor reaches Moscow, meets the tsar, later known as Ivan "The Terrible," and opens a trading relationship between England and Muscovy.

1555 The Mysterie, renamed "The Merchant Adventurers of England for the Discovery of Unknown Lands" and later known as the Muscovy Company, receives its charter; Richard Eden publishes *Decades of the New World,* which draws on the work of the Italian scholar Peter Martyr d'Anghiera, promotes Chancellor's second voyage, and introduces the words "China" and "colony" into the English language.

1557–60 Anthony Jenkinson travels to Moscow and then continues overland towards China, reaching Bokhara (now in Uzbekistan).

1558 The French capture Calais, England's raw wool staple and the last remnant of an empire dating back to the time of the Norman Conquest.

1562 The French, under a Huguenot navigator called Jean Ribault, establish Charlesfort on the coast of modern-day South Carolina. It is abandoned after one year.

1564 The French, this time led by René de Laudonnière, establish Fort Caroline in modern-day Florida.

1565 The Spanish establish San Augustine, the longest-surviving European settlement in North America; they sack the French settlement at Fort Caroline, ending the hopes of Huguenots for a safe haven in the New World.

1566 Humphrey Gilbert completes (but does not publish) *A Discourse of a discoverie for a new passage to Cataia;* his proposals for leading a voyage in search of the Northwest Passage are rejected by the Muscovy Company.

1567–69 Humphrey Gilbert and his associates launch unsuccessful attempts to establish colonies in Ulster and Munster, two provinces in Ireland.

1570 Elizabeth I is excommunicated by Pope Pius V.

1572–74 Thomas Smith and his son make an unsuccessful attempt to establish a colony in Ulster, Ireland.

1576 Humphrey Gilbert's *A Discourse of a discoverie for a new passage to Cataia* is published, ten years after it was first written: it features his map of the world, the earliest by an Englishman; Martin Frobisher leads his first voyage to the New World, bringing back an Inuit, a black rock that is suspected to contain gold, and news that he has found (he claims) the entrance to the Northwest Passage (which he calls Frobisher Strait).

1577 Martin Frobisher, sponsored by the new Company of Cathay, makes a second voyage to the New World; Elizabeth I names the land explored by Frobisher *Meta Incognita,* "Unknown Limit"; John Dee publishes *General and Rare*

Memorials Pertayning to the Perfect Arte of Navigation, and argues for the establishment of a "British Empire"; Francis Drake sets out on his voyage round the world.

1578 Frobisher makes his third and final voyage to *Meta Incognita* and names an illusive island (probably the southern tip of Greenland) "West England" — the first foreign land to be named after the country; Humphrey Gilbert leads an abortive voyage to "annoy" Spain and locate a site for a colony in the New World; George Best publishes his account of Frobisher's three voyages.

1579 Francis Drake claims the northwest coast of America for England and names it *Nova Albion;* Richard Hakluyt produces his first publication, *A Discourse of the Commodity of the Taking of the Straight of Magellanus.*

1580 Drake sails home on the *Golden Hind* after his three-year voyage round the world, the first English captain to circumnavigate.

1581 Philip II is declared king of Portugal, increasing his power and extending Spain's declared right to unclaimed territories worldwide.

1582 Richard Hakluyt publishes *Diverse Voyages touching the discovery of America.*

1583 Humphrey Gilbert sets out on a second voyage to the New World, claims Newfoundland for Elizabeth, but is lost at sea on the journey home.

1584 Walter Ralegh, Gilbert's half brother, receives royal approval to establish a settlement in the land he calls Virginia, after Elizabeth I, the "Virgin Queen"; Richard Hakluyt produces *Discourse on Western Planting* to support Ralegh's venture.

1585 Ralegh's first colony is established on the island of Roanoke; England's long sea war with Spain begins.

1586 Drake arrives at Roanoke and evacuates Ralegh's settlers — so ending the first English colony in America;

Grenville, on a relief voyage to Roanoke, finds the colony deserted and leaves fifteen men to resettle — they are never seen alive again.

1587 John White establishes Ralegh's second colony on Roanoke with a mix of men, women and children; his daughter gives birth to Virginia, the first English child born in America; he returns to England to collect supplies.

1588 The English fleet defeats the Spanish Armada; Thomas Harriot, one of Ralegh's colonists, publishes *A Brief and True Report of the New Found Land of Virginia,* his report on the first Roanoke Colony.

1589 Thomas Smythe, a young London merchant, takes charge of plans to establish the City of Raleigh; the famous Armada portrait of Elizabeth I is completed; Richard Hakluyt publishes the first edition of *Principal Navigations.*

1590 John White returns to Roanoke, but fails to make contact with the colonists he left behind in 1587. They later become known as the "lost colonists."

1592 A great carrack, the *Madre de Dios,* with a hoard of treasure worth £500,000, is captured by English privateers; the Levant Company is established.

1595 Walter Ralegh sails to South America in an unsuccessful search for El Dorado, the city of gold.

1598 Richard Hakluyt publishes the first volume of a revised three-volume edition of *Principal Navigations.*

1600 The English East India Company is established.

1602 Bartholomew Gosnold explores Maine and modern-day Massachusetts, giving Cape Cod and Martha's Vineyard their names; George Waymouth sails in a vain search for the Northwest Passage.

1603 Elizabeth I dies, after reigning for nearly forty-five years, and the throne passes to James VI of Scotland, the son of Mary,

Queen of Scots, who becomes James I of England; Ralegh is sent to the Tower of London, effectively ending his tenure as "Lord and Governor of Virginia."

1604 The Treaty of London is agreed, ending the nineteen-year undeclared war between England and Spain; George Waymouth explores Maine, and kidnaps five Indians, who are sent to live in the households of Ferdinando Gorges and John Popham.

1605 Guy Fawkes and a group of Catholic dissidents are caught attempting to assassinate James I in an event remembered as the Gunpowder Plot.

1606 James I signs the first Charter of Virginia, authorizing the founding of two colonies in North America; Richard Challons, leading an expedition run by the Plymouth Company, sails for the New World but is captured by the Spanish, leading to an international incident.

1607 The first permanent English colony, Jamestown, is founded by settlers from the London Company; Bartholomew Gosnold is among many Jamestown settlers who succumb to disease soon after their arrival; Captain John Smith reports that he is saved from brutal execution by a young Indian princess, Pocahontas; George Popham and Raleigh Gilbert, Humphrey's son, establish the Popham, or Sagadahoc, Colony in Maine.

1608 The settlers of the Popham Colony abandon the New World, ending the hopes of Gorges and the Plymouth Company.

1609 James I signs the second charter of Virginia, which significantly increases the number of investors; the *Sea Venture*, the flagship of a fleet led by the new governor, Sir Thomas Gates, is shipwrecked off the Bermuda Islands, possibly prompting William Shakespeare to write *The Tempest*.

1610 Henry Hudson, funded by the Virginia Company and the English East India Company, explores what later became known as the Hudson Strait. It follows his earlier (1609) navigation of the Hudson River while sailing under the flag of the Dutch East India Company; some London and Bristol merchants receive a charter to colonize Newfoundland, nearly 30 years after Humphrey Gilbert claimed it for England.

1612 James I signs the third Virginia charter, broadening its geographical range to encompass the Bermuda Islands and providing the authority to raise funds through public lotteries; a group of merchants, led by some of the Virginia Company leaders, launch the Northwest Passage Company in order to revive the search for a fast route to Cathay. John Smith publishes *A Map of Virginia, with a description of the countrey, the commodities, people, government and religion.*

1613 The first consignment of Virginian tobacco, grown by John Rolfe, is sent to England.

1614 The first indentured servants, who arrived in Jamestown in 1607, complete their service and are rewarded with a new status as tenant farmers; John Rolfe marries Pocahontas, marking the end of the first Anglo-Powhatan war.

1615 Some leaders of the Virginia Company establish the Bermuda, or Somers Islands, Company.

1616 Pocahontas, now known as Rebecca Rolfe, visits England and meets James I; John Smith writes a treatise on America, and gives New England its name.

1617 The largest private plantation, known as Smith's Hundred, after Sir Thomas Smythe, is established near Jamestown.

1618 The Virginia Company issues the Great Charter, which introduced the ground rules for what was, in effect, a new commonwealth.

1619 Jamestown's settlers hold the first meeting of the House of Burgesses, described by one historian as "the first freely elected parliament of a self-governing people in the Western World."

1620 English separatists, later known as Pilgrims, leave Plymouth in England and sail in the *Mayflower* to New England, where they found New Plymouth.

1621 The Pilgrims mark their first year in the New World with the very first thanksgiving celebration.

A Note to the Reader

There are a number of particular issues involved in writing and reading about the people, events, and ideas of the sixteenth and early seventeenth century that we have made decisions about and that the reader should know about.

Spelling, Writing, and Printing. There was little consistency of spelling, capitalization, grammar, or printing during this period. English was only gradually becoming the standard written language of England, where educated people had long preferred to write and publish in Latin. In 1516, Sir Thomas More chose to write *Utopia* in Latin. It was not until 1551 that it was translated into English. By 1582, Richard Mulcaster, who memorably described Elizabeth I's coronation procession, was calling for an English dictionary, noting that "I do not think that any language . . . is better able to utter all arguments, either with more pith, or greater plainness, than our English tongue is." By way of emphasis, he stated: "I honor the Latin, but I worship the English."[1] It was not until 1604, however, that the first English dictionary was compiled. This tracked many of the new words flooding into the language—not least because of the exploits of the merchant adventurers and their colonial commanders. According to the *Oxford*

English Dictionary (OED), the "number of words 'available' to speakers of English more than doubled between 1550 and 1650."[2]

William Shakespeare, who was born and died during this period, introduced many new words—precisely 1,484, according to the *OED*.[3] Richard Eden introduced words such as "China" and "colony." Several of the English visitors to North America made a point of collecting Indian words. John Smith, for example, was responsible for introducing "tomahawk," "moccasin," and "raccoon," while others introduced "caribou," "moose," "papoose," "powwow," "squaw," "terrapin," and "wigwam."[4] Given the rapid growth of the number of words, it is little wonder that there was inconsistency and complication in the usage and capturing of the English language.

There were other contributing factors. People spelled words phonetically and pronounced them as their particular dialect or regional accent propelled them to; publishers and printers followed their own rules of spelling and punctuation. The result was often a lexical shambles on the page that can be both astonishing and sometimes amusing to read—or try to read. Martin Frobisher's last name was spelled in at least a dozen different ways, many of them by Frobisher himself, and often within the same text: we find Martyne Furbisher, for example, and Ffurbisher and Captayne Frobysher.[5] Walter Ralegh was another famous man whose name was spelled in various ways. We have chosen to spell the great courtier's name with the spelling that he tended to use: Ralegh, not the more standard modern spelling, Raleigh.

In one text, the word "miner" is spelled "moyener" and the word "ore" as "ewr," probably manifesting the vowels of a West Countryman.[6] Also, the skills of the editors, publishers, and printers (often one and the same person) are thrown into high relief on the page. In Daniel Tucker's account of the 1606 voyage of Richard Challons, there is the phrase "we a Rived at a niland" for "we arrived at an island," which could easily have been corrected in the editing process.[7]

Writers and printers of the day also used a number of marks and shortcuts that are unfamiliar today, such as shortening the word "which" into the space-saving wch or indicating a double consonant with a dash: m̄. The letter "s" is often printed with a character that looks to the modern reader like an "f"; a "u" often is printed as a "v"; an "i" indicates a "j." So the word "subject" might be printed "fubicte." "Ing" endings often gain an "e," as in "promisinge." Publishers, especially in the earlier years of this period, might print an entire page of text with no indentations or paragraph breaks, and rarely a comma or period. One likely reason that Hakluyt's *Principal Navigations,* first published in 1589, gained popularity was that the spelling was reasonably consistent and the printing and layout made the accounts relatively easy to read. By this time, printing—introduced into England in 1476 by William Caxton, a cloth merchant and governor of the Merchant Adventurers in Bruges (before the staple moved to Antwerp)—was a well-established technology.

Some of the materials for this book were produced by non-native speakers, such as Bernardino de Mendoza, Spain's ambassador to England for many years, and one of his successors, Pedro de Zúñiga—and they, too, sometimes offer revealing hints about pronunciation and spelling conventions. Zúñiga, for example, wrote to Philip III with news about an English gentleman he referred to as "Vatarrales," meaning—of course—Walter Ralegh.[8]

Given all this, we have generally modernized the original language. In some cases, however, we have retained the original spelling where it was comprehensible and added some meaning or color to the phrase—for example, Dee's "ilandish" empire or Christopher Newport's arm, which was "strooken off" in a sea battle.

Names (1): Indians. Columbus gave the name Indians to the people living in the islands when he first reached the New World in 1492, because he hoped and believed he had arrived in India or the East Indies, although he hadn't. For Europeans, the name stuck for people living in all parts of the New World, including what were then called Peru, Brazil, the West Indies, New Spain, Florida, Virginia, and New

France. English people in the sixteenth and seventeenth centuries referred to the people of the New World with a variety of other terms, none of which are now tolerable.

Today, a number of terms are used, including Native Americans, Amerindians, indigenous peoples or, whenever possible, the name of a specific tribe of peoples, such as Incans or Aztecs, Algonquins, Abenakis, or Inuits. Even during the period of this book, some European visitors to the New World took the trouble to understand and name the local peoples. In his *Generall Historie,* John Smith was careful to list some thirty different New England tribal or regional names, from the Penobscot in the north to the Massachusett in the south.[9]

We have embraced the reasoning of Charles Mann, who uses the word "Indian" in his books *1491* and *1493* for the simple and irrefutable reason that, as he puts it, "The overwhelming majority of the indigenous peoples whom I have met in both North and South America describe themselves as Indians."[10]

Names (2): Aristocratic Titles. We have used family names for people with titles, while often including the title, as well. This is to avoid the problem of having to keep track of a succession of titles and remembering that William Cecil, for example, was one and the same as Lord Burghley, also known as Baron Burghley and sometimes referred to simply as Burghley, whose son was Robert Cecil, who became the first Earl of Salisbury.

Money. We have made no attempt to convert coinage, currency values, or other monetary amounts or financial data into modern-day equivalents because of the great complexity involved and the ultimate futility of the exercise. Our hope is that the reader will gradually get a relative sense of the economy and money and values, through the many examples of costs, investments, incomes, losses, and the like — such as the cost of a suit of armor (£25) or a ship (the *Bark Raleigh* was valued at £2,000); a meager annual income (£8 for a laborer) and a high-end annual salary (£100 for Walsingham as secretary of state); the cost of an overseas venture (£1,500 to £7,000 or so) and the value of a fortune (the £150,000 estimate of the *Madre de Dios* prize).

Distances. There was little standard measurement of much of anything in those days on land or at sea. Distances might be measured by "days walked" or the length of a cannonball's travel. Measures that sound standard were not. A league, for example, was calculated differently in different cultures. One was as one-twenty-fifth of a degree of latitude, or about 2.6 miles. A mariner's league was one-twentieth of a degree. A day's horseback ride was typically figured as seven leagues.[11] Distances at sea are almost impossible to figure, because no ship traveled in a straight line between two points, so time is a better comparative measure.

Dates. Until 1582, the countries of Western Europe followed the Julian calendar, introduced by Julius Caesar in 45 BC and accepted by the Christian Roman emperor Constantine I in AD 325. But then, Pope Gregory XIII introduced a new calendar, and overnight, the calendar leapt forward by ten days. The purpose was to synchronize the holy and feast days with the equinoxes and solstices—after more than one thousand years, they had drifted apart. In particular, the Pope wanted to fix the date of Easter. Spain, as a dutiful Catholic nation, introduced the so-called Gregorian calendar across its empire. France followed suit. But England, deeming this to be a Catholic plot, refused to change its calendar. John Dee was asked to devise an alternative calendar. This he did, calling it "Queen Elizabeth's Perpetual Calendar," fixing the meridian in London and thereby making the Protestant English master of time. But, for various reasons, Dee's calendar was not introduced. It would not be until 1752 that England finally adopted the Gregorian calendar, by which time the calendar had to leap forward by eleven days. So, throughout this book, we use the Julian, or Old Style, dating system—with one difference: the year is assumed to have begun on January 1 rather than March 25.[12]

Acknowledgments

"No man is an island, entire of itself," wrote John Donne, who briefly hankered after the job of secretary of the Jamestown colony. And no writers are either. We leaned heavily on several people throughout the writing of this book.

First comes Henry Jupiter Butman, who worked closely with us over a three-year period, from the development of the publishing proposal through to the submission of the manuscript. He has acted as thought partner, collaborator, and researcher: digging out great sources, drafting copious and compelling research notes, and providing extremely valuable commentary on the entire manuscript. Also, Henry set up and managed the Evernote database of notes and sources, developed an interactive timeline, and mastered the intricacies of the Calendar of State Papers online resource. Henry, thank you: we really couldn't have done this without you.

We would also like to thank John T. "Ike" Williams and Katherine Flynn of the Kneerim & Williams Literary Agency in Boston. Right from the beginning, they have been staunch supporters, encouraging us and guiding us through to publication. Both have a special feeling for historical material, and this period in particular, and contributed their knowledge and analysis of the content, in addition to their professional expertise. John also thanks his colleague, John De Lancey, who conducted valuable research.

We were honored and happy to find a home for the book with Little, Brown. This was entirely down to our editor, Vanessa Mobley. She came in late to the placement process but showed such passion for the topic that she and Little, Brown were the obvious choice. The fact that Little, Brown was the first trade publisher of William Bradford's *Of Plymouth Plantation* in 1856 — which we only realized later — has given us the feeling that our collaboration was written in the stars. Throughout the writing process, Vanessa has proffered wise counsel and her boundless enthusiasm has propelled us forward.

We have also been blessed to have received the support of Little, Brown publisher, Reagan Arthur, and the contributions of editorial assistant Joseph Lee, production editor Michael Noon, publicist Elizabeth Garriga, marketing manager Lauren Velasquez, copyeditor David Coen, and cartographer Jeffrey Ward.

During the writing of *New World Inc.,* we have been constantly aware of the debt we owe the scholars who have done much of the heavy lifting of research in this period, creating a host of essential collections of original manuscripts, monographs, articles, and papers. We hope our extensive bibliography pays tribute to their work. Some of the sources are only accessible in libraries, and we consulted the physical collections at the British Library, Boston Public Library, Boston Athenaeum, Cambridge University Library, London Library, and the National Archives at Kew. But we have been almost ineffably facilitated by online resources — such as the British History Online database (which includes the Calendar of State Papers) and the JSTOR database of articles — and by online tools, such as Evernote, which facilitates the storage, organization, search, and access of huge quantities of information in many forms.

Continuing the digital theme, we would also like to recognize the role played by Skype. This book is an Anglo-American collaboration that would have been difficult, not to say impossible, to accomplish without the face-to-face conversations that we conducted over Skype on a weekly basis over a period of two years.

Above all, we would like to pay tribute to our families for their encouragement, tolerance, understanding, advice, forebearance, interest, and love during the all-consuming process of creating this book. John wishes to thank his family, Nancy, Jeremy, and Henry, for their contributions and support and expresses his deep appreciation to his father, Robert, who instilled in him a fascination with exploration, but did not live to see the publication of this book. Simon would like to thank his parents, Val and Pete, who are no longer here, but who were always there for him when they were, and who fostered his passion for the past. To his family, Alison, Ella, and Martha, who listened enthusiastically to the latest reports from yesteryear and who were never short of constructive criticism, he would like to say the biggest thank-you of all.

Select Bibliography

Primary Sources: Manuscripts, Maps, Printed Books, Collections

"Accounts, with subsidiary documents, of Michael Lok, treasurer, of first, second and third voyages of Martin Frobisher to Cathay by the north-west passage. Composite volume: E 164/35." National Archives. Kew, England.

Acts of the Privy Council of England, Volume II, 1547–1550. Edited by John Roche Dasent. London: Her Majesty's Stationery Office, 1890.

Acts of the Privy Council of England, Volume IX, 1575–1577. Edited by John Roche Dasent. London, Her Majesty's Stationery Office, 1894.

Acts of the Privy Council of England, Volume XI, 1578–1580. Edited by John Roche Dasent. London, Her Majesty's Stationery Office, 1895.

Agricola, Georgius. *De Re Metallica.* Trans. Herbert Clark Hoover and Lou Henry Hoover. New York: Dover Publications, Inc., 1950.

Andrews, Kenneth R. *English Privateering Voyages to the West Indies 1588–95.* London: The Hakluyt Society, 1959.

Arber, Edward, ed. *The First Three English Books on America [?1511]–1555.* Birmingham, 1885.

Aubrey, John. *Brief Lives, chiefly of Contemporaries, set down by John Aubrey, between the years 1669 & 1696.* 2 vols. Edited by Andrew Clark. Oxford: The Clarendon Press, 1898.

————. *Brief Lives by John Aubrey.* Edited by Richard Barber. London: The Folio Society, 1975.

Bacon, Francis. *The Essays.* Edited with an introduction by John Pitcher. London: Penguin Books, 1987.

Bancroft, George, ed. *The Seven Articles from the Church of Leyden 1617 with an introductory letter by George Bancroft.* New York: From the Collections of the New York Historical Society, Second Series, Vol. 3, n.d.

Barbour, Philip L., ed., *The Jamestown Voyages Under the First Charter, 1606–1609.* 2 vols. Cambridge: Cambridge University Press, for The Hakluyt Society, 1969.

————. *The Complete Works of Captain John Smith (1580–1631).* 3 vols. Chapel Hill: University of North Carolina Press, 1986.

Beaven, Alfred P. *The Aldermen of the City of London Temp. Henry III – 1912.* London: Corporation of the City of London, 1908.

Bemiss, Samuel M., *The Three Charters of the Virginia Company of London. With Seven Related Documents: 1606–1621*. Williamsburg, VA: 350th Anniversary Celebration Corporation, 1957; repr. Baltimore: Clearfield Company, 2007.

Benet, Stephen Vincent. *The Devil and Daniel Webster and Other Writings*. London: Penguin Books, 1999.

Blake, John W., ed. *Europeans in West Africa, 1450–1560*. London: The Hakluyt Society, 1942.

Biringuccio, Vannoccio. *The Pirotechnia of Vannoccio Biringuccio*. Trans., with an Introduction and Notes, by Cyril Stanley Smith and Martha Teach Gnudi. New York: Dover Publications Inc., 1990.

Bradford, William, *Of Plymouth Plantation, 1620–1647*. Edited, with introduction and notes, by Samuel Eliot Morison. New York: Random House, The Modern Library, 1952.

Brown, Alexander, editor and compiler. *The Genesis of the United States: A Narrative of the Movement in England, 1605–1616, Which Resulted in the Plantation of North America by Englishmen, Disclosing the Contest Between England and Spain For the Possession of the Soil Now Occupied by the United States of America; Set Forth Through A Series of Historical Manuscripts now first printed: Together with a Reissue of Rare Contemporaneous Tracts, Accompanied by Bibliographical Memoranda, Notes, and Brief Biographies*. 2 vols. Boston: Houghton, Mifflin and Company, 1890.

Byrne, Muriel St. Clare, ed. *The Lisle Letters. An Abridgement. Selected and Arranged by Bridget Boland*. London: Secker & Warburg, 1983.

Calendar of Carew Manuscripts, 1515–1574. Edited by J. S. Brewer and William Bullen. London: Longmans, Green, Reader, & Dyer, 1867.

Calendar of the Cecil Papers in Hatfield House: Volume 18, 1606. Edited by M. S. Giuseppi. London: His Majesty's Stationery Office, 1940.

Calendar of the Cecil Papers in Hatfield House: Volume 19, 1607. Edited by M. S. Giuseppi and D. McN. Lockie. London: Her Majesty's Stationery Office, 1965.

Calendar of the Patent Rolls, Edward VI. Edited by R. H. Brodie. London: His Majesty's Stationery Office, 1924–1929.

Calendar of the Patent Rolls, Philip and Mary. Volume II, 1554–1555. London: His Majesty's Stationery Office, 1936.

Calendar of State Papers Colonial, America and West Indies: Volume 1, 1574–1660. Edited by W. Noel Sainsbury. London: Her Majesty's Stationery Office, 1860.

Calendar of State Papers, Colonial, America and West Indies: Volume 9, 1675–1676 and Addenda 1574–1674. Edited by W. Noel Sainsbury. London: Her Majesty's Stationery Office, 1893.

Calendar of State Papers, Colonial, East Indies, China and Japan: Volume 2, 1513–1616. Edited by W. Noel Sainsbury. London: Longman, Green, Longman & Roberts, 1862.

Calendar of State Papers, Domestic Series, Edward VI., Mary, Elizabeth, 1547–1580. Edited by Robert Lemon. London: Longman, Brown, Green, Longmans & Roberts, 1856.

Calendar of State Papers, Domestic Series, Elizabeth 1581–1590. Edited by Robert Lemon. London: Longman, Green, Longman, Roberts, and Green, 1865.

Calendar of State Papers, Foreign: Elizabeth, Volume 5, 1562. Edited by Joseph Stevenson. London: Her Majesty's Stationery Office, 1887.

Calendar of State Papers, Ireland: Elizabeth, 1574–1585. Edited by Hans Claude Hamilton. London: Longmans, Green, Reader, & Dyer, 1867.

Calendar of State Papers, Ireland: Elizabeth, 1586–1588, July. Edited by Hans Claude Hamilton. London: Longman & Co., Paternoster Row; Trübner & Co., Ludgate Hill; Parker & Co., Oxford; MacMillan & Co., Cambridge; A. & C. Black, Edinburgh; A. Thom, Dublin, 1877.

Calendar of State Papers, Ireland: Henry VIII., Edward VI., Mary, and Elizabeth, 1509–1573. Edited by Hans Claude Hamilton. London: Longman, Green, Longman, & Roberts, 1860.

Calendar of State Papers, Spain (Simancas), Volume 1, 1558–1567. Edited by Martin A.S. Hume. London: Her Majesty's Stationery Office, 1892.

Calendar of State Papers, Spain (Simancas), Volume 2, 1568–1579. Edited by Martin A.S. Hume. London: Her Majesty's Stationery Office, 1894.

Calendar of State Papers, Spain (Simancas), Volume 3, 1580–1586. Edited by Martin A.S. Hume. London: Her Majesty's Stationery Office, 1896.

Calendar of State Papers, Spain, Volume 9, 1547–1549. Edited by Martin A. S. Hume and Royall Tyler. London: His Majesty's Stationery Office, 1912.

Calendar of State Papers, Spain, Volume 10, 1550–1552. Edited by Royall Tyler. London: His Majesty's Stationery Office, 1914.

Calendar of State Papers, Spain, Volume 11, 1553. Edited by Royall Tyler. London: His Majesty's Stationery Office, 1916.

Calendar of State Papers and Manuscripts, Relating to English Affairs, Existing in the Archives and Collections of Venice, and in Other Libraries of Northern Italy, Volume VI, Part I, 1555–1556. Edited by Rawdon Brown. London: Longman & Co., 1877.

Calvin, John. *Institutes of the Christian Religion, Volume I*. 6th ed. Translated by John Allen. Philadelphia: Presbyterian Board of Publication, 1813. Ebook by Project Gutenberg, http://www.gutenberg.org/files/45001/45001-h/45001-h.html.

Campagnac, E. T., ed. *Mulcaster's Elementarie*. Oxford: Clarendon Press, 1925.

Carr, Cecil T., ed. *Select Charters of Trading Companies, A.D. 1530–1707*. London: Bernard Quartich, 1913.

Collinson, Richard. *The Three Voyages of Martin Frobisher, In Search of a Passage to Cathaia and India by the North-West, A.D. 1576–8, Reprinted from the First Edition of Hakluyt's voyages, with selections from Manuscript Documents in the British Museum And State Paper Office*. London: The Hakluyt Society, 1867.

Columbia University. "Document #1: The Written Record of the Voyage of 1524 of Giovanni da Verrazzano as recorded in a letter to Francis I, King of France, July 8th, 1524." Adapted from the translation by Susan Tarrow in *The Voyages of Giovanni da Verrazzano, 1524–1528*, edited by Lawrence C. Wroth. New Haven, CT: Yale University Press, 1970, 133–43.

Croft, Pauline, ed. *The Spanish Company*. London: London Record Society, 1973.

Dee, John. *General and Rare Memorials Pertayning to the Perfect Arte of Navigation*. Edited by Gerald Suster. Berkeley, CA: North Atlantic Books, 2003.

————. *John Dee Essential Readings*. Compiled by Gerald Suster. Berkeley, CA: North Atlantic Books, 2003.

————. *The Limits of the British Empire*. Edited by Ken MacMillan with Jennifer Abeles. Westport, CT: Praeger, 2004.

Dietz, Brian, ed. *The Port and Trade of Early Elizabethan London Documents*. London: London Record Society, 1972.

De las Casas, Bartolomé. *A Short Account of the Destruction of the Indies*. London: Penguin Books, 1992.

Dewar, Mary, ed. *A Discourse of the Commonweal of This Realm of England, Attributed to Sir Thomas Smith*. Charlottesville: The University Press of Virginia, 1969.

D'Ewes, Simonds, ed. *The Journals of All the Parliaments During the Reign of Queen Elizabeth*. Shannon: Irish University Press, 1682.

Díaz, Bernal. *The Conquest of New Spain*. Translated with an introduction by J.M. Cohen. London: Penguin Books, 1963.

Dudley, Edmund. *The Tree of Commonwealth*. Edited by D. M. Brodie. Cambridge: Cambridge University Press, 1948.

Ellis, Henry, ed. *Original Letters Illustrative of English History, in Four Volumes: Volume II*. London: Harding and Lepard, Second Series, 1827.

Fischer, Joseph, Franz von Wieser and Charles George Herbermann, eds., *Cosmographiae Introductio of Martin Waldseemüller in Facsimile Followed By The Four Voyages of Amerigo Vespucci, With Their Translation Into English; to which are added Waldseemüller's Two World Maps of 1507 With An Introduction*. New York: The United States Catholic Historical Society, 1907.

Fletcher, Francis. *The World Encompassed by Sir Francis Drake*. London: Nicholas Bourne, 1628; facsimile edition: Amsterdam: Da Capo Press, 1969.

Fuller, Thomas. *The History of the Worthies of England. A New Edition*. 3 vols. Edited by P. Austin Nuttall. London: Thomas Tegg, 1890.

Grant, W. L., ed. *Voyages of Samuel de Champlain 1604–1618*. New York: Charles Scribner's Sons, 1907.

Hakluyt, Richard, compiler and publisher. *Divers Voyages Touching the Discovery of America and the Islands Adjacent*. Edited by John Winter Jones. Cambridge: Cambridge University Press, 2010.

Hakluyt, Richard. *The Principal Navigations, Voyages, Traffiques & Discoveries of the English Nation, In Twelve Volumes*. Glasgow: James MacLehose & Sons, the University Press, 1903–5.

————. *A Particular Discourse Concerning the Greate Necessitie and Manifolde Commodyties That Are Like to Growe to This Realm of Englande by the Western Discoveries Lately Attempted*. Edited by David B. Quinn. London: The Hakluyt Society, 1993.

Halliwell, James Orchard, ed. *The Private Diary of Dr John Dee and the Catalogue of his Library of Manuscripts, From the Original Manuscripts in the Ashmolean Museum at Oxford, and Trinity College Library, Cambridge*. London: Camden Society, 1842.

Hamor, Ralph. *A True Discourse of the Present Estate of Virginia. Reprinted from the London edition, 1615, with an introduction by A. L. Rowse*. Richmond: The Virginia State Library, 1957.

Harrison, William. *The Description of England. The Classic Contemporary Account of Tudor Social Life*, ed. Georges Edelen. Washington, DC, and New York: Folger Shakespeare Library and Dover Publications, 1994.

Harrisse, Henry. *The Discovery of North America*. London: Henry Stevens & Son, 1892.

Heath, J. B., ed. *An account of the materials furnished for the use of Queen Anne Boleyn and the Princess Elizabeth, by William Loke, the King's Mercer, Volume VII*. London: Philobiblon Society, 1862–3.

Holinshed, Raphael. *Holinshed's Chronicles of England, Scotland and Ireland*. With a new introduction by Vernon F. Snow. 6 vols. New York: AMS Press, 1965.

Homem, Diogo. *Queen Mary Atlas: Facsimile Edition*. Commentary by Peter Barber. London: Folio Society, 2005.

Hood, Thomas. *A Copy of the Speech made by the Mathematical Lecturer at the House of Mr. Thomas Smith*. London, 1588; reprinted in Johnson, Francis R. "Thomas Hood's Inaugural Address as Mathematical Lecturer of the City of London (1588)." *Journal of the History of Ideas* 3, no. 1 (1942): 94–106.

Hunter, Rev. Joseph. *Collections Concerning the Church of Congregation of Protestant Separatists Formed at Scrooby in North Nottinghamshire, in the Time of King James I*. London: John Russell Smith, 1854.

Jefferson, Thomas. *Notes on the State of Virginia. A New Edition*. Richmond, Virginia: J. W. Randolph, 1853.

Jenkinson, Anthony, et al. *Early Voyages and Travels in Russia and Persia*. Edited by E. Delmar Morgan and C. H. Coote. London: The Hakluyt Society, 1886.

[Johnson, Robert.] *The New Life of Virginea: Declaring the former Successe and present estate of that plantation, being the second part of Nova Britannia. Published by the authoritie of his Maiesties Counsell of Virginea*. London, 1612.

Keller, Mary. *Drake's West Indian Voyage, 1585–6*. London: The Hakluyt Society, 1981.

Kingsbury, Susan Myra, ed. *The Records of the Virginia Company of London*. Washington, DC: Library of Congress, 1933.

Klarwill, Victor von, ed. *Queen Elizabeth and Some Foreigners Being a series of hitherto unpublished letters from the archives of the Hapsburg family. Authorized translation by Professor T.H. Nash*. London: John Lane, The Bodley Head, 1928.

Lefroy, Sir J. H., compiler. *Memorials of the discovery and early settlement of the Bermudas or Somers Islands, 1515–1685*. 2 vols. London: Longmans, Green, and Co., 1877–79.

Lincoln, Abraham. "Proclamation 106—Thanksgiving Day, 1863." Published online by Gerhard Peters and John T. Woolley, *The American Presidency Project*, http://www.presidency.ucsb.edu/ws/?pid=69900.

Longfellow, Henry Wadsworth. *The Courtship of Miles Standish*. New York: Grosset & Dunlap, 1910.

Lyell, Laetitia, ed. *Acts of Court of the Mercers' Company 1453–1527*. Cambridge: Cambridge University Press, 1936.

Machyn, Henry, *The Diary of Henry Machyn, Citizen and Merchant-Taylor of London, 1550–1563*. Edited by J. G. Nichols. London: Camden Society, 1848.

Major, R. H., trans. and ed. *Notes upon Russia: Being a translation of the Earliest Account of that Country entitled Rerum Moscoviticarum Commentarii by the Baron Sigismund von Herberstein*. 2 vols. London: Hakluyt Society, 1851.

Martin, Charles Trice, ed. "Journal of Sir Francis Walsingham from December 1570 to April 1583. From the original manuscript in the possession of Lieut.-Colonel Carew" in *The Camden Miscellany*, vol. 6 (London: Camden Society, 1871), 1–99.

Mather, Cotton. *Magnalia Christi Americana: or, the Ecclesiastical History of New-England*. London: Thomas Parkhurst, 1702; republished, Hartford: Silas Andrus, 1820.

Maxwell, Constantia. *Irish History from Contemporary Sources (1509–1610)*. London: George Allen & Unwin Ltd., 1923.

McDermott, James. *The Third Voyage of Martin Frobisher to Baffin Island, 1578*. London: Hakluyt Society, 2001.

Mercator, Gerard. "The Mercator Atlas of Europe – Pages 3 and 4," http://www.bl.uk/onlinegallery/ttp/mercator/accessible/pages3and4.html.

More, Thomas. *Utopia*. Translated from the Latin by Ralph Robinson. With an introduction by Jenny Mezciems. New York: Alfred A. Knopf, 1992.

Morgan, E. Delmar and C. H. Coote, eds. *Early Voyages and Travels into Russia and Persia by Anthony Jenkinson and other Englishmen, with Some Account of the First Intercourse of the English with Russia and Central Asia by way of the Caspian Sea*. 2 vols. London: Hakluyt Society, 1886.

Moseley, C. W. R. D., translator. *The Travels of Sir John Mandeville*. London: Penguin Books, 1983.

Mourt's Relation: A Journal of the Pilgrims at Plymouth. Bedford MA: Applewood Books in cooperation with Plimoth Plantation, 1963.

Munster, Sebastian, *Novae Insulae XXVI Nova Tabula*, https://www.raremaps.com/gallery/detail/28899/Novae_Insulae_XXVI_Nova_Tabula_1st_Map_of_the_continent_of_America/Munster.html.

Naunton, Robert. *Fragmenta Regalia; or Observations on Queen Elizabeth, Her Times and Favourites*. Edited by John S. Cervoski. Washington, DC: Folger Books, 1985.

Neville, Alexander. *Norfolkes Furies or a View of Ketts Campe*. London: William Stansby for Henry Fetherstone, 1615.

Nichols, J. G., ed. *The Chronicle of Calais in the Reigns of Henry VII and Henry VIII to the Year 1540*. London: Camden Society, 1846.

————. *The Chronicle of Queen Jane and of Two Years of Queen Mary and Especially of the Rebellion of Sir Thomas Wyat, Written by a Resident in the Tower of London*. London: Camden Society, 1850.

Nuttall, Zelia, ed. and trans. *New Light on Drake. A Collection of Documents Relating to his Voyage of Circumnavigation 1577–1580*. London: Hakluyt Society, 1914.

Osborn, James M., ed. *The Quenes Maiesties Passage through the Citie of London to Westminster the Day before her Coronation*. New Haven, CT: Yale University Press, 1960.

Pears, Steuart, compiler and translator. A. *The Correspondence of Sir Philip Sidney and Hubert Languet*. London: William Pickering, 1845.

George Percy. "Trewe Relacyon." Reprinted in Mark Nicholls, "George Percy's 'Trewe Relacyon': A Primary Source for the Jamestown Settlement," *The Virginia Magazine of History and Biography* 113, no. 3 (2005): 212–75.

Peterson, Joseph H., ed. *John Dee's Five Books of Mystery: Original Sourcebook of Enochian Magic*. Boston: Weiserbooks, 2003.

Polo, Marco. *The Most Noble and Famous Travels of Marco Polo, Together with the Travels of Nicolo di Conti*. Rev. ed. Edited and translated by John Frampton, with Introduction, Notes, and Appendices by N. M. Penzer. London: A. & C. Black, 1937.

Ptolemy, Claudius. "Ptolemy's World Map: 1407," http://www.bl.uk/learning/timeline/item126360.html.

Purchas, Samuel. *Hakluytus Posthumus or Purchas His Pilgrimes: Contayning a History of the World in Sea Voyages and Lande Travells by Englishmen and Others*. 20 vols. Glasgow: James MacLehose and Sons, the University of Glasgow, 1905–1907.

Quinn, David B. ed. *The Voyages and Colonising Enterprises of Sir Humphrey Gilbert*. 2 vols. London: The Hakluyt Society, 1940.

————, ed. *The Roanoke Voyages 1584–1590*. 2 vols. London: Hakluyt Society, 1955.

————. ed. *New American World: A Documentary History of North America to 1612*. 5 vols. New York: Arno Press and Hector Bye, Inc., 1979.

Quinn, David B., and Alison M. Quinn, eds. *The English New England Voyages, 1602–1608*. London: The Hakluyt Society, 1983.

Quinn, David B., and Neil M. Cheshire, eds. *The New Found Land of Stephen Parmenius*. Toronto: University of Toronto Press, 1972.

Ravin-Heart, R. *Before Van Riebeck: Callers at South Africa from 1488 to 1651*. Cape Town: C. Struik (PTY.) Ltd., 1967.

Ribault, Jean. *The Whole & True Discoverye of Terra Florida. A Facsimile of the London Edition of 1563 together with a transcript of an English version in the British Museum, with notes by H. M. Biggar and a Biography by Jeanette Thurber O'Connor*. Deland, FL: The Florida State Historical Society, 1927.

Rolfe, John. *A True Relation of the state of Virginia lefte by Sir Thomas Dale Knight in May last 1616. Set forth with an Introduction and Notes by a group of Virginia Librarians*. New Haven, CT: Yale University Press, 1951.

Smith, Sir Thomas. "A letter sent by I.B. Gentleman vnto his very frende Maystet [sic] R. C. Esquire vvherin is conteined a large discourse of the peopling & inhabiting the cuntrie called the Ardes, and other adiacent in the north of Ireland, and taken in hand by Sir Thomas Smith one of the Queenes Maiesties priuie Counsel, and Thomas Smith Esquire, his sonne." London: Henry Binneman, 1571.

————. *De Republica Anglorum: A Discourse on the Commonwealth of England*. Edited by Mary Dewar. Cambridge: Cambridge University Press, 1982.

Smyth Family (of Hill Hall Estate in Theydon Mount) Manuscripts. Essex Record Office.

Stefansson, Vilhjalmur, ed. *The Three Voyages of Martin Frobisher*. 2 vols. London: The Argonaut Press, 1938; repr. Amsterdam: N. Israel, and New York: Da Capo Press, 1971.

Stevens, Henry, and George Birdwood, eds. *The Dawn of British Trade to the East Indies, As Recorded in the Court Minutes of the East India Company 1599–1603*. London: Henry Stevens & Son, 1886.

Stow, John. *A Survey of London. Reprinted From the Text of 1603*. 2 vols. Edited by C. L. Kingsford. Oxford: Clarendon, 1908.

————. and Edmund Howes. *Annales, or a General Chronicle of England, begun by John Stow: continued and augmented with matters Forraigne and Domestique, Ancient and Moderne, unto the end of this present yeere*. London: Richard Meighen, 1631.

Strachey, William. *For the Colony in Virginia Britannia: Lawes Divine, Morall and Martiall &c*. London: W. Burre, 1612. Reprinted in *Tracts And Other Papers relating principally to the Origin, Settlement and Progress of the Colonies in North America from the Discovery of the Country to 1776*. Collected by Peter Force. Volume III. Washington, DC: Wm. Q. Force, 1844. No. 2.

————. *The Historie of Travell into Virginia Britania (1612) by William Strachey, gent*. Edited by Louis B. Wright and Virginia Freund. London: The Hakluyt Society, 1853.

Tanner, J. R. *Tudor Constitutional Documents A.D. 1485–1603, with an Historical Commentary*. Cambridge: Cambridge University Press, 1951.

Tawney, R. H., and Eileen Power, eds. *Tudor Economic Documents*. 3 vols. London: Longmans, Green & Co., 1924.

Taylor, E. G. R., ed., *The Original Writings and Correspondence of the Two Richard Hakluyts*, 2 vols. London: The Hakluyt Society, 1935.

————, ed., *The Troublesome Voyage of Captain Edward Fenton 1582–1583*. Cambridge: Hakluyt Society, 1959.

Three Proclamations Concerning the Lottery for Virginia. Boston: Merrymount Press, 1907.

Tocqueville, Alexis de. *Democracy in America*. ed. Olivier Zunz and trans. Arthur Goldhammer. New York: The Library of America, 2004.

Twain, Mark, *Mark Twain's Speeches*. With an Introduction by William Dean Howells. New York: Harper & Brothers, 1910.

Tytler, Patrick F. *England Under the Reigns of Edward VI and Mary*. 2 vols. London: Richard Bentley, 1839.

Waymouth, George. "The Jewell of Artes." Bound manuscript of 1605.

Webster, Daniel. "Plymouth Oration: December 22, 1820," https://www.dartmouth.edu/~dwebster/speeches/plymouth-oration.html.

Whatley, Stephen. *A General Collection of Treatys, Manifestos, Contracts of Marriage, Renunciations, and other Publick Papers, from the Year 1495, to the Year 1712. Vol. 2*. London: Printed for J. J. and P. Knapton, J. Darby, D. Midwinter and A. Ward, A. Bettesworth and C. Hitch, J. Pemberton, J. Osborn and T. Longman, C. Rivington, F. Clay, J. Batley, R. Hett, and T. Hatchett, 1732.

Whitfield, Peter. *New Found Lands: Maps in the History of Exploration*. London: The British Library, 1998.

———. *London: A Life in Maps*. Rev. ed. London: The British Library, 2017.

Willes, Richard. *The History of Travayle in the West and East Indies, and other countreys lying eyther way, towards the fruitfull and ryche Moluccaes. As Moscouia, Persia, Arabia, Syria, AEgypte, Ethiopia, Guineas, China in Cathayo, and Giapan: With a discourse of the Northwest passage. Gathered in oarte, and done into Englyshe by Richard Eden. Newly set in order, augmented, and finished by Richarde Willes*. London: Richard Jugge, 1577.

Williams, Clare, trans. *Thomas Platter's Travels in England, 1599*. London: Jonathan Cape, 1937.

Williamson, G. C. *Lady Anne Clifford, Countess of Dorset, Pembroke & Montgomery, 1590–1676: Her Life, Letters and Work Extracted from all the original documents available, many of which are here printed for the first time*. Kendal, England: Titus Wilson and Sons, 1922.

Williamson, James A. *The Cabot Voyages and Bristol Discovery Under Henry VII*. Cambridge: University Press, for the Hakluyt Society, 1962.

———, ed. *The Observations of Sir Richard Hawkins*. London: The Argonaut Press, 1933.

Wright, Louis B., ed. *A Voyage to Virginia in 1609. Two Narratives. Strachey's "True Reportory" and Jourdain's "Discovery of the Bermudas."* Rev. ed. Charlottesville: University of Virginia Press, 2013.

Yule, Sir Henry, trans. *The Travels of Friar Odoric: A 14th-Century Journal of the Blessed Odoric of Pordenone*. Introduction by Paolo Chiesa. Grand Rapids, MI: William B. Eerdmans Publishing Company, 2002.

Secondary Sources: Books

Ackermann, Silke, ed. *Humphrey Cole: Mint, Measurement and Maps in Elizabethan England*. London: British Museum Press, 1998. Occasional Paper No. 126.

Ackroyd, Peter. *The Life of Thomas More*. London: Chatto & Windus, 1998.

———. *Foundation: The History of England from Its Earliest Beginnings to the Tudors*. New York: Thomas Dunne Books, 2012.

Alford, Stephen. *The Early Elizabethan Polity: William Cecil and the British Succession Crisis, 1558–1569*. Cambridge: Cambridge University Press, 1998; paperback ed., 2002.

———. *Burghley: William Cecil at the Court of Elizabeth I*. New Haven, CT: Yale University Press, 2008.

Ames, Russell A. *Citizen More and His Utopia*. Princeton, NJ: Princeton University Press, 1949.

Andrews, Charles M. *The Colonial Period of American History*. 4 vols. New Haven, CT: Yale University Press, 1934; repr. 1964.

Andrews, Kenneth R. *Elizabethan Privateering: English Privateering During the Spanish War, 1585–1603*. Cambridge: Cambridge University Press, 1964; paperback edition, 2011.

———. *Trade, Plunder and Settlement: Maritime Enterprise and the Genesis of the British Empire, 1480–1630*. Cambridge: Cambridge University Press, 1984; repr. 1991.

Armitage, David. *The Ideological Origins of the British Empire*. Cambridge: Cambridge University Press, 2000.

Ash, Eric H. *Power, Knowledge, and Expertise in Elizabethan England*. Baltimore: Johns Hopkins University Press, 2004.

Aughton, Peter. *Bristol: A People's History*. Lancaster: Carnegie Publishing, 2000.

Bagwell, Richard. *Ireland Under the Tudors: With a Succinct Account of the Earlier History*. London: Longmans, Green, and Co., 1885.

Bailyn, Bernard. *The New England Merchants in the Seventeenth Century*. Cambridge, MA: Harvard University Press, 1955.

Bakewell, Peter. *Miners of the Red Mountain: Indian Labor in Potosí, 1545–1650*. Albuquerque: University of New Mexico Press, 2009.

Baxter, James Phinney, ed. *Sir Ferdinando Gorges and His Province of Maine*. 3 vols. Boston: The Prince Society XVIII, 1890. Reprinted by Burt Franklin: Research and Source Works Series #131, 1967.

Beaven, Alfred P. *The Aldermen of the City of London Temp. Henry III – 1912*. London: Corporation of the City of London, 1908.

Beazley, Charles R. *John and Sebastian Cabot: The Discovery of North America*. London: T. Fisher Unwin, 1898.

Beer, Barrett L. *Northumberland: The Political Career of John Dudley, Earl of Warwick and Duke of Northumberland*. Kent, OH: Kent State University Press, 1973.

————. *Rebellion and Riot: Popular Disorder in England during the Reign of Edward VI*. Kent, OH: Kent State University Press, 1982.

Bennet, H. S. *English Books & Readers 1475–1557*. Cambridge: Cambridge University Press, 1969.

Binyon, Laurence. *English Water-Colours*. London: A. & C. Black, 1933.

Blake, John W. *West Africa: Quest for God and Gold 1454–1578*. London: Curzon Press, 1977.

Boorstein, Daniel J. *The Discoverers: A History of Man's Search to Know His World and Himself*. New York: Vintage Books, 1985.

Borman, Tracy. *Elizabeth's Women: The Hidden Story of the Virgin Queen*. London: Vintage Books, 2009.

Bourne, Henry R. Fox. *English Merchants: Memoirs in Illustration of the Progress of British Commerce*. London: Chatto and Windus, Piccadilly, 1886.

Braudel, Fernand. *The Wheels of Commerce: Civilization & Capitalism, 15th–18th Century*. Translated by Siân Reynolds. New York: Harper & Row/Perennial Library, 1986.

————. *The Perspective of the World*. Berkeley: University of California Press, paperback ed., 1992.

Brenner, Robert. *Merchants and Revolution: Commercial Change, Political Conflict, and London's Overseas Traders, 1550–1653*. London: Verso, 2003.

Brigden, Susan. *New Worlds, Lost Worlds: The Rule of the Tudors 1485–1603*. London: Penguin Books, 2001.

Browning, William S. *The History of the Huguenotes during the Sixteenth Century: A new edition, continued to the present time*. London: Whittaker & Co., 1840.

Bunker, Nick. *Making Haste from Babylon: The Mayflower Pilgrims and Their World: A New History*. New York: Alfred A. Knopf, 2010.

Burgon, John William. *The Life and Times of Sir Thomas Gresham; Compiled Chiefly from His Correspondence Preserved in Her Majesty's State-Paper Office. Volume 1*. London: Robert Jennings, 1839.

Canny, Nicholas P. *The Elizabethan Conquest of Ireland: A Pattern Established 1565–76*. Hassocks: The Harvester Press, 1976.

Chambers, E. K. *William Shakespeare: A Study of Facts and Problems*. Vol. 1. Oxford: The Clarendon Press, 1930.

Chandler, E. J. *Ancient Sagadahoc: A Story of the Englishmen Who Welcomed the Pilgrims to the New World*. Thomaston: In association with the Conservatory of American Letters, 1998.

Chaudhuri, K. N. *The English East India Company. The Study of an Early Joint Stock Company 1600–1640*. London: Frank Cass & Co., 1965.

Churchill, Winston S. *A History of the English-Speaking Peoples. Volume II: The New World*. London: Cassell & Co., 1956; paperback edition, Bloomsbury Academic, 2015.

Clark, P., A. G. R. Smith and N. Tyacke, eds. *The English Commonwealth 1547–1640: Essays in politics and society presented to Joel Hurstfield*. Leicester: Leicester University Press, 1979.

Coldham, Peter Wilson. *Bonded Passengers to America. Two Volumes in One*. Baltimore: Genealogical Publishing Company, 1983.

Cooper, John. *The Queen's Agent: Francis Walsingham at the Court of Elizabeth I*. London: Faber and Faber, 2011.

Craven, Wesley Frank. *Dissolution of the Virginia Company. The Failure of a Colonial Experiment*. New York: Oxford University Press, 1932; repr. 1964.

Cussans, Thomas, et al., eds. *The Times Atlas of European History*. New York: Times Books, 1994.

Dalton, Heather. *Merchants and Explorers: Roger Barlow, Sebastian Cabot, and Networks of Atlantic Exchange, 1500–1560*. Oxford: Oxford University Press, 2016.

Davis, Ralph. *English Overseas Trade 1500–1700*. London: Macmillan, 1973.

Dewar, Mary. *Sir Thomas Smith: A Tudor Intellectual in Office*. London: The Athlone Press, 1964.

Dexter, Henry Martyn. *English Exiles in Amsterdam*. Cambridge: John Wilson and Son, University Press, 1890.

Dexter, Henry Martyn, and Morton Dexter. *The England and Holland of the Pilgrims*. Boston: Houghton, Mifflin and Company; Cambridge: The Riverside Press, 1905.

Díaz, Bernal. *The Conquest of New Spain*. Edited and translated by J. M. Cohen. London: Penguin Books, 1963.

Donald, M. B. *Elizabethan Copper: The History of the Company of Mines Royal, 1568–1605*. London: Pergamon Press, 1955.

————. *Elizabethan Monopolies: The History of the Company of Mineral and Battery Works from 1565 to 1604*. London: Oliver and Boyd, 1961.

Duff, E. Gordon. *A Century of the English Book Trade*. London: Cambridge University Press, 1905. Digital reprint 2011.

Elliott, J., and L. Brockliss, eds. *The World of the Favourite*. New Haven, CT: Yale University Press, 1999.

Ellis, Steven G., *Tudor Ireland. Crown, Community and the Conflict of Cultures, 1470–1603*. London and New York: Longman Group, 1985.

Elton, G. R, ed. *The Reformation, 1520–1559*. Cambridge: Cambridge University Press, 1958; paperback edition, 1975.

Evans, James. *Merchant Adventurers. The voyage of discovery that transformed Tudor England*. London: Weidenfeld & Nicolson, 2013; paperback, Phoenix, 2014.

Firstbrook, Peter. *A Man Most Driven. Captain John Smith, Pocahontas and the Founding of America*. London: Oneworld Publications, 2015.

Fischer, David Hackett. *The Great Wave: Price Revolutions and the Rhythm of History*. New York: Oxford University Press, 1996.

————. *Champlain's Dream: The European Founding of North America*. New York: Simon & Schuster, 2008.

Foster, Roy F. *Modern Ireland 1600–1972*. London: Allen Lane, 1988; paperback edition, Penguin Books, 1989.

Foster, William. *England's Quest of Eastern Trade*. London: A. & C. Black, 1933.

Gaskell, Philip. *Trinity College Library: The First 150 years. The Sandars Lectures 1978–1979*. Cambridge: Cambridge University Press, 1980.

Gasquet, Francis Aidan. *Henry VIII and the English Monasteries*. London: John C. Nimmo, 1899.

Gater, G. H., and Walter H. Godfrey, eds. *Survey of London: Volume 15, All Hallows, Barking-By-The-Tower, Pt II*. London: London City Council, 1934.

Gookin, Warner F. *Bartholomew Gosnold. Discoverer and Planter. New England, 1602. Virginia, 1607*. Completed by Philip L. Barbour. Hamden, Connecticut and London, England: Archon Books, 1963.

Gorges, Raymond. *The Story of a Family Through Eleven Centuries: History of the Family Gorges*. Boston: Privately printed, 1944.

Gosling, William G. *The Life of Sir Humphrey Gilbert: England's First Empire Builder*. London: Constable & Co., 1911.

Gras, N. S. B., and Henrietta M. Larson. *Casebook in American Business History.* New York: Appleton-Century-Crofts, 1939.

Gross, Charles. *The Gild Merchant, Volume I.* Oxford: Oxford University Press, 1890; repr. 1964.

Grummitt, David. *The Calais Garrison: War and Military Service in England, 1436–1558.* Woodbridge, Suffolk: The Boydell Press, 2008.

Guy, John. *Elizabeth: The Forgotten Years.* London: Viking, 2016.

Hall, Hubert. *History of the Custom-Revenue in England from the Earliest Times to the Year 1827.* 2 vols. London: Elliot Stock, 1885.

Hamel, Dr. J. *Early English Voyages to Northern Russia; Comprising the Voyages of John Tradescant the Elder, Sir Hugh Willoughby, Richard Chancellor, Nelson, and Others.* Translated by John Studdy Leigh. London: Richard Bentley, 1857.

Hanke, Lewis. *Aristotle and the American Indians: A Study in Race Prejudice in the Modern World.* London: Hollis and Carter, 1959.

Harisse, Henry. *John Cabot, the Discoverer of North-America, and Sebastian, His Son: A Chapter of the Maritime History of England Under the Tudors, 1496–1557.* London: Benjamin Franklin Stevens, 1896.

Harkness, Deborah E. *The Jewel House: Elizabethan London and the Scientific Revolution.* New Haven, CT: Yale University Press, 2007.

Hibbert, Christopher. *The English: A Social History, 1066–1945.* London: HarperCollins, 1987; paperback, 1994.

The History of Parliament: The House of Commons 1509–1558. 3 vols. Edited by S. T. Bindoff. London: History of Parliament Trust, 1982; online edition.

The History of Parliament: The House of Commons 1558–1603. 3 vols. Edited by P. W. Hasler. London: History of Parliament Trust, 1981; online edition.

The History of Parliament: The House of Commons 1604–1629. 6 vols. Edited by Andrew Thrush and John P. Ferris. London: History of Parliament Trust, 2010; online edition.

Hodge, H. S. Vere. *Sir Andrew Judde.* Tonbridge: Tonbridge School Shop, n.d.

Hogarth, Donald D., Peter W. Boreham, and John G. Mitchell, *Martin Frobisher's Northwest Venture, 1576–1581. Mines, Minerals, Metallurgy.* Hull, Quebec: Canadian Museum of Civilization, 1994.

Holland Rose, J., A. P. Newton and E. A. Benians, eds. *The Cambridge History of the British Empire. Volume I. The Old Empire from the beginnings to 1783.* Cambridge: Cambridge University Press, 1929.

Hope, Valerie, Clive Birch, and Gilbert Torrey, eds. *The Freedom: The Past and Present of the Livery, Guilds and City of London.* Buckingham: Barracuda Books, 1982.

Horn, James. *A Land As God Made It: Jamestown and the Birth of America.* New York: Basic Books, 2005; paperback edition, 2006.

Hosking, Geoffrey. *Russia and the Russians from the Earliest Times to the Present.* Rev. ed. London: Penguin Books, 2012.

Hunt, Alice. *The Drama of Coronation: Medieval Ceremony in Early Modern England.* Cambridge: Cambridge University Press, 2008.

Jones, H. G., ed. *Raleigh and Quinn: The Explorer and his Boswell.* Chapel Hill: North Caroliniana Society, 1987.

Jones, W. R. D. *The Tudor Commonwealth 1529–1559.* London: The Athlone Press, 1970.

Jordan, W. K. *Edward VI. The Young King. The Protectorship of the Duke of Somerset.* London: George Allen and Unwin, 1968.

———. *Edward VI: The Threshold of Power. The Dominance of the Duke of Northumberland.* London: George Allen & Unwin, 1970.

Kelsey, Harry. *Sir Francis Drake. The Queen's Pirate.* New Haven, CT: Yale University Press, 1998.

Kim, W. Chan, and Renee Mauborgne, *Blue Ocean Strategy: How to Create Uncontested Market Space and Make the Competition Irrelevant.* Boston: Harvard Business School Press, 2005.

Kupperman, Karen Ordahl, *The Jamestown Project.* Cambridge, MA: The Belknap Press of Harvard University Press, 2007.

Lacey, Robert. *Sir Walter Ralegh.* London: Weidenfeld & Nicholson, 1973; paperback ed., 1975.

Lach, Donald F. *Asia in the Making of Europe: Volume I: The Century of Discovery*. Chicago: The University of Chicago Press, 1965.

Landes, David S., Joel Mokyr, and William J. Baumol, eds. *The Invention of Enterprise. Entrepreneurship from Ancient Mesopotamia to Modern Times*. Princeton, NJ: Princeton University Press, 2010.

Le Strange, Richard. *A History of Herbal Plants*. New York: Arco Publishing, 1977.

Levathes, Louise. *When China Ruled the Seas: The Treasure Fleet of the Dragon Throne, 1405–1433*. New York: Oxford University Press, 1994.

Lloyd, Rachel. *Elizabethan Adventurer: A Life of Captain Christopher Carleill*. London: Hamish Hamilton, 1974.

Loades, David M. *John Dudley Duke of Northumberland 1504–1553*. Oxford: Clarendon Press, 1996.

———. *England's Maritime Empire: Seapower, Commerce and Policy, 1490–1690*. London: Longman, 2000.

Lynch, Martin. *Mining in World History*. London: Reaktion Books, 2002.

Lynam, Edward, ed. *Richard Hakluyt and His Successors*. London: The Hakluyt Society, 1946. Repr. London: Kraus Reprint Limited, 1967.

MacGregor, Neil. *A History of the World in 100 Objects*. London: Allen Lane, 2010.

———. *Shakespeare's Restless World*. London: Allen Lane, 2013.

Maddison, Angus. *The World Economy: A Millennial Perspective*. Paris: OECD Publications, 2001.

Mancall, Peter C., ed. *The Atlantic World and Virginia, 1550–1624*. Chapel Hill: University of North Carolina Press, 2007.

Mann, Charles C. *1491: New Revelations of the Americas Before Columbus*. New York: Alfred P. Knopf, 2005.

Mayers, Kit. *North-east Passage to Muscovy: Stephen Borough and the First Tudor Explorations*. Stroud, England: Sutton Publishing, 2005.

McDermott, James. *Martin Frobisher: Elizabethan Privateer*. New Haven, CT: Yale University Press, 2001.

McGhee, Robert. *The Arctic Voyages of Martin Frobisher: An Elizabethan Adventure*. Montreal: Canadian Museum of Civilization, 2001.

McIntyre, Ruth A. *Debts Hopeful and Desperate: Financing the Plymouth Colony*. Plymouth: Plimoth Plantation, Inc. 1963.

Mickelthwait, John, and Adrian Wooldridge. *The Company: A Short History of a Revolutionary Idea*. London: Phoenix Books, 2005.

Mills, William J. *Exploring Polar Frontiers: A Historical Encyclopedia*. Santa Barbara: ABC Clio, 2003.

Morison, Samuel Eliot. *The Great Explorers: The European Discovery of America*. New York: Oxford University Press, 1978.

Nicholls, Mark, and Penry Williams, *Sir Walter Raleigh in Life and Legend*. London: Continuum International Publishing, 2011.

Norman, Philip and W. D. Caroe, *Crosby Place*. London: Survey of London, Monograph No. 9, 1908.

Oxford Dictionary of National Biography. Oxford: Oxford University Press. Web.

Oxford English Dictionary. Oxford: Oxford University Press. Web.

Parker, Geoffrey. *The Dutch Revolt*. London: Pelican Books, 1979.

———. *Imprudent King: A New Life of Philip II*. New Haven, CT: Yale University Press, 2014; paperback ed., 2015.

Parker, John. *Books to Build an Empire: A Bibliographical History of English Overseas Interest to 1620*. Amsterdam: N. Israel, 1965.

Parks, George Bruner, *Richard Hakluyt and the English Voyages*. New York: The American Geographical Society of New York, 1928.

Parry, Glyn. *The Arch-Conjuror of England: John Dee*. New Haven, CT: Yale University Press, 2013.

Parry, J. H. *The Discovery of the Sea*. Berkeley: University of California Press, 1981.

Philbrick, Nathaniel. *Mayflower: A Story of Courage, Community, and War*. New York: Penguin, 2006.

Phillips, Kim M. *Before Orientalism: Asian Peoples and Cultures in European Travel Writing, 1245–1510*. Philadelphia: University of Pennsylvania Press, 2014.

Picard, Liza. *Elizabeth's London, Everyday Life in Elizabethan London*. London: Phoenix Books, 2004.

Plooij, D. *Pilgrim Fathers from a Dutch Point of View*. New York: The New York University Press, 1932.

Power, Eileen. *The Wool Trade in English Medieval History*. London: Oxford University Press, 1941.

Preston, Richard Arthur. *Gorges of Plymouth Fort: A life of Sir Ferdinando Gorges, Captain of Plymouth Fort, Governor of New England, and Lord of the Province of Maine*. Toronto: University of Toronto Press, in cooperation with the Royal Military College of Canada, 1953.

Quinn, David B. *Richard Hakluyt, Editor*. Amsterdam: Theatrum Orbis Terrarum, Ltd., 1967.

———. *Ralegh and the British Empire*. Harmondsworth: Pelican Books, 1973.

———. *England and the Discovery of America, 1481–1620*. London: George Allen & Unwin, 1974.

———. *The Hakluyt Handbook*. 2 vols. London: The Hakluyt Society, 1974.

———. *Set Fair for Roanoke: Voyages and Colonies, 1584–1606*. Chapel Hill: The University of North Carolina Press, 1985.

———. *Explorers and Colonies: America, 1500–1625*. London: The Hambledon Press, 1990.

———. *Sebastian Cabot and Bristol Exploration*. Rev. ed. Bristol: The Bristol Branch of the Historical Association, 1997.

Ramsay, G. D. *English Overseas Trade during the Centuries of Emergence*. London: Macmillan, 1957.

———. *The City of London in the International Politics at the Accession of Elizabeth Tudor*. Manchester: Manchester University Press, 1975.

———. *The Queen's Merchants and the Revolt of the Netherlands*. Manchester: Manchester University Press, 1986.

Rappaport, Steve. *Worlds Within Worlds: Structures of Life in Sixteenth-Century London*. Cambridge: Cambridge University Press, 1989.

Rapple, Rory. *Martial Power and Elizabethan Political Culture. Military Men in England and Ireland, 1558–1594*. Cambridge: Cambridge University Press, 2009.

Read, Conyers. *Mr. Secretary Walsingham and the policy of Queen Elizabeth*. 3 vols. Oxford: The Clarendon Press, 1925.

Rich, E. E. *The Ordinance Book of the Merchants of the Staple with an introduction*. Cambridge: Cambridge University Press, 1937.

Rodger, N. A. M. *The Safeguard of the Sea: A Naval History of Britain 600–1649*. London: HarperCollins, 1997; paperback ed., Penguin Books, 2004.

Rose, Susan. *Calais: An English Town in France 1347–1558*. Woodbridge: The Boydell Press, 2008.

Rountree, Helen C. *The Powhatan Indians of Virginia. Their Traditional Culture*. Norman: University of Oklahoma Press, 1989.

Rowse, A. L., *Sir Richard Grenville of the Revenge. An Elizabethan Hero*. London. Jonathan Cape, 1937.

———. *The Expansion of Elizabethan England*. London: Macmillan & Co., Ltd., 1955.

———. *Ralegh and the Throckmortons*. London: MacMillan & Co., 1962.

———. *Shakespeare's Southampton: Patron of Virginia*. London: Macmillan, 1965.

Russell, Frederic William. *Kett's Rebellion in Norfolk: Being a History of the Great Civil Commotion That Occurred at the Time of the Reformation, in the Reign of Edward VI*. London: Longman, Brown, Green, Longmans & Roberts, Paternoster Row; and William Penny, 57, Lincoln's Inn Fields, 1859.

Saunders, Ann, ed. *The Royal Exchange*. London: London Topographical Society, Publication No. 152, 1997.

Scammell, G. V. *The World Encompassed: The First European Maritime Empires, c. 800–1650*. London: Methuen, 1981.

Schreiber, Roy E. *The Political Career of Sir Robert Naunton 1589–1635*. London: Royal Historical Society, 1981.

Scott, William Robert. *The Constitution and Finance of English, Scottish and Irish Joint-Stock Companies to 1720*. 3 vols. Cambridge: University Press, 1910.

Shaffer, Marjorie. *Pepper: A History of the World's Most Influential Spice.* New York: Thomas Dunne Books, 2013.

Sherman, William H. *John Dee: The Politics of Reading and Writing in the English Renaissance.* Amherst: University of Massachusetts Press, 1995.

Shirley, John W. *Thomas Harriot: A Biography.* Oxford: Clarendon Press, 1983.

Simon, Joan. *Education and Society in Tudor England.* Cambridge: Cambridge University Press, 1966.

Skidmore, Chris. *Edward VI: The Lost King of England.* London: Weidenfeld and Nicolson, 2008.

Sloan, Kim, ed. *A New World: England's First View of America.* London: British Museum Press, 2007.

Strong, Roy. *Gloriana: The Portraits of Queen Elizabeth I.* London: Thames & Hudson, 1987.

Sugden, John. *Sir Francis Drake.* London: Barrie & Jenkins, 1990; paperback ed., Pimlico, 2006.

Sutton, Anne F. *The Mercery of London: Trade, Goods and People, 1130–1578.* Farnham, Surrey: Ashgate Publishing, 2005.

Symons, Thomas, ed. *Meta Incognita: A Discourse of Discovery. Martin Frobisher's Arctic Expeditions, 1576–1578.* 2 vols. Hull, Quebec: Canadian Museum of Civilization, 1999.

Taylor, Alan. *American Colonies. The Settling of North America.* New York: Viking Penguin, 2001; paperback, 2002.

Taylor, E. G. R. *Tudor Geography 1485–1583.* London: Methuen & Co., 1930.

Thrower, Norman J. W. *Sir Francis Drake and the Famous Voyage, 1577–1580.* Berkeley: University of California Press, 1984.

Trevelyan, George Macaulay. *Illustrated English Social History, Volume 1: Chaucer's England and the Early Tudors.* London: Longmans and Green, 1949.

Trevelyan, Raleigh. *Sir Walter Raleigh: Being a True and Vivid Account of the Life and Times of the Explorer, Soldier, Scholar, Poet, and Courtier — The Controversial Hero of the Elizabethan Age.* New York: Henry Holt & Co., 2004.

Turner, Jack. *Spice: The History of a Temptation.* New York: Alfred A. Knopf, 2004; Vintage Books, 2005.

Vaughan, Alden T. *Transatlantic Encounters: American Indians in Britain, 1500–1776.* Cambridge: Cambridge University Press, 2006.

Vela, Bartolomé Arzáns de Orsúa. *Tales of Potosí.* Edited by R. C. Padden and translated from the Spanish by Frances M. López-Morillas. Providence, RI: Brown University Press, 1975.

Voyce, Arthur. *The Moscow Kremlin: Its History, Architecture and Art Treasures.* Berkeley: University of California Press, 1954.

Wagner, Henry R. *Sir Francis Drake's Voyage Around the World: Its Aims and Achievements.* San Francisco: John Howell, 1926.

Walton, Timothy R. *The Spanish Treasure Fleets.* Sarasota, FL: Pineapple Press, Inc., 1994.

Whitelock, Anna. *Elizabeth's Bedfellow. An Intimate History of the Queen's Court.* London: Bloomsbury, 2014.

Willan, T. S. *The Muscovy Merchants of 1555.* Manchester: Manchester University Press, 1953; repr. 1973.

————. *The Early History of the Russia Company, 1553–1603.* Manchester: Manchester University Press, 1956; repr. 1968.

————. *Studies in Elizabethan Foreign Trade.* Manchester: Manchester University Press, 1959; repr. 1968.

Williamson, James A. *Hawkins of Plymouth.* Rev. ed. London: A. & C. Black, 1969.

————. *Sir John Hawkins: The Time and the Man.* Oxford: Clarendon Press, 1927.

Willison, George F. *Saints and Strangers: Being the Lives of the Pilgrim Fathers & Their Families, with The Friends & Foes; & an Account of Their Posthumous Wanderings in Limbo, Their Final Resurrection & Rise to Glory, & the Strange Pilgrimages of Plymouth Rock.* New York: Reynal & Hitchcock, 1945.

Wilson, A. N. *The Elizabethans.* London: Hutchinson, 2011; paperback edition, Arrow Books, 2012.

Wilson, Derek. *The World Encompassed: Francis Drake and His Great Voyage.* New York, Harper & Row, 1977.

Wood, Alfred C. *A History of the Levant Company.* Oxford: Oxford University Press, 1935.

Woolley, Benjamin. *The Queen's Conjuror: The Life and Magic of Dr Dee.* London: Flamingo, 2002.
Wootton, David. *The Invention of Science: A New History of the Scientific Revolution.* London: Allen Lane, 2015.

Secondary Sources: Articles

Adams, Simon. "Elizabeth I and the Sovereignty of the Netherlands 1576–1585." *Transactions of the Royal Historical Society* 4 (2004): 309–19.

Andrews, Kenneth R. K. "Christopher Newport of Limehouse, Mariner." *The William and Mary Quarterly* 11, no. 1 (1954): 28–41.

———. "The Aims of Drake's Expedition of 1577–1580." *The American Historical Review* 73, no. 3 (1968): 724–41.

———. "English Voyages to the Caribbean, 1596 to 1604: An Annotated List." *The William and Mary Quarterly* 31, no. 2 (1974): 243–54.

Archer, Ian W. "Sir Thomas Smythe (c. 1558–1625). A lecture delivered at Skinners' Hall, London, November 26, 2007.": Oxford University Research Archive, https://ora.ox.ac.uk/objects/uuid:4a1c5a8a-78f1-4dfa-9c79-6f94a6161659.

Barbour, Philip L. "Captain George Kendall: Mutineer or Intelligencer?" *The Virginia Magazine of History and Biography* 70, no. 3 (1962), 297–313.

Beecher, Donald. "The Legacy of John Frampton: Elizabethan Trader and Translator," *Renaissance Studies* 20, no. 3 (2006), 320–39.

Bernhard, Virginia. "Bermuda and Virginia in the Seventeenth Century: A Comparative View." *Journal of Social History* 19, no. 1 (1985): 57–70.

Blatcher, Maragaret. "Chatham Dockyard and a Little-Known Shipwright, Matthew Baker (1530–1613)." *Archaeologia Cantiana* 107 (1989): 155–72.

Bourque, Bruce J., and Ruth Holmes Whitehead. "Tarrentines and the Introduction of European Trade Goods in the Gulf of Maine." *Ethnohistory* 32, no. 4 (1985): 327–41.

Bowden, P. J. "Wool Supply and the Woollen Industry." *The Economic History Review,* n.s., 9, no. 1 (1956): 44–58.

Brenner, Robert. "The Social Basis of English Commercial Expansion, 1550–1650." *The Journal of Economic History* 32, no. 1 (1972): 361–84.

Caballo, Diego, and F. A. Kirkpatrick. "The First Recorded English Voyage to the West Indies." *The English Historical Review* 20, no. 77 (1905): 115–24.

Carus, E. M. "The English Cloth Industry in the Late Twelfth and Early Thirteenth Centuries," *Economic History Review* 14, no. 1 (1944): 32–50.

Chin, Tamara. "The Invention of the Silk Road, 1877," *Critical Inquiry* 40, no. 1 (2013): 194–219.

Cobb, Gwendolin B. "Supply and Transportation for the Potosí Mines." *The Hispanic American Historical Review* 29, no. 1 (1949): 25–45.

Craven, Wesley Frank. "An Introduction to the History of Bermuda, Part I." *The William and Mary Quarterly* 17, no. 2 (1937): 176–215.

Croft, Pauline. "Trading with the Enemy, 1585–1604," *The Historical Journal* 32, no. 2 (1989): 281–302.

———. 'The Reputation of Robert Cecil: Libels, Political Opinion and Popular Awareness in the Early Seventeenth Century." *Transactions of the Royal Historical Society* 1 (1991): 43–69.

Dewar, Mary. "The Authorship of the 'Discourse of the Commonweal.'" *The Economic History Review,* n.s., 19, no. 2 (1966): 388–400.

Dunlop, Robert. "The Plantation of Munster 1584–1589." *The English Historical Review* 3, no. 10 (1888): 150–69.

———. "Sixteenth Century Schemes for the Plantation of Ulster, Part I." *The Scottish Historical Review* 22, no. 85 (1924): 51–60.

———. "Sixteenth Century Schemes for the Plantation of Ulster, Part II." *The Scottish Historical Review* 22, no. 86 (1925): 115–26.

———. "Sixteenth Century Schemes for the Plantation of Ulster, Part III." *The Scottish Historical Review* 22, no. 87 (1925): 199–212.

Select Bibliography

Drelichman, Mauricio. "American Silver and the Decline of Spain." *The Journal of Economic History* 65, no. 2 (2005): 532–35.

Eldred, Jason. "The Just Will Pay for the Sinners: English Merchants, the Trade with Spain, and Elizabethan Foreign Policy, 1563–1585." *Journal for Early Modern Cultural Studies* 10, no. 1 (2010): 5–28.

Ellison, James. "'Measure for Measure' and the Execution of Catholics in 1604." *English Literary Renaissance* 33, no. 1 (2003): 44–87.

Estes, J. Worth. "The European Reception of the First Drugs from the New World." *Pharmacy in History* 37, no. 1 (1995): 3–23.

Ewan, Joseph. "Plant Resources in Colonial America." *Environmental Review* 1, no. 2 (1976): 44–55.

Fincham, Kenneth, and Peter Lake. "The Ecclesiastical Policy of King James I." *Journal of British Studies* 24, no. 2 (1985): 169–207.

Fisher, F. J. "Commercial Trends and Policy in Sixteenth-Century England," *The Economic History Review* 10, no. 2 (1940): 95–117

Gomes, Peter J. "Pilgrims and Puritans: 'Heroes' and 'Villains' in the Creation of the American Past." *Proceedings of the Massachusetts Historical Society,* third series, 95 (1983): 1–16.

Gookin, Warner F. "Who Was Bartholomew Gosnold?" *The William and Mary Quarterly* 6, no. 3, (1949): 398–415.

———. "The First Leaders at Jamestown." *The Virginia Magazine of History and Biography* 58, no. 2, (1950): 181–93.

Gordon, Eleanora C. "The Fate of Sir Hugh Willoughby and His Companions: A New Conjecture." *The Geographic Journal* 152, no. 2 (1986): 243–47.

Gorman, M. Adele Francis. "Jean Ribault's Colonies in Florida." *The Florida Historical Quarterly* 44, no. ½, Quadricentennial Edition (1965): 51–66.

Gray, Janet G. "The Origin of the Word Huguenot." *The Sixteenth Century Journal* 14, no. 3 (1983): 349–59.

Greninger, Edwin T. "Thanksgiving: An American Holiday." *Social Science* 54, no. 1 (1979): 3–15.

Harkness, Deborah E. "Managing an Experimental Household: The Dees of Mortlake and the Practice of Natural Philosophy." *Isis* 88, no. 2 (1997): 247–62.

Higgins, Pat. "Popham Colony: A Slice of Time." *The Maine Story,* accessed December 19, 2016, http://www.mainestory.info/maine-stories/popham-colony.html.

Jenkins, Raymond. "'Newes out of Munster,' a Document in Spenser's Hand." *Studies in Philology* 32, no. 2 (1935): 125–30.

Jensen, De Lamar. "The Spanish Armada: The Worst-Kept Secret in Europe." *The Sixteenth Century Journal* 19, no. 4 (1988): 621–41.

Johnson, Robert C. "The Lotteries of the Virginia Company, 1612–1621." *The Virginia Magazine of History and Biography* 74, no. 3 (1966): 259–92.

Jones, Evan. "The Matthew of Bristol and the Financiers of John Cabot's 1497 Voyage to North America." *The English Historical Review* 121, no. 492 (2006): 778–95.

Jones, William M. "Two Learned Italians in Elizabethan England." *Italica* 32, no.4 (1955): 242–47.

Kraft, Herbert C. "Sixteenth and Seventeenth Century Indian/White Trade Relations in the Middle Atlantic and Northeast Regions." *Archaeology of Eastern North America* 17 (1989): 1-29.

Lennard, E. W. "Some Intimate Bristol Connections with the Overseas Empire," *Geography* 16, no. 2 (1931): 109–121.

Lough, Susan M. "Trade and Industry in Ireland in the Sixteenth Century." *Journal of Political Economy* 24, no. 7 (1916): 713–30.

MacCaffrey, Wallace T. "The Newhaven Expedition, 1562–1563." *The Historical Journal* 40, no. 1 (1997): 1–21.

MacMillan, Ken. "John Dee's 'Brytanici Imperii Limites.'" *Huntington Library Quarterly* 64, no. ½ (2001): 151–59.

———. "Sovereignty 'More Plainly Described': Early English Maps of North America, 1580–1625." *Journal of British Studies* 42, no. 4 (2003): 413–47.

Marsden, R. G. "The Early Career of Martin Frobisher." *The English Historical Review* 21, no. 83 (1906): 538–44.

McGrath, John T. "Admiral Coligny, Jean Ribault, and the East Coast of North America." *French Colonial History* 1 (2002): 63–76.

Merriman, Roger Bigelow. "Some Notes on the Treatment of English Catholics in the Reign of Elizabeth." *The American Historical Review* 13, no. 3 (1908): 480–500.

Monkhouse, F. J. "Some Features of the Historical Geography of the German Mining Enterprise in Elizabethan Lakeland." *Geography* 28, no. 4, (1943): 107–13.

Morgan, Hiram. "The Colonial Venture of Sit Thomas Smith in Ulster, 1571–1575." *The Historical Journal* 28, no. 2 (1985): 261–78.

Mund, Stephane. "The Discovery of Muscovite Russia in Tudor England," *Revue Belge de Philologie et d'Histoire* 86, no. 2 (2008): 351–73.

Murdock, Kenneth B. "The Pilgrims' Progress." *New York Times Book Review,* September 28, 1952, 15.

Nicholls, Mark. "George Percey's 'Trewe Relacyon': A Primary Source for the Jamestown Settlement." *The Virginia Magazine of History and Biography* 133, no. 3 (2005): 212–75.

————. "Strategy and Motivation in the Gunpowder Plot." *The Historical Journal* 50, no. 4 (2007): 787–807.

Norman, Philip, and W. D. Caroe. "The Architecture of Crosby Hall," in *Survey of London Monograph 9, Crosby Place.* London, 1908. British History Online, http://www.british-history.ac.uk/survey-london/bk9/pp57-63.

————. "The History of Crosby Place," in *Survey of London Monograph 9, Crosby Place.* London, 1908. British History Online, http://www.british-history.ac.uk/survey-london/bk9/pp15-32.

Northrup, David. "Vasco da Gama and Africa: An Era of Mutual Discovery, 1497–1800." *Journal of World History* 9, no. 2 (1998): 189–211.

Owens, Robert R. "The Myth of Anian." *Journal of the History of Ideas* 36, no. 1 (1975): 135–38.

Parks, George B. "George Peele and His Friends as 'Ghost'-Poets." *The Journal of English and Germanic Philology* 41, no. 4 (1942): 527–36.

Pearson, Kathy L. "Nutrition and the Early-Medieval Diet." *Speculum* 72, no. 1 (1997): 1–32.

Pleck, Elizabeth. "The Making of the Domestic Occasion: The History of Thanksgiving in the United States." *Journal of Social History* 32, no. 4 (1999): 773–89.

Poole, Robert. " 'Give Us Our Eleven Days!': Calendar Reform in Eighteenth-Century England." *Past & Present* 149 (1995): 95–139.

Popper, Nicholas. "The English Polydaedali: How Gabriel Harvey Read Late Tudor London." *Journal of the History of Ideas* 66, no. 3 (2005): 351–81.

Potter, David. "The Duc de Guise and the Fall of Calais 1557–1558." *English Historical Review* 98, no. 388 (1983): 481–512.

Quinn, David B. "Sir Thomas Smith (1513–1577) and the Beginning of English Colonial Theory." *Proceedings of the American Philosophical Society* 89, no. 4 (1945): 543–60.

————. "Preparations for the 1585 Virginia Voyage." *The William and Mary Quarterly* 6, no. 2 (1949): 208–36.

————. "Some Spanish Reactions to Elizabethan Colonial Enterprises." *Transactions of the Royal Historical Society* 1 (1951): 1–21.

————. "Thomas Hariot and the Virginia Voyages of 1602." *The William and Mary Quarterly* 27, no. 2 (1970): 268–81.

Read, Conyers. "Queen Elizabeth's Seizure of the Duke of Alva's Pay-Ships." *The Journal of Modern History* 5, no. 4 (1933): 443–64.

Reed, Arthur W. "John Rastell's Voyage in the Year of 1517." *The Mariners Mirror* 9, no. 5 (1923): 137–47.

Rorke, Martin. "English and Scottish Overseas Trade, 1300–1600." *The Economic History Review,* n.s., 59, no. 2 (2006): 265–88.

Sandman, Allison, and Eric H. Ash. "Trading Expertise: Sebastian Cabot between Spain and England." *Renaissance Quarterly* 57, no. 3 (2004): 813–46.

Schnurmann, Claudia. " 'Wherever profit leads us, to every sea and shore...' the VOC, the WIC, and Dutch methods of globalization in the seventeenth century." *Renaissance Studies* 17, no. 3 (2003): 474–93.

Scott, James W. "Technological and Economic Changes in the Metalliferous Mining and Smelting Industries of Tudor England." *Albion: A Quarterly Journal Concerned with British Studies* 4, no. 2 (1972): 94–110.

Stevenson, Edward L. "The Geographical Activities of the Casa de la Contratación." *Annals of the Association of American Geographers* 17, no. 2 (1927): 39–59.

Sutherland, N. M. "Queen Elizabeth and the Conspiracy of Ambiose, March 1560." *The English Historical Review* 81, no. 320 (1966): 474–89.

Sykes, Godfrey. "The Mythical Straits of Anian." *Bulletin of the American Geographical Society* 47, no. 3 (1915): 161–72.

Taylor, E. G. R. "The Missing Draft Project of Drake's Voyage of 1577-90." *The Geographical Journal* 75, no. 1 (1930): 46–47.

Tucker, Edward L. "Longfellow's 'Courtship of Miles Standish': Some Notes and Two Early Versions." *Studies in American Renaissance* (1985): 285–321.

Vaughan, Alden T. "Sir Walter Ralegh's Indian Interpreters, 1584–1618." *The William and Mary Quarterly* 59, no. 2 (2002): 341–76.

Wallis, Helen. "England's Search for the Northern Passages in the Sixteenth and Early Seventeenth Centuries." *Arctic* 37, no. 4 (1984): 453–72.

Wills, Anne Blue. "Pilgrims and Progress: How Magazines Made Thanksgiving." *Church History* 72, no. 1 (2003): 138–58.

Willson, Lawrence. "Another View of the Pilgrims." *The New England Quarterly* 34, no. 2 (1962): 160–77.

Winer, Carol Z. "The Beleaguered Isle. A Study of Elizabethan and Early Jacobean Anti-Catholicism." *Past & Present*, no. 51 (1971): 27–62.

Woodward, Walter W. "Captain John Smith and the Campaign for New England: A Study in Early Modern Identity and Promotion." *The New England Quarterly* 81, no. 1 (2008): 91–125.

Wretts-Smith, Mildred. "The English in Russia during the Second Half of the Sixteenth Century." *Transactions of the Royal Historical Society* 3 (1920): 72–102.

Notes

THE PREQUEL TO THE PILGRIMS

[1] "Pilgrim Fathers," *Oxford English Dictionary*; definition C2.
[2] John Stowe and Edmund Howes, *Annales, or a General Chronicle of England, begun by John Stow: continued and augmented with matters Forraigne and Domestique, Ancient and Moderne, unto the end of this present yeere* (London, 1631), 605.

I. WAXING COLD AND IN DECAY

[1] W. K. Jordan, *Edward VI. The Young King. The Protectorship of the Duke of Somerset* (London: George Allen and Unwin, 1968), 402–3.
[2] John Norden cited in Christopher Hibbert, *The English: A Social History, 1066–1945* (London: HarperCollins, 1987; paperback, 1994), 173.
[3] P. J. Bowden, "Wool Supply and the Woolen Industry," *The Economic History Review*, n.s. 9, no. 1 (1956): 44–58; 45.
[4] David Loades, *England's Maritime Empire: Seapower, Commerce and Policy, 1490–1690* (London: Longman, 2000), 15–16.
[5] Martin Rorke, "English and Scottish Overseas Trade, 1300–1600," *The Economic History Review*, n.s., 59, no. 2 (2006): 265–88; 274.
[6] Sir Edward Coke (1552–1634), speaking in Parliament in 1621; cited in Nick Bunker, *Making Haste from Babylon: The Mayflower Pilgrims and Their World: A New History* (New York: Alfred A. Knopf, 2010), 252.
[7] From the records of the Worshipful Company of Woolmen, http://woolmen.com/home/history/.
[8] Anne F. Sutton, *The Mercery of London: Trade, Goods and People, 1130–1578* (Farnham, Surrey: Ashgate Publishing, 2005), 49; 3–5.
[9] John William Burgon, *The Life and Times of Sir Thomas Gresham; Compiled Chiefly from His Correspondence Preserved in Her Majesty's State-Paper Office*, 2 vols. (London: Robert Jennings, 1839), 1:5–43; Ian Blanchard, "Sir Thomas Gresham (c. 1518–1579), mercer, merchant adventurer, and founder of the Royal Exchange and Gresham College," in *Oxford Dictionary of National Biography* (Oxford: Oxford University Press, online edition); Ian Blanchard, "Sir Richard Gresham (c.1485–1549),

mercer, merchant advengturer and mayor of London," in ibid.; and William Harrison, *The Description of England. The Classic Contemporary Account of Tudor Social Life*, ed. Georges Edelen (Washington and New York: Folger Shakespeare Library and Dover Publications, 1994), 132.

[10] Burgon, *The Life and Times of Sir Thomas Gresham*, 1:72.

[11] Francesco Guicciardini, Florentine statesman and chronicler, cited in Burgon, *The Life and Times of Sir Thomas Gresham*, 1:76. Also: S. T. Bindoff, "The Greatness of Antwerp," in *The New Cambridge Modern History. Volume II. The Reformation 1520–1559*, ed. G. R. Elton (1958; repr. Cambridge: Cambridge University Press, 1975), 50–69.

[12] Thomas Smith to William Cecil, July 19, 1549, in Patrick F. Tytler, *England Under the Reigns of Edward VI and Mary*, 2 vols. (London: Richard Bentley, 1839), 1:185–89; 185.

[13] Mary Dewar, *Sir Thomas Smith. A Tudor Intellectual in Office* (London: Athlone Press, 1964), 29–30 (provost of Eton); 50–51 (case for reform and rejection); 12–13 (Cambridge); 25 (enters Seymour's household); 32 (becomes Secretary of State).

[14] Mary Dewar, ed., *A Discourse of the Commonweal of This Realm of England, Attributed to Sir Thomas Smith* (Charlottesville: The University Press of Virginia, 1969), 18 ("poverty reigns"), ix (prices), 18–19 (imported goods), 34 ("grieved").

[15] Frederic William Russell, *Kett's Rebellion in Norfolk: Being a History of the Great Civil Commotion that Occurred at the Time of the Reformation, in the Reign of Edward VI* (London: Longman, Brown, Green, Longmans, Roberts, and William Penny, 1859), 12.

[16] Thomas Tusser cited in Hibbert, *The English: A Social History*, 172.

[17] Dewar, ed., *A Discourse of the Commonweal*, 49.

[18] G. R. Elton, ed., *The New Cambridge Modern History. Volume II. The Reformation 1520–1559* (1958; repr. Cambridge: Cambridge University Press, 1975), 39.

[19] Dewar, ed., *A Discourse of the Commonweal*, 50.

[20] Russell, *Kett's Rebellion*, 25.

[21] Francis Aidan Gasquet, *Henry VIII and the English Monasteries* (London: John C. Nimmo, 1899), 360.

[22] Burgon, *The Life and Times of Sir Thomas Gresham*, 2:493; 499–500. In his will, Gresham gave Edward Flowerdew, Sir John's son, an annuity of forty shillings for his "counselles."

[23] John Walter, "Robert Kett (c.1492–1549), rebel," *Oxford Dictionary of National Biography*.

[24] Russell, *Kett's Rebellion*, 27–28 ("weal," "misery," "avarice"); 102 (20,000); 69 (sheep); 48 (grievances); 95 ("common-wealth").

[25] Jordan, *Edward VI: The Young King*, 487–88.

[26] David Loades, *John Dudley, Duke of Northumberland 1504–1553* (Oxford: Clarendon Press, 1996); Barret L. Beer, *Northumberland: The Political Career of John Dudley, Earl of Warwick and Duke of Northumberland* (Kent, OH: Kent State University Press, 1973).

[27] Jordan, *Edward VI: The Young King*, 489; Burgon, *The Life and Times of Sir Thomas Gresham*, 1:100–103.

[28] Barrett L. Beer, *Rebellion and Riot. Popular Disorder in England during the Reign of Edward VI* (Kent, OH: Kent State University Press, 1982), 7.

[29] Russell, *Kett's Rebellion*, 147.

[30] Alexander Neville, *Norfolkes Furies or a View of Ketts Campe* (London: William Stansby for Henry Fetherstone, 1615), 18.

[31] Stowe and Howes, *Annales, or a General Chronicle of England*, 601.

[32] Russell, *Kett's Rebellion*, 151.

[33] Beer, *Rebellion and Riot*, 7.

[34] F. J. Fisher, "Commercial Trends and Policy in Sixteenth-Century England," *The Economic History Review* 10, no. 2 (1940): 95–117; 96.

[35] Thomas Edge, "A briefe Discoverie of the Northerne Discoveries of Seas, Coasts, and Countries," in Samuel Purchas, *Hakluytus Posthumus or Purchas His Pilgrimes: Contayning a History of the World in Sea Voyages and Lande Travells by Englishmen and Others*, 20 vols. (Glasgow: James MacLehose & Sons, the University of Glasgow, 1905–1907), 13:5.

[36] G. V. Scammell, *The World Encompassed: The First European Maritime Empires, c. 800–1650* (London: Methuen, 1981), 269–70.

[37] George Macaulay Trevelyan, *Illustrated English Social History, Volume 1: Chaucer's England and the Early Tudors* (London: Longmans and Green, 1949), 33; E. M. Carus-Wilson, "The English Cloth Industry in the Late Twelfth and Early Thirteenth Centuries," *Economic History Review* 14, no. 1 (1944): 32–50; 32–33.

[38] Stephen Alford, *Burghley: William Cecil at the Court of Elizabeth I* (New Haven, CT: Yale University Press, 2008), 3–32.

[39] Thomas Smith to William Cecil, cited in Dewar, ed., *A Discourse of the Commonweal*, xxiv.

[40] Burgon, *The Life and Times of Sir Thomas Gresham*, 1:66.

[41] "Information of Sir Thomas Gresham, Mercer, towching the fall of the exchaunge, MDLVIII: to the Quenes most excellent maiestye," in Burgon, *The Life and Times of Sir Thomas Gresham*, 1:483–86. Gresham's quotes in the next paragraph are taken from this letter too.

[42] Robert Brenner, *Merchants and Revolution: Commercial Change, Political Conflict, and London's Overseas Traders, 1550–1653* (London: Verso, 2003), 7.

[43] W. K. Jordan, *Edward VI: The Threshold of Power. The Dominance of the Duke of Northumberland* (London: George Allen & Unwin, 1970), 482–88.

[44] Clement Adams, "The newe Navigation and discoverie of the kingdom of Moscovia, by the Northeast, in the yeere 1553," in Richard Hakluyt, *The Principal Navigations, Voyages, Traffiques & Discoveries of the English Nation, in Twelve Volumes.* (Glasgow: James MacLehose and Sons, University of Glasgow, 1903–1905), 2:239–70; 239.

2. THE LURE OF CATHAY

[1] Adams, "The newe Navigation," in Hakluyt, *Principal Navigations*, 2:239–40.

[2] Richard Eden, "A Treatyse of the Newe India, with other new founde lands and ilands," in Edward Arber, ed., *The First Three English Books on America, [?1511]–1555 A.D.* (Birmingham, 1885), 6.

[3] Stowe and Howes, *Annales, or a General Chronicle of England*, 609; John Stow, *A Survey of London. Reprinted from the text of 1603. With Introduction and Notes by Charles Lethbridge Kingsford*, 2 vols., edited by C. L. Kingsford. (Oxford: The Clarendon Press, 1908), 1:212.

[4] Judde is ranked second, after Cabot, in a contemporary list of merchants involved in the new company: "A letter of M. Henrie Lane to the woshipfull M. William Sanderson, conteining a briefe discourse of that which passed in the North-east discovery for the space of three and thirtie years," in Hakluyt, *Principal Navigations*, 2:330–36; 331.

[5] Thomas More, *Utopia*, trans. Ralph Robinson, introduction Jenny Mezciems (New York: Alfred A. Knopf, 1992), 25 ("live idle"); 28 ("your sheep").

[6] David Beers Quinn, *England and the Discovery of America, 1481–1620* (London: George Allen and Unwin, 1974), 163–66.

[7] John Rastell, "A new interlude and a mery of the nature of the. iiij. Elementes, &c," in Arber, ed., *The First Three English Books on America*, xxi.

[8] Marco Polo, *The Most Noble and Famous Travels of Marco Polo, Together with the Travels of Nicolo di Conti*, rev. ed., ed. and trans. John Frampton, with Introduction, Notes, and Appendices by N. M. Penzer (London: Adam and Charles Black, 1937), 64–65, 93–94. Also Donald Beecher, "The Legacy of John Frampton: Elizabethan Trader and Translator," *Renaissance Studies* 20, no. 3 (2006), 320–39.

[9] For Chinese exploration, see Louise Levathes, *When China Ruled the Seas: The Treasure Fleet of the Dragon Throne, 1405–1433* (New York: Oxford University Press, 1994), 87–181.

[10] For the state of the world economy in the sixteenth century, see Angus Maddison, *The World Economy: A Millennial Perspective* (Paris: OECD Publications, 2001), 263.

[11] Tamara Chin, "The Invention of the Silk Road, 1877," *Critical Inquiry* 40, no. 1 (2013), 194–219; 196–97.

[12] Jack Turner, *Spice: The History of a Temptation* (New York: Alfred A. Knopf, 2004; Vintage Books, 2005), 5.

[13] Ibid., 102–3.

[14] "The First Letters Patent Granted To John Cabot and his Sons, 5 March 1496," in James A. Williamson, *The Cabot Voyages and Bristol Discovery Under Henry VII* (Cambridge: The University Press, for the Hakluyt Society, 1962), 204–5.

[15] J. H. Parry, *The Discovery of the Sea* (Berkeley: University of California Press, 1981), 219.

[16] For the Isle of Brasil: see the statement from William Worcestre's *Itinerarium*, in Williamson, *The Cabot Voyages*, 187–88. For the discoverers of Newfoundland: see "The booke made by the right worshipful M. Robert Thorne in the yeere 1527 in Sivil, to Doctour Ley, Lord ambassador for king Henry the eight, to Charles the Emperour...," in Hakluyt, *Principal Navigations*, 2:164–80; 178.

[17] Evan Jones, "The *Matthew* of Bristol and the Financiers of John Cabot's 1497 Voyage to North America," *The English Historical Review*, 121, no. 492 (2006), 778–95; 781.

[18] Legend No. 8, in the map of 1544, transcribed in Charles Raymond Beazley, *John and Sebastian Cabot: The Discovery of North America* (London: T. Fisher Unwin, 1898), 222.

[19] John Day to the Lord Grand Admiral, n.d., in Williamson, *The Cabot Voyages*, 211–14.

[20] Williamson, *The Cabot Voyages*, 64 (activities on land); 66–72 (Newfoundland v. Nova Scotia).

[21] Lorenzo Pasqualigo to his Brothers at Venice, 23 August 1497, in Williamson, *The Cabot Voyages*, 207–8.

[22] Raimondo de Raimondi de Soncino to the Duke of Milan, 18 December 1497, in Williamson, *The Cabot Voyages*, 209–11; 210.

[23] Williamson, *The Cabot Voyages*, 103–13.

[24] David B. Quinn, *Sebastian Cabot and Bristol Exploration*, rev. ed. (Bristol: The Bristol Branch of the Historical Association, 1997; original edition 1968), 34.

[25] Williamson, *The Cabot Voyages*, 151, 153, 166–69.

[26] "Marcantonio Contarini's Report on Sebastian Cabot's Voyage," in Williamson, *The Cabot Voyages*, 270.

[27] "King Ferdinand to Sebastian Cabot, 13 September 1512," in Williamson, *The Cabot Voyages*, 281.

[28] Edward L. Stevenson, "The Geographical Activities of the Casa de la Contratación," *Annals of the Association of American Geographers* 17, no. 2 (1927): 40.

[29] Ibid., 42.

[30] "Gasparo Contrarini to the Council of Ten in Venice, 31 December 1522," in Williamson, *The Cabot Voyages*, 282–85; Laetitia Lyell, ed., *Acts of Court of the Mercers' Company 1453–1527* (Cambridge: Cambridge University Press, 1936), 524–25.

[31] Lyell, ed., *Acts of Court of the Mercers' Company*, 524–29.

[32] Extracts from the Wardens Manuscript Accounts of the Drapers Company of London, From March 1 to April 9, 1521, in Henry Harrisse, *The Discovery of North America* (London: Henry Stevens and Son, 1892), 747–50.

[33] Heather Dalton, *Merchants and Explorers: Roger Barlow, Sebastian Cabot, and Networks of Atlantic Exchange, 1500–1560* (Oxford: Oxford University Press, 2016), 76.

[34] Alison Sandman and Eric H. Ash, "Trading Expertise: Sebastian Cabot between Spain and England," *Renaissance Quarterly* 57, no. 3 (2004): 813–46; 839–40.

[35] Dalton, *Merchants and Explorers*, 63–65, 127–28.

[36] John Roche Dasent, ed., *Acts of the Privy Council of England, Volume II, 1547–1550* (London: Her Majesty's Stationery Office, 1890), 137; R. H. Brodie, ed., *Calendar of the Patent Rolls, Edward VI* (London: His Majesty's Stationery Office, 1924–1929), 1:320.

[37] "May 28. Van der Delft to the Emperor," in "Spain: May 1549," in *Calendar of Letters, Despatches, and State Papers, Spain, Volume 9, 1547–1549*, ed. Martin A. S. Hume and Royall Tyler (London: His Majesty's Stationery Office, 1912), 381–83; 381; "January 18, 1550. The Emperor to Van der Delft," in *Calendar of Letters, Dispatches, and State Papers, Spain, Volume 10, Edward VI, 1550–1552*, ed. Royall Tyler (London: His Majesty's Stationery Office, 1914), 11–12; 12.

[38] Cited in Quinn, *Sebastian Cabot and Bristol Exploration*, 29.

[39] Legend No. 12 (massive ears); No. 14 (Bengal); No. 19 (birds/ox), transcribed in Beazley, *John and Sebastian Cabot*, 230.

[40] Joseph Fischer, Franz von Wieser, and Charles George Herbermann, eds., *Cosmographiae Introductio of Martin Waldseemüller in Facsimile Followed By The Four Voyages of Amerigo Vespucci, With Their Translation Into English; to which are added Waldseemüller's Two World Maps of 1507 With An Introduction* (New York: The United States Catholic Historical Society, 1907), 70. While conven-

tion has it that the word "America" was first applied by Martin Waldseemüller, who derived it from the Latin version of Vespucci's first name, there has been some debate about the matter. For instance, it has been speculated that John Cabot came up with the name in recognition of one of his supporters, Richard Ameryk, Sheriff of Bristol in 1503. See E. W. Lennard, "Some Intimate Bristol Connections with the Overseas Empire," *Geography* 16, no. 2 (1931): 109–21; 110–11.

[41] Williamson, *The Cabot Voyages,* 166–70. Also Helen Wallis, "England's Search for the North-ern Passages in the Sixteenth and Early Seventeenth Centuries," *Arctic* 37, no. 4 (1984): 453–72; 457–59. Others suggest that the strait is named after the Portuguese Corte-Real Brothers. See William J. Mills, *Exploring Polar Frontiers: A Historical Encyclopedia,* 1 (Santa Barbara, CA: ABC Clio, 2003), 125.

3. THE MYSTERIE

[1] Adams, "The newe Navigation," in Hakluyt, *Principal Navigations,* 2:240.

[2] Steve Rappaport, *Worlds Within Worlds: Structures of Life in Sixteenth-Century London* (Cambridge: Cambridge University Press, 1989), 29–36, 184–88; Valerie Hope, Clive Birch, and Gilbert Torrey, eds., *The Freedom: The Past and Present of the Livery, Guilds and City of London* (Buckingham: Barracuda Books, 1982), 37–45.

[3] According to the Oxford English Dictionary, "the word may well have been influenced by or con-fused with 'mastery.'" *Oxford English Dictionary* online, definition n.2, 2.a.

[4] The map appeared in 1572 in an atlas of city plans called *Civitates Orbis Terrarum* by Georg Braun and Franz Hogenberg. See Peter Whitfield, *London: A Life in Maps,* rev. ed. (London: The British Library, 2017; original edition 2006), 34–37.

[5] Loades, *John Dudley,* ix; Sutton, *The Mercery of London,* 369–73.

[6] John Munro, "Tawney's Century, 1540–1640," in *The Invention of Enterprise. Entrepreneurship from Ancient Mesopotamia to Modern Times,* ed. David S. Landes, Joel Mokyr, and William J. Baumol (Princeton, NJ: Princeton University Press, 2010), 107–55; 128–32. Munro calls the company the "first (historically verifiable) joint-stock company."

[7] W. R. Scott, *The Constitution of English, Scottish and Irish Joint-Stock Companies to 1720,* 3 vols (Cambridge: Cambridge University Press, 1910), 1:18.

[8] John Mickelthwait and Adrian Wooldridge, *The Company: A Short History of a Revolutionary Idea* (London: Phoenix Books, 2005), 18.

[9] Liza Picard, *Elizabeth's London, Everyday Life in Elizabethan London* (London: Phoenix Books, 2004), 323.

[10] Adams, "The newe Navigation," in Hakluyt, *Principal Navigations,* 2:240–41.

[11] "The copie of the letters missive, which the right noble Prince Edward the sixt sent to the Kings, Princes, and other Potentates, inhabiting the Northeast partes of the world...," in Hakluyt, *Prin-cipal Navigations,* 2:209–11; 210.

[12] The date of his birth is unknown, and his age is based on the evidence of a contemporary por-trait, facing the title page in vol. 2 of Hakluyt's *Principal Navigations.*

[13] Adams, "The newe Navigation," in Hakluyt, *Principal Navigations,* 2:240–41.

[14] J. D. Alsop, "Sir Anthony Aucher (d. 1558), administrator and landowner," in the *Oxford Dictio-nary of National Biography.*

[15] "The voyage of M. Roger Bodenham with the great Barke Aucher to Candia and Chio, in the yeere 1550," in Richard Hakluyt, *Principal Navigations,* 5:71–76; 76.

[16] Adams, "The newe Navigation," in Hakluyt, *Principal Navigations,* 2:242.

[17] For Dee's life, see Glyn Parry, *The Arch-Conjuror of England* (New Haven, CT: Yale University Press, 2013) and Benjamin Woolley, *The Queen's Conjuror: The Life and Magic of Dr Dee* (London: Flamingo, 2002).

[18] John Aubrey, *Brief Lives, chiefly of Contemporaries, set down by John Aubrey, between the years 1669 & 1696,* ed. Andrew Clark, 2 vols. (Oxford: The Clarendon Press, 1898), 1:212, 214.

[19] John Dee, "The Compendious Rehearsal," in Gerald Suster (ed., comp.), *John Dee: Essential Read-ings* (Berkeley, CA: North Atlantic Books, 2003), 9.

[20] Aubrey, *Brief Lives*, 1:27. Aubrey was referring in this passage to Thomas Allen, a scholar of Trinity College, Oxford.

[21] Parry, *The Arch-Conjurer*, 12, 23. Dee gave his two Mercator globes (now lost) to Trinity College, Cambridge. Philip Gaskell, *Trinity College Library: The First 150 Years. The Sandars Lectures 1978–1979* (Cambridge: Cambridge University Press, 1980), 33.

[22] Parry, *The Arch-Conjurer*, 23–24; see E. G. R. Taylor, *Tudor Geography 1485–1583* (London: Methuen & Co., 1930), 91, for a general reference to the making of navigational instruments.

[23] Eden, "A Treatyse of the Newe India," in Arber, ed., *The First Three English Books on America*, 8.

[24] Donald F. Lach, *Asia in the Making of Europe: Volume I: The Century of Discovery* (Chicago: The University of Chicago Press, 1965), 185 n171.

[25] Sir Henry Yule, ed. and trans., *Cathay And The Way Thither, Being a Collection of Medieval Notices of China*, 4 vols. (London: Hakluyt Society, 1913–1916), 2:136.

[26] Ibid., 2:179–80 (Censcalan); 215–22 (Cambalech); 232 (camels).

[27] Kim M. Phillips, *Before Orientalism: Asian Peoples and Cultures in European Travel Writing, 1245–1510* (Philadelphia: University of Pennsylvania Press, 2014), 45.

[28] C. W. R. D. Moseley (trans.), *The Travels of Sir John Mandeville* (London: Penguin Books, 1983; paperback), 150.

[29] Adams, "The newe Navigation," in Hakluyt, *Principal Navigations*, 2:243–44.

[30] The word "Tartar" comes from "Tartarus", the abyss of suffering in classical mythology. It was applied to the Mongols, whose terrifying exploits generated fear among Europeans.

[31] Adams, "The newe Navigation," in Hakluyt, *Principal Navigations*, 2:244.

[32] Eden, "A Treatyse of the Newe India," in Arber, ed., *The First Three English Books on America*, 16–17 ("market town"); 24 ("Cathay"); 26 ("marvelous"); 29 (cannibals).

[33] John Parker, *Books to Build an Empire: A Bibliographical History of English Overseas Interests to 1620* (Amsterdam: N. Israel, 1965), 38; Eden, "A Treatyse of the Newe India," in Arber, ed., *The First Three English Books on America*, 3.

[34] Eden, "A Treatyse of the Newe India," in Arber, ed., *The First Three English Books on America*, 8.

[35] Adams, "The newe Navigation," in Hakluyt, *Principal Navigations*, 2:241.

[36] "Ordinances, instructions, and advertisements of and for the direction of the intended voyage for Cathay, compiled, made, and delivered by the right worshipfull M. Sebastian Cabota...," in Hakluyt, *Principal Navigations*, 2:195–205.

[37] Adams, "The newe Navigation," in Hakluyt, *Principal Navigations*, 2:241.

4. A NEWE AND STRANGE NAVIGATION

[1] "The true copie of a note found written in one of the two ships, to wit, the Speranza, which wintred in Lappia, where Sir Hugh Willoughby and all his companie died, being frozen to death. Anno 1553," in Hakluyt, *Principal Navigations*, 2:212–14.

[2] "The copie of the letters missive," in Hakluyt, *Principal Navigations*, 2:211 ("divers languages"); 209 ("all kings").

[3] Ibid., 210.

[4] Ibid., 211.

[5] In 2005, two professors from INSEAD business school in France wrote an influential book on what they called "blue ocean" strategy—succeeding by creating "blue oceans" of uncontested market space: W. Chan Kim and Renee Mauborgne, *Blue Ocean Strategy: How to Create Uncontested Market Space and Make the Competition Irrelevant* (Boston: Harvard Business School Press, 2005).

[6] "The true copie of a note ... Sir Hugh Willoughby," in Hakluyt, *Principal Navigations*, 2:212–14.

[7] The blue color was derived from local whortleberries (http://www.watchetmuseum.co.uk/social-history/).

[8] Adams, "The newe Navigation," in Hakluyt, *Principal Navigations*, 2:244.

[9] Ibid., 2:245.

[10] Ibid., 2:245.

[11] "The true copie of a note . . . Sir Hugh Willoughby," in Hakluyt, *Principal Navigations*, 2:220.

[12] Adams, "The newe Navigation," in Hakluyt, *Principal Navigations*, 2:247.

[13] Mildred Wretts-Smith, "The English in Russia During the Second Half of the Sixteenth Century," *Transactions of the Royal Historical Society* 3 (1920), 72–102; 90–91, n6.

[14] "The first voyage made by Master Anthonie Jenkinson, from the Citie of London toward the land of Russia, begun the twelfth of May, in the yeere 1557," in Hakluyt, *Principal Navigations*, 2:413–26; 416.

[15] Kit Mayers, *North-East Passage to Muscovy: Stephen Borough and the First Tudor Explorations* (Phoenix Mill: Sutton Publishing, 2005), 65 (map).

[16] "The true copie of a note . . . Sir Hugh Willoughby," in Hakluyt, *Principal Navigations*, 2:221.

[17] Ibid., 223.

[18] "Ordinances . . . Sebastian Cabota," in Hakluyt, *Principal Navigations*, 2:202.

[19] Adams, "The newe Navigation," in Hakluyt, *Principal Navigations*, 2:243 ("home quietly"); 247 ("die the death"); 248 ("held his course").

[20] Ibid., 2:248.

[21] Ibid., 2:249.

[22] Adams, "The newe Navigation," in Hakluyt, *Principal Navigations*, 2:250 ("wares and commodities"); 251 ("loving manner"); 254 ("bignesse," "London"); 255 ("cloth of gold," "chamber of presence," "throne," "precious stones," "out of countenance").

[23] Stephane Mund, "The Discovery of Muscovite Russia in Tudor England," *Revue Belge de Philologie et d'Histoire* 86, no. 2 (2008): 351–73; 351n3.

[24] Geoffrey Hosking, *Russia and the Russians from the Earliest Times to the Present* (London: Penguin Books, rev. ed., 2012), 84, 89, 117, 120.

[25] "The copie of the Duke of Moscovie and Emperour of Russia his letters, sent to King Edward the sixt, by the hands of Richard Chancelour," in Hakluyt, *Principal Navigations*, 2:272.

[26] Letters Patent for the Limitation of the Crown, 21 June 1553: Harleian MSS, 35, fol. 364, in John Gough Nichols, ed., *The Chronicle of Queen Jane and of Two Years of Queen Mary and Especially of the Rebellion of Sir Thomas Wyat, Written by a Resident in the Tower of London* (London: Camden Society, 1850), 91–100.

[27] Hubert Hall, *History of the Custom-Revenue in England from the Earliest Times to the Year 1827*, 2 vols. (London: Elliot Stock, 1885), 1:316; Hakluyt, *Principal Navigations*, 2:201; T. S. Willan, *The Early History of the Russia Company, 1553–1603* (1956; repr. Manchester: Manchester University Press, 1968), 6–7.

[28] "The Charter of the Marchants of Russia, graunted upon the discoverie of the saide Countrey, by King Philipe and Queene Marie," in Hakluyt, *Principal Navigations*, 2:304–16; 315.

[29] For the list of investors: *Calendar of the Patent Rolls, Philip and Mary. Volume II, 1554–1555* (London: His Majesty's Stationery Office, 1936), 55–57. The women were Elizabeth Wilford and Katherine Lomnour. T. S. Willan notes that Wilford may have been the wife of a merchant who sailed with Willoughby and "presumably perished when the ship was frozen in the White Sea": see his *The Muscovy Merchants of 1555* (Manchester: Manchester University Press, 1953; repr. 1973), 10, 110, 127.

[30] H. R. Woudhuysen, "Sir Philip Sidney (1554–1586), author and courtier," *Oxford Dictionary of National Biography*; Susan Brigden, *New Worlds, Lost Worlds. The Rule of the Tudors, 1485–1603* (London: Penguin Books, 2001), 214.

[31] "The names of the twelve Counsellors appointed in this voyage," Hakluyt, *Principal Navigations*, 2:206.

[32] "The letters of king Philip and Queene Marie to Ivan Vasilivich the Emperour of Russia written the first of April 1555 and in the second voyage," in Hakluyt, *Principal Navigations*, 2:278–80; 282 ("Greek").

[33] See the *Oxford English Dictionary* for "China," definition 1a.

[34] Richard Eden, *The Decades of the Newe Worlde or West India*, in Arber, ed., *The First Three English Books on America*, 292.

³⁵ "Articles conceived and determined for the Commission of the Merchants of this company resiant in Russia, and at the Wardhouse, for the second voyage, 1555. The first of May, as followeth," in Hakluyt, *Principal Navigations*, 2:281–89.

³⁶ Ibid., 2:281 ("agents"); 285 ("learned"); 289 ("honor," "public benefit").

³⁷ James Evans, *Merchant Adventurers. The voyage of discovery that transformed Tudor England* (London: Weidenfeld & Nicolson, 2013; paperback, Phoenix, 2014), 260–64.

³⁸ Wretts-Smith, "The English in Russia," 76n4. The port of Arkhangelsk was established at the mouth of the Dvina in 1584 and continued to be a trading center for the English.

³⁹ Arthur Edwards, "Another letter of Arthur Edwards written in Astracan the 16. Of June, 1567, at his return in his first voiage out of Persia, to the right worshipfull Companie trading into Russia, Persia, and other the North and Northeast partes," in Hakluyt, *Principal Navigations*, 3:64–72; 72.

⁴⁰ Eleanora C. Gordon, "The Fate of Sir Hugh Willoughby and His Companions: A New Conjecture," *The Geographical Journal* 152, no. 2 (1986): 243–47; 244.

⁴¹ Evans, *Merchant Adventurers*, 265.

⁴² "Giovanni Michiel, Venetian Ambassador in England, to the Doge and Senate," November 4, 1555, in Rawdon Brown, ed., *Calendar of State Papers and Manuscripts, Relating to English Affairs, Existing in the Archives and Collections of Venice, and in Other Libraries of Northern Italy, Volume VI, Part I, 1555–1556* (London: Longman & Co., 1877), no. 269: 238–40; 240.

⁴³ Wretts-Smith, "The English in Russia," 79.

⁴⁴ "The letter of M. George Killingworth," in Hakluyt, *Principal Navigations*, 2:291 ("wares" and "sold very little").

⁴⁵ Adams, "The newe Navigation," in Hakluyt, *Principal Navigations*, 2:261 (Flemings); "A letter of M. Henrie Lane to M. Richard Hakluit, concerning the first ambassage to our most gracious Queene Elizabeth from the Russian Emperour anno 1567, and other notable matters incident to those places and times," in Hakluyt, *Principal Navigations*, 3:100; R. H. Major, trans. and ed., *Notes upon Russia: Being a translation of the Earliest Account of that Country entitled Rerum Moscoviticarum Commentarii by the Baron Sigismund von Herberstein*, 2 vols. (London: Hakluyt Society, 1851). 2:24.

⁴⁶ "A letter of M. Henrie Lane to the worshipfull M. William Sanderson, conteining a briefe discourse of that which passed in the Northeast discovery for the space of three and thirtie years," in Hakluyt, *Principal Navigations*, 3:330–36; 333.

⁴⁷ "The coines, weights and measures used in Russia, written by John Hasse, in the yere, 1554," in Hakluyt, *Principal Navigations*, 2:273–78.

⁴⁸ The word "Kremlin"—literally "citadel"—refers to the walled complex of buildings and facilities of the tsar and his court in Moscow. Although the word was not often used at the time of the English visits, it had been common for decades before and is still, of course, in use today. See Arthur Voyce, *The Moscow Kremlin: Its History, Architecture and Art Treasures* (Berkeley: University of California Press, 1954).

⁴⁹ "The voyage, wherein Osep Napea the Moscovite Ambassadour returned home into his country, with his entertainement at his arrivall, at Colmogro: and a large description of the maners of the Countrey," in Hakluyt, *Principal Navigations*, 2:425–49; 439.

⁵⁰ "A letter of M. Henrie Lane to . . . William Sanderson," in Hakluyt, *Principal Navigations*, 3:333.

⁵¹ E. Delmar Morgan and C. H. Coote, eds., *Early Voyages and Travels into Russia and Persia by Anthony Jenkinson and other Englishmen, with Some Account of the First Intercourse of the English with Russia and Central Asia by way of the Caspian Sea*, 2 vols. (London: Hakluyt Society, 1886), 1:iv.

⁵² An archaeological survey of the supposed shipwreck site was conducted in 2000, but nothing was found. Aberdeen Council, https://online.aberdeenshire.gov.uk/smrpub/master/detail.aspx?tab=main&refno=NJ96NW0073.

⁵³ "A discourse of the honorable receiving into England of the first Ambassador from the Emperor of Russia, in the yeere of Christ 1556, and in the third yeere of the raigne of Queene Marie, serving for the third voyage to Moscovie. Registred by Master John Incent Protonotarie," in Hakluyt, *Principal Navigations*, 2:350–62; 352. (The year is 1556 in *Principal Navigations* but the narrative continues into 1557.)

[54] Raphael Holinshed, *Holinshed's Chronicles of England, Scotland and Ireland*, 6 vols. (New York: AMS Press, 1965), 4:86.

5. AN ELUSIVE REALM

[1] Alice Hunt, *The Drama of Coronation: Medieval Ceremony in Early Modern England* (Cambridge: Cambridge University Press, 2008), 146–172; James M. Osborn, ed., *The Quenes Maiesties Passage through the Citie of London to Westminster the Day before her Coronation* (New Haven, CT: Yale University Press, 1960), 28.

[2] The words come from Psalm 118. See: A. N. Wilson, *The Elizabethans* (London: Hutchinson, 2011; paperback edition, Arrow Books, 2012), 28.

[3] Brigden, *New Worlds, Lost Worlds*, 219.

[4] Diogo Homem, *Queen Mary Atlas, Facsimile edition with commentary by Peter Barber* (London: Folio Society, 2005), 65–66. Barber notes that Elizabeth "would have been the only person with the authority to perpetrate vandalism on a precious object that had been commissioned by her royal predecessor."

[5] Susan Rose, *Calais: An English Town in France 1347–1558* (Woodbridge: The Boydell Press, 2008), 39–53; Muriel St. Clare Byrne, ed., *The Lisle Letters. An Abridgement. Selected and Arranged by Bridget Boland* (London: Secker & Warburg, 1983), 30; David Grummitt, *The Calais Garrison. War and Military Service in England, 1436–1558* (Woodbridge: The Boydell Press, 2008), 5–6; Paul Slack, rev., "Sir Andrew Judde (c. 1492–1558), merchant," *Oxford Dictionary of National Biography*. For "Pale," see the *Oxford English Dictionary*, definitions 4a, b, c and 5c.

[6] "Report of the Signr Giovanni Michele on his return from England A.D. 1557," in Henry Ellis, ed., *Original Letters Illustrative of English History, in Four Volumes: Volume II* (London: Harding and Lepard, Second Series, 1827), 218–42; 226–27.

[7] "The Queen to the special gentlemen in every shire," [January 7], 1558, in *Calendar of State Papers, Domestic Series, of the Reigns of Edward VI., Mary, Elizabeth, 1547–1580*, ed. Robert Lemon (London: Longman, Brown, Green, Longmans, & Roberts, 1856), vol. 12, #6, 97.

[8] H. S. Vere Hodge, *Sir Andrew Judde* (Tonbridge: Tonbridge School Shop, n.d.), 114–15.

[9] Machyn, Henry, *The Diary of Henry Machyn, Citizen and Merchant-Taylor of London, 1550–1563*, edited by J. G. Nichols (London: Camden Society, 1848), 163.

[10] Holinshed, *Chronicles*, 4:137.

[11] Wallace T. MacCaffrey, "The Newhaven Expedition, 1562–1563," *The Historical Journal* 40, no. 1 (1997), 1–21; 15.

[12] Ibid., 9.

[13] G. D. Ramsay, *The City of London in the International Politics at the Accession of Elizabeth Tudor* (Manchester: Manchester University Press, 1975), 58.

[14] R. F. Foster, *Modern Ireland: 1600–1972* (London: Allen Lane, 1988; paperback edition, Penguin Books, 1989), 30.

[15] "Shane O'Neill to the Queen," undated, in *Calendar of State Papers relating to Ireland, of the Reigns of Henry VIII, Edward VI, Mary, and Elizabeth, 1509–1573*, ed. Hans Claude Hamilton (London: Longman, Green, Longman & Roberts, 1860), vol. 1, #79, 158.

[16] "Proclamation shewing the presumptuous, arrogant, rebellious and traitorous deeds of Shane O'Neill, and denouncing him as a rebel and traitor," 8 June 1561, in *CSP-Ireland, 1509–1573*, vol. 1, #1, 173.

[17] *CSP-Ireland, 1509–1573*, vol. 3, #59, 170 (£3,000); vol. 4, #22, 175 ("nothing hinders"); #39, 178 (released funds); #76, 183 ("ready to embark").

[18] William G. Gosling, *The Life of Sir Humphrey Gilbert: England's First Empire Builder* (London: Constable & Co., 1911), 38.

[19] "Proclamation by the Queen in favour of Shane O'Neill," May 5, 1562, in *CSP-Ireland, 1509–1573*, vol. 6, #6, 194.

[20] Gosling, *The Life of Sir Humphrey Gilbert*, 38.

[21] Foster, *Modern Ireland*, 12.

[22] "Lord Deputy Sidney to the Earl of Leicester," March 1, 1566, in *CSP-Ireland, 1509–1573*, vol. 16, #35, 289.

[23] "Lord Deputy Sidney to [William Cecil]," June 9, 1566, *CSP-Ireland, 1509–1573*, vol. 18, #9, 304.

[24] Tracy Borman, *Elizabeth's Women: The Hidden Story of the Virgin Queen* (London: Vintage, 2009), 62.

[25] David Beers Quinn, ed., *The Voyages and Colonising Enterprises of Sir Humphrey Gilbert*, 2 vols. (London: The Hakluyt Society, 1940), 1:2.

[26] Ibid., 1:3–4.

[27] "[1565]. Petition from Humphrey Gilbert to the Queen," in Quinn, *Voyages and Colonising Enterprises*, 1:105–6. Quinn says the petition was "most probably the autumn of 1565," although it could have been submitted between June 1565 and March 1566.

[28] "A Discourse of a Discoverie for a new passage to Cataia," in Quinn, *Voyages and Colonising Enterprises*, 1:129–64. Date of the original draft: 135.

[29] Humphrey Gilbert to Sir John Gilbert, 30 June 1566, in Quinn, *Voyages and Colonising Enterprises*, 1:134–35; 134.

[30] "[December 1566]. Petition from Humphrey Gilbert to the Queen," in Quinn, *Voyages and Colonising Enterprises*, 1:108–10; 109.

[31] "An Acte for the corporation of merchant Adventurers for the discovering of newe trades, made in the eight yeere of Queene Elizabeth. Anno 1566," in Hakluyt, *Principal Navigations*, 3:83–91.

[32] "[24 January 1567]. Humphrey Gilbert's petition to the Queen, with comments of the Muscovy Company," in Quinn, *Voyages and Colonising Enterprises*, 1:111–15; 113.

[33] Ibid., 1:111–12.

[34] Susan M. Lough, "Trade and Industry in Ireland in the Sixteenth Century," *Journal of Political Economy* 24, no. 7 (1916): 713–30; 721.

[35] Nicholas P. Canny, *The Elizabethan Conquest of Ireland: A Pattern Established, 1565–1576* (Hassocks: The Harvester Press, 1976), 70–72.

[36] Sir Thomas Smith to Sir William Cecil, 7 November 1565, cited in Mary Dewar, *Sir Thomas Smith: A Tudor Intellectual in Office* (London: The Athlone Press, 1964), 157.

[37] "Queen Elizabeth to the Lord Deputy," July 6, 1567, in *CSP-Ireland, 1509–1573*, vol. 21, #49, 340–41.

[38] Christopher Maginn, "Shane O'Neill (c.1530–1567), chieftain," in *Oxford Dictionary of National Biography Online*; Canny, *The Elizabethan Conquest of Ireland*, 59–60.

[39] Quinn, *Voyages and Colonising Enterprises*, 1:13–16.

[40] "12 February 1569. Petition to Sir Henry Sidney," in Quinn, *Voyages and Colonising Enterprises*, 2:490–493. Though the authorship is not stated, Quinn notes that the petition "is written in a hand which is very likely to be Gilbert's."

[41] "[March 1569]. Petition to the Privy Council," in Quinn, *Voyages and Colonising Enterprises*, 2:293–94; 293.

[42] Canny, *The Elizabethan Conquest of Ireland*, 79.

[43] Between September 29, 1558, and September 29, 1574, some £370,779 was paid out of the Exchequer for Ireland. See: "Money paid for Ireland," [September 29], 1574, *Calendar of State Papers relating to Ireland, of the Reign of Elizabeth, 1574–1585*, ed. Hans Claude Hamilton (London: Longmans, Green, Reader & Dyer, 1867), vol. 47, #68, 38.

[44] Brigden, *New Worlds, Lost Worlds*, 254.

[45] Rory Rapple, "Sir Humphrey Gilbert (1537–1583), explorer and soldier," in *Oxford Dictionary of National Biography*; "H. Gylberte to the Lord Deputy," December 6, 1569, in *CSP-Ireland, 1509–1573*, vol. 29, #83, 424; Rory Rapple, *Martial Power and Elizabethan Political Culture: Military Men in England and Ireland, 1558–1594* (Cambridge: Cambridge University Press, 2009), 211.

[46] Thomas Churchyard, *Churchyarde's Choice*, in Canny, *The Elizabethan Conquest of Ireland*, 122.

[47] "H. Gylberte to the Lord Deputy," December 6, 1569, in *CSP-Ireland, 1509–1573*, vol. 29, #83, 424.

[48] J. R. Tanner, *Tudor Constitutional Documents A.D. 1485–1603, with an Historical Commentary* (Cambridge: Cambridge University Press, 1951), 143–46.

[49] Geoffrey Parker, *Imprudent King: A New Life of Philip II* (New Haven, CT: Yale University Press, 2014; paperback ed., 2015), 206–7.

[50] David Beers Quinn, "Sir Thomas Smith (1513–1577) and the Beginnings of English Colonial Theory," *Proceedings of the American Philosophical Society* 89, no. 4 (1945): 543–60, 548.

[51] Ibid., 551.

[52] Sir Thomas Smith, "A letter sent by I.B. Gentleman vnto his very frende Maystet [*sic*] R. C. Esquire vvherin is conteined a large discourse of the peopling & inhabiting the cuntrie called the Ardes, and other adiacent in the north of Ireland, and taken in hand by Sir Thomas Smith one of the Queenes Maiesties priuie Counsel, and Thomas Smith Esquire, his sonne" (London: Henry Binneman, 1571), n.p. The quotes in the following four paragraphs are taken from this pamphlet.

[53] Quinn, "Sir Thomas Smith," 556.

[54] Sir William Fitzwilliam to Thomas Smith, junior, February 1572, cited in Hiram Morgan, "The Colonial Venture of Sir Thomas Smith in Ulster, 1571–1575," *The Historical Journal* 28, no. 2 (1985): 261–78; 265.

[55] "Thomas Smith to Burghley," September 10, 1572, in *CSP-Ireland, 1509–1573*, vol. 27, #54, 482.

[56] "Earl of Essex to the Privy Council," October 20, 1573, in *CSP-Ireland, 1509–1573*, vol. 42, #55, 525.

[57] Steven Ellis, *Tudor Ireland: Crown, Community and the Conflict of Cultures, 1470–1603* (London: Longman, 1985), 266–68; 267.

[58] Robert Dunlop, "Sixteenth Century Schemes for the Plantation of Ulster, Part II," *The Scottish Historical Review* 22, no. 86 (1925): 115–26; 124.

[59] "Orders set out by Sir Thomas Smyth knight…," December 1, 1573. See Dewar, *Sir Thomas Smith*, 165. These have been redated to 1573 — from 1574. The original documents relating to Smith's colonisation are housed in the Essex Record Office.

[60] "Offices necessarie in the Colony of Ardes and orders agreed vppon," December 20, 1573. See Dewar, *Sir Thomas Smith*, 166.

[61] "Deeds of covenant between Sir Thomas Smith, knight, and Sir John Barckley, of Berverstone Castle, Gloucestershire, knight," December 8, 1573. See Dewar, *Sir Thomas Smith*, 168.

[62] "Earl of Essex to the Privy Council," December 11, 1573, in *CSP-Ireland, 1509–1573*, vol. 43, #11, 532; "Earl of Essex to the Queen," November 2, 1573, in *CSP-Ireland, 1509–1573*, vol. 42, #64, 526.

[63] "Sum of payments for the Earl of Essex's affairs," April 1575, in *CSP-Ireland, 1574–1585* (London: Longmans, Green, Reader, & Dyer, 1867), vol. 50, #84, 62.

[64] "Declaration of the revenue of Ireland," [October 26], 1575, in *CSP-Ireland, 1574–1585*, vol. 53, #55, 82.

[65] "[The Queen] to the Earl of Essex," May [22], 1575, in *CSP-Ireland, 1574–1585*, vol. 51, #39, 66.

[66] "Grant by George Smith of Mount Hall, esquire, and John and William, his sons, to Anthony Morley of Lewes, Sussex, esquire," April 16, 1580: Essex Record Office, Smyth Family (of Hill Hall Estate in Theydon Mount) Manuscripts: D/DSh O1/10.

6. THE LAST GREAT CHALLENGE OF THE AGE

[1] Stow, *A Survey of London*, 1:131–32: "Muscovy Court," in G. H. Gater and Walter H. Godfrey, eds., *Survey of London: Volume 15, All Hallows, Barking-By-The-Tower, Pt II* (London: London City Council, 1934), 4–6.

[2] Richard Collinson, *The Three Voyages of Martin Frobisher: In Search of a Passage to Cathaia and India by the North-West A.D. 1576–8* (1867; reprint, Cambridge: Cambridge University Press, 2009), 89.

[3] Ibid.

[4] Ibid.

[5] T. S. Willan, *The Muscovy Merchants of 1555* (Manchester: Manchester University Press, 1953), 78; 98.

[6] "The first voyage made by Master William Towerson Marchant of London, to the coast of Guinea, with two Ships, in the yeere 1555," in Hakluyt, *Principal Navigations*, 6:177–211; 201.

[7] Brian Dietz, ed., *The Port and Trade of Early Elizabethan London Documents* (London: London Record Society, 1972), 43–44; 49.

[8] R. C. D. Baldwin, "Stephen Borough (1525–1584), explorer and naval administrator," in *Oxford Dictionary of National Biography*.

[9] Collinson, *The Three Voyages of Martin Frobisher*, 87; J. B. Heath, ed., *An account of the materials furnished for the use of Queen Anne Boleyn and the Princess Elizabeth, by William Loke, the King's Mercer, Volume VII* (London: Philobiblon Society, 1862–3), 10, 13: James McDermott, "Michael Lok, Mercer and Merchant Adventurer," in Thomas Symons, ed., *Meta Incognita: A Discourse of Discovery. Martin Frobisher's Arcitice Expeditions, 1576–1578*. 2 vols. (Hull, Quebec: Canadian Museum of `civilization, 1999), 1:119–146.

[10] Collinson, *The Three Voyages of Martin Frobisher*, 87.

[11] "List of the Queen's Navy, 20 Feb 1559–1560," *Calendar of State Papers Foreign: Elizabeth, Volume II, 1559–1560*, ed. Joseph Stevenson (London: Longman, Green, Longman, Roberts & Green, 1865), cxxviii–cxxix. The largest ship in the Queen's navy of 34 vessels was the *Mary Rose*, at 600 tons.

[12] Collinson, *The Three Voyages of Martin Frobisher*, 88.

[13] Willan, *The Muscovy Merchants*, 108–9.

[14] "The second voyage to Guinea set out by Sir George Barne, Sir John Yorke, Thomas Lok, Anthonie Hickman and Edward Castelin, in the yeere 1554. The Captaine whereof was M. John Lok," in Hakluyt, *Principal Navigations*, 6:154–77.

[15] Willan, *The Early History of the Russia Company*, 287.

[16] "The 26 Januarye 1578. Michaell Lok Saluteth the Worshipfull Commyssioners and Auditors of his Accounts of the iij Voyages of C. Furbisher," in Collinson, *The Three Voyages of Martin Frobisher*, 332–343; 334.

[17] James McDermott, *Martin Frobisher: Elizabethan Privateer* (New Haven, CT: Yale University Press, 2001), 7–12.

[18] [Michael Lok], "East India by the Northwest[ward]," in Collinson, *Voyages of Martin Frobisher*, 79–87; 80.

[19] J. G. Elzinga, "Sir John Yorke (d. 1569), administrator," *Oxford Dictionary of National Biography*.

[20] [Lok], "East India by the Northwest[ward]," in Collinson, *Voyages of Martin Frobisher*, 80.

[21] "Declaration of Martin Frobisher," in Joseph Stevenson, ed., *Calendar of State Papers Foreign: Elizabeth, Volume 5, 1562* (London: Her Majesty's Stationery Office, 1867), #102, 53.

[22] R. G. Marsden, "The Early Career of Martin Frobisher," *The English Historical Review* 21, no. 83 (1906): 538–44; McDermott, *Martin Frobisher: Elizabethan Privateer*, 56–76.

[23] "Michaell Lok Saluteth the Worshipfull Commyssioners," in Collinson, *The Three Voyages of Martin Frobisher*, 334.

[24] Richard Willes, *The History of Travayle in the West and East Indies, and other countreys lying eyther way, towards the fruitfull and tythe Moluccaes. As Moscouia, Persia, Arabia, Syria, AEgypte, Ethiopia, Guineas, China in Cathayo, and Giapan: With a discourse of the Northwest passage. Gathered in parte, and done into Englyshe by Richard Eden. Newly set in order, augmented, and finished by Richarde Willes* (London: Richard Jugge, 1577), 233.

[25] George Best, *A True Discourse of the Late Voyages of Discoverie for Finding of a Passage to Cathaya* (London: Henry Bynnyman, 1578), in Collinson, *Voyages of Martin Frobisher*, 70. All the quotes in this and the next paragraph are taken from this page.

[26] Collinson, *Voyages of Martin Frobisher*, 89.

[27] Ibid., 89.

[28] Best, *A True Discourse*, in Collinson, *The Three Voyages of Martin Frobisher*, 70–71; Simon Adams, "Ambrose Dudley, Earl of Warwick (c.1530–1590), magnate," *Oxford Dictionary of National Biography*.

[29] G. C. Williamson, *Lady Anne Clifford, Countess of Dorset, Pembroke & Montgomery, 1590–1676: Her Life, Letters and Work Extracted from all the original documents available, many of which are here printed for the first time* (Kendal: Titus Wilson and Sons, 1922), 37; Simon Adams, "Anne Dudley [née Russell], countess of Warwick (1548/9–1604), courtier," *Oxford Dictionary of National Biography*.

[30] "For M. Cap. Furbyshers Passage by the Northwest," in Willes, *History of Travayle*, 230–36.

[31] "Michaell Lok Saluteth the Worshipfull Commyssioners," in Collinson, *The Three Voyages of Martin Frobisher*, 334.

[32] [Lok], "East India by the Northwest[ward]," in Collinson, *The Three Voyages of Martin Frobisher*, 79.

[33] "Michaell Lok Saluteth the Worshipfull Commyssioners," in Collinson, *The Three Voyages of Martin Frobisher*, 334.

[34] "Accounts, with subsidiary documents, of Michael Lok, treasurer, of first, second and third voyages of Martin Frobisher to Cathay by the north-west passage": The National Archives (Kew), E 164/35, fo. 2.

[35] Collinson, *The Three Voyages of Martin Frobisher*, 89–90.

[36] Willan, *The Muscovy Merchants*, 81.

[37] Stow, *Survey of London*, 1:172–173; Philip Norman and W. D. Caroe, "The Architecture of Crosby Hall," in *Survey of London Monograph 9, Crosby Place* (London: Guild & School of Handicraft, 1908), 57–63.

[38] Peter Ackroyd, *The Life of Thomas More* (London: Chatto & Windus, 1998), 234–35; Philip Norman and W. D. Caroe, "The History of Crosby Place," in *Survey of London Monograph 9, Crosby Place*, 15–32.

[39] Ann Saunders, "The Building of the Exchange," in Ann Saunders, ed., *The Royal Exchange* (London: London Topographical Society, Publication No. 152, 1997), 36–47.

[40] "Michaell Lok Saluteth the Worshipfull Commyssioners," in Collinson, *The Three Voyages of Martin Frobisher*, 335.

[41] T. S. Willan, *Studies in Elizabethan Foreign Trade* (1959; repr. Manchester: Manchester University Press, 1968), 148.

[42] "Michaell Lok Saluteth the Worshipfull Commyssioners," in Collinson, *Voyages of Martin Frobisher*, 335 ("took pains," "received such money," "take charge," and "very little credit"); 336 ("merchant and purser" and "did satisfy").

[43] Deborah E. Harkness, *The Jewel House. Elizabethan London and the Scientific Revolution* (New Haven, CT: Yale University Press, 2007).

[44] Margaret Blatcher, "Chatham dockyard and a little-known shipwright, Matthew Baker (1530–1613)," *Archaeologia Cantiana* 107 (1989): 155–72; James McDermott, "Matthew Baker (1529/30–1613, shipwright," *Oxford Dictionary of National Biography*.

[45] Nicholas Popper, "The English Polydaedali: How Gabriel Harvey Read Late Tudor London," *Journal of the History of Ideas* 66, no. 3 (2005): 351–81; 380.

[46] James McDermott, "Humphrey Cole and the Frobisher Voyages," in Silke Ackermann, ed., *Humphrey Cole: Mint, Measurement and Maps in Elizabethan England* (London: British Museum Press, Occasional Paper No. 126, 1998), 15–19.

[47] N. A. M. Rodger, *The Safeguard of the Sea: A Naval History of Britain 660–1649* (London: HarperCollins Publishers, 1997), 234–36.

[48] Dr. J. Hamel and John Studdy Leigh (trans.), *Early English Voyages to Northern Russia; comprising the Voyages of John Tradescent the Elder, Sir Hugh Willoughby, Richard Chancellor, Nelson, and Others* (London: Richard Bentley, 1857), 24.

[49] Sir James Watt, "The Medical Record of the Frobisher Voyages of 1576, 1577 and 1578," in Symons, ed., *Meta Incognita* 2:607–32; 613.

[50] Ibid., 610–12.

[51] Collinson, *The Three Voyages of Martin Frobisher*, 90. Lok mentions "Stephen" Borough rather than "William" Borough. But this is probably an error, given Stephen's earlier skepticism and William's active involvement in the preparations.

[52] Ibid., 90. Also: "Michaell Lok Saluteth the Worshipfull Commyssioners," in Collinson, *The Three Voyages of Martin Frobisher*, 334.

7. THE SUPPOSED STRAIT

[1] Christopher Hall, "The First Voyage of M. Martin Frobisher, to the Northwest, for the search of the straight or passage to China, written by Christopher Hall, Master of the Gabriel, and made in the yeere of our Lord 1576," in Vilhjalmur Stefansson, ed., *The Three Voyages of Martin Frobisher*, 2 vols. (London: The Argonaut Press, 1938; in Amsterdam: N. Israel and New York: Da Capo Press, 1971), 1:147–54; 149.

[2] [Lok], "East India by the Northwest[ward]," in Collinson, *The Three Voyages of Martin Frobisher*, 80; Hall, "The First Voyage of M. Martin Frobisher," in Stefansson, ed., *Voyages of Martin Frobisher*, 1:150.

[3] Frobisher and Hall to Dee, 1576, excerpted in Taylor, *Tudor Geography 1485–1583*, 262–63.

[4] Hall, "The First Voyage of M. Martine Frobisher," in Stefansson, ed., *The Three Voyages of Martin Frobisher*, 1:151.

[5] Helen Wallis, "England's Search for the Northern Passages in the Sixteenth and Early Seventeenth Centuries," *Arctic* 37, no. 4 (1984): 453–72; 463.

[6] Best, *A True Discourse*, in Collinson, *The Three Voyages of Martin Frobisher*, 71 ("swallowed up" and "cast away"); [Lok], "East India by the Northwest[ward]," in Collinson, *The Three Voyages of Martin Frobisher*, 81.

[7] Ibid., 72 ("extreme foul weather"); 70 ("undone," "determined and resolved," and "or else never to return").

[8] Ibid., 71 ("high and ragged land"); 72 ("Queen Elizabeth's Forland" and "conceived no small hope").

[9] Ibid., 73.

[10] Hall, "The First Voyage of M. Martine Frobisher," in Stefansson, ed., *Voyages of Martin Frobisher*, 1:153.

[11] Ibid., 1:154.

[12] [Lok], "East India by the Northwest[ward]," in Collinson, *The Three Voyages of Martin Frobisher*, 83–84.

[13] Ibid., 84.

[14] Best, *A True Discourse*, in Collinson, *The Three Voyages of Martin Frobisher*, 73.

[15] Ibid., 74.

[16] Ibid., 75.

[17] [Lok], "East India by the Northwest[ward]," in Collinson, *The Three Voyages of Martin Frobisher*, 87.

[18] "Accounts, with subsidiary documents, of Michael Lok, treasurer, of first, second and third voyages of Martin Frobisher to Cathay by the north-west passage": The National Archives (Kew), E 164/35, fo. 14; the globe or "sphere" cost 8 shillings. Also: Kenneth R. Andrews, *Trade, Plunder and Settlement: Maritime Enterprise and the Genesis of the British Empire, 1480–1630* (1984; repr., Cambridge: Cambridge University Press, 1991), 173.

[19] "Michaell Lok Saluteth the Worshipfull Commyssioners," in Collinson, *The Three Voyages of Martin Frobisher*, 336.

[20] Alden T. Vaughan, *Transatlantic Encounters: American Indians in Britain, 1500–1776* (Cambridge: Cambridge University Press, 2006), 1–4.

[21] Best, *A True Discourse*, in Collinson, *The Three Voyages of Martin Frobisher*, 74 ("new pray," "strange infidel"); [Lok], "East India by the Northwest[ward]," in Collinson, *The Three Voyages of Martin Frobisher*, 87.

[22] [Lok], "East India by the Northwest[ward]," in Collinson, *The Three Voyages of Martin Frobisher*, 87.

[23] Ibid., 87.

[24] Vaughan, *Transatlantic Encounters*, 3.

[25] "Articles of Graunt from the Queene's Majestie to the Companye of Kathai," in Collinson, *The Three Voyages of Martin Frobisher*, 111–113: 111.

[26] Ibid., 113 ("High Admiral", "wares"); 112 ("to seek, discover"). Also, "Articles consented and fully agreed by the Company of Kathaye," in Collinson, The Three Voyages of Martin Frobisher, 114–115.

[27] "Articles consented and fully agreed by the Company of Cathay", in *Calendar of State Papers Colonial, East Indies, China and Japan: 1513–1616*, ed. W. Noel Sainsbury (London: Longman, Green, Longman & Roberts, 1862), #31, 16–17.

[28] Collinson, *The Three Voyages of Martin Frobisher*, 91.

[29] Sir Humphrey Gilbert, *A Discourse of a Discoverie for a New Passage to Cataia* (London: Henry Middleton, 1576), in Quinn, *Voyages and Colonising Enterprises*, 1:129–64; 134.

[30] Ibid., 135.

[31] Ibid., 1:160–61. The quotes in this and the next paragraph are taken from these pages.

[32] John Roche Dasent, ed., *Acts of the Privy Council of England Volume IX, 1575–1577* (London: Her Majesty's Stationery Office, 1894), 302–3.

[33] McDermott, *Martin Frobisher: Elizabethan Privateer*, 149.

[34] Vaughan, *Transatlantic Encounters*, 3–4.

[35] Collinson, *The Three Voyages of Martin Frobisher*, 110.

[36] Ibid., 108–9.

8. *TRESOR TROUVEE*

[1] The story of the assaying business is told in Lok's letter of April 22, 1577, "Mr. Lockes Discoors Touching the Ewre, 1577," in Collinson, *The Three Voyages of Martin Frobisher*, 92–99; 92.

[2] Donald D. Hogarth, Peter W. Boreham, and John G. Mitchell, *Martin Frobisher's Northwest Venture, 1576–1581. Mines, Minerals, Metallurgy* (Hull, Quebec: Canadian Museum of Civilzation, 1994), 21.

[3] "Mr. Lockes Discoors," in Collinson, *The Three Voyages of Martin Frobisher*, 92. Williams and another assayer, Wheeler, said the stone was "markesyte."

[4] William M. Jones, "Two Learned Italians in Elizabethan England," *Italica* 32, no. 4 (1955): 242–47; 245–46.

[5] "Mr. Lockes Discoors," in Collinson, *The Three Voyages of Martin Frobisher*, 93.

[6] Ibid., 93 ("own use"; "the new land"; "desirous to know").

[7] "Bernardino de Mendoza to the King," March 31, 1578, in *Calendar of Letters and State Papers Relating to English Affairs, preserved principally in the archives of Simancas, Volume 2, Elizabeth: 1568–1579*, ed. Martin A. S. Hume (London: Her Majesty's Stationery Office, 1894), #484, 567–69; 568.

[8] "Mr. Lockes Discoors," in Collinson, *The Three Voyages of Martin Frobisher*, 92–99.

[9] John Cooper, *The Queen's Agent. Francis Walsingham at the Court of Elizabeth I* (London: Faber and Faber, 2012), 26–33 (exile); 39 (elected M.P.); 42, 49 (work with Cecil); 59 (ambassador).

[10] Ibid., 86–87 (sworn in as Secretary of State); 92 (spymaster).

[11] "Mr. Lockes Discoors," in Collinson, *The Three Voyages of Martin Frobisher*, 94.

[12] M. R. P. and P. W. Hasler, "William Wynter (c.1528–89), of Deptford, Kent, and Lydney, Glos.," in P. W. Hasler, ed., *The History of Parliament: The House of Commons 1558–1603* (London: History of Parliament Trust, 1981; online edition).

[13] For Cecil's meetings with Agnello, see Harkness, *The Jewel House*, 142–43, 282n1.

[14] Hogarth et al., *Martin Frobisher's Northwest Venture*, 73; James W. Scott, "Technological and Economic Changes in the Metalliferous Mining and Smelting Industries of Tudor England," *Albion: A Quarterly Journal Concerned with British Studies* 4, no. 2 (1972): 94–110; 100; Robert Baldwin, "Speculative Ambitions and the Reputations of Frobisher's Metallurgists," in Thomas Symons, ed., *Meta Incognita*, 2:401–476; 405–406.

[15] "Mr. Lockes Discoors," in Collinson, *The Three Voyages of Martin Frobisher*, 97–98.

[16] See "A Brieff Note of all the Cost and Charge . . . for the First Voyage . . . in June, Anno 1567," and "The Bryef Account of the Second Voyage," in Collinson, *The Three Voyages of Martin Frobisher*, 115–16 and 166–67, respectively. Lok notes the "whole stok of the adventurers" to be £875 in June 1576 (116) and the sum he's received "of all the venturers" to be £5,150 (166). By March, some forty-five investors had pledged £3,225, meaning that another £1,925 was raised after news of gold was circulated.

[17] See Collinson, *The Three Voyages of Martin Frobisher*, 107, 109.

[18] M. B. Donald, *Elizabethan Copper. The History of the Company of Mines Royal, 1568–1605* (London: Pergamon Press, 1955), 43–47 (Duckett); 52–55 (Wynter).

[19] Cecil T. Carr, ed., *Select Charters of Trading Companies, A.D. 1530–1707* (London: Bernard Quartich, 1913), 16–20. Also: M. B. Donald, *Elizabethan Monopolies: The History of the Company of Mineral and Battery Works from 1765 to 1604* (London: Oliver & Boyd, 1961), 17–18.

[20] Scott, *The Constitution and Finance of English, Scottish and Irish Joint-Stock Companies to 1720*, 1:39–40; 104.

[21] Carr, ed., *Select Charters*, 4. Also, Donald, *Elizabethan Copper*, 15–42.

[22] Ibid., 16. Also, Donald, *Elizabethan Monopolies*, 24–34.

[23] Martin Lynch, *Mining in World History* (London: Reaktion Books, 2002), 16.

[24] Georgius Agricola, *De Re Metallica*, trans. Herbert Clark Hoover and Lou Henry Hoover (New York: Dover Publications Inc., 1950), xxvi.

[25] Ibid., 33 ("obtain"); 38 (frost); 20 (physicians).

[26] "Wm. Humfrey to Sir Wm. Cecill," June 30, 1566, in *CSP-Domestic, 1547–1580*, vol. 40, #17, 275.

[27] "Thos. Thurland to [Cecil]," August 1, 1566, in ibid., vol. 40, #41, 276.

[28] Douglas Grant, "The Sixth Duke of Somerset, Thomas Robinson and the Newlands Mines," in *Transactions of the Cumberland and Westmoreland Antiquarian and Archaeological Society, Series 2*, vol. 85, 1985, 143–62.

[29] Lynch, *Mining in World History*, 28. For a remarkable account of Cortés's exploits in Mexico see Bernal Díaz, *The Conquest of New Spain*, ed. and trans. J. M. Cohen (London: Penguin Books, 1963).

[30] For discussion of the establishment of Spanish mining activity in the New World, see Lynch, *Mining in World History*, 25–29.

[31] Peter Bakewell, *Miners of the Red Mountain: Indian Labor in Potosí, 1545–1650* (Albuquerque: University of New Mexico Press, 2009), 8.

[32] Lynch, *Mining in World History*, 38.

[33] See Bakewell, *Miners of the Red Mountain*, 15–17. Quechua was a dialect spoken by some Incas of the period. It is still spoken today.

[34] Ibid., 16–17.

[35] Bartolomé Arzáns de Orsúa Vela, *Tales of Potosí*, ed. R.C. Padden and trans. Frances M. López-Morillas (Providence, RI: Brown University Press, 1975), xi; xiii.

[36] Ibid., xiv.

[37] Lynch, *Mining in World History*, 38. By 1611, it would boast a population of 100,000: Vela, *Tales of Potosí*, xiii.

[38] Vela, *Tales of Potosí*, xxv.

[39] For a discussion of the Spanish fleet, see Timothy R. Walton, *The Spanish Treasure Fleets* (Sarasota, FL: Pineapple Press Inc., 1994), 47.

[40] Ibid., 51.

[41] Gwendolin B. Cobb, "Supply and Transportation for the Potosí Mines," *The Hispanic American Historical Review* 29, no. 1 (1949): 25–45; 34.

[42] D. B. Quinn, "Some Spanish Reactions to Elizabethan Colonial Enterprises," in *Transactions of the Royal Historical Society* 1 (1951): 1–21; 2.

[43] Fernand Braudel, *The Wheels of Commerce: Civilization & Capitalism, 15th–18th Century, Volume 2*, trans. Siân Reynolds (New York: Harper & Row, 1982; First Perennial Library edition, 1986), 198.

[44] Lynch, *Mining in World History*, 14–15; Braudel, *Wheels of Commerce*, 198.

[45] Braudel, *The Wheels of Commerce*, 198.

[46] Neil MacGregor, *A History of the World in 100 Objects* (London: Allen Lane, 2010), 516–22.

[47] "Instructions given to Martyne Ffurbisher, Gent., for orders to be observed in the viage nowe recommended to him for the North West parts and Cathay," in Collinson, *The Three Voyages of Martin Frobisher*, 117–120. Also, James McDermott, "The Company of Cathay: the financing and organising of the Frobisher voyages," in Symons, ed., *Meta Incognita*, 1:147–178: 163.

[48] "A little bundle of the tryeing of ye Northwest ewre. By D. Burcot, Jonas Schütz, Baptista Agnillo, etc.," in Collinson, *The Three Voyages of Martin Frobisher*, 174–79; 175.

[49] "Instructions," in Collinson, *The Three Voyages of Martin Frobisher*, 119.

[50] Ibid.

[51] George Best, "A True Reporte of such things as hapned in the second voyage of Captayne Frobysher, pretended for the discoverie of a new passage to cataya, China, and the East India, by the North West. Anno Do. 1577," in Collinson, *The Three Voyages of Martin Frobisher*, 121–57; 128.

[52] "Names of the venturars," in Collinson, *The Three Voyages of Martin Frobisher*, 164.

[53] Best, "A True Reporte . . . ," in Collinson, *The Three Voyages of Martin Frobisher*, 137.

[54] Ibid., 152.

[55] Charles Trice Martin, ed., "Journal of Sir Francis Walsingham from December 1570 to April 1583. From the original manuscript in the possession of Lieut.-Colonel Carew," in *The Camden Miscellany*, vol. 6 (London: Camden Society, 1871), 1–99; 32.

[56] George Best, "The Thirde Voyage of Captaine Frobisher, pretended for the discoverie of Cataya, by Meta Incognita. Anno DO. 1578," in Collinson, *The Three Voyages of Martin Frobisher*, 225–89; 225.

[57] Ibid., 226.

[58] Entry for 28 November 1577 in James Orchard Halliwell, ed., *The Private Diary of Dr John Dee and the Catalogue of his Library of Manuscripts, From the Original Manuscripts in the Ashmolean Museum at Oxford, and Trinity College Library, Cambridge* (London: Camden Society, 1842), 4.

[59] Best, "A True Reporte...," in Collinson, *The Three Voyages of Martin Frobisher*, 122.

[60] McDermott, *Frobisher: Elizabethan Privateer*, 210.

[61] Ibid., 459n23.

[62] "Edward Fenton's provisional list for the 1578 Colony," in James McDermott, *The Third Voyage of Martin Frobisher to Baffin Island, 1578* (London: Hakluyt Society, 2001), 66–69.

[63] Steuart A. Pears, *The Correspondence of Sir Philip Sidney and Hubert Languet* (London: William Pickering, 1845), xvi.

[64] Sir Philip Sidney to Hubert Languet, October 1, 1577, in Pears, *The Correspondence of Sir Philip Sidney and Hubert Languet*, 119.

[65] Hubert Languet to Sir Philip Sidney, November 28, 1577, in Pears, *The Correspondence of Sir Philip Sidney and Hubert Languet*, 124–25.

[66] McDermott, *Frobisher: Elizabethan Privateer*, 199.

[67] Collinson, *The Three Voyages of Martin Frobisher*, 199.

[68] "A Little Bundle," in ibid., 177. The amount of time the workmen estimated for completion is not specified.

[69] "11 March, 1577. To the Lord Treasurer and Lord Chamberlayne abowt the North-West Viage," in Collinson, *The Three Voyages of Martin Frobisher*, 182.

[70] "All the stok of the venturers in all the iij voyages," in Collinson, *The Three Voyages of Martin Frobisher*, 358–59; 358.

[71] Bernardino de Mendoza to the King," April 22, 1578, in *CSP-Spain (Simancas), Volume 2, Elizabeth: 1568–1579*, #489, 576.

[72] Best, "The Thirde Voyage," in Collinson, *The Three Voyages of Martin Frobisher*, 232.

[73] Collinson, *The Three Voyages of Martin Frobisher*, xii.

[74] John Roche Dasent, ed. *Acts of the Privy Council of England, Volume XI, 1578–1580* (London: Her Majesty's Stationery Office, 1895), 64–65.

[75] "The Humble Petition of Michael Lok for Charges Disbursed", in Collinson, *The Three Voyages of Martin Frobisher*, 349–50; 350.

[76] For matters touching Lok's accounts of the Frobisher voyages and the trials of the ore, see "State Papers Subsequent to the Third Voyage," in Collinson, *The Three Voyages of Martin Frobisher*, 317–63; 350.

[77] "Bernardino de Mendoza to the King," February 7, 1579, in *CSP-Spain (Simancas), Volume 2, Elizabeth: 1568–1579*, #549, 642.

[78] Robert McGhee, *The Arctic Voyages of Martin Frobisher: An Elizabethan Adventure* (Montreal: Canadian Museum of Civilization, 2001), 146.

9. ILANDISH EMPIRE

[1] Deborah E. Harkness, "Managing an Experimental Household: The Dees of Mortlake and the Practice of Natural Philosophy," *Isis*, 88, no. 2 (1997): 247–62; 247.

[2] Glyn Parry, *The Arch-Conjuror of England: John Dee* (New Haven, CT: Yale University Press, 2013), 20.

[3] Dee spent three thousand pounds: Suster, *John Dee*, 10, 15. According to the 1583 catalog, there were three to four thousand titles: William H. Sherman, *John Dee: The Politics of Reading and Writing*

in the English Renaissance (Amherst: University of Massachusetts Press, 1995), 31. More than one hundred volumes were stolen in his lifetime and are now in the collection of the Royal College of Surgeons in London: see Katie Birkwood, "Scholar, Courtier, Magician: the Lost Library of John Dee," in *Commentary* 6 (2015); 12–15. Cambridge University, by contrast, had 451 titles at the time. Suster, *John Dee*, 15.

4 Quinn, *The Voyages and Colonising Enterprises*, 1:170–75. Quinn suggests that the signature is Gilbert's, though the body of the text may not be his handwriting.

5 See the *Oxford English Dictionary* for "annoy," definition 4a.

6 Suster, *John Dee*, 43.

7 Rappaport, *Worlds Within Worlds*, 7. See the *Oxford English Dictionary* definition 1a, http://www .oed.com/view/Entry/114675?rskey=DNowjO&result=1&isAdvanced=false#eid?? http://www .oed.com/view/Entry/114675?rskey=TAZ6Hz&result=1&isAdvanced=false.

8 "Sir Humfrey Gilbert to the Count Montgomery or Lord Burghley," September 6, 1572, in *Calendar of State Papers Foreign: Elizabeth, Volume 10, 1572–1574*, ed. Allan James Crosby (London: Longman & Co, 1876), #556, 175.

9 "Petition of divers gentlemen of the West parts of England to the Queen," in *CSP-Domestic, 1547–1580*, vol. 95, #63, 475.

10 Quinn, *Voyages and Colonising Enterprises*, 1:102.

11 Geoffrey Parker, *The Dutch Revolt* (London: Pelican Books, 1979), 178.

12 Jason Eldred, "The Just Will Pay for the Sinners: English Merchants, the Trade with Spain, and Elizabethan Foreign Policy, 1563–1585," *Journal for Early Modern Cultural Studies* 10, no. 1 (2010): 5–28; 9.

13 John Dee, *General and Rare Memorials Pertayning to the Perfect Arte of Navigation* (London: John Daye, 1577; Kessinger Legacy Reprint [facsimile], 2003, 10 ("Victorious British Monarchy," "marvellous Security," "wonderfully increase"); 28 ("New Foreign Discoveries," "Ilandish Empire").

14 David Armitage, *The Ideological Origins of the British Empire* (Cambridge: Cambridge University Press, 2000), 42–43.

15 Dewar, *Sir Thomas Smith*, 48.

16 Entry for 28 November 1577 in Halliwell, ed., *The Private Diary of Dr John Dee*, 4. For the first two reports, see John Dee, *The Limits of the British Empire*, edited by Ken MacMillan with Jennifer Abeles (Westport, CT: Praeger, 2004), 5, 10–13, 37–41.

17 Joseph H. Peterson, ed., *John Dee's Five Books of Mystery: Original Sourcebook of Enochian Magic* (Boston: Weiserbooks, 2003), 8; Suster, *John Dee*, 55–6; Glynn Parry, "John Dee and the Elizabethan British Empire in Its European Context," *The Historical Journal*, Vol. 49, No. 3 (2006), 643–75.

18 Humphrey Gilbert, "A Discourse how Hir Majestie May Annoy the King of Spayne," in Quinn, *Voyages and Colonising Enterprises*, 1:170.

19 "A letter written to M. Richard Hakluyt of the middle Temple, conteining a report of the true state and commodities of Newfoundland, by M. Anthonie Parkhurst Gentleman, 1578," in Hakluyt, *Principal Navigations*, 8:9–16; 10–11.

20 Ibid., 10.

21 Gilbert, "A Discourse how Hir Majestie may Annoy the King of Spayne," in Quinn, *Voyages and Colonising Enterprises*, 1:172–80: for this paragraph and the remaining paragraphs in this section.

22 Eldred, "The Just Will Pay for the Sinners," 14. Also, Pauline Croft, "Trading with the Enemy, 1585-1604," *The Historical Journal* 32, no. 2 (1989): 281–302.

23 See Conyers Read, "Queen Elizabeth's Seizure of the Duke of Alva's Pay-Ships," *The Journal of Modern History* 5, no. 4 (1933): 443–64; 443–46.

24 Pauline Croft, "Introduction: The First Spanish Company, 1530–1585," Pauline Croft, ed., *The Spanish Company* (London: London Record Society, 1973), vii–xxix; vi.

25 Ibid., xiii–xiv.

[26] "Bernardino de Mendoza to the King," February 20, 1580, in *Calendar of Letters and State Papers Relating to English Affairs preserved principally in the archives of Simancas, Volume 3, Elizabeth: 1580–1586*, ed. Martin A. S. Hume (London: Her Majesty's Stationery Office, 1896), #6, 8–9; 8.

[27] John Dee, "Unto your Majesties Tytle Royall to these Forene Regions & Ilandes do appertayne 4 poyntes," in Dee, *The Limits of the British Empire*, eds., MacMillan with Abeles, 18; 43.

[28] Ibid., 43–49.

[29] "11 June 1578. Letters Patent to Sir Humphrey Gilbert," in Quinn, *Voyages and Colonising Enterprises*, 1:188–94; 188.

[30] Ibid., 188–89.

[31] Ibid., 191–92.

[32] "Sir Humphrey Gylberte to Secretary Sir Francis Walsingham," September 23, 1578, in *Calendar of State Papers Colonial, America and West Indies: Volume 9, 1675–1676 and Addenda 1574–1674*, ed. W. Noel Sainsbury (London: Her Majesty's Stationery Office, 1893), #4, 3.

[33] "Bernardino de Mendoza to the King," June 3, 1578, in *CSP-Spain (Simancas), Volume 2, Elizabeth: 1568–1579*, #503, 591.

[34] "Castelnau de Mauvissiere to Henry III, 7 July 1578," in Quinn, *Voyages and Colonising Enterprises*, 1:195–97; 195.

[35] "Bernardino de Mendoza to the King," May 16, 1578, in *CSP-Spain (Simancas), Volume 2, Elizabeth: 1568–1579*, #496, 583.

[36] For the list of investors, see Quinn, *Voyages and Colonising Enterprises*, 2:332–33.

[37] "20 December 1578. Sir John Gilbert to Sir Francis Walsingham," in Quinn, *Voyages and Colonising Enterprises*, 1:215.

[38] "Gylberte to Walsingham," in *CSP-Colonial, America & the West Indies, Volume 9*, #4, 3.

[39] "Sir Humphrey Gilbert to Sir Francis Walsingham, 12 November 1578," in *CSP-Colonial, America & the West Indies, Volume 9*, #5, 4.

[40] Quinn, *Voyages and Colonising Enterprises*, 1:44–45.

[41] "The Privy Council Writes to the Sheriff Etc. of Devonshire, 28 May 1579," in Quinn, *Voyages and Colonising Enterprises*, 1:221–22; 222.

IO. NOVA ALBION

[1] K. R. Andrews, "The Aims of Drake's Expedition of 1577–1580," *The American Historical Review* 73, no. 3 (1968): 724–41; 739.

[2] For Drake's early life: John Sugden, *Sir Francis Drake* (London: Barrie & Jenkins, 1990; paperback ed., Pimlico, 2006), 1–38; Harry Kelsey, *Sir Francis Drake: The Queen's Pirate* (New Haven, CT: Yale University Press, 1998), 3–39.

[3] John Hawkins, "The third troublesome voyage made with the *Jesus of Lubeck*, the *Minion*, and foure other ships, to the parts of Guinea, and the West Indies, in the yeeres 1567 and 1568 by M. John Hawkins," in Hakluyt, *Principal Navigations*, 10:64–74; 69.

[4] Ibid., 71.

[5] Ibid., 71 ("without mercy"); 72 (*Minion* and *Judith*'s escape).

[6] E. G .R. Taylor, "The Missing Draft Project of Drake's Voyage of 1577–80," *The Geographical Journal* 75, no. 1 (1930): 46–47.

[7] "Bernardino de Mendoza to the King," October 23, 1580, in *CSP-Spain (Simancas) Volume 3, 1580–1586*, #49, 60–62; 62.

[8] "Bernardino de Mendoza to the King," October 16, 1580, in Martin A. S. Hume, ed., *CSP-Spain (Simancas) Volume 3, 1580–1586*, #44, 54–56; 54–55.

[9] Ibid., 54–55.

[10] For the two primary accounts of Drake's voyage: Hakluyt's account, see "The famous voyage of Sir Francis Drake into the South sea, and therehence about the whole Globe of the earth, begun in the yeere of our Lord, 1577," in Hakluyt, *Principal Navigations*, 11:101–33; Fletcher's account, see Francis Fletcher, *The World Encompassed by Sir Francis Drake* (1628; repr. Amsterdam: Da Capo

Press, 1969). For Drake's pace compared to Magellan, see A. L. Rowse, *The Expansion of Elizabethan England* (London: Macmillan & Co., Ltd., 1955), 201.

[11] Fletcher, *The World Encompassed*, 35. For Drake's prostration: James A. Williamson, ed., *The Observations of Sir Richard Hawkins Knight, in his voyage into the South Sea, Anno Domini 1593* (London: The Argonaut Press, 1933), 96. For the penguins: Derek Wilson, *The World Encompassed: Francis Drake and His Great Voyage* (New York, Harper & Row, 1977), 97.

[12] Sugden, *Sir Francis Drake*, 128.

[13] Fletcher, *The World Encompassed*, 64.

[14] "The famous voyage of Sir Francis Drake," in Hakluyt, *Principal Navigations*, 11:118–19.

[15] In Hakluyt, "The famous voyage," the latitude given is 43 degrees north (118). In Fletcher, it is 48 degrees north (64). Helen Wallis notes, "One of the most authoritative pieces of cartographic evidence, Molyneux's terrestrial globe of 1592, supports the more northerly limit." See her: "The Cartography of Drake's voyages," in Norman J.W. Thrower, *Sir Francis and the Famous Voyage, 1577–1580* (Berkeley, California: University of California Press, 1984), 121–163: 130.

[16] Fletcher, *The World Encompassed*, 64; 67.

[17] Ibid., 64. Exactly where this bay lies is a matter of heated debate, although the consensus is that it is, indeed, Drake's Bay, just north of San Francisco.

[18] Ibid., 69.

[19] "The famous voyage," in Hakluyt, *Principal Navigations*, 11:121–22. Also, Fletcher, *The World Encompassed*, 76.

[20] "The famous voyage," in Hakluyt, *Principal Navigations*, 11:122. Also, Fletcher, *The World Encompassed*, 77.

[21] "The famous voyage," in Hakluyt, *Principal Navigations*, 11:123. Also, Fletcher, *The World Encompassed*, 80.

[22] "The famous voyage," in Hakluyt, *Principal Navigations*, 11:123.

[23] Fletcher, *The World Encompassed*, 85, 89; "The famous voyage," in Hakluyt, *Principal Navigations*, 11:127; Wilson, *The World Encompassed*, 175.

[24] Sugden, *Sir Francis Drake*, 128.

[25] "Bernardino de Mendoza to the King," October 16, 1580, in *CSP-Spain (Simancas), Volume 3, Elizabeth: 1580–1586*, #44, 55.

[26] "Bernardino de Mendoza to the King," January 9, 1581, in *CSP-Spain (Simancas), Volume 3, Elizabeth: 1580–1586*, #60, 73–75; 74–75.

[27] "Letter from Queen Elizabeth to Edmund Tremayne ordering that the sum of £10,000 was to be left in the hands of Francis Drake," 22 October 1580, in Zelia Nuttall, ed. and trans., *New Light on Drake. A Collection of Documents Relating to his Voyage of Circumnavigation 1577–1580* (London: Hakluyt Society, 1914), 429–30.

[28] "Bernardino de Mendoza to the King," January 15, 1581, in Hume, ed., *CSP-Spain (Simancas), Volume 3, Elizabeth, 1580–1586*, #65, 80.

[29] "Bernardino de Mendoza to the King," April 6, 1581, in *CSP-Spain (Simancas), Volume 3, Elizabeth, 1580–1586*, #77, 93–95; 95.

[30] "Bernardino de Mendoza to the King," July 14, 1581, in *CSP-Spain (Simancas), Volume 3, Elizabeth, 1580–1586*, #113, 147–48.

[31] "Bernardino de Mendoza to the King," November 7, 1581, in *CSP-Spain (Simancas), Volume 3, Elizabeth, 1580–1586*, #159, 208–9; 208.

[32] "Bernardino de Mendoza to the King," January 9, 1581, in *CSP-Spain (Simancas), Volume 3, Elizabeth, 1580–1586*, #60, 74 ("50,000 crowns"); 75 ("300 crowns").

[33] "Bernardino de Mendoza to the King," October 20, 1581, in *CSP-Spain (Simancas), Volume 3, Elizabeth, 1580–1586*, #146, 185–90; 188, 190.

[34] "Bernardino de Mendoza to the King," October 16, 1580, in *CSP-Spain (Simancas), Volume 3, Elizabeth, 1580–1586*, #44, 56.

[35] "A Proiect of a Corporatyon of Soche as Shall Venteur vnto Soche Domynions and Contreys Sytuate Bayonde The Equynoctyall Line," in Nuttall, ed. and trans., *New Light on Drake*, 430.

[36] "Bernardino de Mendoza to the King," October 16, 1580, in *CSP-Spain (Simancas), Volume 3, Elizabeth, 1580–1586*, #44, 55.

[37] Parker, *Imprudent King: A New Life of Philip II* (New Haven, CT: Yale University Press, 2014; paperback ed., 2015), 276.

[38] "Bernardino de Mendoza to the King," October 16, 1580, in *CSP-Spain (Simancas), Volume 3, Elizabeth, 1580–1586*, #44, 55–56.

[39] "Bernardino de Mendoza to the King," February 9, 1582, in *CSP-Spain (Simancas), Volume 3, Elizabeth, 1580–1586*, #211, 283–85; 283.

[40] Ibid., 285.

[41] "Narrative of William Hawkins, 6 July 1583," in E. G. R. Taylor, *The Troublesome Voyage of Captain Edward Fenton 1582–1583* (Cambridge: Hakluyt Society, 1959), 277–286; 278.

[42] "Captain Edward Fenton to Lord Treasurer Burghley," June 29, 1583, in *CSP-Colonial, East Indies, Volume 2, 1513–1616*, #225, 88–89.

[43] "Bernardino de Mendoza to the King," October 16, 1580, in *CSP-Spain (Simancas), Volume 3, Elizabeth: 1580–1586*, #44, 55.

[44] "Bernardino de Mendoza to the King," April 20, 1582, in *CSP-Spain (Simancas), Volume 3, Elizabeth: 1580–1586*, #248, 340–42; 341. Also in 1582, Spain learned the full story of Drake's commercial deal with the Sultan from Francisco de Dueñas, a spy who was sent out to learn about the Portuguese-claimed Moluccas after Philip II seized control of the Portuguese throne. See Dueñas's report: Henry R. Wagner, *Sir Francis Drake's Voyage Around The World: Its Aims and Achievements* (San Francisco: John Howell, 1926), 180.

II. TO HEAVEN BY SEA

[1] "6 June 1582. Agreement between Sir Humphrey Gilbert, Sir George Peckham, and Sir Thomas Gerrard," in David Beers Quinn, *The Voyages and Colonising Enterprises of Sir Humphrey Gilbert*, 2 vols. (London: The Hakluyt Society, 1940), 2:245–50; "9 June 1582. Agreement between Sir Humphrey Gilbert, Sir George Peckham and Sir Thomas Gerrard," in Quinn, *Voyages and Colonising Enterprises*, 2:256–57.

[2] "8 July 1582. Grant of authority by Sir Humphrey Gilbert, Regarding his Rights in America, to Sir John Gilbert, Sir George Peckham and William Aucher," in Quinn, *Voyages and Colonising Enterprises*, 2:266–78; 276–77.

[3] "Sir Humphrey Gylberte to Secretary Sir Francis Walsingham," July 11, 1581, in *CSP-Colonial, America and West Indies: Volume 9, Addenda 1574–1674*, #12, 7–88; 7.

[4] "7 July 1582. Agreement between Sir Humphrey Gilbert and Philip Sidney," in Quinn, *Voyages and Colonising Enterprises*, 2:260–66. Sidney seems to have got involved in or before May, when Hakluyt dedicated to him *Divers Voyages*, the book designed to promote Gilbert's voyage.

[5] "Don Bernardino de Mendoza to Philip II, 11 July 1582," in Quinn, *Voyages and Colonising Enterprises*, 2:278–79.

[6] "6 June 1582. Agreement between Sir Humphrey Gilbert, Sir George Peckham, and Sir Thomas Gerrard," in Quinn, *Voyages and Colonising Enterprises*, 2:245–50.

[7] James McDermott, "Sir George Peckham (d. 1608), colonial adventurer," Oxford Dictionary of National Biography; Quinn, *Voyages and Colonising Enterprises*, 2:332, 334.

[8] "Second book and offer of Sir Thomas Gerrarde and companions…," in Hamilton, ed., *CSP-Ireland, 1509–1573*, #32, 428.

[9] "Don Bernardino de Mendoza to Philip II, 11 July 1582," in Quinn, *Voyages and Colonising Enterprises*, 2:278.

[10] Roger Bigelow Merriman, "Some Notes on the Treatment of English Catholics in the Reign of Elizabeth," *The American Historical Review* 13, no. 3 (1908): 480–500; 493.

[11] Ibid. 494.

[12] Susan Brigden, *New Worlds, Lost Worlds. The Rule of the Tudors, 1485–1603* (London: Penguin Books, 2001), 216.

[13] James Ellison, "'Measure for Measure' and the Execution of Catholics in 1604," *English Literary Renaissance* 33, no. 1 (2003): 44–87; 53.

[14] For the land grants, see Quinn, *Voyages and Colonising Enterprises*, 1:60n (all land grants); 2:245–50 (first land grant); 2:256–57 (second land grant); 2:341–46 (third land grant). For an additional grant of 500,000 acres to Peckham: 2:250–54.

[15] "[June 1582]. Petition of Sir George Peckham and Sir Thomas Gerrard to Sir Francis Walsingham," in Quinn, *Voyages and Colonising Enterprises*, 2:255–56.

[16] "Don Bernardino de Mendoza to Philip II, 11 July 1582," in Quinn, *Voyages and Colonising Enterprises*, 2:278–279.

[17] "John Dee's Dealings with Sir George Peckham, 16 July 1582," in Quinn, *Voyages and Colonising Enterprises*, 2:280.

[18] Quinn, *Voyages and Colonising Enterprises*, 1:62–64.

[19] Richard Hakluyt, "A Discourse of the Commodity of the Taking of the Straight of Magellanus," in E. G. R. Taylor, ed., *The Original Writings and Correspondence of the Two Richard Hakluyts*, 2 vols. (London: The Hakluyt Society, 1935), 1:139–46; 140.

[20] Richard Hakluyt, "The Epistle Dedicatorie in the First Edition, 1589. To the Right Honorable Sir Francis Walsingham Knight, Principall Secretarie to her Majestie, Chancellor of the Duchie of Lancaster, and one of her Majesties most honourable Privie Councell," in Richard Hakluyt, *Principal Navigations*, 1:xvii–xxii; xvii.

[21] Richard Hakluyt, "Epistle Dedicatorie in the First Edition, 1589," in Hakluyt, *Principal Navigations*, 1:xviii.

[22] Richard Hakluyt, *Divers Voyages Touching the Discovery of America and the Islands Adjacent*, ed. John Winter Jones (London: Hakluyt Society, 1850), title page ("1582"); 8 (Philip Sidney).

[23] Ibid., 8.

[24] Ibid., 9.

[25] Ibid., 8.

[26] Ibid., 18.

[27] "A letter of Sir Francis Walsingham to M. Richard Hakluyt then of Christchurch in Oxford, incouraging him in the study of Cosmographie, and of furthering new discoveries, &c," in Richard Hakluyt, *Principal Navigations*, 8:131.

[28] See "8 July 1582. Grant of Authority by Sir Humphrey Gilbert, Regarding His Rights in America, to Sir John Gilbert, Sir George Peckham and William Aucher," in Quinn, *Voyages and Colonising Enterprises*, 2:266–278; 274–75.

[29] "Bernardino de Mendoza to the King," April 26, 1582, in *CSP-Spain (Simancas) Volume 3, Elizabeth: 1580–1586*, #254, 349.

[30] The adventurers in Gilbert's voyage are listed in Quinn, *Voyages and Colonising Enterprises*, 2:329–33.

[31] As Quinn puts it: "It is safe to say that the expedition was under-capitalized," *Voyages and Colonising Enterprises*, 1:81–2.

[32] "Sir Humphrey Gylberte to Sec. Sir Francis Walsingham," February 7, 1583, in *CSP-Colonial: America and West Indies*, vol. 9, #21, 17–18; 17.

[33] Walter Ralegh to Sir Humphrey Gilbert, 16 March 1583, in Quinn, ed., *Voyages and Colonising Enterprises*, 2:348.

[34] Quinn, *England and the Discovery of America*, 228–30; Edward Hayes, "[October 1583?] Edward Hayes' Narrative of Sir Humphrey Gilbert's Last Expedition," in Quinn, *Voyages and Colonising Enterprises*, 2:385–423.

[35] Hayes, "Gilbert's Last Expedition," in Quinn, *Voyages and Colonising Enterprises*, 2:396.

[36] Ibid., 2:397.

[37] Ibid., 2:402–3.

[38] See Ken MacMillan, "Sovereignty 'More Plainly Described': Early English Maps of North America, 1580–1625," *Journal of British Studies* 42, no. 4 (2003): 413–47; 428.

[39] Hayes, "Gilbert's Last Expedition," in Quinn, *Voyages and Colonising Enterprises*, 2:408.

[40] Ibid., 2:415.

[41] Ibid., 2:419.

[42] Ibid., 2:420. For the link to More, see: J. Holland Rose, "The Spirit of Adventure," in *The Cambridge History of the British Empire, Volume I, The Old Empire from the Beginnings to 1783*, eds. J. Hol-

land Rose, A. P. Newton, and E. A. Benians (Cambridge: Cambridge University Press, 1929), 93–114; 107.

[43] Winston S. Churchill, *A History of the English-Speaking Peoples. Volume II: The New World* (London: Cassell & Co., 1956; paperback edition, Bloomsbury Academic, 2015), 98.

12. WESTERN PLANTING

[1] George Peckham, "A True Reporte, Of the late discoveries, and possession, taken in the right of the Crowne of Englande, of the Newfound Landes: By that valiaunt and worthye Gentleman, Sir Humfrey Gilbert Knight," in Quinn, *The Voyages and Colonising Enterprises of Sir Humphrey Gilbert*, 2:435–80.

[2] Christopher Carleill, "A Briefe and Summary Discourse upon the Intended Voyage to the Hithermost Parts of America, April 1583," in Quinn, *Voyages and Colonising Enterprises*, 2:351–64. A second edition was published in late 1583 or early 1584: David B. Quinn, ed., *New American World*, 5 vols. (New York: Arno Press and Hector Bye, 1979), 3:262–63. For Carleill's deliberations with the Muscovy Company: Quinn, *Voyages and Colonising Enterprises*, 2:365–69.

[3] Thomas Fuller, *The History of the Worthies of England: A New Edition*, ed. P. Austin Nuttall, 3 vols. (London: Thomas Tegg, 1890), 2:419.

[4] Victor von Klarwill, ed., *Queen Elizabeth and Some Foreigners Being a series of hitherto unpublished letters from the archives of the Hapsburg family. Authorized translation by Professor T.H. Nash* (London: John Lane, The Bodley Head, 1928), 338.

[5] Robert Naunton, *Fragmenta Regalia; or Observations on Queen Elizabeth, Her Times and Favourites*, ed. John S. Cerovski (Washington, DC: Folger Books, 1985), 73.

[6] Aubrey, *Brief Lives*, ed. Clark, 2: 180 ("proper"), 184 ("white satin"), 182 ("trunk of books"); Naunton, *Fragmenta Regalia*, 73 ("an indefatigable reader"); John Aubrey, *Brief Lives by John Aubrey*, ed. Richard Barber (London: The Folio Society, 1975), 265 ("loved a wench" and "up against a tree").

[7] "[Sir Henry] Wallop to Burghley," February 11, 1582, in *Calendar of State Papers relating to Ireland, of the Reign of Elizabeth, Volume II: 1574–1585*, ed. Hans Claude Hamilton (London: Longmans, Green, Reader, & Dyer, 1867), vol. 139, #26, 349.

[8] Mark Nicholls and Penry Williams, *Sir Walter Raleigh in Life and Legend* (London: Continuum International Publishing, 2011), 29–30.

[9] Aubrey, *Brief Lives*, ed. Clark, 2:183.

[10] John W. Shirley, *Thomas Harriot: A Biography* (Oxford: Clarendon Press, 1983), 51–52.

[11] "Sir Edward Stafford to Walsingham," September 29, 1583, in *Calendar of State Papers Foreign: Elizabeth, Volume 18, July 1583–July 1584*, ed. Sophie Crawford Lomas (London: His Majesty's Stationery Office, 1914), #138, 117–18.

[12] "Richard Hakluyt, Preacher [with Sir Edward Stafford], to Sec. Sir Francis Walsingham," January 7, 1584, in *CSP-Colonial, America and West Indies*, vol. 9, #31, 24; David B. Quinn, ed., *The Hakluyt Handbook*, 2 vols. (London: The Hakluyt Society, 1974), 1:280–84.

[13] "Hakluyt to Walsingham," January 7, 1584, in *CSP-Colonial, America and West Indies, Volume 9*, #31, 24; Quinn, ed., *Hakluyt Handbook*, 1:284.

[14] Richard Hakluyt, *A Particular Discourse Concerning the Greate Necessitie and Manifolde Commodyties That Are Like to Growe to This Realm of Englande by the Western Discoveries Lately Attempted*, ed. David B. Quinn and Alison M. Quinn (London: The Hakluyt Society, 1993), 12–15. The rest of the section is based on this publication: 16–28 ("commodities"); 28–35 ("employments"); 43 ("mortally hate"); 44 ("laughing stock"); 76 ("fair") and ("doubtful friends").

[15] "'Articles out of Walter Raleigh's Letters Patent,'" March 25, 1584, in Sainsbury, ed., *CSP-Colonial, America and West Indies*, vol. 9, #33, 26.

[16] Klarwill, ed., *Queen Elizabeth and Some Foreigners*, 323.

[17] "Arthur Barlowe's Discourse of the First Voyage," in David Beers Quinn, *The Roanoke Voyages 1584–1590*, 2 vols. (London: Hakluyt Society, 1955), 1:91–116; 1:94 (claimed possession); 96–7 ("goodly woods", "reddest cedars"); 108 ("earth bringeth"). Also, David Beers Quinn, *Set Fair for Roanoke: Voyages and Colonies, 1584–1606* (Chapel Hill: The University of North Carolina Press, 1985), 28–29.

[18] Ibid., 1:99 ("Winganacoia"); 98 ("shirt"); 101 ("tin dish").

[19] Ibid., 1:108.

[20] Ibid., 1:106 (Roanoke); 115 ("fertile"), ("goodly cedars"), ("sweet woods").

[21] David Beers Quinn, "Preparations for the 1585 Virginia Voyage," *The William and Mary Quarterly* 6, no. 2 (1949): 208–36; 230. Also Simonds d'Ewes, *The Journals of All the Parliaments during the Reign of Queen Elizabeth* (Shannon, Ire: Irish University Press, 1682), 339–341.

[22] Shirley, *Thomas Harriot*, 100–105.

[23] Ibid., 107–12; Alden T. Vaughan, "Sir Walter Ralegh's Indian Interpreters, 1584–1618," *The William and Mary Quarterly* 59, no. 2 (2002): 341–76; 347.

[24] Ruth A. McIntyre, "William Sanderson: Elizabethan Financier of Discovery," *The William and Mary Quarterly* 13, no. 2 (1956), 184–201; 189.

[25] For Walsingham's inheritance of Muscovy Company shares, his licenses, and his profits from Drake's voyage: Conyers Read, *Mr. Secretary Walsingham and the policy of Queen Elizabeth*, 3 vols. (Oxford: The Clarendon Press, 1925), 3:370–71, 381–82, 394–96.

[26] Peckham, "A True Report," in Quinn, *Voyages and Colonising Enterprises*, 2:466.

[27] Anthony Bagot, cited in A. L. Rowse, *Ralegh and the Throckmortons* (London: Macmillan & Co., 1962), 139n1.

[28] Rowse, A. L., *Sir Richard Grenville of the Revenge. An Elizabethan Hero* (London: Jonathan Cape, 1937), 26–47; 83–112.

[29] Richard Hakluyt, "Inducements to the Liking of the Voyage intended towards Virginia in 40 and 42. degrees of latitude, written 1585," in Taylor, *The Original Writings*, 2:327–38; 338.

[30] Quinn, *Set Fair for Roanoke*, 23, 183–84.

[31] "Ralegh on the naming of 'Wingandacon,'" in Quinn, *Roanoke Voyages*, 1:116–17; 117.

[32] "Ralph Lane to Sir Francis Walsingham, 12 August 1585," in Quinn, *Roanoke Voyages*, 1: 199–204; 201.

[33] Nicholas Hilliard, cited in Kim Sloan, "Knowing John White: The Courtier's 'Curious and Gentle Art of Limning,'" in Kim Sloan, ed., *A New World: England's First View of America* (London: British Museum Press, 2007), 23–37; 29.

[34] Kim Sloan, "John White's Watercolours of the North Carolina Algonquians," in Sloan, ed., *A New World*, 107.

[35] Christian F. Freest, "John White's New World," in Sloan, ed., *A New World*, 65–78; 68.

[36] For Harriot's commercial and ethnographical study: Harriot, "A Brief and True Report of the New Found Land of Virginia (1588)," in Quinn, *Roanoke Voyages*, 1:317–87.

[37] "Lane to Walsingham, 12 August 1585," in Quinn, *Roanoke Voyages*, 1:199 ("kingdom"); 200 ("Nature") and ("vast and huge"); 203 ("lose," "noble," "worthy," "conquest").

[38] "Ralph Lane to Sir Philip Sidney," August 12, 1585, in Quinn, *Roanoke Voyages*, 1:204–6; Ralph Lane, "An account of the particularities of the imployments of the English men left in Virginia by Sir Richard Greenevill under the charge of Master Ralfe Lane," in Quinn, *Roanoke Voyages*, 1:255–94; 273.

[39] "A summarie and true discourse of sir Francis Drakes West Indian voyage, begun in the yeere 1858. Wherein were taken the cities of Sant Iago, Santo Domingo, Cartagena, and the towne of Saint Augustine in Florida; Published by M. Thomas Cates," in Hakluyt, *Principal Navigations*, 10:97–134.

[40] Ibid., 131.

[41] Quinn, *Roanoke Voyages*, 1:469.

13. PRINCIPAL NAVIGATIONS

[1] "Bernardino de Mendoza to the King," June 9, 1586, in *CSP-Spain (Simancas), Volume 3, Elizabeth: 1580–1586*, #444, 583–84; 583.

[2] Kenneth R. Andrews, *Elizabethan Privateering: English Privateering during the Spanish War, 1585–1604* (Cambridge: Cambridge University Press, 1964), 4–5.

[3] "Bernardino de Mendoza to the King," November 8, 1586, in *CSP-Spain (Simancas), Volume 3, Elizabeth: 1580–1586*, #503, 648–50; 649.

[4] Mark Nicholls and Penry Williams, *Sir Walter Raleigh in Life and Legend* (London: Continuum International Publishing, 2011), 32.

[5] "Lord Deputy Perrot to the Privy Council," January 31, 1585/6, in *Calendar of State Papers relating to Ireland, of the Reign of Elizabeth, 1586–1588, July*, ed. Hans Claude Hamilton (London: Longman & Co., 1877), vol. 122, #59, 16–19; 16, 17.

[6] "Note of the profit and advancement that may grow to the younger houses of English gentlemen by planting in Munster," December 1585, in *CSP-Ireland, 1574–1585*, vol. 121, #61, 590.

[7] "Mr. George Carew to [Walsyngham]," February 27, 1585/6, in *CSP-Ireland, 1586–1588, July*, vol. 122, #86, 33.

[8] David B. Quinn, *Ralegh and the British Empire* (Harmondsworth: Pelican Books, 1973), 106–7.

[9] "20 February 1591. The Case of the Cape Merchant, Thomas Harvey," in Quinn, *The Roanoke Voyages*, 1:232–34.

[10] Harriot, "A Briefe and True Reporte," in Quinn, *Roanoke Voyages*, 1.322–23.

[11] Lane, "An account," in Quinn, *Roanoke Voyages*, 1:256–57, 273–75.

[12] "22 February 1587. Dedication by Richard Hakluyt to Raleigh," in Quinn, *Roanoke Voyages*, 2:514–15.

[13] "The fourth voyage made to Virginia with three ships, in the yere 1587. Wherein was transported the second Colonie," in Hakluyt, *Principal Navigations*, 8:386–402; 386.

[14] Ibid., 391.

[15] "John White's Narrative of His Voyuage" in Quinn, *Roanoke Voyages*, 2:533 ("great discredit"); 2:534 ("stuff and goods"); 2:535 ("extreme intreating").

[16] "A briefe relation of the notable service performed by Sir Francis Drake upon the Spanish Fleete prepared in the Road of Cadiz...in the yeere 1587," in Hakluyt, *Principal Navigations*, 6:438–43; 438.

[17] Ibid., 439.

[18] De Lamar Jensen, "The Spanish Armada: The Worst-Kept Secret in Europe," *The Sixteenth Century Journal* 19, no. 4 (1988): 621–41; 636.

[19] Quinn, *Roanoke Voyages*, 2:567.

[20] Susan Brigden, *New World, Lost Worlds. The Rule of the Tudors, 1485–1603* (London: Penguin Books, 2001), 291.

[21] "Gold and Ruby Salamander Pendant," in the Ulster Museum Collections, World Cultures; National Museums of Northern Ireland, 2014, https://nmni.com/um/Collections/World-Cultures/The-Armada-Collection.

[22] Roy Strong, *Gloriana: The Portraits of Queen Elizabeth I* (London: Thames & Hudson, 1987), 131–33.

[23] Neil MacGregor, *Shakespeare's Restless World* (London: Allen Lane, 2013), 16.

[24] Hakluyt, "The Epistle Dedicatorie in the First Edition, 1589: To the Right Honorable Sir Francis Walsingham," in Hakluyt, *Principal Navigations*, 1:xviii–xix.

[25] "Richard Hakluyt to the favourable Reader," in Hakluyt, *Principal Navigations*, 1:xxiii–xxiv.

[26] Quinn, *Hakluyt Handbook*, 1:289 (Spanish soldier: July 1586); 290 (Ralegh: December 1586; Grenville: 1596–9); 294–5 (Spanish and Portuguese documents, c. 1587 and after); 302 (Frobisher: c. 1589; Jenkinson, c. 1589; Butts: c. 1589).

[27] Ibid., 265–331; 313.

[28] Hakluyt, "The Epistle Dedicatorie," in Hakluyt, *Principal Navigations*, 1:xix.

[29] Quinn, *Hakluyt Handbook*, 1:101–3.

[30] Hakluyt, "The Epistle Dedicatorie," in Hakluyt, *Principal Navigations*, 1:xxii.

[31] Quinn, *Hakluyt Handbook*, 1:226–27.

[32] E.K. Chambers, *William Shakespeare: A Study of Facts and Problems*, vol. 1 (Oxford: The Clarendon Press, 1930), 270.

[33] Hakluyt, "The Epistle Dedicatorie," in Hakluyt, *Principal Navigations*, 1:xx.

[34] "7 March 1589. Agreement between Sir Walter Raleigh, Thomas Smythe etc., and John White etc, for the continuance of the City of Raleigh venture," in Quinn, *Roanoke Voyages*, 2:569–76.

[35] Quinn, *Set Fair for Roanoke*, 311–12.

[36] "To the Worshipful and my very friend Master Richard Hakluyt," in Hakluyt, *Principal Navigations*, 8:404–6; 405.

[37] "The fifth voyage of M. John White into the West Indies and parts of America called Virginia, in the yeere 1590," in Hakluyt, *Principal Navigations*, 8:406–22; 414.

[38] Ibid., 416 ("curiously carved," "fair Roman letters," "secret token," "signify the place"); 418 ("the place where Manteo"); 417 ("a Cross," "taken down"); 418 ("torn from the covers," "almost eaten through," "goods").

[39] On White living on Ralegh's Ireland estate, see Nicholas Canny, "Raleigh's Ireland," in H. G. Jones, ed., *Raleigh and Quinn: The Explorer and His Boswell* (Chapel Hill: North Caroliniana Society, 1987), 87–101; 95.

[40] [White], "To the Worshipful," in Hakluyt, *Principal Navigations*, 8:404–6.

14. THE OLD EAST AND THE NEW WEST

[1] Stowe, *Annales, or a General Chronicle of England* (London, 1631), 766, 769, 770. Also, Guy, *Elizabeth*, 193, 195, 199.

[2] George Bruner Parks, *Richard Hakluyt and the English Voyages* (New York: The American Geographical Society of New York, 1928), 124–45; 174n4. Also Quinn, *Hakluyt Handbook*, xxv; 101–3.

[3] Pauline Croft, "The Reputation of Robert Cecil: Libels, Political Opinion and Popular Awareness in the Early Seventeenth Century," *Transactions of the Royal Historical Society* 1 (1991): 43–69; 46.

[4] Pauline Croft, "Can a Bureaucrat Be a Favourite?," in J. Elliott and L. Brockliss, eds., *The World of the Favourite*, (New Haven, CT: Yale University Press, 1999), 81–95; 94n9.

[5] Richard Hakluyt, "The Epistle Dedicatorie in the Second Volume of the Second Edition, 1599: To the Right Honorable Sir Robert Cecil Knight, principall Secretarie to her Majestie, master of the Court of Wardes and Liveries, and one of her Majesties most honourable privie Counsell," in Hakluyt, *Principal Navigations, Voyages*, 1:lxxiii.

[6] Ibid., 1:lxxii.

[7] "Certain Reesons why the English Merchants may trade into the East Indies, especially to such rich kingdoms and dominions as are not subject to the kinge of Spayne & Portugal: together with the true limits of the Portugals conquest & Jurisdiction in those oriental parts," in Taylor, *The Original Writings*, 2:465–68.

[8] Adams, Simon. "Elizabeth I and the Sovereignty of the Netherlands 1576–1585," *Transactions of the Royal Historical Society*, vol. 4 (2004): 309–19.

[9] Claudia Schurmann, "'Wherever profit leads us, to every sea and shore...': The VOC, the WIC, and Dutch Methods of Globalization in the Seventeenth Century," *Renaissance Studies* 17, no. 3 (2003): 474–93; 477.

[10] William Foster, *England's Quest of Eastern Trade* (London: A&C Black, 1933), 142–44.

[11] Henry Stevens and George Birdwood, eds., *The Dawn of British Trade to the East Indies As Recorded in the Court Minutes of the East India Company, 1599–1603* (London: Henry Stevens & Son, 1886), 1–7.

[12] Kenneth R. Andrews, *Elizabethan Privateering: English Privateering During the Spanish War, 1585–1603* (1964; repr., Cambridge: Cambridge University Press, 2011), 218, 128.

[13] Stevens and Birdwood, eds., *The Dawn of British Trade*, 5.

[14] Ibid., 8.

[15] Ibid., 10–11.

[16] Alfred P. Beaven, "Chronological List of Aldermen: 1501–1600," in *The Aldermen of the City of London Temp. Henry III–1912* (London: Corporation of the City of London, 1908), 20–47.

[17] Willan, *Early History of the Russia Company*, 286; Alfred C. Wood, *A History of the Levant Company* (London: Routledge, 2013), appendix 4.

[18] "Colemanstreete warde," in Stow, *A Survey of London*, 1:276–285; 283. Foster, *England's Quest for Eastern Trade*, 148; Stevens and Birdwood, eds., *The Dawn of British Trade*, 62. For Smythe: Basil Morgan, "Sir Thomas Smythe (c.1558–1625), merchant," in *Oxford Dictionary of National Biography*.

[19] "A Priviledge for fifteene yeeres granted by her Majestie to certaine Adventurers, for the discoverie of the Trade for the East-Indies, the one and thirtieth of December, 1600," in Samuel Purchas, *Hakluytus Posthumus*, 2:366–91; 368.

[20] Stevens and Birdwood, eds., *The Dawn of British Trade*, 123–24; Richard Hakluyt, "The chief places where sundry sorte of spices do growe in the East Indies, gathered out of sundry the best and latest authours," in Taylor, *The Original Writing*, 2:476–82.

[21] "The first Voyage made to East-India by Master James Lancaster, now Knight, for the merchants of London, Anno 1600. With foure tall Shippes, (to wit) the Dragon, the Hector, the Ascension and Susan, and a Victualler called the Guest," in Purchas, *Hakluytus Posthumus*, 2:392–437; 393.

[22] K. R. Andrews, "Christopher Newport of Limehouse, Mariner," *The William and Mary Quarterly* 11, no. 1 (1954), 28–41; 32.

[23] Cited in Quinn, *England and the Discovery of America*, 444.

[24] Hakluyt, "The Episte Dedicatorie to Sir Robert Cecil," in Hakluyt, *Principal Navigations*, 1:lxvii.

[25] Ibid., 1:lxvi–lxvii.

[26] "A briefe Note of the sending another barke this present yeere 1602. by the honorable knight, Sir Walter Ralegh for the searching out of his Colonie in Virginia," in David Beers Quinn and Alison M. Quinn, eds., *The English New England Voyages, 1602–1608*, (London: The Hakluyt Society, 1983), 166–67.

[27] For Gosnold's privateering: David S. Ransome, "Bartholomew Gosnold (d. 1607), sea captain and explorer," in the *Oxford Dictionary of National Biography*. Also, Warner F. Gookin, *Bartholomew Gosnold. Discoverer and Planter. New England, 1602. Virginia, 1607*, completed by Philip L. Barbour (Hamden, CT: Archon Books, 1963).

[28] William Strachey, *The Historie of Travell into Virginia Britania (1612), by William Strachey, gent*, ed. Louis B. Wright and Virginia Freund (London: Hakluyt Society, 1951), 150.

[29] "The Relation of John de Verrazzano a Florentine 1524," in Hakluyt, *Principal Navigations*, 8:423–38. The word "refugio" appears in a handwritten footnote. See "The Written Record of the Voyage of 1524 of Giovanni da Verrazzano" as recorded in a letter to Francis I, King of France, July 8th, 1524. Adapted from a translation by Susan Tarrow of the Cellere Codex, in Lawrence C. Wroth, ed., *The Voyages of Giovanni da Verrazzano, 1524–1528* (Yale, 1970), 133–43.

[30] "7 September 1602. Bartholomew Gosnold to Anthony Gosnold," in Quinn and Quinn, eds., *The English New England Voyages*, 208–11.

[31] There are two accounts of the voyage: Gabriel Archer, "The Relation of Captaine Gosnolds Voyage to the North Part of Virginia... delivered by Gabriel Archer, a Gentleman of the said voyage," in Quinn and Quinn, eds., *The English New England Voyages*, 114–38; and John Brereton, "A Briefe and Trve Relation of the Discoverie of the North Part of Virginia... made this present yeere 1602, By Captaine Bartholomew Gosnold...," in Quinn and Quinn, eds., *The English New England Voyages*, 143–59.

[32] Quinn and Quinn, eds., *The English New England Voyages*, 146 ("basks"); 158 ("how now Sirrah" and "scholar"). Archer in ibid., 117 ("Christian words").

[33] See Bruce J. Bourque and Ruth Holmes Whitehead, "Tarrentines and the Introduction of European Trade Goods in the Gulf of Maine," *Ethnohistory* 32, no. 4 (1985): 327–41.

[34] Brereton, "A Briefe and Trve Relation," in Quinn and Quinn, eds., *The English New England Voyages*, 147.

[35] Ibid., 150.

[36] Ibid., 150–51, 156.

[37] Archer, "Captaine Gosnolds Voyage," in Quinn and Quinn, eds., *The English New England Voyages*, 134.

[38] Ibid., 135–38.

[39] "21 August 1602. Sir Walter Ralegh to Sir Robert Cecil" in Quinn and Quinn, eds., *The English New England Voyages*, 205–8.

[40] Ibid., 206.

[41] J. Worth Estes, "The European Reception of the First Drugs from the New World," *Pharmacy in History* 37, no. 1 (1995): 3–23; 8.

[42] Harriot, "A Brief and True Report of the New Found Land of Virginia (1588)," in Quinn, *Roanoke Voyages*, 1:329.

[43] Estes, "The European Reception," 8.

[44] David B. Quinn, "Thomas Hariot [*sic*] and the Virginia Voyages of 1602," *The William and Mary Quarterly* 27, no. 2 (1970): 268–21; 278.

[45] Brereton, "A Briefe and Trve Relation," in Quinn and Quinn, eds., *The English New England Voyages,* 159.

[46] Raleigh Trevelyan, *Sir Walter Raleigh: Being a True and Vivid Account of the Life and Times of the Explorer, Soldier, Scholar, Poet, and Courtier—The Controversial Hero of the Elizabethan Age* (New York: Henry Holt, 2004), 357–65.

[47] "The Letters Patent, Granted by the Queenes Majestie to M. Walter Raleigh...," in Hakluyt, *Principal Navigations*, 8:289–96.

15. TWO VIRGINIAS

[1] "A Treaty of Perpetual Peace and Alliance between Philip the III. King of Spain, and the Archduke and Archduchess Albert and Isabella on the one side, and James the I. King of England on the other side. Made in the Year 1604," in *A General Collection of Treatys, Manifesto's, Contracts of Marriage, Renunciations, and other Publick Papers, from the Year 1495, to the Year 1712*, vol. 2 (London: J. J. and P. Knapton, J. Darby et al., 1732), 131–46; 131.

[2] Denmark House was formerly known as Somerset House. The house was demolished in 1775 and in 1779 work began on a new building, known once again as Somerset House, which was constructed in stages and completed in 1801, https://www.somersethouse.org.uk/history. A "queen consort" has no constitutional power. For a detailed discussion of the conference setting, including the carpet and other furnishings, as well as a description of the *Somerset House Conference* painting, see the collections page at the Royal Museums Greenwich, http://collections.rmg .co.uk/collections/objects/14260.html.

[3] A discussion of the attendees accompanies a reproduction of the portrait of the signing ceremony, showing eleven delegates before a large paned window. For the full list of participants, see: "A Treaty of Perpetual Peace and Alliance," in *A General Collection of Treatys*, 132–34.

[4] Parker, *Imprudent King: A New Life of Philip II* (New Haven, CT: Yale University Press, 2014; paperback ed., 2015), 63.

[5] "A Treaty of Perpetual Peace," 131; 134.

[6] Ibid., 141.

[7] Don Juan Fernández de Velasco, Spain's representative at the Treaty of London negotations, as reported in a letter by Pedro de Zúñiga to Philip III, 16 October 1607, in Barbour, ed., *Jamestown Voyages*, 1:121.

[8] Trevelyan, *Sir Walter Raleigh*, 398–405.

[9] David Beers Quinn and Alison M. Quinn, eds., *The English New England Voyages, 1602–1608* (London: The Hakluyt Society, 1983), 58.

[10] George Waymouth, "Jewell of Artes," excerpted in Quinn and Quinn, eds., *The English New England Voyages*, 232–41; 232.

[11] "The jewell of artes," Yale University Library, Beinecke Rare Book & Manuscript Library, 2012, http://brbl-dl.library.yale.edu/vufind/Record/3446439. The authors also inspected the bound manuscript at the British Library.

[12] Henry Stevens and George Birdwood, eds., *The Dawn of British Trade to the East Indies As Recorded in the Court Minutes of the East India Company, 1599–1603* (London: Henry Stevens & Son, 1886), 183.

[13] Ibid., 184.

[14] Ibid., 233.

[15] Quinn and Quinn, eds., *The English New England Voyages*, 233–34. Images are reproduced on 236–41.

[16] Ibid., 56–57.

[17] Ibid., 254, fn4. Quinn speculates that Gilbert may have been involved because Waymouth spent time organizing his expedition in Dartmouth, which is not far from Gilbert's residence in Greenway.

[18] The official account of the voyage was written by James Rosier, "A True Relation of the most prosperous voyage made this present yeere 1605, by Captaine George Waymouth, in the Discovery of the Land of Virginia," in Quinn and Quinn, eds., *The English New England Voyages*, 251–311.

[19] David R. Ransome, "James Rosier (1573–1609), explorer," in *Oxford Dictionary of National Biography*.

[20] Rosier, "A True Relation," in Quinn and Quinn, eds., *The English New England Voyages*, 269.

[21] Nick Bunker, *Making Haste from Babylon: The Mayflower Pilgrims and Their World: A New History* (New York: Alfred A. Knopf, 2010), 9.

[22] Rosier, "A True Relation," in Quinn and Quinn, eds., *The English New England Voyages*, 303.

[23] Fernand Braudel, *The Perspective of the World* (Berkeley: University of California Press, 1992), 189.

[24] Rosier, "A True Relation," in Quinn and Quinn, eds., *The English New England Voyages*, 284.

[25] Ibid., 302.

[26] W. L. Grant, ed., *Voyages of Samuel de Champlain 1604–1618* (New York: Charles Scribner's Sons, 1907), 77.

[27] Rosier, "A True Relation," in Quinn and Quinn, eds., *The English New England Voyages*, 251n5. The exact publication date is not included on the title page of the relation, although Rosier specifies the work was "made" in "this present yeere 1605" which, given the uncertainty of dating, could be as late as March, 1606.

[28] Rosier, "A True Relation," in Quinn and Quinn, eds., *The English New England Voyages*, 292.

[29] Richard Arthur Preston, *Gorges of Plymouth Fort: A Life of Sir Ferdinando Gorges, Captain of Plymouth Fort, Governor of New England, and Lord of the Province of Maine* (Toronto: University of Toronto Press, in cooperation with the Royal Military College of Canada, 1953), 29 (Ann); 126 (children). Also see James Phinney Baxter, ed. *Sir Ferdinando Gorges and His Province of Maine*, 3 vols. (Boston: The Prince Society XVIII, 1890. Reprinted by Burt Franklin: Research and Source Works Series #131, 1967), 2:167.

[30] Preston, *Gorges of Plymouth Fort*, 18.

[31] Ibid., 36.

[32] *The Description of Mawooshen* was obtained by Hakluyt and published by Samuel Purchas in 1625. See *Hakluytus Posthumus*, 19:400–405. Quinn discusses the provenance of the name and the scope of the area it describes. He suggests it lies between Mount Desert Island and the Saco River, in *The New England Voyages*, 470n1–4.

[33] Sir Ferdinando Gorges, "A Briefe Narration of the Originall Undertakings of the Advancement of Plantations into the parts of America," in Baxter, ed., *Sir Ferdinando Gorges and His Province of Maine*, 2:1–81; 8 ("giving life").

[34] Aubrey, *Brief Lives*, ed. Clark, 2:159; P. W. Hasler, "John Popham (c.1532–1607), of Wellington, Som.," in *The History of Parliament: The House of Commons 1558–1603*.

[35] "[Circa January, 1606], Sir Walter Cope to the Earl of Salisbury," in Quinn, ed., *New American World*, 5:166–67.

[36] Clare Williams, trans., *Thomas Platter's Travels in England 1599* (London: Jonathan Cape, 1937), 171–73.

[37] "[Circa January, 1606], Sir Walter Cope to the Earl of Salisbury," in Quinn, ed., *New American World*, 5:166–67.

[38] George Chapman, Ben Jonson, and John Marston, *Eastward Hoe*, extracted in Alexander Brown, ed., *The Genesis of the United States: A Narrative of the Movement in England, 1605–1616, Which Resulted in the Plantation of North America by Englishmen, Disclosing the Contest Between England and Spain for Possession of the Soil Now Occupied by the United States of America; Set Forth Through a Series of Historical Manuscripts now first printed: Together with a Reissue of Rare Contemporary Tracts, Accompanied by Bibliographical Memoranda, Notes, and Brief Biographies*, 2 vols. (Boston: Houghton, Mifflin and Company, 1890), 1:29–32.

[39] "Letters Patent for Sir Thomas Gates, Sir George Somers and others... April 10, 1606," Brown, ed., *The Genesis of the United States*, 1:52–63; 52–53.

[40] "Charter of 1605," in Pauline Croft, ed., *The Spanish Company* (London: London Record Society, 1973), 95–113.

[41] Pauline Croft, "Introduction: The Revival of the Company, 1604–6," in Croft, ed., *The Spanish Company*, xxix–li.

[42] "Articles, Instructions and Orders," in Brown, ed., *The Genesis of the United States*, 1:65–75.

[43] Baxter, ed., *Sir Ferdinando Gorges and His Province of Maine*, 3:122–23.

[44] John Smith, "The Generall Historie of Virginia, New-England, and the Summer Isles," in Philip L. Barbour, ed., *The Complete Works of Captain John Smith (1580–1631) in Three Volumes* (Chapel Hill and London: University of North Carolina Press, 1986), 2:433–75; 428.

16. A PUBLIC PLANTATION

[1] Sir Ferdinando Gorges, "A Briefe Narration of the Originall Undertakings of the Advancement of Plantations into the parts of America," in Baxter, ed., *Sir Ferdinando Gorges and His Province of Maine*, 2:9.

[2] Ibid., 10.

[3] "4 February 1607. The Relation of Daniel Tucker," in David Beers Quinn and Alison M. Quinn, eds., *The English New England Voyages, 1602–1608* (London: The Hakluyt Society, 1983), 360-63. And "[December 1607]. Narrative of John Stoneman, pilot of the *Richard*, after his return to England," in Beers and Quinn, eds., *The English New England Voyages, 1602–1608*, 364–75.

[4] "[December 1607]. Narrative of John Stoneman, pilot of the *Richard*, after his return to England," in Quinn and Quinn, eds., *The English New England Voyages*, 364–75; 368.

[5] "16 February 1606. Deposition of Nicholas Hind, master of the *Richard* in the High Court of Admiralty," in Quinn and Quinn, eds., *The English New England Voyages*, 356–60; 358.

[6] "Narrative of John Stoneman," in Quinn and Quinn, eds., *The English New England Voyages*, 370–71.

[7] "Gorges to Cecil, Feb 4 1606[7]: Report of seizure of ship by Spaniards," in Baxter, ed., *Sir Ferdinando Gorges and His Province of Maine*, 3:126–28.

[8] "Concerning the ship taken at sea going to Virginia," in Baxter, ed., *Sir Ferdinando Gorges and His Province of Maine*, 3:132–33.

[9] "Nevill Davis to Sir John Popham, Lord Chief Justice," January 25/February 4 1606–7, in *Calendar of the Cecil Papers in Hatfield House: Volume 19, 1607*, ed. M.S. Giuseppi and D. McN. Lockie (London: Her Majesty's Stationery Office, 1965), 11–33.

[10] This voyage is not well documented. The name of the ship and the number of crew are unknown. The master was Martin Pring, an experienced navigator.

[11] Sir Ferdinando Gorges, "A briefe Relation of the discovery and plantation of New England," in Baxter, ed., *Sir Ferdinando Gorges and His Province of Maine*, 1:204–5.

[12] "Gorges to Cecil. Feb. 7, 1607," in Baxter, ed., *Sir Ferdinando Gorges and His Province of Maine*, 3:161–64.

[13] "Gorges to the Earl of Salisbury. December 3, 1607," in Baxter, ed., *Sir Ferdinando Gorges and His Province of Maine*, 3:158–60.

[14] Ibid., 158.

[15] "Memoir of Sir Ferdinando Gorges" in Baxter, ed., *Sir Ferdinando Gorges and His Province of Maine*, 1:78. Definition of a "searcher" is in Smith, "The Generall Historie of Virginia," in Barbour, ed., *The Complete Works of Captain John Smith*, 2:398, fn. 4.

[16] The two extant accounts of the voyage are: " 'The Relation of a Voyage unto New-England.' The Journal of Robert Davis (or Davies) of the voyage to North Virginia in 1607 and of the founding of Fort St. George on the Kennebec River, 1 June–26 September 1607," in Quinn and Quinn, eds., *The English New England Voyages*, 416–41; and William Strachey, "The Narrative of the North Virginia Voyage and Colony, 1607–1608," in Quinn and Quinn, eds., *The English New England Voyages*, 397–415.

[17] Baxter, ed., *Sir Ferdinando Gorges and His Province of Maine*, 1:77–8.

[18] Strachey, "The Narrative of the North Virginia voyage and colony," in Quinn and Quinn, eds., *The English New England Voyages*, 414.

[19] "Gorges to Cecil. December 1, 1607," in Baxter, ed., *Sir Ferdinando Gorges and His Province of Maine*, 3:154–7.

[20] "Gorges to Cecil. December 3, 1607," in Ibid., 3:158–60; 160.

[21] "Gorges to Cecil. February 7, 1608," in Ibid., 3:161–64; 161.

[22] The court proceedings are summarized in Quinn and Quinn, eds., *The English New England Voyages*, 334; documents relating to the proceedings can be found on 459–65.

[23] "13 December 1607. Captain George Popham to King James I, from Fort St. George," in Quinn and Quinn, eds., *The English New England Voyages*, 452–54.

[24] "7 February 1608. Sir Ferdinando Gorges to the Earl of Salisbury, reporting the return of the *Gift of God*," in Quinn and Quinn, eds., *The English New England Voyages*, 455–58.

[25] Gorges, "A briefe relation," in Baxter, ed., *Sir Ferdinando Gorges and His Province of Maine*, 1:206–7.

[26] Ibid., 207.

17. FIRST COLONY

[1] Andrews, *Elizabethan Privateering*, 85; Andrews, "Christopher Newport," *The William and Mary Quarterly* 11, no. 1 (1954): 32–33.

[2] Ransome, "Bartholomew Gosnold," in *Oxford Dictionary of National Biography*. Martha's Vineyard was probably named after Gosnold's mother-in-law, a daughter of Sir Andrew Judde, co-founder of the Mysterie.

[3] "24 November 1606, 'Dispensation for Richard Hakluyt,'" in Philip L. Barbour, ed., *The Jamestown Voyages Under the First Charter, 1606–1609*, 2 vols. (Cambridge: Cambridge University Press, for The Hakluyt Society, 1969), 1:62–64.

[4] "Instructions given by way of advice by us whom it hath pleased the King's Majesty to appoint of the Council for the intended voyage to Virginia, to be observed by those Captains and company which are sent at this present to plant there," in Taylor, ed., *The Original Writings*, 2:492–96; 492n1.

[5] Originally, the London Company envisaged 120 settlers and 40 mariners: Brown, ed., *The Genesis of the United States*, 1:82n1. For accounts of the first voyage and the beginnings of the plantation, see George Percy, "Observations gathered out of a Discourse of the Plantation of the Sourtherne Colonie in Virginia by the English, 1606," in Brown, ed., *The Genesis of the United States*, 1:152–68; John Smith, "A true relation of such occurrences and accidents of note as hath happened in Virginia since the first planting of that Colony ...," in Philip L. Barbour, ed. *The Complete Works of Captain John Smith (1580–1631)* 3 vols. (Chapel Hill: University of North Carolina Press, 1986), 1:27–97.

[6] "Certain orders and Directions conceived and set down the tenth day of December ... by His Majesties' Counsel for Virginia," December 10, 1606, in Brown, ed., *The Genesis of the United States*, 1:75–79.

[7] R.C. Simmons, "Edward Maria Wingfield (b. 1550, d. in or after 1619), soldier and colonist in America," *Oxford Dictionary of National Biography*.

[8] "Instructions," Taylor, ed., *The Original Writings*, 2:492 ("strongest"), 493 ("hundred miles"); Smith, "A True Relation," in Barbour, ed., *The Complete Works of Captain John Smith*, 1:29.

[9] "Instructions," in Taylor, ed., *The Original Writings*, 2:493–94.

[10] Gabriel Archer (attributed), "A relatyon of the Discovery of our River, from James Forte into the Maine: made by Captain Christofer Newport: and sincerely written and observed by a gent. of ye Colony," in Barbour, ed., *Jamestown Voyages*, 1:80–98; 95.

[11] "Instructions given by way of advice," in Taylor, ed., *The Original Writings*, 2:496.

[12] "22 June 1607. Letter from the Council in Virginia," in Barbour, ed., *Jamestown Voyages*, 1:78–80.

[13] "12 August 1607: Sir Walter Cope to Lord Salisbury," in Barbour, ed., *Jamestown Voyages*, 1:108–10; "13 August 1607: Sir Walter Cope to Lord Salisbury," in Barbour, ed., *Jamestown Voyages*, 1:111.

[14] "12/22 September 1607: Pedro de Zúñiga to Philip III," in Barbour, ed., *Jamestown Voyages*, 1:114–16.

[15] "12 August 1607: Cope to Salisbury," in Barbour, ed., *Jamestown Voyages*, 1:109; "17 August 1607. Sir Thomas Smythe to Lord Salisbury," in Barbour, ed., *Jamestown Voyages*, 1:112.

[16] Smith, "A True Relation," in Barbour, ed., *The Complete Works of Captain John Smith*, 1:33.

[17] Percy, "Observations," in Brown, ed., *The Genesis of the United States,* 1:167.

[18] Smith, "A True Relation," in Barbour, ed., *The Complete Works of Captain John Smith*, 1:33; Smith, "The Proceedings of the English Colony in Virginia since their first beginning from England in the yeare of our Lord 1606, till this present 1612," in Barbour, ed., *The Complete Works of Captain John Smith*, 1:210.

[19] For Kendall's background: Philip L. Barbour, "Captain George Kendall: Mutineer or Intelligencer?," *The Virginia Magazine of History and Biography* 70, no. 3 (1962): 297–313.

[20] Helen C. Rountree, *The Powhatan Indians of Virginia. Their Traditional Culture* (Norman: University of Oklahoma Press, 1989), 9–15.

[21] Smith, "A True Relation," in Barbour, ed., *The Complete Works of Captain John Smith*, 1:47 (20 or 30 arrows), 49 (bread and venison).

[22] John Smith, "The General Historie," Barbour, ed., *The Complete Works of Captain John Smith*, 2:151.

[23] Karen Ordahl Kupperman, *The Jamestown Project* (Cambridge, MA: The Belknap Press of Harvard University Press, 2007), 230–32.

[24] Smith, "A True Relation," in Barbour, ed., *The Complete Works of Captain John Smith*, 1:35.

[25] Smith, "The Proceedings of the English Colonie in Virginia," in Barbour, ed., *The Complete Works of Captain John Smith*, 1:259.

[26] Smith, "A True Relation," in Barbour, ed., *The Complete Works of Captain John Smith*, 1:53 (raccoon skins), 97 (profitable for commerce).

[27] James Horn, *A Land As God Made It: Jamestown and the Birth of America* (New York: Basic Books, 2005; paperback ed., 2006), 100–101.

[28] "The Copy of a Letter sent to the Treasurer and Councell of Virginia from Captaine Smith, then President of Virginia," in "The General Historie of Virginia, New England, and the Summer Isles," in Barbour, *The Complete Work of Captain John Smith*, 2:53–474; 187–90.

[29] Brown, ed., *The Genesis of the United States*, 1:206.

[30] John Rolfe, *A True Relation of the State of Virginia left by Sir Thomas Dale Knight in May last 1616. Set forth with an Introduction and Notes by a group of Virginian Librarians* (New Haven, CT: Yale University Press, 1951), 34.

[31] "A True and Sincere Declaration of the Purpose and Ends of the Plantation begun in Virginia," December 14, 1609, in Brown, ed., *The Genesis of the United States*, 1:337–53; 342, 345.

[32] See Barbour, ed., *Complete Works of Captain John Smith*, 1:119–90.

[33] Brown, ed., *The Genesis of the United States*, 1:207. For the Second Charter: 208–37.

[34] "A True and Sincere Declaration," in Brown, ed., *Genesis*, 1:349.

[35] "A Letter from His Majesty's Council of Virginia to the Corporation of Plymouth," February 17, 1609, in Brown, ed., *The Genesis of the United States*, 1:238–40.

[36] Robert Johnson, *Nova Britannia: offering most excellent fruites by planting in Virginia. Exciting all such as are well affected to further the same*, in David B. Quinn, ed., *New American: A Documentary History of North America to 1612*, 6 vols. (New York: Arno Press and Hector Bye, Inc., 1979), 5:234–48; 247.

[37] Ibid., 236; 239.

[38] Brown, ed., *The Genesis of the United States*, 1:255–56.

[39] Ibid., 1:282–91.

[40] "Zúñiga to Philip III, April 12, 1609," in Brown, ed., *The Genesis of the United States*, 1:258–59.

[41] Ian W. Archer, "Sir Thomas Smythe (c. 1558–1625). A lecture delivered at Skinners' Hall, London, November 26, 2007." Available from the Oxford University Research Archive, https://ora.ox.ac.uk/objects/uuid:4a1c5a8a-78f1-4dfa-9c79-6f94a6161659.

[42] "A Letter from the Councill and Company of the honourable Plantation in Virginia to the Lord Mayor, Alderman and Companies of London," [Before March 20, 1609], in Brown, ed., *The Genesis of the United States*, 1:252–53.

[43] "The precept of the Lord Mayor of London to the London Companies," in Brown, ed., *The Genesis of the United States*, 1:254.

[44] "An assembly of the persons hereunder named holden the xxiiiith of September 1599," in Stevens and Birdwood, eds., *The Dawn of British Trade*, 7.

[45] Johnson, *Nova Britannia*, in Quinn, ed., *New American World*, 5:246.

[46] Brown, ed., *The Genesis of the United States,* 1:209–28.

[47] "Pedro de Zúñiga to Philip III, March 5, 1609," in Brown, ed., *The Genesis of the United States,* 1:243–47; 245–56.

[48] Brown, ed., *The Genesis of the United States,* 1:206–7.

[49] Francis Bacon, "On Plantations," in his *The Essays,* ed. with an introduction by John Pitcher (London: Penguin Books, 1987), 162. For his role in drafting the second charter: Brown, ed., *The Genesis of the United States,* 1:207.

18. A STAKE IN THE GROUND

[1] "Pedro de Zúñiga to Philip III, March 5, 1609," in Brown, ed., *The Genesis of the United States* 1:243–47; 244; "Virginia Council. 'Instructions, Orders and Constitucions…To Sir Thomas Gates Knight Governor of Virginia.' May 1609," in Samuel M. Bemiss, *The Three Charters of the Virginia Company of London, with Seven Related Documents: 1606–1621* (1957; reprint, Baltimore: Clearfield Company, 2007), 55–69; 60.

[2] Horn, *A Land As God Made It,* 305n1.

[3] "A Letter of M. Gabriel Archer, touching the voyage of the fleet of ships, which arrived at Virginia, without Sir Tho. Gates and Sir George Summers, 1609 [Aug. 31, 1609]," in Brown, ed., *The Genesis of the United States,* 1:328–32; 331.

[4] George Percy, "Trewe Relacyon," in Mark Nicholls, "George Percy's 'Trewe Relacyon': A Primary Source for the Jamestown Settlement," *The Virginia Magazine of History and Biography* 113, no. 3 (2005): 212–75; 246.

[5] Smith, "The Generall Historie of Virginia," in Barbour, ed., *The Complete Works of Captain John Smith,* 2:223.

[6] "A True and Sincere Declaration of the Purpose and Ends of the Plantation begun in Virginia," December 14, 1609, in Brown, ed., *The Genesis of the United States,* 1:338–52; 347.

[7] Susan Myra Kingsbury, ed., *The Records of the Virginia Company of London,* 4 vols. (Washington, DC: Library of Congress, 1933), 3: 89; J. Frederick Fausz, "Thomas West, third Baron De La Warr (1577–1618), colonial governor," in *Oxford Dictionary of National Biography.*

[8] "Virginia Council. 'Instructions, Orders and Constitucions…To…Sir Thomas West, Knight, Lord La Warr.' 1609/10?," in Bemiss, *The Three Charters,* 70–75.

[9] "Instructions for such things as are to be sente from Virginia. 1610," in Brown, ed., *The Genesis of the United States,* 1:384–86.

[10] "Virginia Council. 'Instructions, Orders and Constitucions'" (Thomas West), in Bemiss, *The Three Charters,* 72.

[11] "22 June 1607. Letter from the Council in Virginia," in Barbour, ed. *The Jamestown Voyages,* 1:79.

[12] "Virginia Council. 'Instructions, Orders and Constitucions'" (Thomas West), in Bemiss, *The Three Charters,* 73.

[13] Percy, "Trewe Relacyon," in Mark Nicholls, "George Percy's 'Trewe Relacyon,'" 248.

[14] Ibid., 249.

[15] William Strachey, "A true reportory of the wracke and redemption of Sir Thomas Gates Knight; upon, and from, the Ilands of the Bermudas: his coming to Virginia, and the estate of that Colonie then, and after, under the government of Lord La Warre, July 15. 1610," in Purchas, *Hakluytus Posthumus,* 19:5–72; 5 ("tempest"); 6 ("darkness"); 8 ("all that I had," and "candles").

[16] Ibid., 13. Also Horn, *A Land As God Made It,* 159.

[17] Wesley Frank Craven, "An Introduction to the History of Bermuda," Part I, *The William and Mary Quarterly* 17, no. 2 (1937): 176–215; 182.

[18] Strachey, "A true reportory," in Purchas, *Hakluytus Posthumus,* 19:23.

[19] Ibid., 25–32.

[20] Louis B. Wright, *A Voyage to Virginia in 1609. Two Narratives. Strachey's "True Reportory" and Jourdain's "Discovery of the Bermudas,"* rev. ed. (Charlottesville: University of Virginia Press, 2013), xviii–xix.

[21] "A circular Letter of his Majestie's Counsil for Virginia," in Brown, ed., *The Genesis of the United States,* 1:463–65.

[22] "Resolution of the States General, granting leave of absence to Captain Dale. Thursday 20th January 1611," in Brown, ed., *The Genesis of the United States,* 1:446.

[23] J. Frederick Fausz, "Thomas West, third Baron De La Warr (1577–1618), colonial governor," in *Oxford Dictionary of National Biography.*

[24] Basil Morgan, "Sir Thomas Dale (d. 1619), soldier and administrator," *Oxford Dictionary of National Biography.*

[25] William Strachey, *For the Colony in Virginia Britannia: Lawes Divine, Morall and Martiall &c* (London: W. Burre, 1612), in *Tracts And Other Papers relating principally to the Origin, Settlement and Progress of the Colonies in North America from the Discovery of the Country to 1776. Collected by Peter Force. Volume III* (Washington, DC: WM. Q. Force, 1844), No. 2; Horn, *A Land As God Made It,* 182, 196.

[26] "Sir Thomas Dale to the Earl of Salisbury, August 17th, 1611," in Brown, ed., *The Genesis of the United States,* 1:501–8; 503, 505.

[27] "Virginia Council. 'Instructions, Orders and Constitucions'" (Thomas Gates), in Bemiss, *The Three Charters,* 59–60. Dale was fulfilling the Council's original instructions to Gates.

[28] Ralph Hamor, *A True Discourse of the Present Estate of Virginia. Reprinted from the London edition, 1615, with an introduction by A. L. Rowse* (Richmond: The Virginia State Library, 1957), 30.

[29] "Pedro de Zúñiga to Philip III, 5 March 1609," in Brown, ed., *The Genesis of the United States,* 1:246.

[30] For the advertisement for the first national lottery, see see "The Great Lottery, 1567," http://www.bl.uk/learning/timeline/item102765.html.

[31] Robert C. Johnson, "The Lotteries of the Virginia Company, 1612–1621," *The Virginia Magazine of History and Biography* 74, no. 3 (1966): 259–92; 261; *Three Proclamations concerning the lottery for Virginia 1613–1621* (Boston: Merrymount Press, 1907), 1–2.

[32] [Robert Johnson], *The New Life of Virginea: Declaring the former Successe and present estate of that plantation, being the second part of Nova Britannia. Published by the authoritie of his Maiesties Counsell of Virginea* (London: n.p., 1612).

[33] *Three Proclamations concerning the lottery for Virginia 1613–1621,* 2.

[34] Ibid., 3.

[35] Sir Thomas Dale to Sir Thomas Smith, June 1613, in Brown, ed., *The Genesis of the United States,* 2:639–40.

[36] Ibid., 639.

[37] Horn, *A Land As God Made It,* 233.

[38] Hamor, *A True Discourse,* 24.

[39] Brown, ed., *The Genesis of the United States,* 2:772.

[40] Kupperman, *The Jamestown Project,* 280.

[41] John Rolfe to Sir Thomas Dale, n.d., in Hamor, *A True Discourse,* 61–68; 63.

[42] "Of the Lottery: Sir Thomas Dales returne: the Spaniards in Virginia. Of Pocahantas and Tomocomo: Captaine Yerdley and Captaine Argoll (both since Knighted) their Government; the Lord La-Warrs death, and other occurrents till Anno 1619," in Purchas, *Hakluyt Posthumus,* 19:116–22; 119.

[43] Horn, *A Land As God Made It,* 234.

[44] R. Ravin-Heart, *Before Van Riebeck: Callers at South Africa from 1488 to 1651* (Cape Town: C. Struik [PTY.] Ltd., 1967), 72.

[45] Wesley Frank Craven, *Dissolution of the Virginia Company. The Failure of a Colonial Experiment* (Oxford University Press, 1932; repr., 1964), 39.

[46] K. N. Chaudhuri, *The English East India Company. The Study of an Early Joint Stock Company 1600–1640* (London: Frank Cass & Co., 1965), 209.

[47] Rolfe, *A True Relation,* 38–39.

[48] The Council for Virginia, "A Brief Declaration from the Virginia Company (1616)," in Brown, *The Genesis of the United States,* 2:774–79; 779.

[49] Rolfe, *A True Relation,* 41, 39, 34.

[50] The Council for Virginia, "A Brief Declaration," in Brown, ed., *The Genesis of the United States,* 2:777.

[51] Hamor, *A True Discourse*, 17.

[52] Ibid., 16–17.

[53] Craven, *The Dissolution of the Virginia Company*, 35.

[54] The Council for Virginia, "A Brief Declaration," in Brown, ed., *The Genesis of the United States*, 2:778.

[55] "Virginia Company. Instructions to George Yeardley. (Sometimes called "The Great Charter"). November 18, 1618," in Bemiss, *The Three Charters*, 95–108.

[56] Ibid., 98, 106.

[57] Peter Wilson Coldham, *Bonded Passengers to America. Two Volumes in One* (Baltimore: Genealogical Publishing Company, 1983), 120.

[58] "Virginia Company. Instructions to George Yeardley," in Bemiss, *The Three Charters*, 95, 123.

[59] Bemiss, *The Three Charters*, vi.

19. A WEIGHTY VOYAGE

[1] William Bradford, *Of Plymouth Plantation*, ed. and with notes and an introduction by Samuel Eliot Morison (New York: Random House, Modern Library, 1952), 47.

[2] William Bradford, *Of Plymouth Plantation*, 31 and n4. The text of the Seven Articles is reprinted in George Bancroft, ed., *The Seven Articles from the Church of Leyden 1617 with an introductory letter by George Bancroft* (New York: From the Collections of the New York Historical Society, Second Series, Volume 3, n.d.), 9–10.

[3] Nick Bunker, *Making Haste from Babylon: The Mayflower Pilgrims and Their World: A New History* (New York: Alfred A. Knopf, 2010), 172.

[4] A summary of the law and the debate surrounding it can be found in Simonds d'Ewes, "Journal of the House of Commons: April 1593," in *The Journals of All the Parliaments During the Reign of Queen Elizabeth* (Shannon: Irish University Press, 1682), 513–21.

[5] Cotton Mather, *Magnalia Christi Americana: or, the Ecclesiastical History of New-England. Book 2, Containing the Lives of the Governours, and Names of the Magistrates of New-England* (1702; repr. Hartford: Silas Andrus, 1820), 101.

[6] Bradford, *Of Plymouth Plantation*, 10.

[7] James Howell, cited in Henry M. Dexter, *English Exiles in Amsterdam, 1597–1625* (Cambridge: John Wilson and Son, the University Press, 1890), 4.

[8] Bunker, *Making Haste*, 215.

[9] Bradford, *Of Plymouth Plantation*, 27.

[10] Ibid., 25.

[11] Ibid., 29.

[12] George F. Willison, *Saints and Strangers: Being the Lives of the Pilgrim Fathers & Their Families, with The Friends & Foes; & an Account of Their Posthumous Wanderings in Limbo, Their Final Resurrection & Rise to Glory, & the Strange Pilgrimages of Plymouth Rock* (New York: Reynal & Hitchcock, 1945), 107–8.

[13] Ibid., 32–33.

[14] Bunker, *Making Haste*, 29. Bradford, *Of Plymouth Plantation*, 30n3. For a complete biography of Naunton, see Roy E. Schreiber, *The Political Career of Sir Robert Naunton 1589-1635* (London: Royal Historical Society, 1981).

[15] Willison, *Saints and Strangers*, 108.

[16] Ibid., 109.

[17] "Robert Cushman to the Leyden Congregation May 8, 1619," in Bradford, *Of Plymouth Plantation*, 356.

[18] Bradford, *Of Plymouth Plantation*, 29n2, 34n8.

[19] Willison, *Saints and Strangers*, 111.

[20] Bradford, *Of Plymouth Plantation*, 34n8.

[21] In earlier days, interlopers acted on their own in violation of the rights of the Merchant Adventurers. By this time, however, an interloper acted with permission to trade in certain commodities and routes, for a royalty.

[22] Bradford, *Of Plymouth Plantation*, 38.

[23] Smith, "The General Historie of Virginia," in Barbour, ed., *The Complete Works of Captain John Smith*, 2:473; Ruth A. McIntyre, *Debts Hopeful and Desperate. Financing the Plymouth Colony* (Plymouth, MA: Plimoth Plantation, 1963), 19. McIntyre estimates the amount raised "to cover the expedition's costs" at between twelve and fifteen hundred pounds.

[24] Bunker, *Making Haste,* 259.

[25] Ibid., 668.

[26] Bradford, *Of Plymouth Plantation,* 39n6.

[27] Ibid., 29n2.

[28] Ibid., 38.

[29] Smith mentions "a few Marchants" in his *Description* (Barbour, ed., *The Complete Works of Captain John Smith*, 1:323), but adds that the voyage was "at the charge" of four people (Barbour, ed., *The Complete Works of Captain John Smith*, 2:400) in his *Generall Historie*, published 1624. These were: Captain Marmaduke Roydon, Captain George Langman, Master John Buley, and Master William Skelton. Brown profiles only Roydon as a "great adventurer" to many parts of the world. Brown, *The Genesis of the United States*, 1:988.

[30] Barbour, *The Complete Works,* 2:400 (value of cargo). "Advertisements For the Experienced Planters of New-England, or any where," in Barbour, ed., *The Complete Works of Captain John Smith,* 3: 253–304; writing about and mapping the territory, 278.

[31] Richard Arthur Preston, *Gorges of Plymouth Fort: A Life of Sir Ferdinando Gorges, Captain of Plymouth Fort, Governor of New England, and Lord of the Province of Maine* (Toronto: University of Toronto Press, in cooperation with the Royal Military College of Canada, 1953), 158–59.

[32] John Smith, "A Description of New England, by Captaine John Smith," in Barbour, ed., *The Complete Works of Captain John Smith,* 1:323–61; 324.

[33] John Smith, "The True Travels, Adventures, and Observations of Captaine John Smith," in Barbour, ed., *The Complete Works of Captain John Smith,* 3:123–251; 221.

[34] Bradford, *Of Plymouth Plantation,* 38–39.

[35] Ibid., 36–39.

[36] Ibid. There has been much scholarly debate about the Pilgrims' plan and intended destination. Morison is not convinced they intended to go to New England, even though the majority said they favored that destination, because they did not have the patent to go there (39n7).

[37] Bradford, *Of Plymouth Plantation,* 40–41.

[38] Willison, *Saints and Strangers,* 116.

[39] Bradford, *Of Plymouth Plantation,* 52n1, 28.

[40] Willison, *Saints and Strangers,* 128; 138.

[41] Charles M. Andrews, *The Colonial Period of American History: Settlements,* 4 vols. (New Haven, CT: Yale University Press, 1934; repr., 1964), 1:331n2.

[42] Bradford, *Of Plymouth Plantation,* 120–21.

FORGOTTEN FOUNDERS

[1] Bradford, *Of Plymouth Plantation,* 90n8.

[2] "Plymouth Oration, December 22, 1820," in William S. Kartalopoulos (curator), "Daniel Webster: Dartmouth's Favorite Son: A Hypertext Exhibit on the World Wide Web," Dartmouth College, https://www.dartmouth.edu/~dwebster/speeches/plymouth-oration.html.

[3] Peter J. Gomes, "Pilgrims and Puritans: 'Heroes' and 'Villains' in the Creation of the American Past," *Proceedings of the Massachusetts Historical Society* 95 (1983): 1–16; 2.

[4] Gomes, "Pilgrims and Puritans," 12.

[5] Alexis de Tocqueville, *Democracy in America,* ed. Olivier Zunz and trans. Arthur Goldhammer (New York: The Library of America, 2004), 35–37.

[6] Bradford, *Of Plymouth Plantation,* 23–25.

[7] Nathaniel Philbrick, *Mayflower: A Story of Courage, Community, and War* (New York: Penguin, 2006), 7.

[8] Kenneth B. Murdock, "The Pilgrims' Progress," *New York Times Book Review,* September 28, 1952, 15. This review is of the Morison edition published by Alfred A. Knopf.

[9] Henry Wadsworth Longfellow, *The Courtship of Miles Standish* (New York: Grosset & Dunlap, 1910), 64 (Plymouth Rock); 24 ("patient, courageous, strong"); 30 ("modest"); 42 ("great of heart"); 38 ("tender and trusting"); 42 ("noble and generous"); 54 ("austere").

[10] Edward L. Tucker, "Longfellow's 'The Courtship of Miles Standish': Some Notes and Two Early Versions," *Studies in the American Renaissance* (1985): 285–321; 292.

[11] For a useful overview of the Thanksgiving holiday: Edwin T. Greninger, "Thanksgiving: An American Holiday," *Social Science* 54, no. 1 (1979): 3–15.

[12] Andrew F. Smith, "N.Y.'s place in Thanksgiving Lore: How Gotham Is as Central to Our Modern Conception of the Holiday as New England," *New York Daily News,* November 25, 2015.

[13] Anne Blue Wills, "Pilgrims and Progress: How Magazines Made Thanksgiving," *Church History* 72, no. 1 (2003): 138–58; 144.

[14] Elizabeth Pleck, "The Making of the Domestic Occasion: The History of Thanksgiving in the United States," *Journal of Social History* 32, no. 4 (1999): 773–89; 775.

[15] For a discussion of the interpretation of the Pilgrim story, see Wills, "Pilgrims and Progress," 145; 142.

[16] Joseph Hunter, *Collections Concerning the Church of Congregation of Protestant Separatists Formed at Scrooby in North Nottinghamshire, in the Time of King James I* (London: John Russell Smith, 1854), 2.

[17] Abraham Lincoln, "Proclamation 106 — Thanksgiving Day, 1863," October 3, 1863. Gerhard Peters and John T. Woolley, *The American Presidency Project,* http://www.presidency.ucsb.edu/ws/?pid=69900.

[18] *Mourt's Relation: A Journal of the Pilgrims at Plymouth* (Bedford MA: Applewood Books in cooperation with Plimoth Plantation, 1963), 17–18.

[19] Pleck, "The Making of the Domestic Occasion," 779–80.

[20] Ibid., 780.

[21] Lawrence Willson, "Another View of the Pilgrims," *The New England Quarterly* 34, no. 2 (1961): 160–77; 173.

[22] Michelle Tirado, "The Wampanoag Side of the First Thanksgiving," *Indian Country Today,* November 23, 2011, https://indiancountrymedianetwork.com/news/the-wampanoag-side-of-the-first-thanksgiving-story/.

[23] Mark Twain, "Plymouth Rock and the Pilgrims: 22 December 1881," in *Mark Twain's Speeches,* with an Introduction by William Dean Howells (New York: Harper Brothers, 1910), 17–24.

[24] Willison, *Saints and Strangers,* vi.

[25] Bradford, *Of Plymouth Plantation,* xii.

[26] Philbrick, *Mayflower,* xi.

[27] Thomas Jefferson, *Notes on the State of Virginia. A New Edition* (Richmond, Virginia: J. W. Randolph, 1853), 194 (Cabot), 192 (Ralegh).

[28] Ibid., 118.

[29] N. S. B. Gras and Henrietta M. Larson, *Casebook in American Business History* (New York: Appleton-Century-Crofts, 1939), frontispiece; 29–45.

[30] Smith, "A Description of New England," in Barbour, ed., *The Complete Works of Captain John Smith,* 1:346.

A NOTE TO THE READER

[1] E. T. Campagnac, ed., *Mulcaster's Elementarie* (Oxford: Clarendon Press, 1925), 274 ("greater plainness"), 269 ("worship").

[2] John Simpson, ed., "The first dictionaries of English." http://public.oed.com/aspects-of-english/english-in-time/the-first-dictionaries-of-english/.

[3] Shakespeare is credited with introducing 1,484 words into the English language: see the *Oxford English Dictionary.*

4 Some 496 words come from Native American Indian languages according to the *Oxford English Dictionary*. Also, see James Rosier's list of Indian words in David Beers Quinn and Alison M. Quinn, eds., *The English New England Voyages, 1602–1608* (London: The Hakluyt Society, 1983), 485–93.

5 Collinson, *The Three Voyages of Martin Frobisher*, 117, 121.

6 Ibid., 185, 119.

7 Baxter, ed., *Sir Ferdinando Gorges and His Province of Maine*, 3:129.

8 "5 July 1609. Pedro de Zúñiga to Philip III," in Barbour, ed. *The Jamestown Voyages*, 2:269.

9 "Advertisements," in Barbour, ed., *The Complete Works*, 3:279.

10 Charles Mann, *1491: New Revelations of the Americas Before Columbus* (New York: Alfred A. Knopf, 2005), xi.

11 Bartolomé de las Casas, *A Short Account of the Destruction of the Indies* (London: Penguin Books, 1992), 9 n9.

12 For Dee's calendar reforms: Woolley, *The Queen's Conjuror*, 193-95; and Parry, *The Arch-Conjuror of England*, 147–60.

Index

About the Authors

John Butman is an author, editor, and collaborative writer whose work has appeared in the *Harvard Business Review, The Nation,* and other publications and has been featured in the *New York Times, The Economist,* and media venues around the world. His previous books include *Trading Up: The New American Luxury,* a *BusinessWeek* best-seller, and *Breaking Out: How to Build Influence in a World of Competing Ideas.*

Simon Targett is a writer, historian, and corporate communications adviser. He holds a PhD in history from Cambridge University and has written on British history for various publications. An award-winning journalist, he worked for the *Financial Times* for twelve years, serving variously as features editor, the editor of FT.com, and the editor of supplements and special reports. He subsequently became global editor in chief of The Boston Consulting Group.

Illustration Credits

Page 1: *John Dee*, by unknown artist; c. 1594 (© Ashmolean Museum, University of Oxford); *John Dudley, Duke of Northumberland* (© National Trust Images/John Hammond); Map by Martin Waldseemüller, printed in *Universalis Cosmographia*; 1507 (Geography and Map Division, Library of Congress); Title page of *The Commonwealth of England*, by Thomas Smith, 1609; *Sebastian Cabot*, engraving after Hans Holbein, 1824 (© National Maritime Museum, Greenwich, London)

Page 2: *Martin Frobisher* by Cornelis Ketel, c. 1577 (The Bodleian Library, University of Oxford); *William Cecil, 1st Baron Burghley*, by unknown artist (© National Portrait Gallery, London); *Anne, Countess of Warwick*, attributed to The Master of the Countess of Warwick, 1566–1569 (From The Woburn Abbey Collection); *Matthew Baker*, an image from *Fragments of Ancient English Shipwrightry* (By permission of the Pepys Library, Magdalene College Cambridge)

Page 3: A chart showing Frobisher's straits and surrounding area, from *A True Discourse of the late voyages of discouerie . . .* , 1578 (© British Library Board/Robana/Art Resource, NY); An image from *Accounts, with subsidiary documents, of Michael Lok, treasurer, of first, second and third voyages of Martin Frobisher to Cathay by the north-west passage, 1576–1578* (© The National Archives, UK); *Mining in Potosí*, engraving by Theodor de Bry in *Historia Americae sive Novi Orbis*; 1596 (Image & Sound Collections, International Institute of Social History [Amsterdam])

Page 4: LONDON, c. 1560, Engraving from *Civitates Orbis Terrarum*, by Frans Hogenberg, 1572 (Wikimedia Commons. Public domain. In the collection of the Universitätsbibliothek, Heidelberg); *Portrait of Sir Thomas Gresham*, by Anthonis Mor, c. 1560–c. 1565, (Wikimedia Commons. Public domain. In the collection of the Rijksmuseum, Amsterdam); *The Royal Exchange, London*, by Frans Hogenberg; c. 1569 (Wellcome Library, London. Wellcome Images images@wellcome.ac.uk http://wellcomeimages.org)

Page 5: GILBERT'S MAP OF THE WORLD, 1576, *A general map, made onelye for the particuler declaration of this discovery*, by H. Middleton for R. Jhones, 1576 (British Library/Granger, NYC—All Rights Reserved); *Sir Francis Walsingham*, possibly after John De Critz the Elder; based on a work of circa 1587 (© National Portrait Gallery, London); *Sir Humphrey Gilbert*, by an unknown artist, c.1584 (National Trust Photo Library/Art Resource, NY)

Page 6: *Sir Walter Ralegh (Raleigh)*, by Nicholas Hilliard, circa 1585 (© National Portrait Gallery, London); WHITE'S DRAWINGS OF INDIANS AT ROANOKE, 1585 [The Flyer, left; Woman and Child, right], *Native Indian Conjurer*, by Theodor de Bry, in *America*, after a drawing by John White, 1590 (© The Trustees of the British Museum/Art Resource, NY); *An Indian woman and child of Pomeiooc in Virginia*, by John White, 1585 (© The Trustees of the British Museum/Art Resource, NY)

Page 7: *Sir Francis Drake*, by an unknown artist; circa 1581 (© National Portrait Gallery, London); *Elizabeth I*, attributed to George Gower, c. 1588 (From The Woburn Abbey Collection); *Portrait of Philip II*, by Sofonisba Anguissola, 1565 (Wikimedia Commons. Public domain. In the collection of the Prado Museum, Madrid.)

Page 8: TREATY OF LONDON CEREMONY, 1604, *The Somerset House Conference, 19 August 1604*, by Juan Pantoja de la Cruz, circa 1604 (© National Maritime Museum, Greenwich, London); *Sir Thomas Smythe*, by Simon de Passe, John Woodall, 1616 (© National Portrait Gallery, London); *King James I of England and VI of Scotland*, after John De Critz the Elder, c. 1605 (© National Portrait Gallery, London); *Image of John Smith*, from *A Description of New-England*, by an unknown artist, possibly after Simon de Passe, c. 1617 (National Portrait Gallery, Smithsonian Institution); *Portrait of Pocahontas, aged 21*, by Crispin van de Passe, 1616 (© The Trustees of the British Museum/Art Resource, NY)

THE WORLD
in
1550–1621
with contemporary place names

TERRA INCOGNITA

AFRICA

GREENLAND

NORTHWEST PASSAGE?

META INCOGNITA

ICELAND

Dublin
London
Antwerp
Area of deta
Paris
Cor

FISHING FLEET

NEW
FRANCE

Area of detail opposite

VIRGINIA

NEW
FOUND
LANDS

*Mare
Atlantico*

Azores

Seville
Mediterranea

Nova Albion

Somers
Islands

Barbary Coast

St. Augustine

NEW
SPAIN

FLORIDA
Havana

West Indies

Silver Fleet

Canaries

Mare Pacifico

CUBA
HISPANIOLA

Nombre de Dios
Panama City
Cartagena

Spanish Main

GUINEA

Castle de Mina

Equinoctial

GUIANA

SPAIN ◀ ▶ PORTUGAL

PERU

•Potosí

TREATY OF TORDESILLAS

*Mare del
Sur*

Rio de La Plata

Cape de
Buona Speran

Strait of Magellan

Drake Passage

TER

© 2018 Jeffrey L. Ward